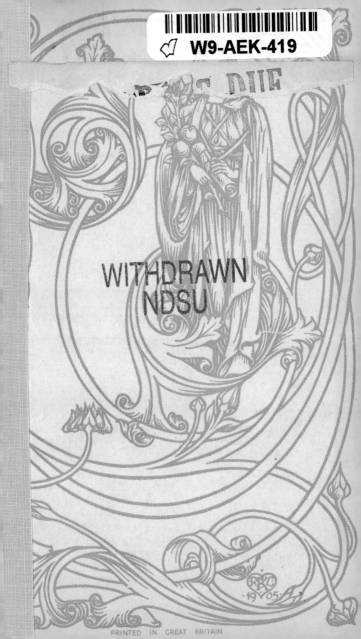

19V05

EVERYMAN'S LIBRARY
EDITED BY ERNEST RHYS

ESSAYS AND
BELLES LETTRES

DRYDEN'S DRAMATIC POESY
AND OTHER ESSAYS
WITH AN INTRODUCTION BY
WILLIAM HENRY HUDSON, M.A.

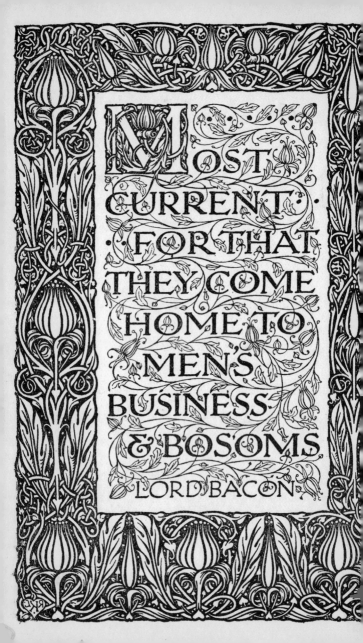

Most current, for that they come home to men's business & bosoms

LORD BACON

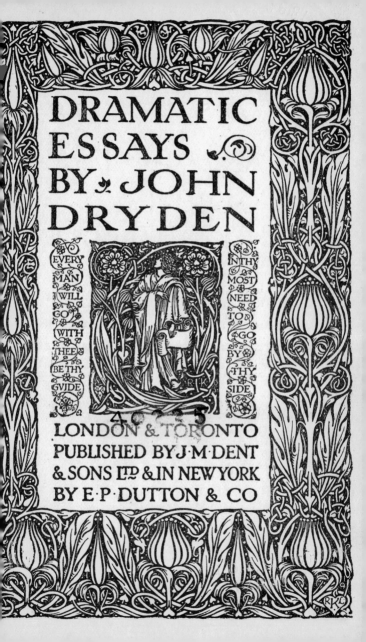

DRAMATIC ESSAYS BY JOHN DRYDEN

EVERY MAN WILL GO WITH THEE BE THY GVIDE

IN THY MOST NEED TO GO BY THY SIDE

LONDON & TORONTO
PUBLISHED BY J·M·DENT
& SONS L^{TD} & IN NEW YORK
BY E·P·DUTTON & CO

First Issue of this Edition . 1912
Reprinted 1921

INTRODUCTION

JOHN DRYDEN was born at Aldwinkle All Saints, Northamptonshire, on the 9th August 1631, and was educated at Westminster and at Trinity College, Cambridge. In 1654, the year in which he took his degree, his father died, leaving him a small property. He then drifted to London, where he seems for a time to have been employed in some secretarial capacity or clerkship. His first substantial experiment in literature—the "Heroic Stanzas on the Death of Oliver Cromwell"—appeared in 1659. In these bombastic verses, with all their crudities, affectations, and "metaphysical" conceits, not even the most prescient critic could have detected any indication of the splendid powers which Dryden's work was presently to reveal. With the return of the Stuarts the young poet found it convenient to change his politics, and his next publications celebrated the "happy restoration" and coronation of Charles II. These are marked indeed by a great advance in form and style, but they are now chiefly valuable as showing that Dryden's genius ripened very slowly. In 1663 he married Lady Elizabeth Howard, sister of his friend, Sir Robert Howard, the Crites of the "Essay of Dramatic Poesy;" but the union was not a fortunate one.

By this time Dryden was working his way steadily into notice as a playwright, though he gained no pronounced success till the production (in collaboration with Howard) of "The Indian Queen" in 1664, and its sequel, "The Indian Emperor," in 1665. Then came the plague, the closing of the theatres, and the composition of the "Essay of Dramatic Poesy" and the long "heroic" poem, "Annus Mirabilis." The faults of the latter work are numerous and glaring; but it has vigour and distinction, and easily placed its author in the front rank of English poets at a time when poetic genius was at a low ebb, and there were few indeed to contest his position.

With the re-opening of the theatres, Dryden returned with great energy to the dramatic field, and for a number of years continued to produce plays of varying merit and of very different styles. But though his dramatic works bulk large in his collected writings, they constitute, taken in the mass, the least vital and permanently interesting portion of his total output. While, as the essays here reprinted show, he devoted much attention to critical questions connected with the drama, and wrote of these with remarkable insight and sagacity, his theoretical knowledge of technical principles was not supported by creative power. His tragedies, belonging for the most part to the melodramatic, or so-called "heroic" class, had little truth of nature to keep them alive when the taste to which they had appealed passed away; and he himself condemned his comedies to well-merited oblivion by his shameless indulgence in the foulness and profanity unfortunately so characteristic of the Restoration stage. His heroic dramas were ridiculed by the Duke of Buckingham and others in their pungent burlesque play, "The Rehearsal," first performed in 1671; many years later—in 1698—he was severely taken to task for the offences of his comedies in the Rev. Jeremy Collier's "Short View of the Immorality and Profaneness of the English Stage." It will be seen that at the very end of his life, in the preface to his Fables, he had the honesty and good sense to acknowledge the substantial justice of Collier's reproaches.

In 1670 Dryden was made poet-laureate and historiographer-royal; and in 1681 opened a new and most important chapter in his career by the publication of the first of his great satires, "Absalom and Achitophel." An outgrowth from the intense excitement caused by the alleged Popish Plot, this was directed immediately against the Earl of Shaftesbury, then intriguing to have the Duke of York excluded from the succession to the crown in favour of Charles II.'s illegitimate son, the young Duke of Monmouth. The sensation produced by this brilliant polemic was immense, and it is still considered, as Scott said, the finest political satire in the language. Master of a marvellously clear and forcible style, and with the power of making every detail tell, Dryden is here shown at his best, though the satires which followed—"The Medal" and "MacFlecknoe"—are scarcely less dexterous and effective. To this period also belong his two great theological poems, which are especially interesting as illustrating his controversial skill, his ability to make the most of any position he might at the time adopt, and his unrivalled facility as a reasoner in verse. The first of these—"Religio Laici"—is a defence of the doctrines of

the Anglican Church, of which he was a member; the second
—"The Hind and the Panther"—is an elaborate argument
in favour of Roman Catholicism, to which he had in the meantime been converted. The question of the sincerity of his
religious change, like that of the real significance of his political
fluctuations, is an intricate one, and space cannot be afforded
for a consideration of it here.[1] But it will be well for the
student of Dryden's literary criticism to note that his mind
was in a state of almost perpetual vacillation about every
subject which he took up, and that emphatic as was his expression of whatever opinion he chanced to hold at any given
moment, his changes of judgment were often rapid and fundamental.

He had once more trimmed his political sails to take advantage of the accession of James II. But the revolution of 1688
swept away all hopes he may have cherished of recognition
and advancement. Deprived of all his offices and of the
income he derived from them, Dryden now accepted with
manly courage and dignity the troubles which darkened his
declining years, and, turning with renewed industry to literature, maintained under the burden of increasing ill-health a
wonderful activity to the end. He produced more plays,
translated Juvenal, Persius, and Virgil, and in his *Fables*
(paraphrases from the "Iliad," Ovid, Boccaccio, and Chaucer)
gave the world some of his finest work. These were published
in November 1899. On the 1st of May of the following year
he died.

Milton excepted—and this older and greater John is really
a survivor of "the mighty race before the flood"—Dryden
is in all respects the most important figure in English literature
during the second half of the seventeenth century. Here he
merits special attention as our first great prose writer and
first systematic critic. English prose before the Restoration—
the prose, for example, of Raleigh and Hooker—was stately,
rich, and at times magnificent; but it was too cumbrous,
intricate, and unwieldy for common use; and it was this kind
of prose which, in Dryden's early manhood, was still being
written by such men as Milton, Clarendon, and Jeremy
Taylor. It was a most important part of the business of the
Restoration period—a business which its pedestrian temper
particularly fitted it to undertake—to perfect and give cur-
rency to an English style which, like the French style by which

[1] It is admirably treated by Scott, in his *Life of Dryden*, § 6.

*

tt was largely influenced, should be clear, simple, direct,
flexible, and serviceable for the ordinary purposes of exposition and discussion; and Dryden beyond all other men is to
be regarded as the leader in this much-needed work of reform.
And as the Restoration was the age of the new prose, so it
was the age of the new criticism; for though a great deal of
criticism had been produced in England before this, it was
now for the first time that men began to be seriously concerned about the principles of literature and to analyse
methods, institute comparisons, investigate rules, and seek
for definite standards of judgment. Here again the power
and weight of Dryden's genius gave him an easy supremacy.
Johnson called him " the Father of English criticism," and we
need scarcely challenge the title.

It was undoubtedly in the dramatic field that Dryden's
best work in criticism was done, and of the value of this work
the reader of the present volume will now be in a position to
judge for himself. To read his essays profitably, however, it
is essential that we should place ourselves at the point of view
of the time when they were written. It must be remembered
that, largely as a result of England's new political and social
relations, a great enthusiasm for all things French grew up
in this country after the Restoration. Adopting many of the
habits, manners, and ideals of their neighbours across the
Channel, our cultured classics learned to regard their drama
also with the utmost admiration. Now the French drama—
the " neo-classic drama " as it is called—was specially marked
by structural correctness, respect for decorum, dignity of mode
and speech, love of high-flown rhetoric, and strict adherence,
in theory at any rate, to the classic unities of time, place, and
action. It was thus inevitable that the newly-bred interest
in a form of dramatic art so unlike that of our older stage
should bring about a widespread neglect of the free romantic
type of play, and lead to openly expressed contempt of the
work of the pre-Restoration men, including Shakespeare
himself. At the same time, various questions connected with
the practice of the French playwrights came naturally to the
front: as to the value of the unities, for example, the significance of the love-motive, and the use of narrative instead of
action and of rhyme instead of blank verse. Furthermore,
throughout the current discussion of these, as of all other
similar matters, it was the habit of the age to consult the
precedents furnished by antiquity and invoke the authority

of classic writers for rule and guidance. Hence there was another problem which arose from time to time, and which presently filled the French world of letters with excitement and indirectly inspired Swift's famous satire, "The Battle of Books," the problem of the comparative merits of the ancients and the moderns, and of the right of the moderns to break away from classic leading-strings, assert the freedom of individual genius, and work out the principles of a new literature for themselves.

These were some of the subjects most prominent in the literary discussions of the time when Dryden wrote his essays in dramatic criticism, and it was perfectly natural, therefore, that his own mind should be full of them. What are the relative values of the ancient and modern dramas? How does the French drama (based in theory on the ancient) compare with the romantic drama of the older English stage? What in turn may be said for and against this romantic drama itself when it is set beside the drama of Dryden's own time? What is the real significance of the unities? Has tragi-comedy any justification? What is the proper place and what the proper treatment of love in the modern drama? What are the advantages and drawbacks of action and narrative? of rhyme and blank verse? Such are the topics which recur in Dryden's pages; and if for most of us to-day they are scarcely living issues, the historical importance, and even the critical value, of what Dryden says about them are not the less on that account.

The foundations of his dramatic criticisms are laid in the earliest and at the same time the most masterly of all his writings on the subject—the "Essay of Dramatic Poesy." That this essay was largely based upon three treatises by the great French playwright Corneille, and that Dryden also draws freely for it from other authors, is a fact that must be mentioned in passing. His indebtedness to those who had been before him in the field makes little difference, however, to the individuality of his own work, for he had a rare faculty for making borrowed material entirely his own and for leaving his personal impress upon it. In the present essay, it will be noted, the discussion is thrown into the form of a dialogue— a favourite device since the revival of learning, when all over Europe men had begun to imitate Plato and Cicero. The critical value of this form is of course to be found in the opportunity it affords for the consideration of any given subject from different points of view; and it doubtless commended itself to Dryden both for this reason and because it fell in with the curious flexibility of his own judgment. "You see it is a dialogue," he afterwards explained, "sustained by persons of several opinions, all of them left doubtful, to be determined by readers in general." [1] Hence the employment of the controversial method may very probably have been suggested in the first instance by the writer's characteristically sceptical spirit. But however that may be, it is important to observe that as literary principles are thus treated, not as fixed and final, but as open to varying interpretations, the older critical dogmatism is abandoned, and the comparative line of investigation adopted instead. The fact adds much to the historical significance of the essay.

There are four interlocutors—Crites, Eugenius, Lisideius, and Neander, representing respectively, it is now generally admitted, Sir Robert Howard, Lord Buckhurst, Sir Charles Sedley, and Dryden himself. [2] Crites asserts the superiority of the ancients to the moderns, in virtue of their closer imitation of nature, and upholds the unities. Eugenius defends the French drama against the classicists; maintains that with the ancient playwrights poetic justice was imperfectly realised, and points out the deficiency of the classic drama in one important respect—its neglect of love. Lisideius in turn undertakes the advocacy of the French drama against the English, on the ground of its adherence to the unities, great structural regularity, and use of rhyme. Neander protests against this: the English, he declares, excel in "lively imitation of nature," richness of invention, variety. He further insists that the French drama has lost more than it has gained by undue regard for decorum and obedience to the rules, and argues that in English plays—even when most "irregular"—there is more "masculine fancy" and a "greater spirit in the writing" than are ever to be found on the French stage.

Other matters are drawn into the argument, but these are the main points discussed. The result, as we have seen Dryden acknowledge, is left in some uncertainty; for while superstitious veneration for classical antiquity and the current admiration of the French drama are boldly challenged, and

---

[1] "Defence," prefixed to second edition of *The Indian Emperor*.

[2] It is probable that he assumed this name (which means "novus homo"—νέος ἀνήρ—or "parvenu") to mark the difference between himself and the other speakers, all of whom belonged to a higher social rank.

while too the older English dramatists are defended, yet the ancients and the French are alike treated with the greatest respect; the value of rhyme (one of the salient features of French tragedy) is emphasised; and the unities are practically admitted as essential principles of a good play. On the conservative side the argument is, that while dramatic rules may be derived immediately from the ancients, the ancients in turn derived them directly from nature; so that to imitate the ancients and to follow nature turn out to be one and the same thing.[1] On the other hand, a strong case is made out for the irregular English drama, and therefore for the right of the individual playwright to go straight to nature for himself. The general purpose of the "Essay," however, may be said to be two-fold — to defend rhyme in the drama against Sir Robert Howard,[2] and to "vindicate the honour of our English writers, from the censure of those who unjustly prefer the French before them."[3] It should be observed that these two aims are, strictly speaking, incompatible.

While the "Essay of Dramatic Poesy" holds the place of pre-eminence among Dryden's writings on the drama, it does not record his final or unswerving judgment upon the questions raised in it. It has therefore to be supplemented by his prefaces and dedications to various plays, in studying which we have an ample opportunity of following the always interesting and sometimes rather puzzling evolutions of his thought. Thus in the "Defence" of the essay he traverses again much of the ground which he had already covered in the essay itself, re-stating his views about rhyme and the "rules," without however adding anything of much importance on either point. In his preface to "All for Love" ("Antony and Cleopatra and the Art of Tragedy") he seems to be seeking some kind of compromise between the classic and the romantic dramas, advocating adherence to ancient tragedy, yet admitting that something of "larger compass" is required on the English stage, and under the influence of "divine Shakespeare" repudiating rhyme, which hitherto has had his ardent support. In considering "The Grounds of Criticism in Tragedy" in the preface to *Troilus and Cressida*, he takes

---

[1] Compare Pope's well-known couplet:

> Learn hence for ancient rules a just esteem;
> To copy nature is to copy them.—*Essay on Criticism.*

[2] "Defence of an Essay of Dramatic Poesy."
[3] "To the Reader," prefixed to "Essay of Dramatic Poesy."

his stand even more firmly on Aristotle, Longinus, and Horace; sets out at length the commonplaces of the classic school of criticism; upholds the "rules," which are now treated (in a phrase of Rapin's afterwards adopted by Pope) as "made only to reduce Nature into method;" and finds fault with Shakespeare and Fletcher for defects in technique. This decisive utterance in favour of the classic doctrine dates from the year after "All for Love" had marked the swing of the critic's mind towards the Shakespearean type of play. Two years later, in the preface to "The Spanish Friar" ("Nature and Dramatic Art"), he so far abandons the classic ideal as to defend double-plots and the "mixed" drama, or tragi-comedy, of the romantic stage. Then, in an "Examen Poeticum" prefixed to the third part of a *Miscellany* published in 1693, he enters the lists as the champion of the English drama against all comers; repeats some of Neander's arguments regarding the poverty of the French playwrights and their too servile dependence on "mechanic rules"; and yet at the same time enters a protest against those who pay lip-service to the "*Manes* of Shakespeare, Fletcher, and Jonson" in order only that they may "throw dirt on the writers of this age." This last particular suggests an interesting point in connection with Dryden's critical position. In the Battle of the Books he is so far a modern that, however much he may himself find to blame in the older English drama, he is in general solicitous to protect it against its detractors. But he is equally solicitous to defend the achievements of his own day against those who regarded the efforts of the greater pre-Restoration playwrights as the high-water mark of English dramatic genius. This opinion he boldly challenged in the Epilogue to the second part of his "Conquest of Granada." The rather reckless language which he there used exposed him to severe attack; he found himself compelled in cold blood to make good assertions which he had flung out in hot blood; and the "Defence of the Epilogue, or an Essay on the Dramatic Poetry of the Last age" was the result. On the whole, this essay is disappointing; too much space is wasted upon verbal criticisms of a singularly petty and profitless kind. Yet a larger purpose is apparent in the argument; the writer is anxious to show that if the modern dramatist cannot compare with the great pre-Restoration men in mere quality of genius, he gains greatly from the superior culture and taste of his time, and that therefore he has a right to work independently.

This contention is closely associated with Dryden's belief (already incidentally set forth in his preface to "An Evening Love"), that there was at least one special achievement in which the modern dramatists might justly claim precedence of those of the foregoing period—the Heroic Play. Hence the significance of Dryden's concern with this extraordinary form of over-blown tragedy or melodrama which, arising from the combined influences of the older English theatre, the epic poem, French heroic romance, and French rhyming tragedy, enjoyed for a time immense popularity on the London boards. For his own exposition of the theory and principles of this curious type of drama we may turn to his essays "Of Heroic Plays" prefixed to the first part of "The Conquest of Granada," and "On Heroic Poetry and Heroic Licence," published with his operatic version (or perversion) of "Paradise Lost," "The State of Innocence." Of course we cannot now accept Dryden's estimate of the Heroic Drama. As a matter of detail, therefore, it should be remembered that he himself finally grew tired of it. In his preface to "The Spanish Friar" he repents, among his other sins, the monstrous extravagances into which it had temporarily seduced him.

Between Dryden's essays on dramatic and those on non-dramatic subjects, the connection is very close. In particular, the problems of what constitutes the "heroic" whether in tragedy or epic, of how the "heroic" should be treated, and of the relations of Art and Nature, are common to both; while more broadly, the questions which otherwise come up for consideration, being products of the same literary interests and conditions, belong to the same general class and are regarded from the same point of view. Dryden's pre-occupation with the elements of heroic poetry in the preface to "Annus Mirabilis;" with the principles of translation in the prefaces to "Ovid's Epistles" and "Sylvæ;" with the characteristics of leading classic writers in the last-named essay and elsewhere; with the moral functions of epic and tragedy in the discourse on "Virgil and the Æneid;" and other similar topics, is thus explained. It is rarely that in these non-dramatic writings Dryden reaches his highest level as a critic. His treatment of the epic, for example, is on the whole rather tame and conventional; the learning which he parades is for the most part second-hand learning; and, except in his analysis of the character of Æneas, which may still be read with profit, there is little that is fresh or striking in the opinions expressed.

In any general statement about the relative inferiority of this portion of Dryden's work, however, exception must be made in favour of one essay—the noble preface to the *Fables* (" On translating the Poets "). This comes from the very last year of his life; and we might therefore have expected to find traces in it of flagging energies and a hesitating hand. On the contrary, in strength and dexterity alike it holds its place secure beside, if not above, the " Essay of Dramatic Poesy." To these two splendid examples of his powers—the one from nearly the beginning, the other from quite the end of his long and strenuous career as a man of letters—we may well turn if we want to realise the greatness of Dryden as a critic and prose-writer. His defects were many and obvious; his inability to distinguish between the essential and the non-essential is frequently very marked; he sometimes wrote from insufficient knowledge and blundered sadly in consequence; he was often hasty in judgment, and was habitually careless about details. He was also emphatically a man of his time; as his views of literature were circumscribed by the limitations and prejudices of that time, they are now in many cases quite obsolete; much of his writing has, therefore, to-day an historical interest only. Yet the more carefully we consider his criticism the more we are likely to be impressed by its substantial and permanent qualities: by the massive good sense which he brings to bear upon every subject he touches; by his honesty, sagacity, and penetration; by the clearness, manly vigour, and fine felicity of his style.

WILLIAM HENRY HUDSON.

The following is a list of the works of John Dryden:—

DRAMATIC WORKS.—The Wild Gallant, acted 1663; published 1669; The Rival Ladies, acted 1663 (?), published 1664; The Indian Queen (in part attributed to Dryden), acted 1664, printed 1665; The Indian Emperor, or, The Conquest of Mexico by the Spaniards (a sequel to the Indian Queen), acted 1665, published 1667; second edition 1668, to which was added A Defence of an Essay of Dramatic Poesy; Secret Love, or, The Maiden Queen, acted 1667, published 1668; Sir Martin Mar-all, or, The Feigned Innocence, acted 1667, published 1668; The Tempest, or, The Enchanted Island — alteration of Shakespeare's play by Sir William Davenant in which Dryden had a share — acted 1667, published 1670; An Evening's Love, or, The Mock Astrologer, acted 1668, published 1671; Tyrannic Love, or, The Royal Martyr, acted 1668-9, published 1670, revised 1672; Almanzor and Almahide, or, The Conquest of Granada by the Spaniards (two parts), acted 1669 or 1670, published 1672; The Essay on Heroic Plays, and The Defence of the Epilogue, or, An Essay on the Dramatic Poetry of the Last Age, were published with this play. Marriage à la Mode, acted 1672, published 1673; The Assignation, or, Love in a Nunnery, acted 1672, published 1673; Amboyna, or, The Cruelties of the Dutch to the English Merchants, acted and published 1673; The State of Innocence and the Fall of Man: an opera, published 1674, with The Author's Apology for Heroic Poetry and Poetic Licence; Aurengzebe, acted 1675, published 1676; All for Love, or, The World Well Lost, acted and printed 1678; Mr. Limberham, or, The Kind Keeper, acted and published 1678; Œdipus (in collaboration with Nat. Lee), acted and published 1679; Troilus and Cressida, or, Truth Found Too Late, acted and published 1679; The Spanish Friar, or, The Double Discovery, acted and published 1681; The Duke of Guise (in collaboration with Nat. Lee), acted 1682, published 1683; The Vindication of the Duke of Guise was published separately, 1683; Albion and Albanius, acted and published 1685; Don Sebastian, acted and published 1690; Amphitryon, or, The Two Sosias, acted and published 1690; King Arthur, or, The British Worthy: an opera, acted and published 1691; Cleomenes, the Spartan Hero, acted and published 1692 (with Life of Cleomenes by T. Creech); Love Triumphant, or, Nature will Prevail, acted and published 1693-94; Secular Masque, with Prologue, Song, and Epilogue, written for Beaumont and Fletcher's Pilgrim, when revised in 1700. The Mall, or, The Modish Lovers, and The Mistaken Husband are doubtful plays.

POETICAL WORKS.—Heroic Stanzas to the Memory of Oliver Cromwell: one of three poems upon the death of the Protector, the two others being by Edmund Waller and Mr. Sprat, two editions in 1659; Astræa Redux, 1660; A Panegyric on the Coronation, 1661; Address to Lord Chancellor Hyde, New Year's Day, 1662; Annus Mirabilis, the Year of Wonders, 1666; prefixed by An Account of the Ensuing Poem addressed to Sir Robert Howard; Absalom and Achitophel, part I., 1681; part II. in collaboration with Nahum Tate, 1682; The Medal, a Satire against Sedition, 1682; Mac-Flecknoe, or, A Satire upon the True Blue Protestant Poet, 1682; Religio Laici, or, A Layman's Faith, 1862; Threnodia Augustatis (to the memory of Charles II.), 1685; The Hind and the Panther, 1687; Britannia Rediviva, a poem on the Birth of the Prince, 1688; Eleonora: a Panegyrical Poem, dedicated to the Memory of the late Countess of Abingdon, 1692; Alexander's Feast, or, The Power of Music, 1697.

Prologues and epilogues (to the number of nearly a hundred), epistles, elegies, and epigrams, odes, lyrical pieces, and hymns are included in Dryden's verse. Among these are a poem on the Death of Lord Hastings, first printed in Lachrymæ Musarum, 1649, and an Ode to the Pious

Memory of the Accomplished Young Lady, Mrs. Anne Killigrew, first printed with her collected poems, 1686; Introductory poems to Hoddesden's Sion and Parnassus, to Sir R. Howard's poems, Charleton's Chorea Gigantum, Lee's Alexander, Roscommon's Essay on Translated Verse, and Congreve's Double Dealer. A few, with Satires and Translations, were published in volumes of the Miscellany Verse, which came out in six volumes from 1684-1706; vol. 2 had additional title of Sylvæ and vol. 3 of Examen Poeticum.

Dryden is believed to have contributed poems to the New Court Songs and Poems, 1672, and to the Covent Garden Drollery, 1672. His Te Deum and hymn on St. John's Eve were first printed in Scott's edition of his works; other hymns have been recently attributed to him.

TRANSLATIONS AND ADAPTATIONS.—Ovid: Epistles (Preface and two epistles by Dryden), 1680; Metamorphoses, published in the Third Miscellany (Examen Poeticum), 1693; Juvenal and Persius, prefixed by Essay on Satire, 1693 ; Virgil: works (Pastorals, Georgics, Aeneid), 1697, fol. and later editions, revised and corrected by J. Carey, 1803, and later editions; The Aeneid, edited with Introduction by H. Morley (Morley's Universal Library), 1884, and in Lubbock's Hundred Best Books, 1891; edited with Introduction by A. J. Church, 1910. Fables, Ancient and Modern, translated into verse from Homer, Ovid, Boccace, and Chaucer, with original poems (Palamon and Arcite, Meleager and Atalanta, Sigismonda and Guiscardo, Baucis and Philemon, Pigmalion and the Statue, Ciniras and Myrrha, 1st Book of Homer's Iliad, The Cock and the Fox, or, The Nun's Priest's Tale, Theodore and Honoria, Ceyx and Alcyone, The Flower and the Leaf, Alexander's Feast, 12th book of Ovid's Metamorphoses, Speeches of Ajax and Ulysses, The Wife of Bath, Of the Pythagorean Philosophy, The Character of a Good Parson, The Monument of a Fair Maiden Lady, Cymon and Iphigenia), 1700; edited by H. Morley (The Companion Poets), 1891.

PROSE WORKS.—Essay on Dramatic Poesy, 1668 (see The Indian Emperor), 2nd edition, 1684; Essay on Heroic Plays, 1672 (see Conquest of Granada); Notes and Observations on the Empress of Morocco, 1674; Apology for Heroic Poetry, 1674 (see State of Innocence); Vindication of the Duke of Guise, 1683; see also under Annus Mirabilis, account of, etc.; Translations of Juvenal and Persius (Essay on Satire); and Translation of Art of Painting (Preface).

Life of Plutarch, prefixed to the Translation of the Lives by various hands, 1683; Controversy between Dryden and Stillingfleet, 1686; Preface to a Dialogue concerning Women, being a Defence of the Sex, 1691; Character of St. Evremond, prefixed to the latter's Miscellaneous Essays, 1692; Character of Polybius, prefixed to Sir Henry Sheere's translation, 1693; Life of Lucian, not printed till 1711; Letters, published in editions of Works.

PROSE TRANSLATIONS.—Maimbourg History of the League, 1684; Bohours Life of St. Francis Xavier, 1688; Dufresnoy Art of Painting, with Preface, A Parallel between Painting and Poetry, 1695.

WORKS.—Edited by Sir Walter Scott, 18 vols., 1808, 1821; re-edited by G. Saintsbury, 1882-93; World's Classics, 1903, etc.

Dramatic Works.—Published by Tonson, 1 vol. fol., 1701; 6 vols. edited by Congreve, 1717; Eight Plays, edited by G. Saintsbury (Mermaid Series), 1904; Selected Dramas, edited G. R. Noyes (with The Rehearsal by G. Villiers), 1910.

Poetical Works.—See Miscellany Verse above; Poems on various occasions, published by Tonson, 1 vol. fol., 1701; 2 vols., 1742; in 4 vols., edited by S. Derrick (with Life), 1760, 1767; edited by Dr. Johnson, The Works of the English Poets, vols. 13-19, 1779; vols. 18-24, 1790;

with Notes by J. Warton and others, and Johnson's Life, 4 vols., 1811; Aldine Edition (with Mitford's Life), vols. 21-25, 1832-3; and with Life by R. Hooper, 1865, 1866; Annotated Edition, with Life by R. Bell, 1854; Globe Edition, with Memoir, revised text, and notes by W. D. Christie, 1870; with Life and Critical Dissertation by G. Gilfillan (Cassell's Library Edition), edited by C. C. Clarke, 1874; Lubbock's Hundred Best Books, 1892; Albion Edition, with additional lyrics from the plays, and with Memoir, 1893; with Introduction and Textual Notes by J. Sargeaunt, 1910.

Selections.—Edited by W. D. Christie (Clarendon Press), 1871; 5th edition revised by C. H. Firth, 1893; edited with Introduction by H. Morley (Cassell's National Library), 1905; Satires, edited by J. Churton Collins, 1893; Dryden Anthology, 1675-1700 (British Anthologies, No. 7), edited by E. Arber, 1901.

Prose Works.—Critical and Miscellaneous Prose Works, 4 vols., published by Malone, 1800; Discourses on Satire and on Epic Poetry, with Introduction by H. Morley (Cassell's National Library), 1888; Essays, selected and edited by W. P. Ker, 2 vols., 1900; Essays on the Drama, with Introduction and Notes by W. Strunk (English Readings), 1908; Selections, by G. E. Hadow, 1908.

Dryden's chief poems were published singly in many later editions after their first appearance. The Hind and the Panther has been edited by W. H. Williams, 1900, and Palamon and Arcite by P. Chubb, 1908. (Macmillan Series of Classics.)

LIFE.—In Cibber's Lives of the Poets, 1753; Derrick's edition of poems, 1760; Johnson's Lives of the Poets, 1779-81; Malone's edition of Prose Works, 1800; Scott's edition of Works, 1808; R. Bell's edition of Poems, 1854; W. D. Christie (Globe edition), 1870; G. Saintsbury (English Men of Letters), 1881; Alex. Beljame, Le public et les hommes de lettres en Angleterre (1660-1744), 1881.

CONTENTS

DRAMATIC POESY

EPISTLE DEDICATORY TO THE RIGHT HONOURABLE
CHARLES, LORD BUCKHURST

My Lord,—As I was lately reviewing my loose papers, amongst the rest I found this Essay, the writing of which, in this rude and indigested manner wherein your lordship now sees it, served as an amusement to me in the country, when the violence of the last plague had driven me from the town. Seeing then our theatres shut up, I was engaged in these kind of thoughts with the same delight with which men think upon their absent mistresses. I confess I find many things in this Discourse which I do not now approve; my judgment being not a little altered since the writing of it; but whether for the better or the worse, I know not: neither indeed is it much material, in an essay, where all I have said is problematical. For the way of writing plays in verse, which I have seemed to favour, I have, since that time, laid the practice of it aside, till I have more leisure, because I find it troublesome and slow. But I am no way altered from my opinion of it, at least with any reasons which have opposed it. For your lordship may easily observe, that none are very violent against it, but those who either have not attempted it, or who have succeeded ill in their attempt. It is enough for me to have your lordship's example for my excuse in that little which I have done in it; and I am sure my adversaries can bring no such arguments against verse, as those with which the fourth act of *Pompey* will furnish me in its defence. Yet, my lord, you must suffer me a little to complain of you, that you too soon withdraw from us a contentment, of which we expected the continuance, because you gave it us so early. It is a revolt, without occasion, from your party, where your merits had already raised you to the highest commands, and where you have not the excuse of other men, that you have been ill used, and therefore laid down arms. I know no other quarrel you can have to verse, than that which Spurina had to his beauty, when he tore and mangled the features of his face, only because they pleased too well the sight. It was an honour which seemed to wait for you, to lead out a new colony of writers from the mother nation: and upon the first spreading of your ensigns, there had been many in a readiness to have followed so fortunate a leader; if not all, yet the better part of poets:

> pars, indocili melior grege; mollis et exspes
> Inominata perprimat cubilia.

I am almost of opinion, that we should force you to accept of the command, as sometimes the Praetorian bands have compelled their captains to receive the empire. The court, which is the best and surest judge of writing, has generally allowed of verse; and in the town it has found favourers of wit and quality. As for your own particular, my lord, you have yet youth and time enough to give part of them to the divertisement of the public, before you enter into the serious and more unpleasant business of the world. That which the French poet said of the temple of Love, may be as well applied to the temple of the Muses. The words, as near as I can remember them, were these:

> Le jeune homme à mauvaise grace,
> N'ayant pas adoré dans le Temple d'Amour;
> Il faut qu'il entre; et pour le sage,
> Si ce n'est pas son vrai séjour,
> C'est un gîte sur son passage.

I leave the words to work their effect upon your lordship in their own language, because no other can so well express the nobleness of the thought; and wish you may be soon called to bear a part in the affairs of the nation, where I know the world expects you, and wonders why you have been so long forgotten; there being no person amongst our young nobility, on whom the eyes of all men are so much bent. But in the meantime your lordship may imitate the course of Nature, who gives us the flower before the fruit: that I may speak to you in the language of the muses, which I have taken from an excellent poem to the king:

> As Nature, when she fruit designs, thinks fit
> By beauteous blossoms to proceed to it;
> And while she does accomplish all the spring,
> Birds to her secret operations sing.

I confess I have no greater reason, in addressing this Essay to your lordship, than that it might awaken in you the desire of writing something, in whatever kind it be, which might be an honour to our age and country. And methinks it might have the same effect on you, which Homer tells us the fight of the Greeks and Trojans before the fleet had on the spirit of Achilles; who, though he had resolved not to engage, yet found a martial warmth to steal upon him at the sight of blows, the sound of trumpets, and the cries of fighting men.

For my own part, if, in treating of this subject, I sometimes dissent from the opinion of better wits, I declare it is not so much to combat their opinions, as to defend my own, which were first made public. Sometimes, like a scholar in a fencing-school, I put forth myself, and show my own ill play, on purpose to be better taught. Sometimes I stand desperately to my arms, like the foot when deserted by their horse; not in hope to overcome, but only to yield on more honourable terms. And yet, my lord, this war of opinions, you well know, has fallen out among the writers of all ages, and sometimes betwixt friends. Only it has been prosecuted by some, like pedants, with violence of words, and managed by others, like gentlemen, with candour and civility. Even Tully had a controversy with his dear Atticus; and in one of his Dialogues, makes him sustain the part of an enemy in philosophy, who, in his letters, is his confidant of state, and made privy to the most weighty affairs of the Roman senate. And the same respect which was paid by Tully to Atticus, we find returned to him afterwards by Cæsar on a like occasion, who, answering his book in praise of Cato, made it not so much his business to condemn Cato, as to praise Cicero.

But that I may decline some part of the encounter with my adversaries, whom I am neither willing to combat, nor well able to resist; I will give your lordship the relation of a dispute betwixt some of our wits on the same subject, in which they did not only speak of plays in verse, but mingled, in the freedom of discourse, some things of the ancient, many of the modern, ways of writing; comparing those with these, and the wits of our nation with those of others: it is true they differed in their opinions, as it is probable they would: neither do I take upon me to reconcile, but to relate them; and that as Tacitus professes of himself, *sine studio partium, aut ira*, without passion or interest; leaving your lordship to decide it in favour of which part you shall judge most reasonable, and withal, to pardon the many errors of

Your Lordship's
Most obedient humble servant,
JOHN DRYDEN.

TO THE READER

THE drift of the ensuing discourse was chiefly to vindicate the honour of our English writers, from the censure of those who unjustly prefer the French before them. This I intimate, lest any should think me so exceedingly vain, as to teach others an art which they understand much better than myself. But if this incorrect Essay, written in the country without the help of books or advice of friends, shall find any acceptance in the world, I promise to myself a better success of the Second Part, wherein I shall more fully treat of the virtues and faults of the English poets, who have written either in this, the epic, or the lyric way.

DRYDEN'S ESSAYS

AN ESSAY OF DRAMATIC POESY

It was that memorable day, in the first summer of the late war, when our navy engaged the Dutch; a day wherein the two most mighty and best appointed fleets which any age had ever seen, disputed the command of the greater half of the globe, the commerce of nations, and the riches of the universe: while these vast floating bodies, on either side, moved against each other in parallel lines, and our countrymen, under the happy conduct of his royal highness, went breaking, by little and little, into the line of the enemies; the noise of the cannon from both navies reached our ears about the city, so that all men being alarmed with it, and in a dreadful suspense of the event, which they knew was then deciding, every one went following the sound as his fancy led him; and leaving the town almost empty, some took towards the park, some cross the river, others down it; all seeking the noise in the depth of silence.

Among the rest, it was the fortune of Eugenius, Crites, Lisideius, and Neander, to be in company together; three of them persons whom their wit and quality have made known to all the town; and whom I have chose to hide under these borrowed names, that they may not suffer by so ill a relation as I am going to make of their discourse.

2. Taking then a barge, which a servant of Lisideius had provided for them, they made haste to shoot the bridge, and left behind them that great fall of waters which hindered them from hearing what they desired: after which, having disengaged themselves from many vessels which rode at anchor in the Thames, and almost blocked up the passage towards Greenwich, they ordered the watermen to let fall their oars more gently; and then, every one favouring his own curiosity with a strict silence, it was not long ere they perceived the air to break about them like the noise of distant thunder, or of swallows in a chimney: those little undulations of sound, though almost vanishing before

they reached them, yet still seeming to retain somewhat of their first horror, which they had betwixt the fleets. After they had attentively listened till such time as the sound by little and little went from them, Eugenius, lifting up his head, and taking notice of it, was the first who congratulated to the rest that happy omen of our nation's victory: adding, that we had but this to desire in confirmation of it, that we might hear no more of that noise, which was now leaving the English coast. When the rest had concurred in the same opinion, Crites, a person of a sharp judgment, and somewhat too delicate a taste in wit, which the world have mistaken in him for ill-nature, said, smiling to us, that if the concernment of this battle had not been so exceeding great, he could scarce have wished the victory at the price he knew he must pay for it, in being subject to the reading and hearing of so many ill verses as he was sure would be made on that subject. Adding, that no argument could scape some of those eternal rhymers, who watch a battle with more diligence than the ravens and birds of prey; and the worst of them surest to be first in upon the quarry: while the better able, either out of modesty writ not at all, or set that due value upon their poems, as to let them be often desired and long expected. "There are some of those impertinent people of whom you speak," answered Lisideius, "who to my knowledge are already so provided, either way, that they can produce not only a panegyric upon the victory, but, if need be, a funeral elegy on the duke; wherein, after they have crowned his valour with many laurels, they will at last deplore the odds under which he fell, concluding that his courage deserved a better destiny." All the company smiled at the conceipt of Lisideius; but Crites, more eager than before, began to make particular exceptions against some writers, and said, the public magistrate ought to send betimes to forbid them; and that it concerned the peace and quiet of all honest people, that ill poets should be as well silenced as seditious preachers. "In my opinion," replied Eugenius, "you pursue your point too far; for as to my own particular, I am so great a lover of poesy, that I could wish them all rewarded who attempt but to do well; at least, I would not have them worse used than one of their brethren was by Sylla the Dictator:—*Quem in concione vidimus* (says Tully), *cum ei libellum malus poeta de populo subjecisset, quod epigramma in eum fecisset tantummodo alternis versiculis longiusculis, statim ex iis rebus quas tunc vendebat jubere ei praemium tribui, sub ea conditione ne quid postea scriberet.*" "I could wish with all my heart," replied Crites, " that many whom we know were as bountifully thanked upon the same condition,—that they would never trouble us again. For amongst others, I have a moral apprehension of two poets, whom this victory, with the help of both her wings, will never be able to escape." " 'Tis easy to guess whom you intend," said Lisideius; " and without naming them, I ask you, if one of them does not perpetually pay us with clenches upon words, and a certain clownish kind of railery? if now and then he does not offer at a catachresis or Clevelandism, wresting and torturing a word into another meaning: in fine, if he be not one of those whom the French would call *un mauvais buffon;* one who is so much a well-willer to the satire, that he intends at least to spare no man; and though he cannot strike a blow to hurt any, yet he ought to be punished for the malice of the action, as our witches are justly hanged, because they think themselves to be such; and suffer deservedly for believing they did mischief, because they meant it." " You have described him," said Crites, " so exactly, that I am afraid to come after you with my other extremity of poetry. He is one of those who, having had some advantage of education and converse, knows better than the other what a poet should be, but puts it into practice more unluckily than any man; his style and matter are every where alike: he is the most calm, peaceable writer you ever read: he never disquiets your passions with the least concernment, but still leaves you in as even a temper as he found you; he is a very leveller in poetry: he creeps along with ten little words in every line, and helps out his numbers with *For to,* and *Unto,* and all the pretty expletives he can find, till he drags them to the end of another line; while the sense is left tired half way behind it: he doubly starves all his verses, first for want of thought, and then of expression; his poetry neither has wit in it, nor seems to have it; like him in Martial:

Pauper videri Cinna vult, et est pauper.

" He affects plainness, to cover his want of imagination: when he writes the serious way, the highest flight of his fancy is some miserable antithesis, or seeming contradiction; and in the comic he is still reaching at some thin conceit, the ghost of a jest, and that too flies before him, never to be caught; these swallows which we see before us on the Thames are the just resemblance of his wit: you may observe how near the water they stoop, how many proffers they make to dip, and yet how seldom they touch it; and when they do, it is but the surface:

they skim over it but to catch a gnat, and then mount into the air and leave it."

3. "Well, gentlemen," said Eugenius, "you may speak your pleasure of these authors; but though I and some few more about the town may give you a peaceable hearing, yet assure yourselves, there are multitudes who would think you malicious and them injured: especially him whom you first described; he is the very Withers of the city: they have bought more editions of his works than would serve to lay under all their pies at the lord mayor's Christmas. When his famous poem first came out in the year 1660, I have seen them reading it in the midst of 'Change time; nay so vehement they were at it, that they lost their bargain by the candles' ends; but what will you say if he has been received amongst great persons? I can assure you he is, this day, the envy of one who is lord in the art of quibbling, and who does not take it well that any man should intrude so far into his province." "All I would wish," replied Crites, "is, that they who love his writings, may still admire him, and his fellow poet: *Qui Bavium non odit, etc.*, is curse sufficient." "And farther," added Lisideius, "I believe there is no man who writes well, but would think he had hard measure, if their admirers should praise anything of his: *Nam quos contemnimus, eorum quoque laudes contemnimus.*" "There are so few who write well in this age," says Crites, "that methinks any praises should be welcome; they neither rise to the dignity of the last age, nor to any of the ancients: and we may cry out of the writers of this time, with more reason than Petronius of his, *Pace vestra liceat dixisse, primi omnium eloquentium perdidistis:* you have debauched the true old poetry so far, that Nature, which is the soul of it, is not in any of your writings."

4. "If your quarrel," said Eugenius, "to those who now write, be grounded only on your reverence to antiquity, there is no man more ready to adore those great Greeks and Romans than I am: but on the other side, I cannot think so contemptibly of the age in which I live, or so dishonourably of my own country, as not to judge we equal the ancients in most kinds of poesy, and in some surpass them; neither know I any reason why I may not be as zealous for the reputation of our age as we find the ancients themselves were in reference to those who lived before them. For you hear your Horace saying,

> Indignor quidquam reprehendi, non quia crassé
> Compositum, illepidève putetur, sed quia nuper.

And after:

Si meliora dies, ut vina, poemata reddit,
Scire velim, pretim chartis quotus arroget annus?

" But I see I am engaging in a wide dispute, where the arguments are not like to reach close on either side; for poesy is of so large an extent, and so many both of the ancients and moderns have done well in all kinds of it, that in citing one against the other, we shall take up more time this evening than each man's occasions will allow him: therefore I would ask Crites to what part of poesy he would confine his arguments, and whether he would defend the general cause of the ancients against the moderns, or oppose any age of the moderns against this of ours? "

5. Crites, a little while considering upon this demand, told Eugenius, that if he pleased, he would limit their dispute to Dramatic Poesy; in which he thought it not difficult to prove, either that the ancients were superior to the moderns, or the last age of ours.

Eugenius was somewhat surprised, when he heard Crites make choice of that subject. "For ought I see," said he, " I have undertaken a harder province than I imagined; for though I never judged the plays of the Greek or Roman poets comparable to ours, yet, on the other side, those we now see acted come short of many which were written in the last age: but my comfort is, if we are overcome, it will be only by our own countrymen: and if we yield to them in this one part of poesy, we more surpass them in all the other: for in the epic or lyric way, it will be hard for them to show us one such amongst them, as we have many now living, or who lately were: they can produce nothing so courtly writ, or which expresses so much the conversation of a gentleman, as Sir John Suckling; nothing so even, sweet, and flowing as Mr. Waller; nothing so majestic, so correct, as Sir John Denham; nothing so elevated, so copious, and full of spirit as Mr. Cowley; as for the Italian, French, and Spanish plays, I can make it evident, that those who now write surpass them; and that the drama is wholly ours."

All of them were thus far of Eugenius his opinion, that the sweetness of English verse was never understood or practised by our fathers; even Crites himself did not much oppose it; and every one was willing to acknowledge how much our poesy is improved by the happiness of some writers yet living; who first taught us to mould our thoughts into easy and significant words,—to retrench the superfluities of expression,—and to make our rhyme so properly a part of the verse, that it should never mislead the sense, but itself be led and governed by it.

6. Eugenius was going to continue this discourse, when Lisideius told him that it was necessary, before they proceeded further, to take a standing measure of their controversy; for how was it possible to be decided who writ the best plays before we know what a play should be? But, this once agreed on by both parties, each might have recourse to it, either to prove his own advantages, or to discover the failings of his adversary.

He had no sooner said this, but all desired the favour of him to give the definition of a play; and they were the more importunate, because neither Aristotle, nor Horace, nor any other, who had writ of that subject, had ever done it.

Lisideius, after some modest denials, at last confessed he had a rude notion of it; indeed, rather a description than a definition; but which served to guide him in his private thoughts, when he was to make a judgment of what others writ: that he conceived a play ought to be, *A just and lively image of human nature, representing its passions and humours, and the changes of fortune to which it is subject, for the delight and instruction of mankind.*

This definition, though Crites raised a logical objection against it—that it was only *genere et fine*, and so not altogether perfect, was yet well received by the rest; and after they had given order to the watermen to turn their barge, and row softly, that they might take the cool of the evening in their return, Crites, being desired by the company to begin, spoke on behalf of the ancients, in this manner:—

" If confidence presage a victory, Eugenius, in his own opinion, has already triumphed over the ancients: nothing seems more easy to him, than to overcome those whom it is our greatest praise to have imitated well; for we do not only build upon their foundations, but by their models. Dramatic Poesy had time enough, reckoning from Thespis (who first invented it) to Aristophanes, to be born, to grow up, and to flourish in maturity. It has been observed of arts and sciences, that in one and the same century they have arrived to great perfection; and no wonder, since every age has a kind of universal genius, which inclines those that live in it to some particular studies: the work then, being pushed on by many hands, must of necessity go forward.

" Is it not evident, in these last hundred years, when the study of philosophy has been the business of all the Virtuosi in Christendom, that almost a new nature has been revealed to us? That more errors of the school have been detected, more useful experiments in philosophy have been made, more noble secrets in optics, medicine, anatomy, astronomy, discovered, than in all those credulous and doting ages from Aristotle to us?—so true it is, that nothing spreads more fast than science, when rightly and generally cultivated.

" Add to this, the more than common emulation that was in those times of writing well; which though it be found in all ages and all persons that pretend to the same reputation, yet poesy, being then in more esteem than now it is, had greater honours decreed to the professors of it, and consequently the rivalship was more high between them; they had judges ordained to decide their merit, and prizes to reward it; and historians have been diligent to record of Eschylus, Euripides, Sophocles, Lycophron, and the rest of them, both who they were that vanquished in these wars of the theatre, and how often they were crowned: while the Asian kings and Grecian commonwealths scarce afforded them a nobler subject than the unmanly luxuries of a debauched court, or giddy intrigues of a factious city:—*Alit æmulatio ingenia* (says Paterculus), *et nunc invidia, nunc admiratio incitatio nem accendit :* Emulation is the spur of wit; and sometimes envy, sometimes admiration, quickens our endeavours.

" But now, since the rewards of honour are taken away, that virtuous emulation is turned into direct malice; yet so slothful, that it contents itself to condemn and cry down others, without attempting to do better: it is a reputation too unprofitable, to take the necessary pains for it; yet, wishing they had it, that desire is incitement enough to hinder others from it. And this, in short, Eugenius, is the reason why you have now so few good poets, and so many severe judges. Certainly, to imitate the ancients well, much labour and long study is required; which pains, I have already shown, our poets would want encouragement to take, if yet they had ability to go through the work. Those ancients have been faithful imitators and wise observers of that nature which is so torn and ill represented in our plays; they have handed down to us a perfect resemblance of her; which we, like ill copiers, neglecting to look on, have rendered monstrous, and disfigured. But, that you may know how much you are indebted to those your masters, and be ashamed to have so ill requited them, I must remember you, that all the rules by which we practise the drama at this day (either such as relate to the justness and symmetry of the plot, or the episodical ornaments, such as descriptions, narrations, and other beauties, which are not essential to the play), were delivered to us from the observations which Aristotle made, of those poets, who either lived before him, or were his contemporaries: we have added nothing of our own, except we have the confidence to say our wit is better; of which, none boast in this our age, but such as understand not theirs. Of that book which Aristotle has left us, περὶ τῆς Ποιητικῆς, Horace his Art of Poetry is an excellent comment, and, I believe, restores to us that Second Book of his concerning Comedy, which is wanting in him.

"Out of these two have been extracted the famous Rules, which the French call *Des Trois Unités*, or, The Three Unities, which ought to be observed in every regular play; namely, of Time, Place, and Action.

"The unity of time they comprehend in twenty-four hours, the compass of a natural day, or as near as it can be contrived; and the reason of it is obvious to every one,—that the time of the feigned action, or fable of the play, should be proportioned as near as can be to the duration of that time in which it is represented: since, therefore, all plays are acted on the theatre in the space of time much within the compass of twenty-four hours, that play is to be thought the nearest imitation of nature, whose plot or action is confined within that time; and, by the same rule which concludes this general proportion of time, it follows, that all the parts of it are (as near as may be) to be equally subdivided; namely, that one act take not up the supposed time of half a day, which is out of proportion to the rest; since the other four are then to be straitened within the compass of the remaining half: for it is unnatural that one act, which being spoke or written is not longer than the rest, should be supposed longer by the audience; it is therefore the poet's duty, to take care that no act should be imagined to exceed the time in which it is represented on the stage; and that the intervals and inequalities of time be supposed to fall out between the acts.

"This rule of time, how well it has been observed by the ancients, most of their plays will witness; you see them in their tragedies (wherein to follow this rule is certainly most difficult), from the very beginning of their plays, falling close into that part of the story which they intend for the action or principal object of it, leaving the former part to be delivered by narration: so that they set the audience, as it were, at the post where the race is to be concluded; and, saving them the tedious expecta-

ion of seeing the poet set out and ride the beginning of the
ourse, they suffer you not to behold him, till he is in sight
f the goal, and just upon you.

"For the second unity, which is that of Place, the ancients
neant by it, that the scene ought to be continued through the
lay, in the same place where it was laid in the beginning: for,
he stage on which it is represented being but one and the same
lace, it is unnatural to conceive it many,—and those far distant
rom one another. I will not deny but, by the variation of
ainted scenes, the fancy, which in these cases will contribute
o its own deceit, may sometimes imagine it several places, with
ome appearance of probability; yet it still carries the greater
ikelihood of truth if those places be supposed so near each
ther as in the same town or city; which may all be compre-
ended under the larger denomination of one place; for a
reater distance will bear no proportion to the shortness of time
vhich is allotted, in the acting, to pass from one of them to
nother; for the observation of this, next to the ancients, the
'rench are to be most commended. They tie themselves so
trictly to the unity of place that you never see in any of their
lays a scene changed in the middle of an act: if the act begins
1 a garden, a street, or chamber, 'tis ended in the same place;
nd that you may know it to be the same, the stage is so supplied
vith persons, that it is never empty all the time: he who enters
econd, has business with him who was on before; and before
he second quits the stage, a third appears who has business
vith him. This Corneille calls *la liaison des scènes*, the con-
inuity or joining of the scenes; and 'tis a good mark of a well-
ontrived play, when all the persons are known to each other,
nd every one of them has some affairs with all the rest.

"As for the third unity, which is that of Action, the ancients
neant no other by it than what the logicians do by their *finis*,
he end or scope of any action; that which is the first in inten-
on, and last in execution: now the poet is to aim at one great
nd complete action, to the carrying on of which all things in his
lay, even the very obstacles, are to be subservient; and the
eason of this is as evident as any of the former. For two
ctions, equally laboured and driven on by the writer, would
estroy the unity of the poem; it would be no longer one play,
ut two: not but that there may be many actions in a play, as
en Jonson has observed in his *Discoveries*; but they must be
ll subservient to the great one, which our language happily
xpresses in the name of *under-plots*: such as in Terence's

Eunuch is the difference and reconcilement of Thais and Phædria
which is not the chief business of the play, but promotes th
marriage of Chærea and Chremes's sister, principally intende
by the poet.   There ought to be but one action, says Corneille
that is, one complete action, which leaves the mind of th
audience in a full repose; but this cannot be brought to pas
but by many other imperfect actions, which conduce to it, an
hold the audience in a delightful suspence of what will be.

"If by these rules (to omit many other drawn from th
precepts and practice of the ancients) we should judge ou
modern plays, 'tis probable that few of them would endure th
trial: that which should be the business of a day, takes up i
some of them an age; instead of one action, they are th
epitomes of a man's life; and for one spot of ground, which th
stage should represent, we are sometimes in more countries tha
the map can show us.

"But if we allow the Ancients to have contrived well, we mus
acknowledge them to have written better.   Questionless we ar
deprived of a great stock of wit in the loss of Menander amon
the Greek poets, and of Cæcilius, Afranius, and Varius, amon
the Romans; we may guess at Menander's excellency by th
plays of Terence, who translated some of his; and yet wante
so much of him, that he was called by C. Cæsar the hal
Menander; and may judge of Varius, by the testimonies
Horace, Martial, and Velleius Paterculus.   'Tis probable tha
these, could they be recovered, would decide the controversy
but so long as Aristophanes and Plautus are extant, while th
tragedies of Euripides, Sophocles, and Seneca, are in our hand
I can never see one of those plays which are now written b
it increases my admiration of the ancients.   And yet I mu
acknowledge further, that to admire them as we ought, we shoul
understand them better than we do.   Doubtless many thin
appear flat to us, the wit of which depended on some custom
story, which never came to our knowledge; or perhaps on som
criticism in their language, which being so long dead, and on
remaining in their books, 'tis not possible they should make
understand perfectly.   To read Macrobius, explaining the pr
priety and elegancy of many words in Virgil, which I had befo
passed over without consideration as common things, is enoug
to assure me that I ought to think the same of Terence; a
that in the purity of his style (which Tully so much valued th
he ever carried his works about him) there is yet left in him gre
room for admiration, if I knew but where to place it.   In th

meantime I must desire you to take notice that the greatest
man of the last age, Ben Jonson, was willing to give place to
them in all things: he was not only a professed imitator of
Horace, but a learned plagiary of all the others; you track him
everywhere in their snow: if Horace, Lucan, Petronius Arbiter,
Seneca, and Juvenal, had their own from him, there are few
serious thoughts which are new in him: you will pardon me,
therefore, if I presume he loved their fashion, when he wore
their clothes. But since I have otherwise a great veneration
for him, and you, Eugenius, prefer him above all other poets,
I will use no farther argument to you than his example: I will
produce before you Father Ben, dressed in all the ornaments
and colours of the ancients; you will need no other guide to our
party, if you follow him; and whether you consider the bad
plays of our age, or regard the good plays of the last, both the
best and worst of the modern poets will equally instruct you to
admire the ancients."

Crites had no sooner left speaking, but Eugenius, who had
waited with some impatience for it, thus began:

"I have observed in your speech, that the former part of it
is convincing as to what the moderns have profited by the rules
of the ancients; but in the latter you are careful to conceal
how much they have excelled them; we own all the helps we
have from them, and want neither veneration nor gratitude,
while we acknowledge that, to overcome them, we must make
use of the advantages we have received from them: but to these
assistances we have joined our own industry; for, had we sat
down with a dull imitation of them, we might then have lost
somewhat of the old perfection, but never acquired any that
was new. We draw not therefore after their lines, but those
of nature; and having the life before us, besides the experience
of all they knew, it is no wonder if we hit some airs and features
which they have missed. I deny not what you urge of arts and
sciences, that they have flourished in some ages more than
others; but your instance in philosophy makes for me: for if
natural causes be more known now than in the time of Aristotle,
because more studied, it follows that poesy and other arts may,
with the same pains, arrive still nearer to perfection; and, that
granted, it will rest for you to prove that they wrought more
perfect images of human life than we; which seeing in your
discourse you have avoided to make good, it shall now be my
task to show you some part of their defects, and some few
excellencies of the moderns. And I think there is none among

us can imagine I do it enviously, or with purpose to detrac
from them; for what interest of fame or profit can the living los
by the reputation of the dead? On the other side, it is a grea
truth which Velleius Paterculus affirms: *Audita visis libentiu
laudamus ; et præsentia invidia præterita admiratione prose
quimur ; et his nos obrui, illis instrui credimus :* that praise o
censure is certainly the most sincere, which unbribed posterit
shall give us.

"Be pleased then in the first place to take notice that th
Greek poesy, which Crites has affirmed to have arrived to per
fection in the reign of the old comedy, was so far from it tha
the distinction of it into acts was not known to them; or if i
were, it is yet so darkly delivered to us that we cannot make i
out.

"All we know of it is from the singing of their Chorus; and
that too is so uncertain, that in some of their plays we hav
reason to conjecture they sung more than five times. Aristotl
indeed divides the integral parts of a play into four. First, th
Protasis, or entrance, which gives light only to the character
of the persons, and proceeds very little into any part of th
action. Secondly, the *Epitasis*, or working up of the plot
where the play grows warmer, the design or action of it i
drawing on, and you see something promising that it will com
to pass. Thirdly, the *Catastasis*, called by the Romans, *Status*
the height and full growth of the play: we may call it properly
the counter-turn, which destroys that expectation, imbroils th
action in new difficulties, and leaves you far distant from tha
hope in which it found you; as you may have observed in a
violent stream resisted by a narrow passage,—it runs round
to an eddy, and carries back the waters with more swiftnes
than it brought them on. Lastly, the *Catastrophe*, which th
Grecians called λύσις, the French *le dénouement*, and we th
discovery, or unravelling of the plot: there you see all thing
settling again upon their first foundations; and, the obstacle
which hindered the design or action of the play once removed
it ends with that resemblance of truth and nature, that th
audience are satisfied with the conduct of it. Thus this grea
man delivered to us the image of a play; and I must confes
it is so lively, that from thence much light has been derived t
the forming it more perfectly into acts and scenes: but wha
poet first limited to five the number of the acts, I know not
only we see it so firmly established in the time of Horace, tha
he gives it for a rule in comedy,—*Neu brevior quinto, neu si*

productior actu. So that you see the Grecians cannot be said to have consummated this art; writing rather by entrances than by acts, and having rather a general indigested notion of a play, than knowing how and where to bestow the particular graces of it.

"But since the Spaniards at this day allow but three acts, which they call *Jornadas*, to a play, and the Italians in many of theirs follow them, when I condemn the ancients, I declare it is not altogether because they have not five acts to every play, but because they have not confined themselves to one certain number: it is building an house without a model; and when they succeeded in such undertakings, they ought to have sacrificed to Fortune, not to the Muses.

"Next, for the plot, which Aristotle called τό μυθος, and often τῶν πραγμάτων σύνθεσις, and from him the Romans *Fabula;* it has already been judiciously observed by a late writer, that in their tragedies it was only some tale derived from Thebes or Troy, or at least something that happened in those two ages; which was worn so threadbare by the pens of all the epic poets, and even by tradition, itself of the talkative Greeklings (as Ben Jonson calls them), that before it came upon the stage it was already known to all the audience: and the people, so soon as ever they heard the name of Œdipus, knew as well as the poet, that he had killed his father by a mistake, and committed incest with his mother, before the play; that they were now to hear of a great plague, an oracle, and the ghost of Laius: so that they sat with a yawning kind of expectation, till he was to come with his eyes pulled out, and speak a hundred or more verses in a tragic tone, in complaint of his misfortunes. But one Œdipus, Hercules, or Medea, had been tolerable: poor people, they escaped not so good cheap; they had still the *chapon bouillé* set before them, till their appetites were cloyed with the same dish, and, the novelty being gone, the pleasure vanished; so that one main end of Dramatic Poesy in its definition, which was to cause delight, was of consequence destroyed.

"In their comedies, the Romans generally borrowed their plots from the Greek poets; and theirs was commonly a little girl stolen or wandered from her parents, brought back unknown to the city, there [falling into the hands of] some young fellow, who, by the help of his servant, cheats his father; and when her time comes, to cry,—*Juno Lucina, fer opem,*—one or other sees a little box or cabinet which was carried away with her, and so discovers her to her friends, if some god do not prevent it, by coming down in a machine, and taking the thanks of it to himself.

"By the plot you may guess much of the characters of the persons. An old father, who would willingly, before he dies, see his son well married; his debauched son, kind in his nature to his mistress, but miserably in want of money; a servant or slave, who has so much wit to strike in with him, and help to dupe his father; a braggadocio captain, a parasite, and a lady of pleasure.

"As for the poor honest maid, on whom the story is built, and who ought to be one of the principal actors in the play, she is commonly a mute in it: she has the breeding of the old Elizabeth way, which was for maids to be seen and not to be heard; and it is enough you know she is willing to be married, when the fifth act requires it.

"These are plots built after the Italian mode of houses,—you see through them all at once: the characters are indeed the imitation of nature, but so narrow, as if they had imitated only an eye or an hand, and did not dare to venture on the lines of a face, or the proportion of a body.

"But in how strait a compass soever they have bounded their plots and characters, we will pass it by, if they have regularly pursued them, and perfectly observed those three unities of time, place, and action; the knowledge of which you say is derived to us from them. But in the first place give me leave to tell you, that the unity of place, however it might be practised by them, was never any of their rules: we neither find it in Aristotle, Horace, or any who have written of it, till in our age the French poets first made it a precept of the stage. The unity of time, even Terencè himself, who was the best and most regular of them, has neglected: his *Heauton-timorumenos*, or Self-Punisher, takes up visibly two days, says Scaliger; the two first acts concluding the first day, the three last the day ensuing; and Euripides, in tying himself to one day, has committed an absurdity never to be forgiven him; for in one of his tragedies he has made Theseus go from Athens to Thebes, which was about forty English miles, under the walls of it to give battle, and appear victorious in the next act; and yet, from the time of his departure to the return of the Nuntius, who gives the relation of his victory, Æthra and the Chorus have but thirty-six verses; which is not for every mile a verse.

"The like error is as evident in Terence his *Eunuch*, when Laches, the old man, enters by mistake into the house of Thais;

where, betwixt his exit and the entrance of Pythias, who comes to give ample relation of the disorders he has raised within, Parmeno, who was left upon the stage, has not above five lines to speak. *C'est bien employer un temps si court*, says the French poet, who furnished me with one of the observations: and almost all their tragedies will afford us examples of the like nature.

" It is true, they have kept the continuity, or, as you called it, *liaison des scènes*, somewhat better: two do not perpetually come in together, talk, and go out together; and other two succeed them, and do the same throughout the act, which the English call by the name of single scenes; but the reason is, because they have seldom above two or three scenes, properly so called, in every act; for it is to be accounted a new scene, not only every time the stage is empty; but every person who enters, though to others, makes it so; because he introduces a new business. Now the plots of their plays being narrow, and the persons few, one of their acts was written in a less compass than one of our well-wrought scenes; and yet they are often deficient even in this. To go no further than Terence; you find in the *Eunuch*, Antipho entering single in the midst of the third act, after Chremes and Pythias were gone off; in the same play you have likewise Dorias beginning the fourth act alone; and after she had made a relation of what was done at the Soldiers' entertainment (which by the way was very inartificial, because she was presumed to speak directly to the audience, and to acquaint them with what was necessary to be known, but yet should have been so contrived by the poet as to have been told by persons of the drama to one another, and so by them to have come to the knowledge of the people), she quits the stage, and Phædria enters next, alone likewise: he also gives you an account of himself, and of his returning from the country, in monologue; to which unnatural way of narration Terence is subject in all his plays. In his *Adelphi*, or Brothers, Syrus and Demea enter after the scene was broken by the departure of Sostrata, Geta, and Canthara; and indeed you can scarce look unto any of his comedies, where you will not presently discover the same interruption.

" But as they have failed both in laying of their plots, and in the management, swerving from the rules of their own art by misrepresenting nature to us, in which they have ill satisfied one intention of a play, which was delight; so in the instructive part they have erred worse: instead of punishing vice and rewarding virtue, they have often shewn a prosperous wickedness, and an unhappy piety: they have set before us a bloody image of revenge in Medea, and given her dragons to convey her safe from punishment; a Priam and Astyanax murdered, and Cassandra ravished, and the lust and murder ending in the victory of him who acted them: in short, there is no indecorum in any of our modern plays, which if I would excuse, I could not shadow with some authority from the ancients.

"And one farther note of them let me leave you: tragedies and comedies were not writ then as they are now, promiscuously, by the same person; but he who found his genius bending to the one, never attempted the other way. This is so plain, that I need not instance to you, that Aristophanes, Plautus, Terence, never any of them writ a tragedy; Æschylus, Euripides, Sophocles, and Seneca, never meddled with comedy: the sock and buskin were not worn by the same poet. Having then so much care to excel in one kind, very little is to be pardoned them, if they miscarried in it; and this would lead me to the consideration of their wit, had not Crites given me sufficient warning not to be too bold in my judgment of it; because, the languages being dead, and many of the customs and little accidents on which it depended lost to us, we are not competent judges of it. But though I grant that here and there we may miss the application of a proverb or a custom, yet a thing well said will be wit in all languages; and though it may lose something in the translation, yet to him who reads it in the original, 'tis still the same: he has an idea of its excellency, though it cannot pass from his mind into any other expression or words than those in which he finds it. When Phædria, in the *Eunuch*, had a command from his mistress to be absent two days, and, encouraging himself to go through with it, said, *Tandem ego non illa caream, si sit opus, vel totum triduum?*—Parmeno, to mock the softness of his master, lifting up his hands and eyes, cries out, as it were in admiration, *Hui! universum triduum!* the elegancy of which *universum*, though it cannot be rendered in our language, yet leaves an impression on our souls: but this happens seldom in him; in Plautus oftener, who is infinitely too bold in his metaphors and coining words, out of which many times his wit is nothing; which questionless was one reason why Horace falls upon him so severely in those verses:

> Sed proavi nostri Plautinos et numeros et
> Laudavere sales, nimium patiemter utrumque.
> Ne dicam stolidè.

For Horace himself was cautious to obtrude a new word on his readers, and makes custom and common use the best measure of receiving it into our writings:

> Multa renascentur quæ nunc [jam] cecidere, cadentque
> Quæ nunc sunt in honore vocabula, si volet usus,
> Quem penes arbitrium est, et jus, et norma loquendi.

" The not observing this rule is that which the world has blamed in our satirist, Cleveland: to express a thing hard and unnaturally, is his new way of elocution. 'Tis true, no poet but may sometimes use a catachresis: Virgil does it—

> Mistaque ridenti colocasia fundet acantho—

in his eclogue of Pollio; and in his seventh Æneid:

> mirantur et undæ,
> Miratur nemus insuetum fulgentia louge
> Scuta virum fluvio pictasque innare carinas.

And Ovid once so modestly, that he asks leave to do it:

> quem, si verbo audacia detur,
> Haud metuam summi dixisse Palatia cæli.

calling the court of Jupiter by the name of Augustus his palace; though in another place he is more bold, where he says,—*et longas visent Capitolia pompas.* But to do this always, and never be able to write a line without it, though it may be admired by some few pedants, will not pass upon those who know that wit is best conveyed to us in the most easy language; and is most to be admired when a great thought comes dressed in words so commonly received, that it is understood by the meanest apprehensions, as the best meat is the most easily digested: but we cannot read a verse of Cleveland's without making a face at it, as if every word were a pill to swallow: he gives us many times a hard nut to break our teeth, without a kernel for our pains. So that there is this difference betwixt his Satires and doctor Donne's; that the one gives us deep thoughts in common language, though rough cadence; the other gives us common thoughts in abstruse words: 'tis true, in some places his wit is independent of his words, as in that of the rebel Scot:

> Had Cain been Scot, God would have chang'd his doom;
> Not forc'd him wander, but confin'd him home.

" *Si sic omnia dixisset !* This is wit in all languages: it is like Mercury, never to be lost or killed:—and so that other—

> For beauty, like white powder, makes no noise,
> And yet the silent hypocrite destroys.

You see the last line is highly metaphorical, but it is so soft and gentle, that it does not shock us as we read it.

"But, to return from whence I have digressed, to the consideration of the ancients' writing, and their wit (of which by this time you will grant us in some measure to be fit judges). Though I see many excellent thoughts in Seneca, yet he of them who had a genius most proper for the stage, was Ovid; he had a way of writing so fit to stir up a pleasing admiration and concernment, which are the objects of a tragedy, and to show the various movements of a soul combating betwixt two different passions, that, had he lived in our age, or in his own could have writ with our advantages, no man but must have yielded to him; and therefore I am confident the *Medea* is none of his: for, though I esteem it for the gravity and sententiousness of it, which he himself concludes to be suitable to a tragedy,—*Omne genus scripti gravitate tragædia vincit,*—yet it moves not my soul enough to judge that he, who in the epic way wrote things so near the drama as the story of Myrrha, of Caunus and Biblis, and the rest, should stir up no more concernment where he most endeavoured it. The masterpiece of Seneca I hold to be that scene in the *Troades*, where Ulysses is seeking for Astyanax to kill him: there you see the tenderness of a mother so represented in Andromache, that it raises compassion to a high degree in the reader, and bears the nearest resemblance of anything in the tragedies of the ancients to the excellent scenes of passion in Shakspeare, or in Fletcher: for love-scenes, you will find few among them; their tragic poets dealt not with that soft passion, but with lust, cruelty, revenge, ambition, and those bloody actions they produced; which were more capable of raising horror than compassion in an audience: leaving love untouched, whose gentleness would have tempered them; which is the most frequent of all the passions, and which, being the private concernment of every person, is soothed by viewing its own image in a public entertainment.

"Among their comedies, we find a scene or two of tenderness, and that where you would least expect it, in Plautus; but to speak generally, their lovers say little, when they see each other, but *anima mea vita mea*; Ζωὴ καὶ ψυχῆ, as the women in Juvenal's time used to cry out in the fury of their kindness. Any sudden gust of passion (as an ecstasy of love in an unexpected meeting) cannot better be expressed than in a word and a sigh, breaking one another. Nature is dumb on such occasions; and to make her speak would be to represent her unlike herself. But there are a thousand other concernments of lovers, as jealousies, complaints, contrivances, and the like, where not to open their minds at large to each other, were to be wanting to their own love, and to the expectation of the audience; who watch the movements of their minds, as much as the changes of their fortunes. For the imaging of the first is properly the work of a poet; the latter he borrows from the historian."

Eugenius was proceeding in that part of his discourse, when Crites interrupted him. "I see," said he, "Eugenius and I are never like to have this question decided betwixt us; for he maintains, the moderns have acquired a new perfection in writing; I can only grant they have altered the mode of it. Homer described his heroes men of great appetites, lovers of beef broiled upon the coals, and good fellows; contrary to the practice of the French Romances, whose heroes neither eat, nor drink, nor sleep, for love. Virgil makes Æneas a bold avower of his own virtues:

Sum pius Æneas, fama super æthera notus;

which, in the civility of our poets is the character of a fanfaron or Hector: for with us the knight takes occasion to walk out, or sleep, to avoid the vanity of telling his own story, which the trusty 'squire is ever to perform for him. So in their love-scenes, of which Eugenius spoke last, the ancients were more hearty, were more talkative: they writ love as it was then the mode to make it; and I will grant thus much to Eugenius, that perhaps one of their poets had he lived in our age, *si foret hoc nostrum fato delapsus in ævum* (as Horace says of Lucilius), he had altered many things; not that they were not natural before, but that he might accommodate himself to the age in which he lived. Yet in the meantime, we are not to conclude anything rashly against those great men, but preserve to them the dignity of masters, and give that honour to their memories, *quos Libitina sacravit*, part of which we expect may be paid to us in future times."

This moderation of Crites, as it was pleasing to all the company, so it put an end to that dispute; which Eugenius, who seemed to have the better of the argument, would urge no farther: but Lisideius, after he had acknowledged himself of Eugenius his opinion concerning the ancient, yet told him, he had forborne, till his discourse were ended, to ask him why he preferred the English plays above those of other nations? and whether we ought not to submit our stage to the exactness of our next neighbours?

" Though," said Eugenius, " I am at all times ready to defend the honour of my country against the French, and to maintain, we are as well able to vanquish them with our pens, as our ancestors have been with their swords; yet, if you please," added he, looking upon Neander, " I will commit this cause to my friend's management; his opinion of our plays is the same with mine, and besides, there is no reason, that Crites and I, who have now left the stage, should re-enter so suddenly upon it; which is against the laws of comedy."

" If the question had been stated," replied Lisideius, " who had writ best, the French or English, forty years ago, I should have been of your opinion, and adjudged the honour to our own nation; but since that time " (said he, turning towards Neander), " we have been so long together bad Englishmen that we had not leisure to be good poets. Beaumont, Fletcher, and Jonson (who were only capable of bringing us to that degree of perfection which we have), were just then leaving the world; as if in an age of so much horror, wit, and those milder studies of humanity, had no farther business among us. But the Muses, who ever follow peace, went to plant in another country: it was then that the great Cardinal Richelieu began to take them into his protection; and that, by his encouragement, Corneille, and some other Frenchmen, reformed their theatre (which before was as much below ours, as it now surpasses it and the rest of Europe). But because Crites in his discourse for the ancients has prevented me, by observing many rules of the stage which the moderns have borrowed from them, I shall only, in short, demand of you, whether you are not convinced that of all nations the French have best observed them? In the unity of time you find them so scrupulous that it yet remains a dispute among their poets, whether the artificial day of twelve hours, more or less, be not meant by Aristotle, rather than the natural one of twenty-four; and consequently, whether all plays ought not to be reduced into that compass. This I can testify, that in all their dramas writ within these last twenty years and upwards, I have not observed any that have extended the time to thirty hours: in the unity of place they are full as scrupulous; for many of their critics limit it to that very spot of ground where the play is supposed to begin; none of them exceed the compass of the same town or city. The unity of action in all plays is yet more conspicuous; for they do not burden them with under-plots, as the English do: which is the reason why many scenes of our tragi-comedians carry on a design that is nothing of kin to the main plot; and that we see two distinct webs in a play, like those in ill-wrought stuffs; and two actions, that is, two plays, carried on together, to the confounding of the audience; who, before they are warm in their concernments for one part, are diverted to another; and by that means espouse the interest of neither. From hence likewise it arises that the one half of our actors are not known to the other. They keep their distances, as if they were Montagues and Capulets, and seldom begin an acquaintance till the last scene of the fifth act, when they are all to meet upon the stage. There is no theatre in the world has anything so absurd as the English tragi-comedy; 'tis a drama of our own invention, and the fashion of it is enough to proclaim it so; here a course of mirth, there another of sadness and passion, and a third of honour and a duel: thus, in two hours and a half, we run through all the fits of Bedlam. The French affords you as much variety on the same day, but they do it not so unseasonably, or *mal à propos*, as we: our poets present you the play and the farce together; and our stages still retain somewhat of the original civility of the Red Bull:

> Atque ursum et pugiles media inter carmina poscunt.

The end of tragedies or serious plays, says Aristotle, is to beget admiration, compassion, or concernment; but are not mirth and compassion things incompatible? and is it not evident that the poet must of necessity destroy the former by intermingling of the latter? that is, he must ruin the sole end and object of his tragedy, to introduce somewhat that is forced into it, and is not of the body of it. Would you not think that physician mad, who, having prescribed a purge, should immediately order you to take restringents?

" But to leave our plays, and return to theirs. I have noted one great advantage they have had in the plotting of their tragedies; that is, they are always grounded upon some known history: according to that of Horace, *Ex noto fictum carmen sequar ;* and in that they have so imitated the ancients that they have surpassed them. For the ancients, as was observed before, took for the foundation of their plays some poetical fiction, such as under that consideration could move but little concernment in the audience, because they already knew the event of it. But the French goes farther:

> Atque ita mentitur, sic veris falsa remiscet
> Primo ne medium, medio ne discrepet imum.

He so interweaves truth with probable fiction that he puts a pleasing fallacy upon us; mends the intrigues of fate, and dispenses with the severity of history, to reward that virtue which has been rendered to us there unfortunate. Sometimes the story has left the success so doubtful that the writer is free, by the privilege of a poet, to take that which of two or more relations will best suit with his design: as for example, in the death of Cyrus, whom Justin and some others report to have perished in the Scythian war, but Xenophon affirms to have died in his bed of extreme old age. Nay more, when the event is past dispute, even then we are willing to be deceived, and the poet, if he contrives it with appearance of truth, has all the audience of his party; at least during the time his play is acting: so naturally we are kind to virtue, when our own interest is not in question, that we take it up as the general concernment of mankind. On the other side, if you consider the historical plays of Shakspeare, they are rather so many chronicles of kings, or the business many times of thirty or forty years, cramped into a representation of two hours and a half; which is not to imitate or paint nature, but rather to draw her in miniature, to take her in little; to look upon her through the wrong end of a perspective, and receive her images not only much less, but infinitely more imperfect than the life: this, instead of making a play delightful, renders it ridiculous:—

> Quodcunque ostendis mihi sic, incredulus odi.

For the spirit of man cannot be satisfied but with truth, or at least verisimility; and a poem is to contain, if not τὰ ἔτυμα yet ἐτύμοισιν ὁμοῖα, as one of the Greek poets has expressed it.

" Another thing in which the French differ from us and from the Spaniards, is that they do not embarrass, or cumber themselves with too much plot; they only represent so much of a story as will constitute one whole and great action sufficient for a play; we, who undertake more, do but multiply adventures, which, not being produced from one another, as effects from causes, but rarely following, constitute many actions in the drama, and consequently make it many plays.

" But by pursuing closely one argument, which is not cloyed with many turns, the French have gained more liberty for verse, in which they write; they have leisure to dwell on a subject which deserves it; and to represent the passions (which we have acknowledged to be the poet's work), without being hurried from one thing to another, as we are in the plays of Calderon, which we have seen lately upon our theatres under the name of Spanish plots. I have taken notice but of one tragedy of ours whose plot has that uniformity and unity of design in it, which I have commended in the French; and that is *Rollo,* or rather, under the name of Rollo, the Story of Bassianus and Geta in Herodian: there indeed the plot is neither large nor intricate, but just enough to fill the minds of the audience, not to cloy them. Besides, you see it founded upon the truth of history, —only the time of the action is not reduceable to the strictness of the rules; and you see in some places a little farce mingled, which is below the dignity of the other parts, and in this all our poets are extremely peccant: even Ben Jonson himself, in *Sejanus* and *Catiline,* has given us this oleo of a play, this un-natural mixture of comedy and tragedy; which to me sounds just as ridiculously as the history of David with the merry humours of Golia's. In *Sejanus* you may take notice of the scene betwixt Livia and the physician which is a pleasant satire upon the artificial helps of beauty: in *Catiline* you may see the parliament of women; the little envies of them to one another; and all that passess betwixt Curio and Fulvia: scenes admirable in their kind, but of an ill mingle with the rest.

" But I return again to the French writers, who, as I have said, do not burden themselves too much with plot, which has been reproached to them by an ingenious person of our nation as a fault; for, he says, they commonly make but one person considerable in a play; they dwell on him, and his concern-ments, while the rest of the persons are only subservient to set him off. If he intends this by it,—that there is one person in the play who is of greater dignity than the rest, he must tax, not only theirs, but those of the ancients, and which he would be loth to do, the best of ours; for it is impossible but that one person must be more conspicuous in it than any other, and con-sequently the greatest share in the action must devolve on him. We see it so in the management of all affairs; even in the most equal aristocracy, the balance cannot be so justly poised but some one will be superior to the rest, either in parts, fortune, interest, or the consideration of some glorious exploit; which will reduce the greatest part of business into his hands.

" But, if he would have us to imagine, that in exalting one character the rest of them are neglected, and that all of them have not some share or other in the action of the play, I desire him to produce any of Corneille's tragedies, wherein every person, like so many servants in a well-governed family, has not some employment, and who is not necessary to the carrying on of the plot, or at least to your understanding it.

"There are indeed some protatic persons in the ancients, whom they make use of in their plays, either to hear or give the relation: but the French avoid this with great address, making their narrations only to, or by such, who are some way interested in the main design. And now I am speaking of relations, I cannot take a fitter opportunity to add this in favour of the French, that they often use them with better judgment and more *à propos* than the English do. Not that I commend narrations in general,—but there are two sorts of them. One, of those things which are antecedent to the play, and are related to make the conduct of it more clear to us. But 'tis a fault to choose such subjects for the stage as will force us on that rock because we see they are seldom listened to by the audience and that is many times the ruin of the play; for, being once let pass without attention, the audience can never recover themselves to understand the plot: and indeed it is somewhat unreasonable that they should be put to so much trouble, as that, to comprehend what passes in their sight, they must have recourse to what was done, perhaps, ten or twenty years ago.

"But there is another sort of relations, that is, of things happening in the action of the play, and supposed to be done behind the scenes; and this is many times both convenient and beautiful; for by it the French avoid the tumult to which we are subject in England, by representing duels, battles, and the like; which renders our stage too like the theatres where they fight prizes. For what is more ridiculous than to represent an army with a drum and five men behind it; all which the hero of the other side is to drive in before him; or to see a duel fought, and one slain with two or three thrusts of the foils, which we know are so blunted that we might give a man an hour to kill another in good earnest with them.

"I have observed that in all our tragedies, the audience cannot forbear laughing when the actors are to die; it is the most comic part of the whole play. All *passions* may be lively represented on the stage, if to the well-writing of them the actor supplies a good commanded voice, and limbs that move easily, and without stiffness; but there are many *actions* which can never be imitated to a just height: dying especially is a thing which none but a Roman gladiator could naturally perform on the stage, when he did not imitate or represent, but do it; and therefore it is better to omit the representation of it.

"The words of a good writer, which describe it lively, will make a deeper impression of belief in us than all the actor can insinuate into us, when he seems to fall dead before us; as a poet in the description of a beautiful garden, or a meadow, will please our imagination more than the place itself can please our sight. When we see death represented, we are convinced it is but fiction; but when we hear it related, our eyes, the strongest witnesses, are wanting, which might have undeceived us; and we are all willing to favour the sleight, when the poet does not too grossly impose on us. They therefore who imagine these relations would make no concernment in the audience, are deceived, by confounding them with the other, which are of things antecedent to the play: those are made often in cold blood, as I may say, to the audience; but these are warmed with our concernments, which were before awakened in the play. What the philosophers say of motion, that, when it is once begun, it continues of itself, and will do so to eternity, without some stop put to it, is clearly true on this occasion: the soul being already moved with the characters and fortunes of those imaginary persons, continues going of its own accord; and we are no more weary to hear what becomes of them when they are not on the stage, than we are to listen to the news of an absent mistress. But it is objected, that if one part of the play may be related, then why not all? I answer, some parts of the action are more fit to be represented, some to be related. Corneille says judiciously that the poet is not obliged to expose to view all particular actions which conduce to the principal: he ought to select such of them to be seen, which will appear with the greatest beauty, either by the magnificence of the show, or the vehemence of passions which they produce, or some other charm which they have in them; and let the rest arrive to the audience by narration. 'Tis a great mistake in us to believe the French present no part of the action on the stage; every alteration or crossing of a design, every new-sprung passion, and turn of it, is a part of the action, and much the noblest, except we conceive nothing to be action till the players come to blows; as if the painting of the hero's mind were not more properly the poet's work than the strength of his body. Nor does this anything contradict the opinion of Horace, where he tells us,

Segnius irritant animos demissa per aurem,
Quam quæ sunt oculis subjecta fidelibus.

For he says immediately after,

> Non tamen intus
> Digna geri promes in scenam; *multaq;* tolles
> Ex oculis, quæ mox narret facundia præsens.

Among which many he recounts some:

> Nec pueros coram populo Medea trucidet,
> Aut in avem Progne mutetur, Cadmus in anguem, etc.

That is, those actions which by reason of their cruelty will cause aversion in us, or by reason of their impossibility, unbelief, ought either wholly to be avoided by a poet, or only delivered by narration. To which we may have leave to add, such as, to avoid tumult (as was before hinted), or to reduce the plot into a more reasonable compass of time, or for defect of beauty in them, are rather to be related than presented to the eye. Examples of all these kinds are frequent, not only among all the ancients, but in the best received of our English poets. We find Ben Jonson using them in his *Magnetic Lady*, where one comes out from dinner, and relates the quarrels and disorders of it, to save the undecent appearance of them on the stage, and to abbreviate the story; and this in expresss imitation of Terence, who had done the same before him in his *Eunuch*, where Pythias makes the like relation of what had happened within at the Soldiers' entertainment. The relations likewise of Sejanus's death, and the prodigies before it, are remarkable; the one of which was hid from sight, to avoid the horror and tumult of the representation; the other, to shun the introducing of things impossible to be believed. In that excellent play, *The King and no King*, Fletcher goes yet farther; for the whole unravelling of the plot is done by narration in the fifth act, after the manner of the ancients; and it moves great concernment in the audience, though it be only a relation of what was done many years before the play. I could multiply other instances, but these are sufficient to prove that there is no error in choosing a subject which requires this sort of narrations; in the ill management of them, there may.

" But I find I have been too long in this discourse, since the French have many other excellencies not common to us; as that you never see any of their plays end with a conversion, or simple change of will, which is the ordinary way which our poets use to end theirs. It shows little art in the conclusion of a dramatic poem, when they who have hindered the felicity during the four acts, desist from it in the fifth, without some powerful cause to take them off their design; and though I deny not but such reasons may be found, yet it is a path that is cautiously to be trod, and the poet is to be sure he convinces the audience that the motive is strong enough. As for example, the conversion of the Usurer in *The Scornful Lady* seems to me a little forced; for, being an Usurer, which implies a lover of money to the highest degree of covetousness,—and such the poet has represented him,—the account he gives for the sudden change is, that he has been duped by the wild young fellow; which in reason might render him more wary another time, and make him punish himself with harder fare and coarser clothes, to get up again what he had lost: but that he should look on it as a judgment, and so repent, we may expect to hear in a sermon, but I should never endure it in a play.

" I pass by this; neither will I insist on the care they take that no person after his first entrance shall ever appear, but the business which brings him upon the stage shall be evident; which rule, if observed, must needs render all the events in the play more natural; for there you see the probability of every accident, in the cause that produced it; and that which appears chance in the play, will seem so reasonable to you, that you will there find it almost necessary: so that in the exit of the actor you have a clear account of his purpose and design in the next entrance (though, if the scene be well wrought, the event will commonly deceive you); for there is nothing so absurd, says Corneille, as for an actor to leave the stage only because he has no more to say.

" I should now speak of the beauty of their rhyme, and the just reason I have to prefer that way of writing in tragedies before ours in blank verse; but because it is partly received by us, and therefore not altogether peculiar to them, I will say no more of it in relation to their plays. For our own, I doubt not but it will exceedingly beautify them; and I can see but one reason why it should not generally obtain, that is, because our poets write so ill in it. This indeed may prove a more prevailing argument than all others which are used to destroy it, and therefore I am only troubled when great and judicious poets, and those who are acknowledged such, have writ or spoke against it: as for others, they are to be answered by that one sentence of an ancient author:—*Sed ut primo ad consequendos eos quos priores ducimus, accendimur, ita ubi aut proeteriri, aut æquari eos posse desperavimus, studium cum spe senescit: quod, scilicet, assequi non potest, sequi desinit;* . . . *praeteritoque eo in quo eminere non possumus, aliquid in quo nitamur, conquirimus.*"

Lisideius concluded in this manner; and Neander, after a little pause, thus answered him:

"I shall grant Lisideius, without much dispute, a great part of what he has urged against us; for I acknowledge that the French contrive their plots more regularly, and observe the laws of comedy, and decorum of the stage (to speak generally), with more exactness than the English. Farther, I deny not but he has taxed us justly in some irregularities of ours, which he has mentioned; yet, after all, I am of opinion that neither our faults nor their virtues are considerable enough to place them above us.

"For the lively imitation of nature being in the definition of a play, those which best fulfil that law ought to be esteemed superior to the others. 'Tis true, those beauties of the French poesy are such as will raise perfection higher where it is, but are not sufficient to give it where it is not: they are indeed the beauties of a statue, but not of a man, because not animated with the soul of poesy, which is imitation of humour and passions: and this Lisideius himself, or any other, however biassed to their party, cannot but acknowledge, if he will either compare the humours of our comedies, or the characters of our serious plays, with theirs. He who will look upon theirs which have been written till these last ten years, or thereabouts, will find it a hard matter to pick out two or three passable humours amongst them. Corneille himself, their arch-poet, what has he produced except *The Liar*, and you know how it was cried up in France; but when it came upon the English stage, though well translated, and that part of Dorant acted to so much advantage as I am confident it never received in its own country, the most favourable to it would not put it in competition with many of Fletcher's or Ben Jonson's. In the rest of Corneille's comedies you have little humour; he tells you himself, his way is, first to show two lovers in good intelligence with each other; in the working up of the play to embroil them by some mistake, and in the latter end to clear it, and reconcile them.

"But of late years Molière, the younger Corneille, Quinault, and some others, have been imitating afar off the quick turns and graces of the English stage. They have mixed their serious plays with mirth, like our tragi-comedies, since the death of Cardinal Richelieu; which Lisideius and many others not observing, have commended that in them for a virtue which they themselves no longer practise. Most of their new plays are, like some

f ours, derived from the Spanish novels. There is scarce one of
hem without a veil, and a trusty Diego, who drolls much after
he rate of *The Adventures*. But their humours, if I may grace
hem with that name, are so thin-sown, that never above one of
hem comes up in any play. I dare take upon me to find more
variety of them in some one play of Ben Jonson's than in all
heirs together; as he who has seen *The Alchemist, The Silent
Woman*, or *Bartholomew-Fair*, cannot but acknowledge with me.

"I grant the French have performed what was possible on
he ground-work of the Spanish plays; what was pleasant
before, they have made regular: but there is not above one good
play to be writ on all those plots; they are too much alike to
please often; which we need not the experience of our own
stage to justify. As for their new way of mingling mirth with
serious plot, I do not, with Lisideius, condemn the thing, though I
cannot approve their manner of doing it. He tells us, we cannot
so speedily recollect ourselves after a scene of great passion and
concernment, as to pass to another of mirth and humour, and to
enjoy it with any relish: but why should he imagine the soul of
man more heavy than his senses? Does not the eye pass from
an unpleasant object to a pleasant in a much shorter time than
is required to this? and does not the unpleasantness of the first
commend the beauty of the latter? The old rule of logic might
have convinced him, that contraries, when placed near, set off
each other. A continued gravity keeps the spirit too much
bent; we must refresh it sometimes, as we bait in a journey
that we may go on with greater ease. A scene of mirth, mixed
with tragedy, has the same effect upon us which our music has
betwixt the acts; which we find a relief to us from the best plots
and language of the stage, if the discourses have been long. I
must therefore have stronger arguments, ere I am convinced
that compassion and mirth in the same subject destroy each
other; and in the meantime cannot but conclude, to the honour
of our nation, that we have invented, increased, and perfected
a more pleasant way of writing for the stage, than was ever
known to the ancients or moderns of any nation, which is tragi-
comedy.

"And this leads me to wonder why Lisideius and many others
should cry up the barrenness of the French plots above the
variety and copiousness of the English. Their plots are single;
they carry on one design, which is pushed forward by all the
actors, every scene in the play contributing and moving towards
it. Our plays, besides the main design, have under-plots or by-

concernments, of less considerable persons and intrigues, which
are carried on with the motion of the main plot: as they say the
orb of the fixed stars, and those of the planets, though they have
motions of their own, are whirled about by the motion of the
primum mobile, in which they are contained. That similitude
expresses much of the English stage; for if contrary motions
may be found in nature to agree; if a planet can go east and
west at the same time;—one way by virtue of his own motion,
the other by the force of the first mover;—it will not be difficult
to imagine how the under-plot, which is only different, not
contrary to the great design, may naturally be conducted along
with it.

"Eugenius has already shown us, from the confession of the
French poets, that the unity of action is sufficiently preserved
if all the imperfect actions of the play are conducing to the main
design; but when those petty intrigues of a play are so ill
ordered, that they have no coherence with the other, I must
grant that Lisideius has reason to tax that want of due connection; for co-ordination in a play is as dangerous and unnatural as in a state. In the meantime he must acknowledge
our variety, if well ordered, will afford a greater pleasure to the
audience.

"As for his other argument, that by pursuing one single
theme they gain an advantage to express and work up the
passions, I wish any example he could bring from them would
make it good; for I confess their verses are to me the coldest
I have ever read. Neither, indeed, is it possible for them, in the
way they take, so to express passion, as that the effects of it
should appear in the concernment of an audience, their speeches
being so many declamations, which tire us with the length; so
that instead of persuading us to grieve for their imaginary
heroes, we are concerned for our own trouble, as we are in tedious
visits of bad company; we are in pain till they are gone. When
the French stage came to be reformed by Cardinal Richelieu,
those long harangues were introduced to comply with the
gravity of a churchman. Look upon the *Cinna* and the *Pompey;*
they are not so properly to be called plays, as long discourses of
reason of state; and *Polieucte* in matters of religion is as solemn
as the long stops upon our organs. Since that time it is grown
into a custom, and their actors speak by the hour-glass, like our
parsons; nay, they account it the grace of their parts, and
think themselves disparaged by the poet, if they may not twice
or thrice in a play entertain the audience with a speech of an

hundred lines. I deny not but this may suit well enough with the French; for as we, who are a more sullen people, come to be diverted at our plays, so they, who are of an airy and gay temper, come thither to make themselves more serious: and this I conceive to be one reason why comedies are more pleasing to us, and tragedies to them. But to speak generally: it cannot be denied that short speeches and replies are more apt to move the passions and beget concernment in us, than the other; for it is unnatural for any one in a gust of passion to speak long together, or for another in the same condition to suffer him, without interruption. Grief and passion are like floods raised in little brooks by a sudden rain; they are quickly up; and if the concernment be poured unexpectedly in upon us, it over-flows us: but a long sober shower gives them leisure to run out as they came in, without troubling the ordinary current. As for comedy, repartee is one of its chiefest graces; the greatest pleasure of the audience is a chase of wit, kept up on both sides, and swiftly managed. And this our forefathers, if not we, have had in Fletcher's plays, to a much higher degree of perfection than the French poets can reasonably hope to reach.

" There is another part of Lisideius his discourse, in which he rather excused our neighbours than commended them; that is, for aiming only to make one person considerable in their plays. 'Tis very true what he has urged, that one character in all plays, even without the poet's care, will have advantage of all the others; and that the design of the whole drama will chiefly depend on it. But this hinders not that there may be more shining characters in the play: many persons of a second magnitude, nay, some so very near, so almost equal to the first, that greatness may be opposed to greatness, and all the persons be made considerable, not only by their quality, but their action. 'Tis evident that the more the persons are, the greater will be the variety of the plot. If then the parts are managed so regularly, that the beauty of the whole be kept entire, and that the variety become not a perplexed and confused mass of accidents, you will find it infinitely pleasing to be led in a laby-rinth of design, where you see some of your way before you, yet discern not the end till you arrive at it. And that all this is practicable, I can produce for examples many of our English plays: as The Maid's Tragedy, The Alchemist, The Silent Woman: I was going to have named The Fox, but that the unity of design seems not exactly observed in it; for there appear two actions in the play; the first naturally ending with the fourth act; the second forced from it in the fifth; which yet is the less to be condemned in him, because the disguise of Volpone, though it suited not with his character as a crafty or covetous person, agreed well enough with that of a voluptuary; and by it the poet gained the end at which he aimed, the punishment of vice, and the reward of virtue, both which that disguise produced. So that to judge equally of it, it was an excellent fifth act, but not so naturally proceeding from the former.

"But to leave this, and pass to the latter part of Lisideius his discourse, which concerns relations: I must acknowledge with him, that the French have reason to hide that part of the action which would occasion too much tumult on the stage, and to choose rather to have it made known by narration to the audience. Farther, I think it very convenient, for the reasons he has given, that all incredible actions were removed; but whether custom has so insinuated itself into our countrymen, or nature has so formed them to fierceness, I know not; but they will scarcely suffer combats and other objects of horror to be taken from them. And indeed, the indecency of tumults is all which can be objected against fighting: for why may not our imagination as well suffer itself to be deluded with the probability of it, as with any other thing in the play? For my part, I can with as great ease persuade myself that the blows are given in good earnest, as I can that they who strike them are kings or princes, or those persons which they represent. For objects of incredibility,—I would be satisfied from Lisideius, whether we have any so removed from all appearance of truth, as are those of Corneille's *Andromede*; a play which has been frequented the most of any he has writ. If the Perseus, or the son of a heathen god, the Pegasus, and the Monster, were not capable to choke a strong belief, let him blame any representation of ours hereafter. Those indeed were objects of delight; yet the reason is the same as to the probability: for he makes it not a ballet or masque, but a play, which is to resemble truth. But for death, that it ought not to be represented, I have, besides the arguments alleged by Lisideius, the authority of Ben Jonson, who has forborne it in his tragedies; for both the death of Sejanus and Catiline are related: though in the latter I cannot but observe one irregularity of that great poet; he has removed the scene in the same act from Rome to Catiline's army, and from thence again to Rome; and besides, has allowed a very inconsiderable time, after Catiline's speech, for the striking of the battle, and the return of Petreius, who is to relate the event of it to the senate: which I should not animadvert on him, who was otherwise a painful observer of τὸ πρέπον, or the *decorum* of the stage, if he had not used extreme severity in his judgment on the incomparable Shakspeare for the same fault.—To conclude on this subject of relations; if we are to be blamed for showing too much of the action, the French are as faulty for discovering too little of it: a mean betwixt both should be observed by every judicious writer, so as the audience may neither be left unsatisfied by not seeing what is beautiful, or shocked by beholding what is either incredible or undecent.

" I hope I have already proved in this discourse, that though we are not altogether so punctual as the French in observing the laws of comedy, yet our errors are so few, and little, and those things wherein we excel them so considerable, that we ought of right to be preferred before them. But what will Lisideius say, if they themselves acknowledge they are too strictly bounded by those laws, for breaking which he has blamed the English? I will allege Corneille's words, as I find them in the end of his Discourse of the three Unities: *Il est facile aux spéculatifs d'estre sévères, etc.* 'Tis easy for speculative persons to judge severely; but if they would produce to public view ten or twelve pieces of this nature, they would perhaps give more latitude to the rules than I have done, when by experience they had known how much we are limited and constrained by them, and how many beauties of the stage they banished from it.' To illustrate a little what he has said: By their servile observations of the unities of time and place, and integrity of scenes, they have brought on themselves that dearth of plot, and narrowness of imagination, which may be observed in all their plays. How many beautiful accidents might naturally happen in two or three days, which cannot arrive with any probability in the compass of twenty-four hours? There is time to be allowed also for maturity of design, which, amongst great and prudent persons, such as are often represented in tragedy, cannot, with any likelihood of truth, be brought to pass at so short a warning. Farther; by tying themselves strictly to the unity of place, and unbroken scenes, they are forced many times to omit some beauties which cannot be shown where the act began; but might, if the scene were interrupted, and the stage cleared for the persons to enter in another place; and therefore the French poets are often forced upon absurdities; for if the act begins in a chamber, all the persons in the play must have some business or other to come thither, or else they are not to be shown that act; and some times their characters are very unfitting to appear there: as suppose it were the king's bed-chamber; yet the meanest man in the tragedy must come and dispatch his business there, rather than in the lobby or courtyard (which is fitter for him), for fear the stage should be cleared, and the scenes broken. Many times they fall by it in a greater inconvenience; for they keep their scenes unbroken, and yet change the place; as in one of their newest plays, where the act begins in the street. There a gentle man is to meet his friend; he sees him with his man, coming out from his father's house; they talk together, and the first goes out: the second, who is a lover, has made an appointment with his mistress; she appears at the window, and then we are to imagine the scene lies under it. This gentleman is called away, and leaves his servant with his mistress; presently her father is heard from within; the young lady is afraid the serving-man should be discovered, and thrusts him into a place of safety, which is supposed to be her closet. After this, the father enters to the daughter, and now the scene is in a house; for he is seeking from one room to another for this poor Philipin, or French Diego, who is heard from within, drolling and break-ing many a miserable conceit on the subject of his sad condition. In this ridiculous manner the play goes forward, the stage being never empty all the while: so that the street, the window, the houses, and the closet, are made to walk about, and the persons to stand still. Now what, I beseech you, is more easy than to write a regular French play, or more difficult than to write an irregular English one, like those of Fletcher, or of Shakspeare?

" If they content themselves, as Corneille did, with some flat design, which, like an ill riddle, is found out ere it be half proposed, such plots we can make every way regular, as easily as they; but whenever they endeavour to rise to any quick turns and counterturns of plot, as some of them have attempted, since Corneille's plays have been less in vogue, you see they write as irregularly as we, though they cover it more speciously. Hence the reason is perspicuous why no French plays, when trans-lated, have, or ever can succeed on the English stage. For, if you consider the plots, our own are fuller of variety; if the writing, ours are more quick and fuller of spirit; and therefore 'tis a strange mistake in those who decry the way of writing plays in verse, as if the English therein imitated the French. We have borrowed nothing from them; our plots are weaved in English looms: we endeavour therein to follow the variety and

reatness of characters which are derived to us from Shakspeare
nd Fletcher; the copiousness and well-knitting of the intrigues
ve have from Jonson; and for the verse itself we have English
recedents of elder date than any of Corneille's plays. Not to
ame our old comedies before Shakspeare, which were all writ
n verse of six feet, or Alexandrines, such as the French now
se,—I can show in Shakspeare many scenes of rhyme together,
nd the like in Ben Jonson's tragedies: in *Catiline* and *Sejanus*
ometimes thirty or forty lines,—I mean besides the Chorus, or
he monologues; which, by the way, showed Ben no enemy to
his way of writing, especially if you read his *Sad Shepherd*,
vhich goes sometimes on rhyme, sometimes on blank verse,
ike an horse who eases himself on trot and amble. You find
iim likewise commending Fletcher's pastoral of *The Faithful
Shepherdess*, which is for the most part rhyme, though not
efined to that purity to which it hath since been brought. And
these examples are enough to clear us from a servile imitation of
the French.

"But to return whence I have digressed: I dare boldly affirm
these two things of the English drama;—First, that we have
many plays of ours as regular as any of theirs, and which, besides,
have more variety of plot and characters; and secondly, that in
most of the irregular plays of Shakspeare or Fletcher (for Ben
Jonson's are for the most part regular), there is a more masculine
fancy and greater spirit in the writing than there is in any of the
French. I could produce, even in Shakspeare's and Fletcher's
works, some plays which are almost exactly formed; as *The
Merry Wives of Windsor*, and *The Scornful Lady*: but because
(generally speaking) Shakspeare, who writ first, did not
perfectly observe the laws of comedy, and Fletcher, who came
nearer to perfection, yet through carelessness made many faults;
I will take the pattern of a perfect play from Ben Jonson, who
was a careful and learned observer of the dramatic laws, and
from all his comedies I shall select *The Silent Woman;* of which
I will make a short examen, according to those rules which the
French observe."

As Neander was beginning to examine *The Silent Woman*,
Eugenius, earnestly regarding him; "I beseech you, Neander,"
said he, "gratify the company, and me in particular, so far, as
before you speak of the play, to give us a character of the author;
and tell us frankly your opinion, whether you do not think all
writers, both French and English, ought to give place to him."

"I fear," replied Neander, "that in obeying your commands

I shall draw some envy on myself. Besides, in performing them
it will be first necessary to speak somewhat of Shakspeare and
Fletcher, his rivals in poesy; and one of them, in my opinion
at least his equal, perhaps his superior.

"To begin, then, with Shakspeare. He was the man who of
all modern, and perhaps ancient poets, had the largest and most
comprehensive soul. All the images of nature were still present
to him, and he drew them, not laboriously, but luckily; when
he describes anything, you more than see it, you feel it too.
Those who accuse him to have wanted learning, give him the
greater commendation: he was naturally learned; he needed
not the spectacles of books to read nature; he looked inwards,
and found her there. I cannot say he is everywhere alike;
were he so, I should do him injury to compare him with the
greatest of mankind. He is many times flat, insipid; his comic
wit degenerating into clenches, his serious swelling into bombast.
But he is always great, when some great occasion is presented
to him; no man can say he ever had a fit subject for his wit,
and did not then raise himself as high above the rest of poets,

> Quantum lenta solent inter viburna cupressi.

The consideration of this made Mr. Hales of Eaton say, that
there was no subject of which any poet ever writ, but he would
produce it much better done in Shakspeare; and however
others are now generally preferred before him, yet the age
wherein he lived, which had contemporaries with him Fletcher
and Jonson, never equalled them to him in their esteem: and
in the last king's court, when Ben's reputation was at highest,
Sir John Suckling, and with him the greater part of the courtiers,
set our Shakspeare far above him.

"Beaumont and Fletcher, of whom I am next to speak, had,
with the advantage of Shakspeare's wit, which was their precedent, great natural gifts, improved by study: Beaumont
especially being so accurate a judge of plays, that Ben Jonson,
while he lived, submitted all his writings to his censure, and,
'tis thought, used his judgment in correcting, if not contriving, all
his plots. What value he had for him, appears by the verses he
writ to him; and therefore I need speak no farther of it. The
first play that brought Fletcher and him in esteem was their
Philaster: for before that, they had written two or three very
unsuccessfully, as the like is reported of Ben Jonson, before he
writ *Every Man in his Humour*. Their plots were generally
more regular than Shakspeare's, especially those which were

made before Beaumont's death; and they understood and imitated the conversation of gentlemen much better; whose wild debaucheries, and quickness of wit in repartees, no poet before them could paint as they have done. Humour, which Ben Jonson derived from particular persons, they made it not their business to describe: they represented all the passions very lively, but above all, love. I am apt to believe the English language in them arrived to its highest perfection: what words have since been taken in, are rather superfluous than ornamental. Their plays are now the most pleasant and frequent entertainments of the stage; two of theirs being acted through the year for one of Shakspeare's or Jonson's: the reason is, because there is a certain gaiety in their comedies, and pathos in their more serious plays, which suit generally with all men's humours. Shakspeare's language is likewise a little obsolete, and Ben Jonson's wit comes short of theirs.

" As for Jonson, to whose character I am now arrived, if we look upon him while he was himself (for his last plays were but his dotages), I think him the most learned and judicious writer which any theatre ever had. He was a most severe judge of himself, as well as others. One cannot say he wanted wit, but rather that he was frugal of it. In his works you find little to retrench or alter. Wit, and language, and humour also in some measure, we had before him; but something of art was wanting to the drama till he came. He managed his strength to more advantage than any who preceded him. You seldom find him making love in any of his scenes, or endeavouring to move the passions; his genius was too sullen and saturnine to do it gracefully, especially when he knew he came after those who had performed both to such an height. Humour was his proper sphere; and in that he delighted most to represent mechanic people. He was deeply conversant in the ancients, both Greek and Latin, and he borrowed boldly from them: there is scarce a poet or historian among the Roman authors of those times whom he has not translated in *Sejanus* and *Catiline*. But he has done his robberies so openly, that one may see he fears not to be taxed by any law. He invades authors like a monarch; and what would be theft in other poets is only victory in him. With the spoils of these writers he so represents old Rome to us, in its rites, ceremonies, and customs, that if one of their poets had written either of his tragedies, we had seen less of it than in him. If there was any fault in his language, 'twas that he weaved it too closely and laboriously, in his comedies especially:

perhaps, too, he did a little too much Romanise our tongue, leaving the words which he translated almost as much Latin as he found them: wherein, though he learnedly followed their language, he did not enough comply with the idiom of ours. If I would compare him with Shakspeare, I must acknowledge him the more correct poet, but Shakspeare the greater wit. Shakspeare was the Homer, or father of our dramatic poets; Jonson was the Virgil, the pattern of elaborate writing; I admire him, but I love Shakspeare. To conclude of him; as he has given us the most correct plays, so in the precepts which he has laid down in his *Discoveries*, we have as many and profitable rules for perfecting the stage, as any wherewith the French can furnish us.

"Having thus spoken of the author, I proceed to the examination of his comedy, *The Silent Woman*.

EXAMEN OF THE SILENT WOMAN

"To begin first with the length of the action; it is so far from exceeding the compass of a natural day, that it takes not up an artificial one. 'Tis all included in the limits of three hours and a half, which is no more than is required for the presentment on the stage: a beauty perhaps not much observed; if it had, we should not have looked on the Spanish translation of *Five Hours* with so much wonder. The scene of it is laid in London; the latitude of place is almost as little as you can imagine; for it lies all within the compass of two houses, and after the first act, in one. The continuity of scenes is observed more than in any of our plays, except his own *Fox* and *Alchemist*. They are not broken above twice or thrice at most in the whole comedy; and in the two best of Corneille's plays, the *Cid* and *Cinna*, they are interrupted once. The action of the play is entirely one; the end or aim of which is the settling Morose's estate on Dauphine. The intrigue of it is the greatest and most noble of any pure unmixed comedy in any language; you see in it many persons of various characters and humours, and all delightful. As first, Morose, or an old man, to whom all noise but his own talking is offensive. Some who would be thought critics, say this humour of his is forced: but to remove that objection, we may consider him first to be naturally of a delicate hearing, as many are, to whom all sharp sounds are unpleasant; and secondly, we may attribute much of it to the peevishness of his age, or the wayward authority of an old man in his own house, where he may make himself obeyed; and to this the poet seems to allude in his name Morose. Besides this, I am assured from divers persons, that Ben Jonson was actually acquainted with such a man, one altogether as ridiculous as he is here represented. Others say, it is not enough to find one man of such an humour; it must be common to more, and the more common the more natural. To prove this, they instance in the best of comical characters, Falstaff. There are many men resembling him; old, fat, merry, cowardly, drunken, amorous, vain, and lying. But to convince these people, I need but tell them that humour is the ridiculous extravagance of conversation, wherein one man differs from all others. If then it be common, or communicated to many, how differs it from other men's? or what indeed causes it to be ridiculous so much as the singularity of it? As for Falstaff, he is not properly one humour, but a miscellany of humours or images, drawn from so many several men: that wherein he is singular is his wit, or those things he says *præter expectatum*, unexpected by the audience; his quick evasions, when you imagine him surprised, which, as they are extremely diverting of themselves, so receive a great addition from his person; for the very sight of such an unwieldy old debauched fellow is a comedy alone. And here, having a place so proper for it, I cannot but enlarge somewhat upon this subject of humour into which I am fallen. The ancients had little of it in their comedies; for the τὸ γελοῖον of the old comedy, of which Aristophanes was chief, was not so much to imitate a man, as to make the people laugh at some odd conceit, which had commonly somewhat of unnatural or obscene in it. Thus, when you see Socrates brought upon the stage, you are not to imagine him made ridiculous by the imitation of his actions, but rather by making him perform something very unlike himself; something so childish and absurd, as by comparing it with the gravity of the true Socrates, makes a ridiculous object for the spectators. In their new comedy which succeeded, the poets sought indeed to express the ἦθος, as in their tragedies the πάθος of mankind. But this ἦθος contained only the general characters of men and manners; as old men, lovers, serving-men, courtezans, parasites, and such other persons as we see in their comedies; all which they made alike: that is, one old man or father, one lover, one courtezan, so like another, as if the first of them had begot the rest of every sort: *Ex homine hunc natum dicas*. The same custom they observed likewise in their tragedies. As for the French, though they have the word *humeur* among them, yet they have small use of it in their comedies or farces; they being but ill imitations of the *ridiculum*, or that which stirred up laughter in the old comedy. But among the English 'tis otherwise: where by humour is meant some extravagant habit, passion, or affection, particular (as I said before) to some one person, by the oddness of which, he is immediately distinguished from the rest of men; which being lively and naturally represented, most frequently begets that malicious pleasure in the audience which is testified by laughter; as all things which are deviations from customs are ever the aptest to produce it: though by the way this laughter is only accidental, as the person represented is fantastic or bizarre; but pleasure is essential to it, as the imitation of what is natural. The description of these humours, drawn from the knowledge and observation of particular persons, was the peculiar genius and talent of Ben Jonson; to whose play I now return.

" Besides Morose, there are at least nine or ten different characters and humours in *The Silent Woman;* all which persons have several concernments of their own, yet are all used by the poet to the conducting of the main design to perfection. I shall not waste time in commending the writing of this play; but I will give you my opinion, that there is more wit and acuteness of fancy in it than in any of Ben Jonson's. Besides that he has here described the conversation of gentlemen in the persons of True-Wit, and his friends, with more gaiety, air, and freedom, than in the rest of his comedies. For the contrivance of the plot, 'tis extreme, elaborate, and yet withal easy; for the λύσις, or untying of it, 'tis so admirable, that when it is done, no one of the audience would think the poet could have missed it; and yet it was concealed so much before the last scene, that any other way would sooner have entered into your thoughts. But I dare not take upon me to commend the fabric of it, because it is altogether so full of art, that I must unravel every scene in it to commend it as I ought. And this excellent contrivance is still the more to be admired, because 'tis comedy, where the persons are only of common rank, and their business private, not elevated by passions or high concernments, as in serious plays. Here every one is a proper judge of all he sees, nothing is represented but that with which he daily converses: so that by consequence all faults lie open to discovery, and few are pardonable. 'Tis this which Horace has judiciously observed:

> Creditur, ex medio quia res arcessit, habere
> Sudoris minimum; sed habet Comedia tanto
> Plus oneris, quanto veniæ minus.

But our poet who was not ignorant of these difficulties has made use of all advantages; as he who designs a large leap takes his rise from the highest ground. One of these advantages is that which Corneille has laid down as the greatest which can arrive to any poem, and which he himself could never compass above thrice in all his plays; viz., the making choice of some signal and long-expected day, whereon the action of the play is to depend. This day was that designed by Dauphine for the settling of his uncle's estate upon him; which to compass, he contrives to marry him. That the marriage had been plotted by him long beforehand, is made evident by what he tells Truewit in the second act, that in one moment he had destroyed what he had been raising many months.

"There is another artifice of the poet, which I cannot here omit, because by the frequent practice of it in his comedies he has left it to us almost as a rule; that is, when he has any character or humour wherein he would show a *coup de Maistre*, or his highest skill, he recommends it to your observation by a pleasant description of it before the person first appears. Thus, in *Bartholomew-Fair* he gives you the pictures of Numps and Cokes, and in this those of Daw, Lafoole, Morose, and the Collegiate Ladies; all which you hear described before you see them. So that before they come upon the stage, you have a longing expectation of them, which prepares you to receive them favourably; and when they are there, even from their first appearance you are so far acquainted with them, that nothing of their humour is lost to you.

"I will observe yet one thing further of this admirable plot; the business of it rises in every act. The second is greater than the first; the third than the second; and so forward to the fifth. There too you see, till the very last scene, new difficulties arising to obstruct the action of the play; and when the audience is brought into despair that the business can naturally be effected, then, and not before, the discovery is made. But that the poet might entertain you with more variety all this while, he reserves some new characters to show you, which he opens not till the second and third act; in the second Morose, Daw, the Barber, and Otter; in the third the Collegiate Ladies: all which he moves afterwards in by-walks, or under-plots, as diversions to the main design, lest it should grow tedious, though they are still naturally joined with it, and somewhere or other subservient to it. Thus, like a skilful chess-player, by little and little he draws out his men, and makes his pawns of use to his greater persons.

" If this comedy and some others of his were translated into French prose (which would now be no wonder to them, since Molière has lately given them plays out of verse, which have not displeased them), I believe the controversy would soon be decided betwixt the two nations, even making them the judges. But we need not call our heroes to our aid. Be it spoken to the honour of the English, our nation can never want in any age such who are able to dispute the empire of wit with any people in the universe. And though the fury of a civil war, and power for twenty years together abandoned to a barbarous race of men, enemies of all good learning, had buried the muses under the ruins of monarchy; yet, with the restoration of our happiness, we see revived poesy lifting up its head, and already shaking off the rubbish which lay so heavy on it. We have seen since his majesty's return, many dramatic poems which yield not to those of any foreign nation, and which deserve all laurels but the English. I will set aside flattery and envy: it cannot be denied but we have had some little blemish either in the plot or writing of all those plays which have been made within these seven years; (and perhaps there is no nation in the world so quick to discern them, or so difficult to pardon them, as ours:) yet if we can persuade ourselves to use the candour of that poet, who, though the most severe of critics, has left us this caution by which to moderate our censures—

> ubi plura nitent in carmine, non ego paucis
> Offendar maculis;—

if, in consideration of their many and great beauties, we can wink at some slight and little imperfections, if we, I say, can be thus equal to ourselves, I ask no favour from the French. And if I do not venture upon any particular judgment of our late plays, 'tis out of the consideration which an ancient writer gives me: *vivorum, ut magna admiratio, ita censura difficilis:* betwixt the extremes of admiration and malice, 'tis hard to judge uprightly of the living. Only I think it may be permitted me to say, that as it is no lessening to us to yield to some plays, and those not many, of our own nation in the last age, so can it be no addition to pronounce of our present poets, that they have far surpassed all the ancients, and the modern writers of other countries."

This was the substance of what was then spoken on that occasion; and Lisideius, I think, was going to reply, when he was prevented thus by Crites: " I am confident," said he, "that the most material things that can be said have been already urged on either side; if they have not, I must beg of Lisideius that he will defer his answer till another time: for I confess I have a joint quarrel to you both, because you have concluded, without any reason given for it, that rhyme is proper for the stage. I will not dispute how ancient it hath been among us to write this way; perhaps our ancestors knew no better till Shakspeare's time. I will grant it was not altogether left by him, and that Fletcher and Ben Jonson used it frequently in their Pastorals, and sometimes in other plays. Farther,—I will not argue whether we received it originally from our own countrymen, or from the French; for that is an inquiry of as little benefit, as theirs who, in the midst of the great plague, were not so solicitous to provide against it, as to know whether we had it from the malignity of our own air, or by transportation from Holland. I have therefore only to affirm, that it is not allowable in serious plays; for comedies, I find you already concluding with me. To prove this, I might satisfy myself to tell you, how much in vain it is for you to strive against the stream of the people's inclination; the greatest part of which are prepossessed so much with those excellent plays of Shakspeare, Fletcher, and Ben Jonson, which have been written out of rhyme, that except you could bring them such as were written better in it, and those too by persons of equal reputation with them, it will be impossible for you to gain your cause with them, who will still be judges. This it is to which, in fine, all your reasons must submit. The unanimous consent of an audience is so powerful, that even Julius Cæsar (as Macrobius reports of him), when he was perpetual dictator, was not able to balance it on the other side; but when Laberius, a Roman Knight, at his request contended in the *Mime* with another poet, he was forced to cry out, *Etiam favente me victus es, Laberi*. But I will not on this occasion take the advantage of the greater number, but only urge such reasons against rhyme, as I find in the writings of those who have argued for the other way. First, then, I am of opinion that rhyme is unnatural in a play, because dialogue there is presented as the effect of sudden thought: for a play is the imitation of nature; and since no man, without premeditation, speaks in rhyme, neither ought he to do it on the stage. This hinders not but the fancy may be there elevated to an higher pitch of thought than it is in ordinary discourse; for there is a probability that men of excellent and quick parts may speak noble things *extempore*:

but those thoughts are never fettered with the numbers or sound of verse without study, and therefore it cannot be but unnatural to present the most free way of speaking in that which is the most constrained. For this reason, says Aristotle, 'tis best to write tragedy in that kind of verse which is the least such, or which is nearest prose: and this amongst the ancients was the Iambic, and with us is blank verse, or the measure of verse kept exactly without rhyme. These numbers therefore are fittest for a play; the others for a paper of verses, or a poem; blank verse being as much below them as rhyme is improper for the drama. And if it be objected that neither are blank verses made *extempore*, yet, as nearest nature, they are still to be preferred.—But there are two particular exceptions, which many besides myself have had to verse; by which it will appear yet more plainly how improper it is in plays. And the first of them is grounded on that very reason for which some have commended rhyme; they say, the quickness of repartees in argumentative scenes receives an ornament from verse. Now what is more unreasonable than to imagine that a man should not only light upon the wit, but the rhyme too, upon the sudden? This nicking of him who spoke before both in sound and measure, is so great an happiness, that you must at least suppose the persons of your play to be born poets: *Arcades omnes, et cantare pares, et respondere parati:* they must have arrived to the degree of *quicquid conabar dicere;*—to make verses almost whether they will or no. If they are anything below this, it will look rather like the design of two, than the answer of one: it will appear that your actors hold intelligence together; that they perform their tricks like fortune-tellers, by confederacy. The hand of art will be too visible in it, against that maxim of all professions—*Ars est celare artem;* that it is the greatest perfection of art to keep itself undiscovered. Nor will it serve you to object, that however you manage it, 'tis still known to be a play; and, consequently, the dialogue of two persons understood to be the labour of one poet. For a play is still an imitation of nature; we know we are to be deceived, and we desire to be so; but no man ever was deceived but with a probability of truth; for who will suffer a gross lie to be fastened on him? Thus we sufficiently understand that the scenes which represent cities and countries to us are not really such, but only painted on boards and canvas; but shall that excuse the ill painture or designment of them? Nay, rather ought they not be laboured with so much the more diligence and exactness, to help the imagination? since the mind of man does naturally tend to truth; and therefore the nearer anything comes to the imitation of it, the more it pleases.

"Thus, you see, your rhyme is incapable of expressing the greatest thoughts naturally, and the lowest it cannot with any grace: for what is more unbefitting the majesty of verse, than to call a servant, or bid a door be shut in rhyme? and yet you are often forced on this miserable necessity. But verse, you say, circumscribes a quick and luxuriant fancy, which would extend itself too far on every subject, did not the labour which is requried to well-turned and polished rhyme, set bounds to it. Yet this argument, if granted, would only prove that we may write better in verse, but not more naturally. Neither is it able to evince that; for he who wants judgment to confine his fancy in blank verse, may want it as much in rhyme: and he who has it will avoid errors in both kinds. Latin verse was as great a confinement to the imagination of those poets as rhyme to ours; and yet you find Ovid saying too much on every subject. *Nescivit* (says Seneca) *quod bene cessit relinquere:* of which he gives you one famous instance in his description of the deluge:

> *Omnia pontus erat, deerant quoque litora ponto.*
> Now all was sea, nor had that sea a shore.

Thus Ovid's fancy was not limited by verse, and Virgil needed not verse to have bounded his.

"In our own language we see Ben Jonson confining himself to what ought to be said, even in the liberty of blank verse; and yet Corneille, the most judicious of the French poets, is still varying the same sense an hundred ways, and dwelling eternally on the same subject, though confined by rhyme. Some other exceptions I have to verse; but since these I have named are for the most part already public, I conceive it reasonable they should first be answered."

"It concerns me less than any," said Neander (seeing he had ended), "to reply to this discourse; because when I should have proved that verse may be natural in plays, yet I should always be ready to confess, that those which I have written in this kind come short of that perfection which is required. Yet since you are pleased I should undertake this province, I will do it, though with all imaginable respect and deference, both to that person from whom you have borrowed your strongest arguments, and to whose judgment, when I have said all, I finally submit. But before I proceed to answer your objections, I must first remember you, that I exclude all comedy from my defence; and next that I deny not but blank verse may be also used; and content myself only to assert, that in serious plays where the subject and characters are great, and the plot unmixed with mirth, which might allay or divert these concernments which are produced, rhyme is there as natural and more effectual than blank verse.

" And now having laid down this as a foundation,—to begin with Crites,—I must crave leave to tell him, that some of his arguments against rhyme reach no farther than, from the faults or defects of ill rhyme, to conclude against the use of it in general. May not I conclude against blank verse by the same reason? If the words of some poets who write in it are either ill chosen, or ill placed, which makes not only rhyme, but all kind of verse in any language unnatural, shall I, for their vicious affectation, condemn those excellent lines of Fletcher, which are written in that kind? Is there anything in rhyme more constrained than this line in blank verse?—*I heaven invoke, and strong resistance make;* where you see both the clauses are placed unnaturally, that is, contrary to the common way of speaking, and that without the excuse of a rhyme to cause it: yet you would think me very ridiculous, if I should accuse the stubbornness of blank verse for this, and not rather the stiffness of the poet. Therefore, Crites, you must either prove that words, though well chosen, and duly placed, yet render not rhyme natural in itself; or that, however natural and easy the rhyme may be, yet it is not proper for a play. If you insist on the former part, I would ask you, what other conditions are required to make rhyme natural in itself, besides an election of apt words, and a right disposition of them? For the due choice of your words expresses your sense naturally, and the due placing them adapts the rhyme to it. If you object that one verse may be made for the sake of another, though both the words and rhyme be apt, I answer, it cannot possibly so fall out; for either there is a dependence of sense betwixt the first line and the second, or there is none: if there be that connection, then in the natural position of the words the latter line must of necessity flow from the former; if there be no dependence, yet still the due ordering of words makes the last line as natural in itself as the other: so that the necessity of a rhyme never forces any but bad or lazy writers to say what they would not otherwise. 'Tis true, there is both care and art required to write in verse. A good poet never establishes the first line till he has sought out such a rhyme as may fit the sense, already prepared to heighten the second: many times the close of the sense falls into the middle of the next verse, or farther off, and he may often prevail himself of the same advantages in English which Virgil had in Latin,— he may break off in the hemistich, and begin another line. Indeed, the not observing these two last things makes plays which are writ in verse so tedious: for though, most commonly, the sense is to be confined to the couplet, yet nothing that does *perpetuo tenore fluere*, run in the same channel, can please always. 'Tis like the murmuring of a stream, which not varying in the fall, causes at first attention, at last drowsiness. Variety of cadences is the best rule; the greatest help to the actors, and refreshment to the audience.

" If then verse may be made natural in itself, how becomes it unnatural in a play? You say the stage is the representation of nature, and no man in ordinary conversation speaks in rhyme. But you foresaw when you said this, that it might be answered —neither does any man speak in blank verse, or in measure without rhyme. Therefore you concluded, that which is nearest nature is still to be preferred. But you took no notice that rhyme might be made as natural as blank verse, by the well placing of the words, etc. All the difference between them, when they are both correct, is, the sound in one, which the other wants; and if so, the sweetness of it, and all the advantage resulting from it, which are handled in the Preface to *The Rival Ladies*, will yet stand good. As for that place of Aristotle, where he says, plays should be writ in that kind of verse which is nearest prose, it makes little for you; blank verse being properly but measured prose. Now measure alone, in any modern language, does not constitute verse; those of the ancients in Greek and Latin consisted in quantity of words, and a determinate number of feet. But when, by the inundation of the Goths and Vandals into Italy, new languages were introduced, and barbarously mingled with the Latin, of which the Italian, Spanish, French, and ours (made out of them and the Teutonic) are dialects, a new way of poesy was practised; new, I say, in those countries, for in all probability it was that of the conquerors in their own nations: at least we are able to prove, that the eastern people have used it from all antiquity. This new way consisted in measure or number of feet, and rhyme; the sweetness of rhyme, and observation of accent, supplying the place of quantity in words, which could neither exactly be observed by those barbarians, who knew not the rules of it, neither was it suitable to their tongues, as it had been to the Greek and Latin. No man is tied in modern poesy to observe any farther rule in the feet of his verse, but that they be dissyllables; whether Spondee, Trochee, or Iambic, it matters not; only he is obliged to rhyme: neither do the Spanish, French, Italian, or Germans, acknowledge at all, or very rarely, any such kind of poesy as blank verse amongst them. Therefore, at most 'tis but a poetic prose, a *sermo pedestris;* and as such, most fit for comedies, where I acknowledge rhyme to be improper.—Farther; as to that quotation of Aristotle, our couplet verses may be rendered as near prose as blank verse itself, by using those advantages I lately named,—as breaks in an hemistich, or running the sense into another line,—thereby making art and order appear as loose and free as nature: or not tying ourselves to couplets strictly, we may use the benefit of the Pindaric way practised in *The Siege of Rhodes;* where the numbers vary, and the rhyme is disposed carelessly, and far from often chiming. Neither is that other advantage of the ancients to be despised, of changing the kind of verse when they please, with the change of the scene, or some new entrance; for they confine not themselves always to iambics, but extend their liberty to all lyric numbers, and sometimes even to hexameter. But I need not go so far to prove that rhyme, as it succeeds to all other offices of Greek and Latin verse, so especially to this of plays, since the custom of nations at this day confirms it; the French, Italian, and Spanish tragedies are generally writ in it; and sure the universal consent of the most civilised parts of the world, ought in this, as it doth in other customs, to include the rest.

" But perhaps you may tell me, I have proposed such a way to make rhyme natural, and consequently proper to plays, as is unpracticable; and that I shall scarce find six or eight lines together in any play, where the words are so placed and chosen as is required to make it natural. I answer, no poet need constrain himself at all times to it. It is enough he makes it his general rule; for I deny not but sometimes there may be a greatness in placing the words otherwise; and sometimes they may sound better; sometimes also the variety itself is excuse enough. But if, for the most part, the words be placed as they are in the negligence of prose, it is sufficient to denominate the way practicable; for we esteem that to be such, which in the trial oftener succeeds than misses. And thus far you may find the practice made good in many plays: where you do not, remember still, that if you cannot find six natural rhymes together, it will be as hard for you to produce as many lines in blank verse, even among the greatest of our poets, against which I cannot make some reasonable exception.

" And this, Sir, calls to my remembrance the beginning of your discourse, where you told us we should never find the audience favourable to this kind of writing, till we could produce as good plays in rhyme as Ben Jonson, Fletcher, and Shakspeare had writ out of it. But it is to raise envy to the living, to compare them with the dead. They are honoured, and almost adored by us, as they deserve; neither do I know any so presumptuous of themselves as to contend with them. Yet give me leave to say thus much, without injury to their ashes; that not only we shall never equal them, but they could never equal themselves, were they to rise and write again. We acknowledge them our fathers in wit; but they have ruined their estates themselves, before they came to their children's hands. There is scarce an humour, a character, or any kind of plot, which they have not used. All comes sullied or wasted to us: and were they to entertain this age, they could not now make so plenteous treatments out of such decayed fortunes. This therefore will be a good argument to us, either not to write at all, or to attempt some other way. There is no bays to be expected in their walks: *tentanda via est, quà me quoque possum tollere humo.*

" This way of writing in verse they have only left free to us; our age is arrived to a perfection in it, which they never knew; and which (if we may guess by what of theirs we have seen in verse, as *The Faithful Shepherdess*, and *Sad Shepherd*) 'tis probable they never could have reached. For the genius of every age is different; and though ours excel in this, I deny not but to imitate nature in that perfection which they did in prose, is a greater commendation than to write in verse exactly. As for what you have added—that the people are not generally inclined to like this way,—if it were true, it would be no wonder, that betwixt the shaking off an old habit, and the introducing of a new, there should be difficulty. Do we not see them stick to Hopkins' and Sternhold's psalms, and forsake those of David, I mean Sandys his translation of them? If by the people you understand the multitude, the οἱ πολλοί, 'tis no matter what they think; they are sometimes in the right, sometimes in the wrong: their judgment is a mere lottery. *Est ubi plebs rectè putat, est ubi peccat.* Horace says it of the vulgar, judging poesy. But if you mean the mixed audience of the populace and the noblesse, I dare confidently affirm that a great part of the latter sort are already favourable to verse; and that no serious plays written since the king's return have been more kindly received by them than *The Siege of Rhodes*, the *Mustapha*, *The Indian Queen*, and *Indian Emperor*.

"But I come now to the inference of your first argument. You said that the dialogue of plays is presented as the effect of sudden thought, but no man speaks suddenly, or *extempore*, in rhyme; and you inferred from thence, that rhyme, which you acknowledge to be proper to epic poesy, cannot equally be proper to dramatic, unless we could suppose all men born so much more than poets, that verses should be made in them, not by them.

"It has been formerly urged by you, and confessed by me, that since no man spoke any kind of verse *extempore*, that which was nearest nature was to be preferred. I answer you, therefore, by distinguishing betwixt what is nearest to the nature of comedy, which is the imitation of common persons and ordinary speaking, and what is nearest the nature of a serious play: this last is indeed the representation of nature, but 'tis nature wrought up to a higher pitch. The plot, the characters, the wit, the passions, the descriptions, are all exalted above the level of common converse, as high as the imagination of the poet can carry them, with proportion to verisimility. Tragedy, we know, is wont to image to us the minds and fortunes of noble persons, and to portray these exactly; heroic rhyme is nearest nature, as being the noblest kind of modern verse.

> Indignatur enim privatis et prope socco
> Dignis carminibus narrari cœna Thyestæ

says Horace: and in another place,

> Effutire leves indigna tragœdia versus.

Blank verse is acknowledged to be too low for a poem, nay more, for a paper of verses; but if too low for an ordinary sonnet, how much more for tragedy, which is by Aristotle, in the dispute betwixt the epic poesy and the dramatic, for many reasons he there alleges, ranked above it?

"But setting this defence aside, your argument is almost as strong against the use of rhyme in poems as in plays; for the epic way is everywhere interlaced with dialogue, or discoursive scenes; and therefore you must either grant rhyme to be improper there, which is contrary to your assertion, or admit it into plays by the same title which you have given it to poems. For though tragedy be justly preferred above the other, yet there is a great affinity between them, as may easily be discovered in that definition of a play which Lisideius gave us. The *genus* of them is the same—a just and lively image of human nature, in its actions, passions, and traverses of fortune: so is the end—namely, for the delight and benefit of mankind. The characters and persons are still the same, viz., the greatest of both sorts; only the manner of acquainting us with those actions, passions, and fortunes, is different. Tragedy performs it *viva voce*, or by action, in dialogue; wherein it excels the epic poem, which does it chiefly by narration, and therefore is not so lively an image of human nature. However, the agreement betwixt them is such, that if rhyme be proper for one, it must be for the other. Verse, 'tis true, is not the effect of sudden thought; but this hinders not that sudden thought may be represented in verse, since those thoughts are such as must be higher than nature can raise them without premeditation, especially to a continuance of them, even out of verse; and consequently you cannot imagine them to have been sudden either in the poet or in the actors. A play, as I have said, to be like nature, is to be set above it; as statues which are placed on high are made greater than the life, that they may descend to the sight in their just proportion.

"Perhaps I have insisted too long on this objection; but the clearing of it will make my stay shorter on the rest. You tell us, Crites, that rhyme appears most unnatural in repartees, or short replies: when he who answers (it being presumed he knew not what the other would say, yet) makes up that part of the verse which was left incomplete, and supplies both the sound and measure of it. This, you say, looks rather like the confederacy of two, than the answer of one.

"This, I confess, is an objection which is in every man's mouth, who loves not rhyme: but suppose, I beseech you, the repartee were made only in blank verse, might not part of the same argument be turned against you? for the measure is as often supplied there as it is in rhyme; the latter half of the hemistich as commonly made up, or a second line subjoined as a reply to the former; which any one leaf in Jonson's plays will sufficiently clear to you. You will often find in the Greek tragedians, and in Seneca, that when a scene grows up into the warmth of repartees, which is the close fighting of it, the latter part of the trimeter is supplied by him who answers; and yet it was never observed as a fault in them by any of the ancient or modern critics. The case is the same in our verse, as it was in theirs; rhyme to us being in lieu of quantity to them. But if no latitude is to be allowed a poet, you take from him not only his licence of *quidlibet audendi*, but you tie him up in a straiter compass than you would a philosopher. This is indeed *Musas colere severiores*. You would have him follow nature, but he must follow her on foot: you have dismounted him from his Pegasus. But you tell us, this supplying the last half of a verse, or adjoining a whole second to the former, looks more like the design of two, than the answer of one. Suppose we acknowledge it: how comes this confederacy to be more displeasing to you, than in a dance which is well contrived? You see there the united design of many persons to make up one figure: after they have separated themselves in many petty divisions, they rejoin one by one into a gross: the confederacy is plain amongst them, for chance could never produce anything so beautiful; and yet there is nothing in it that shocks your sight. I acknowledge the hand of art appears in repartee, as of necessity it must in all kind of verse. But there is also the quick and poignant brevity of it (which is an high imitation of nature in those sudden gusts of passion) to mingle with it; and this, joined with the cadency and sweetness of the rhyme, leaves nothing in the soul of the hearer to desire. 'Tis an art which appears; but it appears only like the shadowings of painture, which being to cause the rounding of it, cannot be absent; but while that is considered, they are lost: so while we attend to the other beauties of the matter, the care and labour of the rhyme is carried from us, or at least drowned in its own sweetness, as bees are sometimes buried in their honey. When a poet has found the repartee, the last perfection he can add to it, is to put it into verse. However good the thought may be, however apt the words in which 'tis couched, yet he finds himself at a little unrest, while rhyme is wanting: he cannot leave it till that comes naturally, and then is at ease, and sits down contented.

" From replies, which are the most elevated thoughts of verse, you pass to those which are most mean, and which are common with the lowest of household conversation. In these, you say, the majesty of verse suffers. You instance in the calling of a servant, or commanding a door to be shut, in rhyme. This, Crites, is a good observation of yours, but no argument: for it proves no more but that such thoughts should be waived. as often as may be, by the address of the poet. But suppose they are necessary in the places where he uses them, yet there is no need to put them into rhyme. He may place them in the beginning of a verse, and break it off, as unfit, when so debased, for any other use: or granting the worst,—that they require more room than the hemistich will allow, yet still there is a choice to be made of the best words, and least vulgar (provided they be apt), to express such thoughts. Many have blamed rhyme in general, for this fault, when the poet with a little care might have redressed it. But they do it with no more justice than if English poesy should be made ridiculous for the sake of the Water-poet's rhymes. Our language is noble, full, and significant; and I know not why he who is master of it may not clothe ordinary things in it as decently as the Latin, if he use the same diligence in his choice of words: *delectus verborum origo est eloquentiæ.* It was the saying of Julius Cæsar, one so curious in his, that none of them can be changed but for a worse. One would think, *unlock the door*, was a thing as vulgar as could be spoken; and yet Seneca could make it sound high and lofty in his Latin:

> *Reserate clusos regii postes laris.*
> Set wide the palace gates.

" But I turn from this conception, both because it happens not above twice or thrice in any play that those vulgar thoughts are used; and then too (were there no other apology to be made, yet), the necessity of them, which is alike in all kind of writing, may excuse them. For if they are little and mean in rhyme, they are of consequence such in blank verse. Besides that the great eagerness and precipitation with which they are spoken, makes us rather mind the substance than the dress; that for which they are spoken, rather than what is spoken. For they are always the effect of some hasty concernment, and something of consequence depends on them.

" Thus, Crites, I have endeavoured to answer your objections; it remains only that I should vindicate an argument for verse, which you have gone about to overthrow. It had formerly been said that the easiness of blank verse renders the poet too luxuriant, but that the labour of rhyme bounds and circumscribes an over-fruitful fancy; the sense there being commonly confined to the couplet, and the words so ordered that the rhyme naturally follows them, not they the rhyme. To this you answered, that it was no argument to the question in hand; for the dispute was not which way a man may write best, but which is most proper for the subject on which he writes.

"First, give me leave, Sir, to remember you that the argument against which you raised this objection was only secondary: it was built on this hypothesis,—that to write in verse was proper for serious plays. Which supposition being granted (as it was briefly made out in that discourse, by showing how verse might be made natural), it asserted, that this way of writing was an help to the poet's judgment, by putting bounds to a wild overflowing fancy. I think, therefore, it will not be hard for me to make good what it was to prove on that supposition. But you add, that were this let pass, yet he who wants judgment in the liberty of his fancy, may as well show the defect of it when he is confined to verse; for he who has judgment will avoid errors, and he who has it not, will commit them in all kinds of writing

"This argument, as you have taken it from a most acute person, so I confess it carries much weight in it: but by using the word judgment here indefinitely, you seem to have put a fallacy upon us. I grant, he who has judgment, that is, so profound, so strong, or rather so infallible a judgment, that he needs no helps to keep it always poised and upright, will commit no faults either in rhyme or out of it. And on the other extreme, he who has a judgment so weak and crazed that no helps can correct or amend it, shall write scurvily out of rhyme, and worse in it. But the first of these judgments is nowhere to be found, and the latter is not fit to write at all. To speak therefore of judgment as it is in the best poets; they who have the greatest proportion of it, want other helps than from it, within. As for example, you would be loth to say that he who is endued with a sound judgment has no need of history, geography, or moral philosophy, to write correctly. Judgment is indeed the masterworkman in a play; but he requires many subordinate hands, many tools to his assistance. And verse I affirm to be one of these; 'tis a rule and line by which he keeps his building compact and even, which otherwise lawless imagination would raise either irregularly or loosely; at least, if the poet commits errors with this help, he would make greater and more without it: 'tis, in short, a slow and painful, but the surest kind of working. Ovid, whom you accuse for luxuriancy in verse, had perhaps been farther guilty of it, had he writ in prose. And for your instance of Ben Jonson, who, you say, writ exactly without the help of rhyme; you are to remember, 'tis only an aid to a luxuriant fancy, which his was not: as he did not want imagination, so none ever said he had much to spare. Neither was verse then refined so much, to be an help to that age, as it is to ours. Thus then the second thoughts being usually the best, as receiving the maturest digestion from judgment, and the last and most mature product of those thoughts being artful and laboured verse, it may well be inferred, that verse is a great help to a luxuriant fancy; and this is what that argument which you opposed was to evince."

Neander was pursuing this discourse so eagerly that Eugenius had called to him twice or thrice, ere he took notice that the barge stood still, and that they were at the foot of Somerset-stairs, where they had appointed it to land. The company were all sorry to separate so soon, though a great part of the evening was already spent; and stood a-while looking back on the water, upon which the moonbeams played, and made it appear like floating quicksilver: at last they went up through a crowd of French people, who were merrily dancing in the open air, and nothing concerned for the noise of guns which had alarmed the town that afternoon. Walking thence together to the Piazze, they parted there; Eugenius and Lisideius to some pleasant appointment they had made, and Crites and Neander to their several lodgings.

A DEFENCE OF AN ESSAY OF
DRAMATIC POESY

The former edition of *The Indian Emperor* being full of faults, which had escaped the printer, I have been willing to overlook this second with more care; and though I could not allow myself so much time as was necessary, yet, by that little I have done, the press is freed from some gross errors which it had to answer for before. As for the more material faults of writing, which are properly mine, though I see many of them, I want leisure to amend them. 'Tis enough for those who make one poem the business of their lives, to leave that correct: yet excepting Virgil, I never met with any which was so in any language.

But while I was thus employed about this impression, there came to my hands a new printed play called *The Great Favourite, or The Duke of Lerma ;* the author of which, a noble and most ingenious person, has done me the favour to make some observations and animadversions upon my *Dramatic Essay*. I must confess he might have better consulted his reputation, than by matching himself with so weak an adversary. But if his honour be diminished in the choice of his antagonist, it is sufficiently recompensed in the election of his cause: which being the weaker, in all appearance, as combating the received opinions of the best ancient and modern authors, will add to his glory, if he overcome, and to the opinion of his generosity, if he be vanquished: since he engages at so great odds, and, so like a cavalier, undertakes the protection of the weaker party. I have only to fear on my own behalf that so good a cause as mine may not suffer by my ill management, or weak defence; yet I cannot in honour but take the glove, when 'tis offered me: though I am only a champion by succession; and no more able to defend the right of Aristotle and Horace than an infant Dimock to maintain the title of a king.

For my own concernment in the controversy, it is so small that I can easily be contented to be driven from a few notions of Dramatic Poesy; especially by one who has the reputation oi understanding all things: and I might justly make that excuse for my yielding to him, which the Philosopher made to the Emperor,—*why should I offer to contend with him who is master of more than twenty legions of arts and sciences?* But I am forced to fight, and therefore it will be no shame to be overcome.

Yet I am so much his servant, as not to meddle with anything which does not concern me in his Preface; therefore, I leave the good sense and other excellencies of the first twenty lines to be considered by the critics. As for the play of *The Duke of Lerma*, having so much altered and beautified it, as he has done, it can justly belong to none but him. Indeed, they must be extreme ignorant as well as envious, who would rob him of that honour; for you see him putting in his claim to it, even in the first two lines:

> Repulse upon repulse, like waves thrown back,
> That slide to hang upon obdurate rocks.

After this, let detraction do its worst; for if this be not his, it deserves to be. For my part, I declare for distributive justice; and from this and what follows, he certainly deserves *those advantages which he acknowledges to have received from the opinion of sober men.*

In the next place, I must beg leave to observe his great address in courting the reader to his party. For intending to assault all poets, both ancient and modern, he discovers not his whole design at once, but seems only to aim at me, and attacks me on my weakest side, my defence of verse.

To begin with me,—he gives me the compellation of *The Author of a Dramatic Essay*, which is a little discourse in dialogue, for the most part borrowed from the observations of others: therefore, that I may not be wanting to him in civility, I return his compliment by calling him *The Author of the Duke of Lerma*.

But (that I may pass over his salute) he takes notice of my great pains to prove rhyme as natural in a serious play, and more effectual than blank verse. Thus, indeed, I did state the question; but he tells me, *I pursue that which I call natural in a wrong application: for 'tis not the question whether rhyme or not rhyme be best or most natural for a serious subject, but what is nearest the nature of that it represents.*

If I have formerly mistaken the question, I must confess my ignorance so far, as to say I continue still in my mistake: but he ought to have proved that I mistook it; for it is yet but *gratis dictum :* I still shall think I have gained my point, if I can prove that rhyme is best or most natural for a serious subject. As for the question as he states it, whether rhyme be nearest the nature of what it represents, I wonder he should think me so ridiculous as to dispute whether prose or verse be nearest to ordinary conversation.

It still remains for him to prove his inference,—that, since verse is granted to be more remote than prose from ordinary conversation, therefore no serious plays ought to be writ in verse: and when he clearly makes that good, I will acknowledge his victory as absolute as he can desire it.

The qustion now is, which of us two has mistaken it; and if it appear I have not, the world will suspect *what gentleman that was, who was allowed to speak twice in Parliament, because he had not yet spoken to the question ;* and perhaps conclude it to be the same, who, 'tis reported, maintained a contradiction *in terminis,* in the face of three hundred persons.

But to return to verse; whether it be natural or not in plays, is a problem which is not demonstrable of either side: 'tis enough for me that he acknowledges he had rather read good verse than prose: for if all the enemies of verse will confess as much, I shall not need to prove that it is natural. I am satisfied, if it cause delight: for delight is the chief, if not the only, end of poesy: instruction can be admitted but in the second place; for poesy only instructs as it delights. 'Tis true, that to imitate well is a poet's work; but to affect the soul, and excite the passions, and above all to move admiration, which is the delight of serious plays, a bare imitation will not serve. The converse, therefore, which a poet is to imitate, must be heightened with all the arts and ornaments of poesy, and must be such, as, strictly considered, could never be supposed spoken by any without premeditation.

As for what he urges, that *a play will still be supposed to be a composition of several persons speaking* ex tempore; *and that good verses are the hardest things which can be imagined to be so spoken ;* I must crave leave to dissent from his opinion, as to the former part of it: for, if I am not deceived, a play is supposed to be the work of the poet, imitating or representing the conversation of several persons; and this I think to be as clear as he thinks the contrary.

But I will be bolder, and do not doubt to make it good, though a paradox, that one great reason why prose is not to be used in serious plays, is, because it is too near the nature of converse:

there may be too great a likeness; as the most skilful painters affirm, that there may be too near a resemblance in a picture: to take every lineament and feature, is not to make an excellent piece; but to take so much only as will make a beautiful resemblance of the whole; and, with an ingenious flattery of nature, to heighten the beauties of some parts, and hide the deformities of the rest. For so says Horace:

> Ut pictura poesis erit. . . .
> Hæc amat obscurum, vult hæc sub luce videri,
> Judicis argutum quæ non formidat acumen.
>   et quæ
> Desperat tractata nitescere posse, relinquit.

In *Bartholomew Fair*, or the lowest kind of comedy, that degree of heightening is used, which is proper to set off that subject. 'Tis true the author was not there to go out of prose, as he does in his higher arguments of comedy, *The Fox*, and *Alchymist*; yet he does so raise his matter in that prose as to render it delightful; which he could never have performed had he only said or done those very things that are daily spoken or practised in the Fair; for then the Fair itself would be as full of pleasure to an ingenious person as the play; which we manifestly see it is not. But he hath made an excellent lazar of it: the copy is of price, though the original be vile. You see in *Catiline* and *Sejanus*, where the argument is great, he sometimes ascends to verse, which shows he thought it not unnatural in serious plays; and had his genius been as proper for rhyme as it was for humour, or had the age in which he lived attained to as much knowledge in verse as ours, it is probable he would have adorned those subjects with that kind of writing.

Thus prose, though the rightful prince, yet is by common consent deposed, as too weak for the government of serious plays; and he failing, there now start up two competitors; one the nearer in blood, which is blank verse; the other more fit for the ends of government, which is rhyme. Blank verse is, indeed, the nearer prose, but he is blemished with the weakness of his predecessor. Rhyme (for I will deal clearly) has somewhat of the usurper in him; but he is brave and generous, and his dominion pleasing. For this reason of delight, the ancients (whom I will still believe as wise as those who so confidently correct them) wrote all their tragedies in verse, though they knew it most remote from conversation.

But I perceive I am falling into the danger of another rebuke from my opponent; for when I plead that the Ancients used verse, I prove not that they would have admitted rhyme, had it then been written: all I can say is only this; that it seems to have succeeded verse by the general consent of poets in all modern languages: for almost all their serious plays are written in it: which, though it be no demonstration that therefore they ought to be so, yet at least the practice first, and then the continuation of it, shows that it attained the end,—which was to please; and if that cannot be compassed here, I will be the first who shall lay it down. For I confess my chief endeavours are to delight the age in which I live. If the humour of this be for low comedy, small accidents, and raillery, I will force my genius to obey it, though with more reputation I could write in verse. I know I am not so fitted by nature to write comedy: I want that gaiety of humour which is required to it. My conversation is slow and dull, my humour saturnine and reserved: in short, I am none of those who endeavour to break jests in company, or make repartees. So that those who decry my comedies do me no injury, except it be in point of profit: reputation in them is the last thing to which I shall pretend. I beg pardon for entertaining the reader with so ill a subject; but before I quit that argument, which was the cause of this digression, I cannot but take notice how I am corrected for my quotation of Seneca, in my defence of plays in verse. My words are these: "Our language is noble, full, and significant; and I know not why he who is master of it, may not clothe ordinary things in it as decently as the Latin, if he use the same diligence in his *choice of words*. One would think, *unlock a door*, was a thing as vulgar as could be spoken; yet Seneca could make it sound high and lofty in his Latin:

Reserate clusos regii postes laris."

But he says of me, *That being filled with the precedents of the Ancients, who writ their plays in verse, I commend the thing; declaring our language to be full, noble, and significant, and charging all defects upon the* ill placing of words, *which I prove by quoting Seneca loftily expressing such an ordinary thing as* shutting a door.

Here he manifestly mistakes; for I spoke not of the placing, but of the choice of words; for which I quoted that aphorism of Julius Cæsar:

Delectus verborum est origo eloquentiæ :

but *delectus verborum* is no more Latin for the placing of words, an *reserate* is Latin for *shut the door*, as he interprets it, which ignorantly construed *unlock* or *open* it.

He supposes I was highly affected with the sound of those ords; and I suppose I may more justly imagine it of him; r if he had not been extremely satisfied with the sound, he ould have minded the sense a little better.

But these are now to be no faults; for ten days after his book s published, and that his mistakes are grown so famous that hey are come back to him, he sends his *Errata* to be printed, nd annexed to his play; and desires, that instead of *shutting* ou would read *opening;* which, it seems, was the printer's ault. I wonder at his modesty, that he did not rather say it vas Seneca's, or mine; and that in some authors, *reserare* was o *shut* as well as to *open*, as the word *barach*, say the learned, s both to *bless* and *curse*.

Well, since it was the printer, he was a naughty man to com-nit the same mistake twice in six lines: I warrant you *delectus* erborum for *placing of words* was his mistake too, though the uthor forgot to tell him of it: if it were my book, I assure you should. For those rascals ought to be the proxies of every ;entleman author, and to be chastised for him, when he is not oleased to own an error. Yet since he has given the *Errata*, wish he would have enlarged them only a few sheets more, and hen he would have spared me the labour of an answer: for this ursed printer is so given to mistakes, that there is scarce a entence in the Preface without some false grammar or hard ense in it; which will all be charged upon the poet, because ie is so good-natured as to lay but three errors to the printer's ccount, and to take the rest upon himself, who is better able to support them. But he needs not apprehend that I should strictly examine those little faults, except I am called upon to lo it: I shall return therefore to that quotation of Seneca, and answer, not to what he writes, but to what he means. I never ntended it as an argument, but only as an illustration of what I had said before concerning the election of words: and all he can charge me with is only this,—that if Seneca could make an ordinary thing sound well in Latin by the choice of words, the same, with the like care, might be performed in English: if it cannot, I have committed an error on the right hand, by commending too much the copiousness and well-sounding of our language; which I hope my countrymen will pardon me. At least the words which follow in my Dramatic Essay will plead somewhat in my behalf; for I say there, that this objection happens but seldom in a play; and then too either the meanness of the expression may be avoided, or shut out from the verse b breaking it in the midst.

But I have said too much in the defence of verse; for afte all, it is a very indifferent thing to me, whether it obtain or not I am content hereafter to be ordered by his rule, that is, t write it sometimes, because it pleases me; and so much th rather, because he has declared that it pleases him. But h has taken his last farewell of the Muses, and he has done it civilly by honouring them with the name of *his long acquaintances* which is a compliment they have scarce deserved from him For my own part, I bear a share in the public loss; and hov emulous soever I may be of his fame and reputation, I canno but give this testimony of his style,—that it is extreme poetical even in oratory; his thoughts elevated sometimes above commor apprehension; his notions politic and grave, and tending to th instruction of princes, and reformation of states; that they are abundantly interlaced with variety of fancies, tropes, and figures, which the critics have enviously branded with the name of obscurity and false grammar.

Well, he is now fettered in business of more unpleasant nature the Muses have lost him, but the commonwealth gains by it the corruption of a poet is the generation of a statesman.

He will not venture again into the civil wars of censure; ub . . . nullos habitura triumphos: if he had not told us he had left the Muses, we might have half suspected it by that word *ubi,* which does not any way belong to them in that place; the rest of the verse is indeed Lucan's; but that *ubi,* I will answer for it, is his own. Yet he has another reason for this disgust of Poesy; for he says immediately after, that *the manner of plays which are now in most esteem, is beyond his power to perform .* to perform the manner of a thing, I confess is new English to me. *However, he condemns not the satisfaction of others; but rather their unnecessary understanding, who, like Sancho Pança's doctor prescribe too strictly to our appetites;* for, says he, *in the difference* of Tragedy *and* Comedy, *and of* Farce *itself, there can be no determination but by the taste, nor in the manner of their composure.*

We shall see him now as great a critic as he was a poet; and the reason why he excelled so much in poetry will be evident, for it will appear to have proceeded from the exactness of his judgment. *In the difference of Tragedy, Comedy, and Farce itself, there can be no determination but by the taste.* I will not quarrel with the obscurity of his phrase, though I justly might; but beg his pardon if I do not rightly understand him: if he means, that there is no essential difference betwixt comedy, tragedy, and farce, but what is only made by the people's taste, which distinguishes one of them from the other, that is so manifest an error, that I need not lose time to contradict it. Were there neither judge, taste, nor opinion in the world, yet they would differ in their natures; for the action, character, and language of tragedy, would still be great and high; that of comedy lower and more familiar; admiration would be the delight of one, and satyr of the other.

I have but briefly touched upon these things, because, whatever his words are, I can scarce imagine, that *he who is always concerned for the true honour of reason, and would have no spurious issue fathered upon her,* should mean anything to absurd as to affirm, *that there is no difference betwixt comedy and tragedy, but what is made by the taste only :* unless he would have us understand the comedies of my Lord L., where the first act should be pottages, the second Fricassees, etc., and the fifth a *chere entiere* of women.

I rather guess he means, that betwixt one comedy or tragedy and another, there is no other difference but what is made by the liking or disliking of the audience. This is indeed a less error than the former, but yet it is a great one. The liking or disliking of the people gives the play the denomination of good or bad; but does not really make or constitute it such. To please the people ought to be the poet's aim, because plays are made for their delight; but it does not follow that they are always pleased with good plays, or that the plays which please them are always good. The humour of the people is now for comedy; therefore, in hope to please them, I write comedies rather than serious plays; and so far their taste prescribes to me: but it does not follow from that reason, that comedy is to be preferred before tragedy in its own nature; for that which is so in its own nature cannot be otherwise; as a man cannot but be a rational creature: but the opinion of the people may alter, and in another age, or perhaps in this, serious plays may be set up above comedies.

This I think a sufficient answer: if it be not, he has provided me of an excuse; it seems, in his wisdom, he foresaw my weakness, and has found out this expedient for me, *That it is not necessary for poets to study strict reason ; since they are so used to a greater latitude than is allowed by that severe inquisition, that*

*they must infringe their own jurisdiction, to profess themselve
obliged to argue well.*

I am obliged to him for discovering to me this back-door
but I am not yet resolved on my retreat: for I am of opinion tha
they cannot be good poets who are not accustomed to argu
well. False reasonings and colours of speech are the certai
marks of one who does not understand the stage; for mora
truth is the mistress of the poet, as much as of the philosopher
Poesy must resemble natural truth, but it must *be* ethical
Indeed the poet dresses truth, and adorns nature, but does no
alter them:

> Ficta voluptatis causa sint proxima veris.

Therefore, that is not the best poesy which resembles notions
of things that are not to things that are: though the fancy may
be great, and the words flowing, yet the soul is but half satisfied
when there is not truth in the foundation. This is that which
makes Virgil be preferred before the rest of Poets: in variety of
fancy and sweetness of expression, you see Ovid far above him;
for Virgil rejected many of those things which Ovid wrote. *A
great wit's great work is to refuse*, as my worthy friend, Sir John
Berkenhead, has ingeniously expressed it: you rarely meet
with anything in Virgil but truth, which therefore leaves the
strongest impression of pleasure in the soul. This I thought
myself obliged to say in behalf of Poesy; and to declare, though
it be against myself, that when poets do not argue well, the
defect is in the workman, not in the art.

And now I come to the boldest part of his discourse, wherein
he attacks not me, but all the ancients and moderns; and under-
mines, as he thinks, the very foundations on which Dramatic
Poesy is built. I could wish he would have declined that envy
which must of necessity follow such an undertaking, and contented himself with triumphing over me in my opinions of verse,
which I will never hereafter dispute with him; but he must
pardon me, if I have that veneration for Aristotle, Horace,
Ben Jonson, and Corneille, that I dare not serve him in such a
cause, and against such heroes, but rather fight under their
protection, as Homer reports of little Teucer, who shot the
Trojans from under the large buckler of Ajax Telamon:

> Στῆ δ' ἄρ' ὑπ' Αἴαντος σάκεϊ Τελαμωνιάδαο.

> He stood beneath his brother's ample shield,
> And cover'd there, shot death through all the field.

The words of my noble adversary are these:

But if we examine the general rules laid down for plays by strict reason, we shall find the errors equally gross ; for the great foundation which is laid to build upon, is nothing, as it is generally stated, as will appear upon the examination of the particulars.

These particulars, in due time, shall be examined: in the meanwhile, let us consider what this great foundation is, which he says is nothing, as it is generally stated. I never heard of any other foundation of Dramatic Poesy than the imitation of nature; neither was there ever pretended any other by the ancients, or moderns, or me, who endeavour to follow them in that rule. This I have plainly said in my definition of a play; that it is a just and lively image of human nature, etc. Thus the foundation, as it is generally stated, will stand sure, if this definition of a play be true; if it be not, he ought to have made his exception against it, by proving that a play is not an imitation of nature, but somewhat else which he is pleased to think it.

But it is very plain that he has mistaken the foundation for that which is built upon it, though not immediately: for the direct and immediate consequence is this; if nature be to be imitated, then there is a rule for imitating nature rightly; otherwise there may be an end, and no means conducing to it. Hitherto I have proceeded by demonstration; but as our divines when they have proved a Deity, because there is order, and have inferred that this Deity ought to be worshipped, differ afterwards in the manner of the worship; so, having laid down that nature is to be imitated, and that proposition proving the next, that then there are means which conduce to the imitating of nature, I dare proceed no farther positively; but have only laid down some opinions of the ancients and moderns, and of my own, as means which they used, and which I thought probable for the attaining of that end. Those means are the same which my antagonist calls the foundations,—how properly, the world may judge; and to prove that this is his meaning, he clears it immediately to you, by enumerating those rules or propositions against which he makes his particular exceptions,—as namely, those of time, and place,—in these words: *First, we are told the plot should not be so ridiculously contrived, as to crowd two several countries into one stage : secondly, to cramp the accidents of many years or days into the representation of two hours and an half ; and lastly, a conclusion drawn, that the only remaining dispute is, concerning time, whether it should be contained in twelve or twenty-four hours ; and the place to be limited to that spot of ground where*

*the play is supposed to begin : and this is called nearest nature
for that is concluded most natural, which is most probable, an
nearest to that which it presents.*

Thus he has only made a small mistake of the means con
ducing to the end, for the end itself; and of the superstructur
for the foundation: but he proceeds: *To show, therefore, upo*
what ill grounds they dictate laws for Dramatic Poesy, etc. H
is here pleased to charge me with being magisterial, as he ha
done in many other places of his Preface. Therefore in vindica
tion of myself, I must crave leave to say, that my whole discours
was sceptical, according to that way of reasoning which wa
used by Socrates, Plato, and all the Academicques of old, whic
Tully and the best of the ancients followed, and which is imitate
by the modest inquisitions of the Royal Society. That it is so
not only the name will show, which is, *An Essay,* but the fram
and composition of the work. You see, it is a dialogue sustaine
by persons of several opinions, all of them left doubtful, to b
determined by the readers in general; and more particularly
deferred to the accurate judgment of my Lord Buckhurst, to
whom I made a dedication of my book. These are my words i
my Epistle, speaking of the persons whom I introduced in my
dialogue: It is true, they differed in their opinions, as it i
probable they would; neither do I take upon me to reconcile
but to relate them, leaving your lordship to decide it in favou
of that part which you shall judge most reasonable. And afte
that, in my Advertisement to the Reader, I said this: The drif
of the ensuing discourse is chiefly to vindicate the honour of ou
English writers from the censure of those who unjustly prefe
the French before them. This I intimate, lest any should think
me so exceeding vain, as to teach others an art which they
understand much better than myself. But this is more than
necessary to clear my modesty in that point; and I am very
confident that there is scarce any man who has lost so much
time as to read that trifle, but will be my compurgator as to
that arrogance whereof I am accused. The truth is, if I had
been naturally guilty of so much vanity as to dictate my opinions
yet I do not find that the character of a positive or self-conceited
person is of such advantage to any in this age, that I should
labour to be publicly admitted of that order.

But I am not now to defend my own cause, when that of all
the ancients and moderns is in question: for this gentleman
who accuses me of arrogance, has taken a course not to be taxed
with the other extreme of modesty. Those propositions which

re laid down in my discourse, as helps to the better imitation
of nature, are not mine (as I have said) nor were ever pretended
to be, but derived from the authority of Aristotle and Horace,
and from the rules and examples of Ben Jonson and Corneille.
These are the men with whom properly he contends, and against
*whom he will endeavour to make it evident, that there is no such
thing as what they all pretend.*

His argument against the unities of place and time is this:
*That it is as impossible for one stage to present two rooms or houses
truly, as two countries or kingdoms ; and as impossible that five
hours or twenty-four hours should be two hours, as that a thousand
hours or years should be less than what they are, or the greatest
part of time to be comprehended in the less : for all of them being
impossible, they are none of them nearest the truth or nature of
what they present ; for impossibilities are all equal, and admit
of no degree.*

This argument is so scattered into parts that it can scarce
be united into a syllogism; yet, in obedience to him, *I will
abbreviate* and comprehend as much of it as I can in few words,
that my answer to it may be more perspicuous. I conceive his
meaning to be what follows, as to the unity of place: (if I mistake, I beg his pardon, professing it is not out of any design
to play the *Argumentative Poet*). If one stage cannot properly
present two rooms or houses, much less two countries or kingdoms, then there can be no unity of place; but one stage cannot
properly perform this: therefore there can be no unity of place.

I plainly deny his minor proposition; the force of which, if
I mistake not, depends on this; that the stage being one place
cannot be two. This, indeed, is as great a secret as that we
are all mortal; but to requite it with another, I must crave
leave to tell him, that though the stage cannot be two places,
yet it may properly represent them, successively, or at several
times. His argument is indeed no more than a mere fallacy,
which will evidently appear, when we distinguish place, as it
relates to plays, into real and imaginary. The real place is
that theatre, or piece of ground, on which the play is acted.
The imaginary, that house, town, or country, where the action
of the *Drama* is supposed to be; or more plainly, where the
scene of the play is laid. Let us now apply this to that Hercu-
lean argument, *which, if strictly and duly weighed, is to make it
evident that there is no such thing as what they all pretend.* It is
impossible, he says, for one stage to present two rooms or houses:
I answer, it is neither impossible, nor improper, for one real

place to represent two or more imaginary places, so it be done successively; which in other words is no more than this; That the imagination of the audience, aided by the words of the poet and painted scenes, may suppose the stage to be sometimes one place, sometimes another; now a garden, or wood, and immediately a camp: which, I appeal to every man's imagination if it be not true. Neither the ancients nor moderns, as much fools as he is pleased to think them, ever asserted that they could make one place two; but they might hope, by the good leave of this author, that the change of a scene might lead the imagination to suppose the place altered: So that he cannot fasten those absurdities upon this scene of a play, or imaginary place of action, that it is one place, and yet two. And this being so clearly proved, that it is past any show of a reasonable denial, it will not be hard to destroy that other part of his argument which depends upon it; namely, that it is as impossible for a stage to represent two rooms or houses, as two countries or kingdoms; for his reason is already overthrown, which was, because both were alike impossible. This is manifestly otherwise; for it is proved that a stage may properly represent two rooms or houses; for the imagination being judge of what is represented, will in reason be less chocked with the appearance of two rooms in the same house, or two houses in the same city, than with two distant cities in the same country, or two remote countries in the same universe. Imagination in a man or reasonable creature is supposed to participate of reason; and when that governs, as it does in the belief of fiction, reason is not destroyed, but misled, or blinded: that can prescribe to the reason, during the time of the representation, somewhat like a weak belief of what it sees and hears; and reason suffers itself to be so hoodwinked, that it may better enjoy the pleasures of the fiction: but it is never so wholly made a captive, as to be drawn headlong into a persuasion of those things which are most remote from probability: 'tis in that case a free-born subject, not a slave; it will contribute willingly its assent, as far as it sees convenient, but will not be forced. Now there is a greater vicinity in nature betwixt two rooms than betwixt two houses, betwixt two houses than betwixt two cities, and so of the rest; Reason therefore can sooner be led by Imagination to step from one room into another, than to walk to two distant houses, and yet rather to go thither, than to fly like a witch through the air, and be hurried from one region to another. Fancy and Reason go hand in hand; the first cannot leave the last behind; and though Fancy, when it sees the wide gulf, would venture over as the nimbler, yet it is withheld by Reason, which will refuse to take the leap, when the distance over it appears too large. If Ben Jonson himself will remove the scene from Rome into Tuscany in the same act, and from thence return to Rome, in the scene which immediately follows, reason will consider there is no porportionable allowance of time to perform the journey, and therefore will choose to stay at home. So, then, the less change of place there is, the less time is taken up in transporting the persons of the drama, with analogy to reason; and in that analogy, or resemblance of fiction to truth, consists the excellency of the play.

For what else concerns the unity of place, I have already given my opinion of it in my *Essay;*—that there is a latitude to be allowed to it,—as several places in the same town or city, or places adjacent to each other in the same country, which may all be comprehended under the larger denomination of one place; yet with this restriction, that the nearer and fewer those imaginary places are, the greater resemblance they will have to truth; and reason, which cannot make them one, will be more easily led to suppose them so.

What has been said of the unity of place, may easily be applied to that of time: I grant it to be impossible that the greater part of time should be comprehended in the less, that twenty-four hours should be crowded into three; but there is no necessity of that supposition. For as *Place*, so *Time* relating to a play, is either imaginary or real: the real is comprehended in those three hours, more or less, in the space of which the play is represented; the imaginary is that which is supposed to be taken up in the representation, as twenty-four hours more or less. Now no man ever could suppose that twenty-four real hours could be included in the space of three: but where is the absurdity of affirming that the feigned business of twenty-four imagined hours may not more naturally be represented in the compass of three real hours, than the like feigned business of twenty-four years in the same proportion of real time? For the proportions are always real, and much nearer, by his permission, of twenty-four to three, than of four thousand to it.

I am almost fearful of illustrating anything by similitude, lest he should confute it for an argument; yet I think the comparison of a glass will discover very aptly the fallacy of his argument, both concerning time and place. The strength of his reason depends on this, That the less cannot comprehend the greater. I have already answered, that we need not suppose it does: I say not that the less can comprehend the greater, but only that it may represent it: as in a glass or mirror of half a yard diameter, a whole room and many persons in it may be seen at once; not that it can comprehend that room or those persons, but that it represents them to the sight.

But the author of *The Duke of Lerma* is to be excused for his declaring against the unity of time; for, if I be not much mistaken, he is an interested person; the time of that play taking up so many years as the favour of the Duke of Lerma continued; nay, the second and third act including all the time of his prosperity, which was a great part of the reign of Philip the Third: for in the beginning of the second act he was not yet a favourite, and before the end of the third was in disgrace. I say not this with the least design of limiting the stage too servilely to twenty-four hours, however he be pleased to tax me with dogmatising in that point. In my dialogue, as I before hinted, several persons maintained their several opinions: one of them, indeed, who supported the cause of the French poesy, said, how strict they were in that particular; but he who answered in behalf of our nation, was willing to give more latitude to the rule; and cites the words of Corneille himself, complaining against the severity of it, and observing what beauties it banished from the stage. In few words, my own opinion is this (and I willingly submit it to my adversary, when he will please impartially to consider it), that the imaginary time of every play ought to be contrived into as narrow a compass as the nature of the plot, the quality of the persons, and variety of accidents will allow. In comedy I would not exceed twenty-four or thirty hours: for the plot, accidents, and persons of comedy are small, and may be naturally turned in a little compass: But in tragedy the design is weighty, and the persons great; therefore there will naturally be required a greater space of time in which to move them. And this though Ben Jonson has not told us, yet it is manifestly his opinion: for you see that to his comedies he allows generally but twenty-four hours; to his two tragedies, *Sejanus* and *Catiline*, a much larger time: though he draws both of them into as narrow a compass as he can: for he shows you only the latter end of Sejanus his favour, and the conspiracy of Catiline already ripe, and just breaking out into action.

But as it is an error on the one side, to make too great a disproportion betwixt the imaginary time of the play, and the

eal time of its representations; so on the other side, it is an
oversight to compress the accidents of a play into a narrower
compass than that in which they could naturally be produced.
Of this last error the French are seldom guilty, because the
thinness of their plots prevents them from it; but few Englishmen, except Ben Jonson, have ever made a plot with variety of
design in it, included in twenty-four hours, which was altogether
natural. For this reason, I prefer *The Silent Woman* before all
other plays, I think justly; as I do its author, in judgment,
above all other poets. Yet of the two, I think that error the
most pardonable, which in too straight a compass crowds
together many accidents; since it produces more variety, and
consequently more pleasure to the audience; and because the
nearness of proportion betwixt the imaginary and real time
does speciously cover the compression of the accidents.

Thus I have endeavoured to answer the meaning of his argument; for as he drew it, I humbly conceive that it was none;
as will appear by his proposition, and the proof of it. His
proposition was this.

*If strictly and duly weighed, it is as impossible for one stage to
present two rooms or houses, as two countries or kingdoms,* etc.
And his proof this: *For all being impossible, they are none of
them nearest the truth or nature of what they present.*

Here you see, instead of proof or reason, there is only *petitio
principii :* for in plain words, his sense is this, The things are as
impossible as one another, because they are both equally impossible: but he takes those two things to be granted as impossible which he ought to have proved such, before he had
proceeded to prove them equally impossible: he should have
made out first, that it was impossible for one stage to represent
two houses, and then have gone forward to prove that it was as
equally impossible for a stage to present two houses as two
countries.

After all this, the very absurdity to which he would reduce me
is none at all: for he only drives at this, that if his argument be
true, I must then acknowledge that there are degrees in impossibilities, which I easily grant him without dispute: and if I
mistake not, Aristotle and the School are of my opinion. For
there are some things which are absolutely impossible, and
others which are only so *ex parte ;* as it is absolutely impossible
for a thing *to be,* and *not be,* at the same time; but for a stone
to move naturally upward, is only impossible *ex parte materiæ ;*
but it is not impossible for the first mover to alter the nature of it.

His last assault, like that of a Frenchman, is most feeble for whereas I have observed that none have been violent against verse, but such only as have not attempted it, or have succeeded ill in their attempt, he will needs, according to his usual custom improve my observation to an argument, that he might have the glory to confute it. But I lay my observation at his feet as I do my pen, which I have often employed willingly in his deserved commendations, and now most unwillingly against his judgment. For his person and parts, I honour them as much as any man living, and have had so many particular obligations to him, that I should be very ungrateful if I did not acknowledge them to the world. But I gave not the first occasion of this difference in opinions. In my Epistle Dedicatory before my *Rival Ladies*, I had said somewhat in behalf of verse, which he was pleased to answer in his Preface to his plays: that occasioned my reply in my Essay; and that reply begot this rejoinder of his in his Preface to *The Duke of Lerma*. But as I was the last who took up arms, I will be the first to lay them down. For what I have here written, I submit it wholly to him; and if I do not hereafter answer what may be objected against this paper, I hope the world will not impute it to any other reason than only the due respect which I have for so noble an opponent.

ON COMEDY, FARCE, AND TRAGEDY

The Preface to "An Evening's Love; or, The Mock Astrologer" (1671)

I HAD thought, reader, in this Preface, to have written somewhat concerning the difference betwixt the plays of our age and those of our predecessors on the English stage: to have shown in what parts of Dramatic Poesy we were excelled by Ben Jonson, I mean, humour, and contrivance of Comedy; and in what we may justly claim precedence of Shakspeare and Fletcher, namely in Heroic Plays: but this design I have waved on second considerations; at least, deferred it till I publish *The Conquest of Granada*, where the discourse will be more proper. I had also prepared to treat of the improvement of our language since Fletcher's and Jonson's days, and consequently of our refining the courtship, raillery, and conversation of plays: but as I am willing to decline that envy which I should draw on myself from some old opiniatre judges of the stage, so likewise I am pressed in time so much that I have not leisure, at present, to go through with it.

Neither, indeed, do I value a reputation gained from Comedy, so far as to concern myself about it, any more than I needs must in my own defence: for I think it, in its own nature, inferior to all sorts of dramatic writing. Low comedy especially requires, on the writer's part, much of conversation with the vulgar, and much of ill nature in the observation of their follies. But let all men please themselves according to their several tastes: that which is not pleasant to me, may be to others who judge better. And, to prevent an accusation from my enemies, I am sometimes ready to imagine that my disgust of low comedy proceeds not so much from my judgment as from my temper; which is the reason why I so seldom write it; and that when I succeed in it (I mean so far as to please the audience), yet I am nothing satisfied with what I have done; but am often vexed to hear the people laugh and clap, as they perpetually do, where I intended 'em no jest; while they let pass the better things without taking notice of them. Yet even this confirms me in my opinion of slighting popular applause, and of contemning that approbation which those very people give, equally with me, to the zany of a mountebank; or to the appearance of an antic on the theatre, without wit on the poet's part, or any occasion of laughter from the actor, besides the ridiculousness of his habit and his grimaces.

But I have descended, before I was aware, from Comedy to Farce which consists principally of grimaces. That I admire not any comedy equally with tragedy, is, perhaps, from the sullenness of my humour; but that I detest those farces, which are now the most frequent entertainments of the stage, I am sure I have reason on my side. Comedy consists, though of low persons, yet of natural actions and characters; I mean such humours, adventures, and designs, as are to be found and met with in the world. Farce, on the other side, consists of forced humours, and unnatural events. Comedy presents us with the imperfections of human nature: Farce entertains us with what is monstrous and chimerical. The one causes laughter in those who can judge of men and manners, by the lively representation of their folly or corruption: the other produces the same effect in those who can judge of neither, and that only by its extravagancies. The first works on the judgment and fancy; the latter on the fancy only: there is more of satisfaction in the former kind of laughter, and in the latter more of scorn. But, how it happens that an impossible adventure should cause our mirth, I cannot so easily imagine. Something there may be in the oddness of it, because on the stage it is the common effect of things unexpected to surprise us into a delight: and that is to be ascribed to the strange appetite, as I may call it, of the fancy; which, like that of a longing woman, often runs out into the most extravagant desires; and is better satisfied sometimes with loam, or with the rinds of trees, than with the wholesome nourishments of life. In short, there is the same difference betwixt Farce and Comedy, as betwixt an empiric and a true physician: both of them may attain their ends; but what the one performs by hazard, the other does by skill. And as the artist is often unsuccessful, while the mountebank succeeds; so farces more commonly take the people than comedies. For to write unnatural things is the most probable way of pleasing them, who understand not Nature. And a true poet often misses of applause, because he cannot debase himself to write so ill as to please his audience.

After all, it is to be acknowledged, that most of those comedies which have been lately written, have been allied too much to Farce: and this must of necessity fall out, till we forbear the translation of French plays: for their poets, wanting judgment to make or to maintain true characters, strive to cover their defects with ridiculous figures and grimaces. While I say this, I accuse myself as well as others: and this very play would rise up in judgment against me, if I would defend all things I have written to be natural: but I confess I have given too much to the people in it, and am ashamed for them as well as for myself, that I have pleased them at so cheap a rate. Not that there is anything here which I would not defend to an ill-natured judge (for I despise their censures, who I am sure would write worse on the same subject): but, because I love to deal clearly and plainly, and to speak of my own faults with more criticism than I would of another poet's. Yet I think it no vanity to say, that this comedy has as much of entertainment in it, as many others which have been lately written: and, if I find my own errors in it, I am able, at the same time, to arraign all my contemporaries for greater. As I pretend not that I can write humour, so none of them can reasonably pretend to have written it as they ought. Jonson was the only man, of all ages and nations, who has performed it well, and that but in three or four of his comedies: the rest are but a *crambe bis cocta;* the same humours a little varied and written worse. Neither was it more allowable in him, than it is in our present poets, to represent the follies of particular persons; of which many have accused him. *Parcere personis, dicere de vitiis,* is the rule of plays. And Horace tells you, that the Old Comedy amongst the Grecians was silenced for the too great liberties of the poets:

> . . . In vitium libertas excidit et vim
> Dignam lege regi: Lex est accepta, chorusque
> Turpiter obticuit, sublato jure nocendi.

Of which he gives you the reason in another place: where, having given the precept,

> Neve immunda crepent, ignominiosaque dicta,

he immediately subjoins,

> Offenduntur enim quibus est equus, et pater, et res.

But Ben Jonson is to be admired for many excellencies; and can be taxed with fewer failings than any English poet. I know I have been accused as an enemy of his writings; but without any other reason than that I do not admire him blindly, and without looking into his imperfections. For why should he only be exempted from those frailties, from which Homer and Virgil are not free? Or why should there be any *Ipse dixit* in our poetry, any more than there is in our philosophy? I admire and applaud him where I ought: those who do more, do but value themselves in their admiration of him; and, by telling you they extol Ben Jonson's way, would insinuate to you that they can practise it. For my part, I declare that I want judgment to imitate him; and should think it a great impudence in myself to attempt it. To make men appear pleasantly ridiculous on the stage, was, as I have said, his talent; and in this he needed not the acumen of wit but that of judgment. For the characters and representations of folly are only the effects of observation; and observation is an effect of judgment. Some ingenious men, for whom I have a particular esteem, have thought I have much injured Ben Jonson, when I have not allowed his wit to be extraordinary: but they confound the notion of what is witty, with what is pleasant. That Ben Jonson's plays were pleasant, he must want reason who denies: but that pleasantness was not properly wit, or the sharpness of conceit, but the natural imitation of folly; which I confess to be excellent in its kind, but not to be of that kind which they pretend. Yet if we will believe Quintilian, in his chapter *de movendo risu*, he gives his opinion of both in these following words: *Stulta reprehendere facillimum est ; nam per se sunt ridicula, et a derisu non procul abest risus : sed rem urbanam facit aliqua ex nobis adjectio.*

And some perhaps would be apt to say of Jonson, as it was said of Demosthenes, *non displicuisse illi jocos, sed non contigisse.* I will not deny, but that I approve most the mixed way of Comedy; that which is neither all wit, nor all humour, but the result of both. Neither so little of humour as Fletcher shows, nor so little of love and wit as Jonson; neither all cheat, with which the best plays of the one are filled, nor all adventure, which is the common practice of the other. I would have the characters well chosen, and kept distant from interfering with each other; which is more than Fletcher or Shakspeare did: but I would have more of the *urbana, venusta, salsa, faceta,* and the rest which Quintilian reckons up as the ornaments of wit; and these are extremely wanting in Ben Jonson. As for repartee, in particular; as it is the very soul of conversation, so it is the greatest grace of Comedy, where it is proper to the characters. There may be much of acuteness in a thing well said; but there is more in a quick reply: *sunt enim longe venustiora omnia in respondendo puam in provocando*. Of one thing I am sure, that no man ever will decry wit, but he who despairs of it himself; and who has no other quarrel to it, but that which the fox had to the grapes. Yet, as Mr. Cowley (who had a greater portion of it than any man I know) tells us in his *Character of Wit*, rather than all wit, let there be none. I think there is no folly so great in any poet of our age, as the superfluity and waste of wit was in some of our predecessors: particularly we may say of Fletcher and of Shakspeare, what was said of Ovid, *in omni ejus ingenio, facilius quod rejici, quam quod adjici potest, invenies*. The contrary of which was true in Virgil, and our incomparable Jonson.

Some enemies of repartee have observed to us, that there is a great latitude in their characters, which are made to speak it: and that it is easier to write wit than humour; because, in the characters of humour, the poet is confined to make the person speak what is only proper to it. Whereas, all kind of wit is proper in the charatcer of a witty person. But, by their favour, there are as different characters in wit as in folly. Neither is all kind of wit proper in the mouth of every ingenious person. A witty coward, and a witty brave, must speak differently. Falstaff and the Liar speak not like Don John in the *Chances*, and Valentine in *Wit without Money*. And Jonson's Truewit in the *Silent Woman* is a character different from all of them. Yet it appears that this one character of wit was more difficult to the author than all his images of humour in the play: for those he could describe and manage from his observations of men; this he has taken, at least a part of it, from books: witness the speeches in the first act, translated *verbatim* out of Ovid *de Arte Amandi*; to omit what afterwards he borrowed from the sixth satire of Juvenal against women.

However, if I should grant that there were a greater latitude in characters of wit than in those of humour; yet that latitude would be of small advantage to such poets who have too narrow an imagination to write it. And to entertain an audience perpetually with humour, is to carry them from the conversation of gentlemen, and treat them with the follies and extravagancies of Bedlam.

I find I have launched out farther than I intended in the beginning of this preface; and that, in the heat of writing, I have touched at something which I thought to have avoided. 'Tis time now to draw homeward; and to think rather of defend-

ing myself than assaulting others. I have already acknowledged that this play is far from perfect: but I do not think
myself obliged to discover the imperfections of it to my adversaries, any more than a guilty person is bound to accuse himself
before his judges. It is charged upon me that I make debauched
persons (such as, they say, my Astrologer and Gamester are) my
protagonists, or the chief persons of the drama; and that I
make them happy in the conclusion of my play; against the
law of Comedy, which is to reward virtue, and punish vice. I
answer, first, that I know no such law to have been constantly
observed in Comedy, either by the ancient or modern poets.
Chærea is made happy in the *Eunuch*, after having deflowered
a virgin; and Terence generally does the same through all his
plays, where you perpetually see, not only debauched young
men enjoy their mistresses, but even the courtesans themselves
rewarded and honoured in the catastrophe. The same may be
observed in Plautus almost everywhere. Ben Jonson himself,
after whom I may be proud to err, has given me more than once
the example of it. That in *The Alchemist* is notorious, where
Face, after having contrived and carried on the great cozenage
of the play, and continued in it without repentance to the last,
is not only forgiven by his master, but enriched, by his consent,
with the spoils of those whom he had cheated. And, which is
more, his master himself, a grave man, and a widower, is introduced taking his man's counsel, debauching the widow first, in
hope to marry her afterward. In the *Silent Woman*, Dauphine
(who, with the other two gentlemen, is of the same character
with my Celadon in the *Maiden Queen*, and with Wildblood in
this) professes himself in love with all the Collegiate Ladies:
and they likewise are all of the same character with each other,
excepting only Madam Otter, who has something singular: yet
this naughty Dauphine is crowned in the end with the possession
of his uncle's estate, and with the hopes of enjoying all his
mistresses; and his friend, Mr. Truewit (the best character of a
gentleman which Ben Jonson ever made), is not ashamed to
pimp for him. As for Beaumont and Fletcher, I need not allege
examples out of them; for that were to quote almost all their
comedies. But now it will be objected, that I patronise vice by
the authority of former poets, and extenuate my own faults by
recrimination. I answer, that as I defend myself by their
example, so that example I defend by reason, and by the end of
all dramatic poesy.

In the first place, therefore, give me leave to show you their mistake who have accused me. They have not distinguished, as they ought, betwixt the rules of Tragedy and Comedy. In Tragedy, where the actions and persons are great, and the crimes horrid, the laws of justice are more strictly observed; and examples of punishment to be made, to deter mankind from the pursuit of vice. Faults of this kind have been rare amongst the ancient poets: for they have punished in Œdipus, and in his posterity, the sin which he knew not he had committed. Medea is the only example I remember at present who escapes from punishment after murder. Thus Tragedy fulfils one great part of its institution; which is, by example, to instruct. But in Comedy it is not so; for the chief end of it is divertisement and delight: and that so much, that it is disputed, I think, by Heinsius, before Horace his *Art of Poetry*, whether instruction be any part of its employment. At least I am sure it can be but its secondary end: for the business of the poet is to make you laugh: when he writes humour, he makes folly ridiculous; when wit, he moves you, if not always to laughter, yet to a pleasure that is more noble. And if he works a cure on folly, and the small imperfections in mankind, by exposing them to public view, that cure is not performed by an immediate operation. For it works first on the ill-nature of the audience; they are moved to laugh by the representation of deformity; and the shame of that laughter teaches us to amend what is ridiculous in our manners. This being then established, that the first end of Comedy is delight, and instruction only the second; it may reasonably be inferred, that Comedy is not so much obliged to the punishment of faults which it represents, as Tragedy. For the persons in Comedy are of a lower quality, the action is little, and the faults and vices are but the sallies of youth, and the frailties of human nature, and not premeditated crimes: such to which all men are obnoxious, not such as are attempted only by few, and those abandoned to all sense of virtue: such as move pity and commiseration, not detestation and horror: such, in short, as may be forgiven, not such as must of necessity be punished. But, lest any man should think that I write this to make libertinism amiable, or that I cared not to debase the end and institution of Comedy, so I might thereby maintain my own errors, and those of better poets, I must further declare, both for them and for myself, that we make not vicious persons happy, but only as Heaven makes sinners so; that is, by reclaiming them first from vice. For so it is to be supposed they are, when they resolve to marry; for then, enjoying what they desire in one, they cease to pursue the love of many. So Chærea is made happy by Terence, in marrying her whom he had deflowered: and so are Wildblood and the Astrologer in this play.

There is another crime with which I am charged, at which I am yet much less concerned, because it does not relate to my manners, as the former did, but only to my reputation as a poet: a name of which I assure the reader I am nothing proud; and therefore cannot be very solicitous to defend it. I am taxed with stealing all my plays, and that by some who should be the last men from whom I would steal any part of 'em. There is one answer which I will not make; but it has been made for me, by him to whose grace and patronage I owe all things,—

Et spes et ratio studiorum in Caesare tantum—

and without whose command they should no longer be troubled with anything of mine:—that he only desired, that they, who accused me of theft, would always steal him plays like mine. But though I have reason to be proud of this defence, yet I should waive it, because I have a worse opinion of my own comedies than any of my enemies can have. 'Tis true, that wherever I have liked any story in a romance, novel, or foreign play, I have made no difficulty, nor ever shall, to take the foundation of it, to build it up, and to make it proper for the English stage. And I will be so vain to say, it has lost nothing in my hands: but it always cost me so much trouble to heighten it for our theatre (which is incomparably more curious in all the ornaments of dramatic poesy than the French or Spanish), that when I had finished my play, it was like the hulk of Sir Francis Drake, so strangely altered, that there scarcely remained any plank of the timber which first built it. To witness this, I need go no farther than this play: it was first Spanish, and called *El Astrologo Fingido;* then made French by the younger Corneille; and is now translated into English, and in print, under the name of *The Feigned Astrologer.* What I have performed in this will best appear by comparing it with those: you will see that I have rejected some adventures which I judged were not divertising; that I have heightened those which I have chosen; and that I have added others, which were neither in the French nor Spanish. And, besides, you will easily discover, that the walk of the Astrologer is the least considerable in my play: for the design of it turns more on the parts of Wildblood and Jacintha, who are the chief persons in it. I have farther to add, that I seldom use the wit and language of any romance or play which I undertake to alter: because my own invention (as bad as it is) can furnish me with nothing so dull as what is there. Those who have called Virgil, Terence, and Tasso, plagiaries (though they much injured them), had yet a better colour for their accusation; for Virgil has evidently translated Theocritus, Hesiod, and Homer, in many places; besides what he has taken from Ennius in his own language. Terence was not only known to translate Menander (which he avows also in his prologues), but was said also to be helped in those translations by Scipio the African, and Lælius. And Tasso, the most excellent of modern poets, and whom I reverence next to Virgil, has taken both from Homer many admirable things, which were left untouched by Virgil, and from Virgil himself, where Homer could not furnish him. Yet the bodies of Virgil's and Tasso's poems were their own; and so are all the ornaments of language and elocution in them. The same (if there were anything commendable in this play) I could say for it. But I will come nearer to our own countrymen. Most of Shakspeare's plays, I mean the stories of them, are to be found in the *Hecatommuthi*, or *Hundred Novels* of Cinthio. I have myself read in his Italian, that of *Romeo and Juliet*, the *Moor of Venice*, and many others of them. Beaumont and Fletcher had most of theirs from Spanish novels: witness *The Chances*, *The Spanish Curate*, *Rule a Wife and have a Wife*, *The Little French Lawyer*, and so many others of them as compose the greatest part of their volume in folio. Ben Jonson, indeed, has designed his plots himself; but no man has borrowed so much from the Ancients as he has done: and he did well in it, for he has thereby beautified our language.

But these little critics do not well consider what is the work of a poet, and what the graces of a poem: the story is the least part of either: I mean the foundation of it, before it is modelled by the art of him who writes it; who forms it with more care, by exposing only the beautiful parts of it to view, than a skilful lapidary sets a jewel. On this foundation of the story, the characters are raised: and, since no story can afford characters enough for the variety of the English stage, it follows that it is to be altered and enlarged with new personal accidents, and designs, which will almost make it new. When this is done, the forming it into acts and scenes, disposing of actions and passions into their proper places, and beautifying both with descriptions, similitudes, and propriety of language, is the

principal employment of the poet; as being the largest field of
fancy, which is the principal quality required in him: for so
much the word ποιητής implies. Judgment, indeed, is necessary in him; but 'tis fancy that gives the life-touches, and the
secret graces to it; especially in serious plays, which depend
not much on observation. For, to write humour in comedy
(which is the theft of poets from mankind), little of fancy is
required; the poet observes only what is ridiculous and pleasant
folly, and by judging exactly what is so, he pleases in the
representation of it.

But in general, the employment of a poet is like that of a
curious gunsmith, or watchmaker: the iron or silver is not his
own; but they are the least part of that which gives the value:
the price lies wholly in the workmanship. And he who works
dully on a story, without moving laughter in a comedy, or raising
concernment in a serious play, is no more to be accounted a
good poet, than a gunsmith of the Minories is to be compared
with the best workman of the town.

But I have said more of this than I intended; and more,
perhaps, than I needed to have done: I shall but laugh at them
hereafter, who accuse me with so little reason; and withal
contemn their dulness, who, if they could ruin that little reputation I have got, and which I value not, yet would want both wit
and learning to establish their own; or to be remembered in after
ages for anything, but only that which makes them ridiculous
in this.

OF HEROIC PLAYS

PREFATORY ESSAY TO " THE CONQUEST OF GRANADA " (1672)

WHETHER heroic verse ought to be admitted into serious plays is not now to be disputed: 'tis already in possession of the stage; and I dare confidently affirm that very few tragedies, in this age, shall be received without it. All the arguments which are formed against it can amount to no more than this, that it is not so near conversation as prose, and therefore not so natural. But it is very clear to all who understand poetry, that serious plays ought not to imitate conversation too nearly. If nothing were to be raised above that level, the foundation of poetry would be destroyed. And if you once admit of a latitude, that thoughts may be exalted, and that images and actions may be raised above the life, and described in measure without rhyme, that leads you insensibly from your own principles to mine: you are already so far onward on your way, that you have forsaken the imitation of ordinary converse. You are gone beyond it; and to continue where you are is to lodge in the open fields betwixt two inns. You have lost that which you call natural, and have not acquired the last perfection of art. But it was only custom which cozened us so long; we thought, because Shakspeare and Fletcher went no farther, that there the pillars of poetry were to be erected; that, because they excellently described passion without rhyme, therefore rhyme was not capable of describing it. But time has now convinced most men of that error. 'Tis indeed so difficult to write verse that the adversaries of it have a good plea against many who undertake that task, without being formed by art or nature for it. Yet, even they who have written worst in it, would have written worse without it: they have cozened many with their sound, who never took the pains to examine their sense. In fine, they have succeeded; though, it is true, they have more dishonoured rhyme by their good success, than they have done by their ill. But I am willing to let fall this argument: 'tis free for every man to write, or not to write, in verse, as he judges it to be, or not to be, his talent; or as he imagines the audience will receive it.

For Heroic Plays (in which only I have used it without the mixture of prose), the first light we had of them, on the English theatre, was from the late Sir William D'Avenant. It being forbidden him in the rebellious times to act tragedies and comedies, because they contained some matter of scandal to those good people, who could more easily dispossess their lawful sovereign than endure a wanton jest, he was forced to turn his thoughts another way, and to introduce the examples of moral virtue, writ in verse, and performed in recitative music. The original of this music, and of the scenes which adorned his work, he had from the Italian operas; but he heightened his characters (as I may probably imagine) from the example of Corneille and some French poets. In this condition did this part of poetry remain at his Majesty's return; when, growing bolder, as being now owned by a public authority, he reviewed his *Siege of Rhodes*, and caused it be acted as a just drama. But as few men have the happiness to begin and finish any new project, so neither did he live to make his design perfect: there wanted the fulness of a plot, and the variety of characters to form it as it ought; and, perhaps, something might have been added to the beauty of the style. All which he would have performed with more exactness had he pleased to have given us another work of the same nature. For myself and others, who come after him, we are bound, with all veneration to his memory, to acknowledge what advantage we received from that excellent groundwork which he laid: and, since it is an easy thing to add to what already is invented, we ought all of us, without envy to him, or partiality to ourselves, to yield him the precedence in it.

Having done him this justice, as my guide, I may do myself so much, as to give an account of what I have performed after him. I observed then, as I said, what was wanting to the perfection of his *Siege of Rhodes*; which was design, and variety of characters. And in the midst of this consideration, by mere accident, I opened the next book that lay by me, which was an Ariosto in Italian; and the very first two lines of that poem gave me light to all I could desire:

> Le donne, i cavalier, l'arme, gli amori,
> Le cortesie, l'audaci imprese io canto, etc.

For the very next reflection which I made was this, that an

heroic play ought to be an imitation, in little, of an heroic poem; and, consequently, that love and valour ought to be the subject of it. Both these Sir William D'Avenant had begun to shadow; but it was so, as first discoverers draw their maps, with headlands, and promontories, and some few outlines of somewhat taken at a distance, and which the designer saw not clearly. The common drama obliged him to a plot well formed and pleasant, or, as the ancients call it, one entire and great action. But this he afforded not himself in a story, which he neither filled with persons, nor beautified with characters, nor varied with accidents. The laws of an heroic poem did not dispense with those of the other, but raised them to a greater height, and indulged him a further liberty of fancy, and of drawing all things as far above the ordinary proportion of the stage as that is beyond the common words and actions of human life; and, therefore, in the scanting of his images and design, he complied not enough with the greatness and majesty of an heroic poem.

I am sorry I cannot discover my opinion of this kind of writing, without dissenting much from his, whose memory I love and honour. But I will do it with the same respect to him, as if he were now alive, and overlooking my paper while I write. His judgment of an heroic poem was this: *That it ought to be dressed in a more familiar and easy shape; more fitted to the common actions and passions of human life; and, in short, more like a glass of Nature, showing us ourselves in our ordinary habits, and figuring a more practicable virtue to us, than was done by the ancients or moderns.* Thus he takes the image of an heroic poem from the drama, or stage poetry; and accordingly intended to divide it into five books, representing the same number of acts; and every book into several cantos, imitating the scenes which compose our acts.

But this, I think, is rather a play in narration, as I may call it, than an heroic poem; if at least you will not prefer the opinion of a single man to the practice of the most excellent authors, both of ancient and latter ages. I am no admirer of quotations; but you shall hear, if you please, one of the ancients delivering his judgment on this question; it is Petronius Arbiter, the most elegant, and one of the most judicious authors of the Latin tongue; who, after he had given many admirable rules for the structure and beauties of an epic poem, concludes all in these following words:—

Non enim res gestæ versibus comprehendendæ sunt, quod longe melius historici faciunt : sed, per ambages, deorumque ministeria, præcipitandus est liber spiritus, ut potius furentis animi vaticinatio appareat, quam religiosæ orationis, sub testibus, fides.

In which sentence, and his own essay of a poem, which immediately he gives you, it is thought he taxes Lucan, who followed too much the truth of history, crowded sentences together, was too full of points, and too often offered at somewhat which had more of the sting of an epigram, than of the dignity and state of an heroic poem. Lucan used not much the help of his heathen deities: there was neither the ministry of the gods, nor the precipitation of the soul, nor the fury of a prophet (of which my author speaks), in his *Pharsalia ;* he treats you more like a philosopher than a poet, and instructs you, in verse, with what he had been taught by his uncle Seneca in prose. In one word, he walks soberly afoot, when he might fly. Yet Lucan is not always this religious historian. The oracle of Appius, and the witchcraft of Erictho, will somewhat atone for him, who was, indeed, bound up by an ill-chosen and known argument, to follow truth with great exactness. For my part, I am of opinion that neither Homer, Virgil, Statius, Ariosto, Tasso, nor our English Spencer, could have formed their poems half so beautiful, without those gods and spirits, and those enthusiastic parts of poetry, which compose the most noble parts of all their writings. And I will ask any man who loves heroic poetry (for I will not dispute their tastes who do not), if the ghost of *Polydorus* in Virgil, the *Enchanted Wood* in Tasso, and the *Bower of Bliss* in Spencer (which he borrows from that admirable Italian) could have been omitted, without taking from their works some of the greatest beauties in them. And if any man object the improbabilities of a spirit appearing, or of a palace raised by magic, I boldly answer him, that an heroic poet is not tied to a bare representation of what is true, or exceeding probable; but that he may let himself loose to visionary objects, and to the representation of such things as depending not on sense, and therefore not to be comprehended by knowledge, may give him a freer scope for imagination. 'Tis enough that, in all ages and religions, the greatest part of mankind have believed the power of magic, and that there are spirits or spectres which have appeared. This, I say, is foundation enough for poetry; and I dare further affirm that the whole doctrine of separated beings, whether those spirits are incorporeal substances (which Mr. Hobbs, with some reason, thinks to imply a contradiction), or that they are a thinner or more aërial sort of bodies (as some of the fathers have conjectured), may better be explicated by poets than by philosophers or divines. For their speculations on this subject are wholly poetical; they have only their fancy for their guide; and that, being sharper in an excellent poet, than it is likely it should in a phlegmatic, heavy gownman, will see further in its own empire, and produce more satisfactory notions on those dark and doubtful problems.

Some men think they have raised a great argument against the use of spectres and magic in heroic poetry by saying they are unnatural; but whether they or I believe there are such things is not material; 'tis enough that, for aught we know, they may be in nature; and whatever is or may be, is not properly unnatural. Neither am I much concerned at Mr. Cowley's verses before *Gondibert* (though his authority is almost sacred to me): 'tis true, he has resembled the epic poetry to a fantastic fairy-land; but he has contradicted himself by his own example. For he has himself made use of angels and visions in his *Davideis*, as well as Tasso in his *Godfrey*.

What I have written on this subject will not be thought a digression by the reader, if he please to remember what I said in the beginning of this essay, that I have modelled my heroic plays by the rules of an heroic poem. And if that be the most noble, the most pleasant, and the most instructive way of writing in verse, and withal the highest pattern of human life, as all poets have agreed, I shall need no other argument to justify my choice in this imitation. One advantage the drama has above the other, namely, that it represents to view what the poem only does relate; and, *Segnius irritant animum demissa per aures, quam quae sunt oculis subjecta fidelibus*, as Horace tells us.

To those who object my frequent use of drums and trumpets, and my representations of battles, I answer, I introduced them not on the English stage: Shakspeare used them frequently; and though Jonson shows no battle in his *Catiline*, yet you hear from behind the scenes the sounding of trumpets, and the shouts of fighting armies. But I add farther, that these warlike instruments, and even their presentations of fighting on the stage, are no more than necessary to produce the effects of an heroic play; that is, to raise the imagination of the audience, and to persuade them, for the time, that what they behold on the theatre is really performed. The poet is then to endeavour an absolute dominion over the minds of the spectators; for, though our fancy will contribute to its own deceit, yet a writer ought to help its operation: and that the *Red Bull* has formerly done the same, is no more an argument against our practice, than it would be for a physician to forbear an approved medicine, because a mountebank has used it with success.

Thus I have given a short account of heroic plays. I might now, with the usual eagerness of an author, make a particular defence of this. But the common opinion (how unjust soever) has been so much to my advantage, that I have reason to be satisfied, and to suffer with patience all that can be urged against it.

For, otherwise, what can be more easy for me than to defend the character of Almanzor, which is one great exception that is made against the play? 'Tis said, that Almanzor is no perfect pattern of heroic virtue, that he is a contemner of kings, and that he is made to perform impossibilities.

I must therefore avow, in the first place, from whence I took the character. The first image I had of him, was from the *Achilles* of Homer; the next from Tasso's *Rinaldo* (who was a copy of the former), and the third from the *Artaban* of Monsieur Calprenède, who has imitated both. The original of these, Achilles, is taken by Homer for his hero; and is described by him as one, who in strength and courage surpassed the rest of the Grecian army; but withal of so fiery a temper, so impatient of an injury, even from his king and general, that when his mistress was to be forced from him by the command of Agamemnon, he not only disobeyed it, but returned him an answer full of contumely, and in the most opprobrious terms he could imagine. They are Homer's words which follow, and I have cited but some few amongst a multitude:

Οἰνοβαρές, κυνὸς ὄμματ' ἔχων, κραδίην δ' ἐλάφοιο—*Il*. A. v. 225.

Δημοβόρος βασιλεύς, etc.—*Il*. A. v. 231.

Nay, he proceeded so far in his insolence, as to draw out his sword, with intention to kill him:

Ἕλκετο δ' ἐκ κολεοῖο μέγα ξίφος.—*Il*. A. v. 194.

And, if Minerva had not appeared, and held his hand, he had executed his design; and it was all she could do to dissuade him from it. The event was, that he left the army, and would fight no more. Agamemnon gives his character thus to Nestor:

Ἀλλ' ὅδ' ἀνὴρ ἐθέλει περὶ πάντων ἔμμεναι ἄλλων,
Πάντων μὲν κρατέειν ἐθέλει, πάντεσσι δ' ἀνάσσειν—*Il*. A. v. 287, 288.

and Horace gives the same description of him in his *Art of Poetry*:

> Honoratum si fortè reponis Achillem,
> Impiger, iracundus, inexorabilis, acer,
> Jura neget sibi nata, nihil non arroget armis.

Tasso's chief character, Rinaldo, was a man of the same temper; for, when he had slain Gernando in his heat of passion, he not only refused to be judged by Godfrey, his general, but threatened that if he came to seize him, he would right himself by arms upon him; witness these following lines of Tasso:

> Venga egli, o mandi, io terrò fermo il piede:
> Giudici fian tra noi la sorte, e l'arme;
> Fera tragedia vuol che s'appresenti,
> Per lor diporto, alle nemiche genti.

You see how little these great authors did esteem the *point of honour*, so much magnified by the French, and so ridiculously aped by us. They made their heroes men of honour; but so as not to divest them quite of human passions and frailties: they contented themselves to show you what men of great spirits would certainly do when they were provoked, not what they were obliged to do by the strict rules of moral virtue. For my own part, I declare myself for Homer and Tasso, and am more in love with Achilles and Rinaldo, than with Cyrus and Oroondates. I shall never subject my characters to the French standard, where love and honour are to be weighed by drachms and scruples. Yet, where I have designed the patterns of exact virtues, such as in this play are the parts of Almahide, of Ozmyn, and Benzayda, I may safely challenge the best of theirs.

But Almanzor is taxed with changing sides: and what tie has he on him to the contrary? He is not born their subject whom he serves, and he is injured by them to a very high degree. He threatens them, and speaks insolently of sovereign power; but so do Achilles and Rinaldo, who were subjects and soldiers to Agamemnon and Godfrey of Bulloigne. He talks extravagantly in his passion; but, if I would take the pains to quote an hundred passages of Ben Jonson's Cethegus, I could easily show you that the rodomontades of Almanzor are neither so irrational as his, nor so impossible to be put in execution; for Cethegus threatens to destroy Nature, and to raise a new one out of it; to kill all the Senate for his part of the action; to look Cato dead; and a thousand other things as extravagant he says, but performs not one action in the play.

But none of the former calumnies will stick: and, therefore, 'tis at last charged upon me, that Almanzor does all things; or if you will have an absurd accusation, in their nonsense who make it, that he performs impossibilities. They say, that being a stranger, he appeases two fighting factions, when the authority of their lawful sovereign could not. This is indeed the most improbable of all his actions, but 'tis far from being impossible. Their king had made himself contemptible to his people, as the history of Granada tells us; and Almanzor, though a stranger, yet was already known to them by his gallantry, in the *juego de toros*, his engagement on the weaker side, and more especially by the character of his person and brave actions, given by Abdalla just before; and, after all, the greatness of the enterprise consisted only in the daring, for he had the king's guards to second him. But we have read both of Cæsar, and many other generals, who have not only calmed a mutiny with a word, but have presented themselves single before an army of their enemies; which upon sight of them has revolted from their own leaders and come over to their trenches. In the rest of Almanzor's actions you see him for the most part victorious; but the same fortune has constantly attended many heroes who were not imaginary. Yet you see it no inheritance to him; for, in the first place, he is made a prisoner, and, in the last, defeated, and not able to preserve the city from being taken. If the history of the late Duke of Guise be true, he hazarded more, and performed not less in Naples, than Almanzor is feigned to have done in Granada.

I have been too tedious in this apology; but to make some satisfaction, I will leave the rest of my play exposed to the critics without defence.

The concernment of it is wholly passed from me, and ought to be in them who have been favourable to it, and are somewhat obliged to defend their own opinions. That there are errors in it, I deny not:

Ast opere in tanto fas est obrepere somnum.

But I have already swept the stakes; and, with the common good fortune of prosperous gamesters, can be content to sit quietly; to hear my fortune cursed by some, and my faults arraigned by others, and to suffer both without reply.

THE DRAMATIC POETRY OF THE
LAST AGE

They, who have best succeeded on the stage,
Have still conform'd their genius to their age.
Thus *Jonson* did mechanic humour show,
When men were dull, and conversation low.
Then, *Comedy* was faultless, but 'twas coarse:
Cobb's tankard was a jest, and *Otter's* horse.
And, as their *Comedy*, their love was mean;
Except, by chance, in some one labour'd scene,
Which must atone for an ill-written play:
They rose, but at their height could seldom stay.
Fame then was cheap, and the first comer sped;
And they have kept it since, by being dead.
But, were they now to write, when critics weigh
Each line, and ev'ry word, throughout a play,
None of them, no, not *Jonson* in his height,
Could pass, without allowing grains for weight.
Think it not envy, that these truths are told;
Our poet's not malicious, though he's bold.
'Tis not to brand 'em that their faults are shown,
But, by their errors, to excuse his own.
If *Love* and *Honour* now are higher rais'd,
'Tis not the poet, but the age is prais'd.
Wit's now arriv'd to a more high degree;
Our native language more refin'd and free.
Our ladies and our men now speak more wit
In conversation, than those poets writ.
Then, one of these is, consequently, true;
That what this poet writes comes short of you,
And imitates you ill (which most he fears),
Or else his writing is not worse than theirs.

Yet, though you judge (as sure the critics will),
That some before him writ with greater skill,
In this one praise he has their fame surpast,
To please an age more gallant than the last.

THE promises of authors, that they will write again, are, in effect, a threatening of their readers with some new impertinence; and they who perform not what they promise, will have their pardon on easy terms. It is from this consideration that I could be glad to spare you the trouble, which I am now giving you, of a postscript, if I were not obliged, by many reasons, to write somewhat concerning our present plays, and those of our predecessors on the English stage. The truth is, I have so far engaged myself in a bold *Epilogue* to this play, wherein I have somewhat taxed the former writing, that it was necessary for me either not to print it, or to show that I could defend it. Yet I would so maintain my opinion of the present age, as not to be wanting in my veneration for the past: I would ascribe to dead authors their just praises in those things wherein they have excelled us; and in those wherein we contend with them for the pre-eminence, I would acknowledge our advantages to the age, and claim no victory from our wit. This being what I have proposed to myself, I hope I shall not be thought arrogant when I inquire into their errors. For we live in an age so sceptical, that as it determines little, so it takes nothing from antiquity on trust; and I profess to have no other ambition in this *Essay* than that poetry may not go backward, when all other arts and sciences are advancing. Whoever censures me for this inquiry, let him hear his character from Horace:

Ingeniis non ille favet, plauditque sepultis,
Nostra sed impugnat; nos nostraque lividus odit.

He favours not dead wits, but hates the living.

It was upbraided to that excellent poet, that he was an enemy to the writings of his predecessor Lucilius, because he had said, *Lucilium lutulentum fluere*, that he ran muddy; and that he ought to have retrenched from his satires many unnecessary verses. But Horace makes Lucilius himself to justify him from the imputation of envy, by telling you that he would have done the same, had he lived in an age which was more refined:

Si foret hoc nostrum fato delapsus in aevum,
Detereret sibi multa, recideret omne quod ultra
Perfectum traheretur, etc.

And, both in the whole course of that satire, and in his most admirable *Epistle to Augustus*, he makes it his business to prove that antiquity alone is no plea for the excellency of a poem; but that, one age learning from another, the last (if we can suppose an equality of wit in the writers) has the advantage of knowing more and better than the former. And this, I think, is the state of the question in dispute. It is therefore my part to make it clear, that the language, wit, and conversation of our age are improved and refined above the last; and then it will not be difficult to infer that our plays have received some part of those advantages.

In the first place, therefore, it will be necessary to state, in general, what this refinement is, of which we treat; and that, I think, will not be defined amiss: *An improvement of our Wit, Language, and Conversation; or, an alteration in them for the better.*

To begin with Language. That an alteration is lately made in ours, or since the writers of the last age (in which I comprehend Shakspeare, Fletcher, and Jonson), is manifest. Any man who reads those excellent poets, and compares their language with what is now written, will see it almost in every line; but that this is an improvement of the language, or an alteration for the better, will not so easily be granted. For many are of a contrary opinion, that the English tongue was then in the height of its perfection; that from Jonson's time to ours it has been in a continual declination, like that of the Romans from the age of Virgil to Statius, and so downward to Claudian; of which, not only Petronius, but Quintilian himself so much complains, under the person of Secundus, in his famous dialogue *de Causis corruptae Eloquentiae.*

But, to show that our language is improved, and that those people have not a just value for the age in which they live, let us consider in what the refinement of a language principally consists: that is, *either in rejecting such old words, or phrases, which are ill sounding, or improper; or in admitting new, which are more proper, more sounding, and more significant.*

The reader will easily take notice, that when I speak of rejecting improper words and phrases, I mention not such as are antiquated by custom only, and, as I may say, without any fault of theirs. For in this case the refinement can be but accidental; that is, when the words and phrases which are rejected happen to be improper. Neither would I be understood, when I speak of impropriety of language, either wholly to accuse the last age, or to excuse the present, and least of all myself; for all writers have their imperfections and failings: but I may safely conclude in the general, that our improprieties are less frequent and less gross than theirs. One testimony of this is undeniable, that we are the first who have observed them; and, certainly, to observe errors is a great step in the correcting of them. But, malice and partiality set apart, let any man who understands English, read diligently the works of Shakspeare and Fletcher, and I dare undertake that he will find in every page either some solecism of speech, or some notorious flaw in sense; and yet these men are reverenced, when we are not forgiven. That their wit is great, and many times their expressions noble, envy itself cannot deny:

> Neque ego illis detrahere ausim
> Haerentem capiti multâ cum laude coronam.

But the times were ignorant in which they lived. Poetry was then, if not in its infancy among us, at least not arrived to its vigour and maturity: witness the lameness of their plots; many of which, especially those which they writ first (for even that age refined itself in some measure), were made up of some ridiculous incoherent story, which in one play many times took up the business of an age. I suppose I need not name *Pericles, Prince of Tyre,* nor the historical plays of Shakspeare: besides many of the rest, as the *Winter's Tale, Love's Labour's Lost, Measure for Measure,* which were either grounded on impossibilities, or at least so meanly written, that the comedy neither caused your mirth, nor the serious part your concernment. If I would expatiate on this subject, I could easily demonstrate, that our admired Fletcher, who writ after him, neither understood correct plotting, nor that which they call *the decorum of the stage.* I would not search in his worst plays for examples: he who will consider his *Philaster,* his *Humorous Lieutenant,* his *Faithful Shepherdess,* and many others which I could name, will find them much below the applause which is now given them. He will see Philaster wounding his mistress, and afterwards his boy, to save himself; not to mention the Clown, who enters immediately, and not only has the advantage of the combat against the hero, but diverts you from your serious concernment with his ridiculous and absurd raillery. In his *Humorous Lieutenant,* you find his Demetrius and Leontius staying in the midst of a routed army, to hear the cold mirth of the Lieutenant; and Demetrius afterwards appearing with a pistol in his hand, in the next age to Alexander the Great. And for his Shepherd, he falls twice into the former indecency of wounding women. But these absurdities, which those poets committed, may more properly be called the age's fault than theirs: for, besides the want of education and learning (which was their particular unhappiness), they wanted the benefit of converse: but of that I shall speak hereafter, in a place more proper for it. Their audiences knew no better; and therefore were satisfied with what they brought. Those, who call theirs *the Golden Age of Poetry*, have only this reason for it, that they were then content with acorns before they knew the use of bread, or that ἅλις δρυὸς was become a proverb. They had many who admired them, and few who blamed them; and certainly a severe critic is the greatest help to a good wit: he does the office of a friend, while he designs that of an enemy; and his malice keeps a poet within those bounds which the luxuriancy of his fancy would tempt him to overleap.

But it is not their plots which I meant principally to tax; I was speaking of their sense and language; and I dare almost challenge any man to show me a page together which is correct in both. As for Ben Jonson, I am loath to name him, because he is a most judicious writer; yet he very often falls into these errors: and I once more beg the reader's pardon for accusing him of them. Only let him consider, that I live in an age where my least faults are severely censured; and that I have no way left to extenuate my failings, but by showing as great in those whom we admire:

> Cædimus, inque vicem præbemus crura sagittis.

I cast my eyes but by chance on *Catiline ;* and in the three or four last pages found enough to conclude that Jonson writ not correctly:—

> Let the long-hid seeds
> Of treason, in thee, now shoot forth in deeds
> Ranker than horror.

In reading some bombast speeches of Macbeth, which are not to be understood, he used to say that it was horror; and I am much afraid that this is so.

> Thy parricide late on thy only son,
> After his mother, to make empty way
> For thy last wicked nuptials, worse than they
> That blaze that act of thy incestuous life,
> Which gained thee at once a daughter and a wife.

The sense is here extremely perplexed; and I doubt the word *they* is false grammar.

> And be free
> Not heaven itself from thy impiety.

A *synchysis*, or ill-placing of words, of which Tully so much complains in oratory.

> The waves and dens of beasts could not receive
> The bodies that those souls were frighted from.

The preposition in the end of the sentence; a common fault with him, and which I have but lately observed in my own writings.

> What all the several ills, that visit earth,
> Plague, famine, fire, could not reach unto,
> The sword, nor surfeits, let thy fury do.

Here are both the former faults: for, besides that the preposition *unto* is placed last in the verse, and at the half period, and is redundant, there is the former synchysis in the words *the sword, nor surfeits,* which in construction ought to have been placed before the other.

Catiline says of Cethegus, that for his sake he would

> Go on *upon* the Gods, kiss lightning, wrest
> The engine from the Cyclops, and give fire
> At face of a full cloud, and stand his ire.

To *go on upon*, is only to go on twice. To *give fire at face of a full cloud*, was not understood in his own time; *and stand his ire,* besides the antiquated word *ire,* there is the article *his,* which makes false construction: and *giving fire at the face of a cloud*, is a perfect image of shooting, however it came to be known in those days to Catiline.

> Others there are,
> Whom envy to the state draws and pulls on,
> For contumelies received; and such are sure ones.

Ones, in the plural number: but that is frequent with him; for he says, not long after,

> Cæsar and Crassus, if they be ill men,
> Are mighty ones—
> Such men, they do not succour more the cause, etc.

They redundant.

> Though Heaven should speak with all his wrath at once,
> We should stand upright and unfear'd.

His is ill syntax with *Heaven ;* and by *unfeared* he means *unafraid :* words of quite a contrary signification.

The ports are open.

He perpetually uses *ports* for gates; which is an affected error in him, to introduce Latin by the loss of the English idiom; as in the translation of Tully's speeches he usually does.

Well-placing of words, for the sweetness of pronunciation, was not known till Mr. Waller introduced it; and, therefore, it is not to be wondered if Ben Jonson has many such lines as these:

But being bred up in his father's needy fortunes ; brought up in's sister's prostitution, etc.

But meanness of expression one would think not to be his error in a tragedy, which ought to be more high and sounding than any other kind of poetry; and yet, amongst others in *Catiline,* I find these four lines together:

> So Asia, thou art cruelly even
> With us, for all the blows thee given;
> When we, whose virtues conquered thee,
> Thus by thy vices ruin'd be.

Be there is false English for *are ;* though the rhyme hides it.

But I am willing to close the book, partly out of veneration to the author, partly out of weariness to pursue an argument which is so fruitful, in so small a compass. And what correctness, after this, can be expected from Shakspeare or from Fletcher, who wanted that learning and care which Jonson had? I will, therefore, spare my own trouble of inquiring into their faults; who, had they lived now, had doubtless written more correctly. I suppose it will be enough for me to affirm (as I think I safely may), that these, and the like errors, which I taxed in the most correct of the last age, are such into which we do not ordinarily fall. I think few of our present writers would have left behind them such a line as this:

> Contain your spirit in more stricter bounds.

But that gross way of two comparatives was then ordinary; and, therefore, more pardonable in Jonson.

As for the other part of refining, which consists in receiving new words and phrases, I shall not insist much on it. It is obvious that we have admitted many, some of which we wanted, and therefore our language is the richer for them, as it would be by importation of bullion: others are rather ornamental than necessary; yet by their admission, the language is become more courtly, and our thoughts are better dressed. These are to be found scattered in the writers of our age, and it is not my business to collect them. They, who have lately written with most care, have, I believe, taken the rule of Horace for their guide; that is, not to be too hasty in receiving of words, but rather to stay till custom has made them familiar to us:

Quem penes arbitrium est, et jus, et norma loquendi.

For I cannot approve of their way of refining, who corrupt our English idiom by mixing it too much with French: that is a sophistication of language, not an improvement of it; a turning English into French, rather than a refining of English by French. We meet daily with those fops who value themselves on their travelling, and pretend they cannot express their meaning in English, because they would put off to us some French phrase of the last edition; without considering that, for aught they know, we have a better of our own. But these are not the men who are to refine us; their talent is to prescribe fashions, not words: at best, they are only serviceable to a writer, so as Ennius was to Virgil. He may *aurum ex stercore colligere:* for 'tis hard if, amongst many insignificant phrases, there happen not something worth preserving; though they themselves, like Indians, know not the value of their own commodity.

There is yet another way of improving language, which poets especially have practised in all ages; that is, by applying received words to a new signification; and this, I believe, is meant by Horace, in that precept which is so variously construed by expositors:

Dixeris egregie, notum si callida verbum
Reddiderit junctura novum.

And, in this way, he himself had a particular happiness; using all the tropes, and particular metaphors, with that grace which is observable in his *Odes*, where the beauty of expression is often greater than that of thought; as, in that one example, amongst an infinite number of others, *Et vultus nimium lubricus aspici*.

And therefore, though he innovated little, he may justly be called a great refiner of the Roman tongue. This choice of words, and heightening of their natural signification, was observed in him by the writers of the following ages; for Petronius says of him, *et Horatii curiosa felicitas*. By this graffing, as I may call it, on old words, has our tongue been beautified by the three fore-mentioned poets, Shakspeare, Fletcher, and Jonson, whose excellencies I can never enough admire; and in this they have been followed, especially by Sir John Suckling and Mr. Waller, who refined upon them. Neither have they, who succeeded them, been wanting in their endeavours to adorn our mother tongue: but it is not so lawful for me to praise my living contemporaries, as to admire my dead predecessors.

I should now speak of the refinement of Wit; but I have been so large on the former subject, that I am forced to contract myself in this. I will therefore only observe to you, that the wit of the last age was yet more incorrect than their language. Shakspeare, who many times has written better than any poet, in any language, is yet so far from writing wit always, or expressing that wit according to the dignity of the subject, that he writes, in many places, below the dullest writer of ours, or any precedent age. Never did any author precipitate himself from such height of thought to so low expressions, as he often does. He is the very Janus of poets; he wears almost everywhere two faces; and you have scarce begun to admire the one, ere you despise the other. Neither is the luxuriance of Fletcher (which his friends have taxed in him) a less fault than the carelessness of Shakspeare. He does not well always; and, when he does, he is a true Englishman; he knows not when to give over. If he wakes in one scene, he commonly slumbers in another; and, if he pleases you in the first three acts, he is frequently so tired with his labour, that he goes heavily in the fourth, and sinks under his burden in the fifth.

For Ben Jonson, the most judicious of poets, he always writ properly, and as the character required; and I will not contest farther with my friends who call that wit: it being very certain, that even folly itself, well represented, is wit in a larger signification; and that there is fancy, as well as judgment, in it, though not so much or noble: because all poetry being imitation, that of folly is a lower exercise of fancy, though perhaps as difficult as the other; for 'tis a kind of looking downward in the poet, and representing that part of mankind which is below him.

In these low characters of vice and folly lay the excellency of that inimitable writer; who, when at any time he aimed at wit in the stricter sense, that is, sharpness of conceit, was forced either to borrow from the Ancients, as to my knowledge he did very much from Plautus; or, when he trusted himself alone, often fell into meanness of expression. Nay, he was not free from the lowest and most grovelling kind of wit, which we call clenches, of which *Every Man in his Humour* is infinitely full; and, which is worse, the wittiest persons in the drama speak them. His other comedies are not exempt from them. Will you give me leave to name some few? Asper, in which character he personates himself (and he neither was nor thought himself a fool), exclaiming against the ignorant judges of the age, speaks thus:

> How monstrous and detested is't, to see
> A fellow, that has neither art nor brain,
> Sit like an *Aristarchus*, or *stark-ass*,
> Taking men's lines, with a *tobacco face*,
> In *snuff*, etc.

And presently after: *I mar'le whose wit 'twas to put a prologue in yond Sackbut's mouth. They might well think he would be out of tune, and yet you'd play upon him too.*—Will you have another of the same stamp? *O, I cannot abide these limbs of* sattin, *or rather* Satan.

But, it may be, you will object that this was Asper, Macilente, or Carlo Buffone: you shall, therefore, hear him speak in his own person, and that in the two last lines or sting of an epigram. 'Tis inscribed to *Fine Grand*, who, he says, was indebted to him for many things which he reckons there; and concludes thus:

> Forty things more, dear *Grand*, which you know true,
> For which, or pay me quickly, or I'll pay you.

This was then the mode of wit, the vice of the age, and not Ben Jonson's; for you see, a little before him, that admirable wit, Sir Philip Sidney, perpetually playing with his words. In his time, I believe, it ascended first into the pulpit, where (if you will give me leave to clench too) it yet finds the benefit of its clergy; for they are commonly the first corrupters of eloquence, and the last reformed from vicious oratory; as a famous Italian has observed before me, in his *Treatise of the Corruption of the Italian Tongue;* which he principally ascribes to priests and preaching friars.

But, to conclude with what brevity I can, I will only add this, in defence of our present writers, that, if they reach not some excellencies of Ben Jonson (which no age, I am confident, ever shall), yet, at least, they are above that meanness of thought which I have taxed, and which is frequent in him.

That the wit of this age is much more courtly, may easily be proved by viewing the characters of gentlemen which were written in the last. First, for Jonson:—Truewit, in the *Silent Woman*, was his masterpiece; and Truewit was a scholar-like kind of man, a gentleman with an alloy of pedantry, a man who seems mortified to the world by much reading. The best of his discourse is drawn, not from the knowledge of the town, but books; and, in short, he would be a fine gentleman in an university. Shakspeare showed the best of his skill in his Mercutio; and he said himself, that he was forced to kill him in the third act to prevent being killed by him. But, for my part, I cannot find he was so dangerous a person: I see nothing in him but what was so exceeding harmless, that he might have lived to the end of the play, and died in his bed, without offence to any man.

Fletcher's Don John is our only bugbear; and yet I may affirm, without suspicion of flattery, that he now speaks better, and that his character is maintained with much more vigour in the fourth and fifth acts, than it was by Fletcher in the three former. I have always acknowledged the wit of our predecessors, with all the veneration which becomes me; but, I am sure, their wit was not that of gentlemen; there was ever somewhat that was ill-bred and clownish in it, and which confessed the conversation of the authors.

And this leads me to the last and greatest advantage of our writing, which proceeds from *conversation*. In the age wherein those poets lived, there was less of gallantry than in ours; neither did they keep the best company of theirs. Their fortune has been much like that of Epicurus, in the retirement of his gardens; to live almost unknown, and to be celebrated after their decease. I cannot find that any of them had been conversant in courts, except Ben Jonson; and his genius lay not so much that way as to make an improvement by it. Greatness was not then so easy of access, nor conversation so free, as now it is. I cannot, therefore, conceive it any insolence to affirm that, by the knowledge and pattern of their wit who writ before us, and by the advantage of our own conversation, the discourse and raillery of our comedies excel what has been written by them. And this will be denied by none, but some few old fellows who value themselves on their acquaintance with the Black Friars; who, because they saw their plays, would pretend a right to judge ours. The memory of these grave gentlemen is their only plea for being wits. They can tell a story of Ben Jonson, and, perhaps, have had fancy enough to give a supper in the Apollo, that they might be called his sons; and, because they were drawn in to be laughed at in those times, they think themselves now sufficiently entitled to laugh at ours. Learning I never saw in any of them; and wit no more than they could remember. In short, they were unlucky to have been bred in an unpolished age, and more unlucky to live to a refined one. They have lasted beyond their own, and are cast behind ours; and, not contented to have known little at the age of twenty, they boast of their ignorance at threescore.

Now, if they ask me, whence it is that our conversation is so much refined? I must freely, and without flattery, ascribe it to the court; and, in it, particularly to the King, whose example gives a law to it. His own misfortunes, and the nation's, afforded him an opportunity, which is rarely allowed to sovereign princes, I mean of travelling, and being conversant in the most polished courts of Europe; and, thereby, of cultivating a spirit which was formed by nature to receive the impressions of a gallant and generous education. At his return, he found a nation lost as much in barbarism as in rebellion; and, as the excellency of his nature forgave the one, so the excellency of his manners reformed the other. The desire of imitating so great a pattern first awakened the dull and heavy spirits of the English from their natural reservedness; loosened them from their stiff forms of conversation, and made them easy and pliant to each other in discourse. Thus, insensibly, our way of living became more free; and the fire of the English wit, which was before stifled under a constrained, melancholy way of breeding, began first to display its force, by mixing the solidity of our nation with the air and gaiety of our neighbours. This being granted to be true, it would be a wonder if the poets, whose work is imitation, should be the only persons in three kingdoms who should not receive advantage by it; or, if they should not more easily imitate the wit and conversation of the present age than of the past.

Let us therefore admire the beauties and the heights of Shakspeare, without falling after him into a carelessness, and, as I may call it, a lethargy of thought, for whole scenes together. Let us imitate, as we are able, the quickness and easiness of Fletcher, without proposing him as a pattern to us, either in the redundancy of his matter, or the incorrectness of his language. Let us admire his wit and sharpness of conceit; but let us at the same time acknowledge that it was seldom so fixed, and made proper to his character, as that the same things might not be spoken by any person in the play. Let us applaud his scenes of love; but let us confess that he understood not either greatness or perfect honour in the parts of any of his women. In fine, let us allow that he had so much fancy, as when he pleased he could write wit; but that he wanted so much judgment, as seldom to have written humour, or described a pleasant folly. Let us ascribe to Jonson the height and accuracy of judgment in the ordering of his plots, his choice of characters, and maintaining what he had chosen to the end.   But let us not think him a perfect pattern of imitation, except it be in humour; for love, which is the foundation of all comedies in other languages, is scarcely mentioned in any of his plays; and for humour itself, the poets of this age will be more wary than to imitate the meanness of his persons.   Gentlemen will now be entertained with the follies of each other; and, though they allow Cobb and Tib to speak properly, yet they are not much pleased with their tankard or with their rags.   And surely their conversation can be no jest to them on the theatre, when they would avoid it in the street.

To conclude all, let us render to our predecessors what is their due, without confining ourselves to a servile imitation of all they writ; and, without assuming to ourselves the title of better poets, let us ascribe to the gallantry and civility of our age the advantage which we have above them, and to our knowledge of the customs and manner of it the happiness we have to please beyond them.

HEROIC POETRY AND POETIC LICENCE

THE AUTHOR'S APOLOGY PREFIXED TO "THE STATE OF INNOCENCE AND FALL OF MAN," AN OPERA (1677)

To satisfy the curiosity of those who will give themselves the trouble of reading the ensuing poem, I think myself obliged to render them a reason why I publish an opera which was never acted. In the first place, I shall not be ashamed to own that my chiefest motive was the ambition which I acknowledged in the Epistle. I was desirous to lay at the feet of so beautiful and excellent a Princess a work which, I confess, was unworthy her, but which, I hope, she will have the goodness to forgive. I was also induced to it in my own defence; many hundred copies of it being dispersed abroad without my knowledge or consent: so that every one gathering new faults, it became at length a libel against me; and I saw, with some disdain, more nonsense than either I, or as bad a poet, could have crammed into it at a month's warning; in which time 'twas wholly written, and not since revised. After this, I cannot, without injury to the deceased author of *Paradise Lost*, but acknowledge that this poem has received its entire foundation, part of the design, and many of the ornaments, from him. What I have borrowed will be so easily discerned from my mean productions, that I shall not need to point the reader to the places: and truly I should be sorry, for my own sake, that any one should take the pains to compare them together; the original being undoubtedly one of the greatest, most noble, and most sublime poems which either this age or nation has produced. And though I could not refuse the partiality of my friend, who is pleased to commend me in his verses, I hope they will rather be esteemed the effect of his love to me, than of his deliberate and sober judgment. His genius is able to make beautiful what he pleases: yet, as he has been too favourable to me, I doubt not but he will hear of his kindness from many of our contemporaries; for we are fallen into an age of illiterate, censorious, and detracting people, who, thus qualified, set up for critics.

In the first place, I must take leave to tell them, that they wholly mistake the nature of criticism who think its business is principally to find fault. Criticism, as it was first instituted by Aristotle, was meant a standard of judging well; the chiefest part of which is, to observe those excellencies which should delight a reasonable reader. If the design, the conduct, the thoughts, and the expressions of a poem, be generally such as proceed from a true genius of Poetry, the critic ought to pass his judgment in favour of the author. 'Tis malicious and unmanly to snarl at the little lapses of a pen, from which Virgil himself stands not exempted. Horace acknowledges that honest Homer nods sometimes: he is not equally awake in every line; but he leaves it also as a standing measure for our judgments,

> Non, ubi plura nitent in carmine, paucis
> Offendi maculis, quas aut incuria fudit,
> Aut humana parum cavit natura. . . .

And Longinus, who was undoubtedly, after Aristotle, the greatest critic amongst the Greeks, in his twenty-seventh chapter ΠΕΡΙ ΎΨΟΥΣ, has judiciously preferred the sublime genius that sometimes errs, to the middling or indifferent one, which makes few faults, but seldom or never rises to any excellence. He compares the first to a man of large possessions, who has not leisure to consider of every slight expense, will not debase himself to the management of every trifle: particular sums are not laid out, or spared, to the greatest advantage in his economy; but are sometimes suffered to run to waste, while he is only careful of the main. On the other side, he likens the mediocrity of wit to one of a mean fortune, who manages his store with extreme frugality, or rather parsimony; but who, with fear of running into profuseness, never arrives to the magnificence of living. This kind of genius writes indeed correctly. A wary man he is in grammar, very nice as to solecism or barbarism, judges to a hair of little decencies, knows better than any man what is not to be written, and never hazards himself so far as to fall, but plods on deliberately, and, as a grave man ought, is sure to put his staff before him; in short, he sets his heart upon it, and with wonderful care makes his business sure; that is, in plain English, neither to be blamed nor praised.—I could, says my author, find out some blemishes in Homer; and am perhaps as naturally inclined to be disgusted at a fault

E

as another man; but, after all, to speak impartially, his failings are such as are only marks of human frailty: they are little mistakes, or rather negligences, which have escaped his pen in the fervour of his writing; the sublimity of his spirit carries it with me against his carelessness; and though Apollonius his *Argonauts*, and Theocritus his *Eidullia*, are more free from errors, there is not any man of so false a judgment who would choose rather to have been Apollonius or Theocritus than Homer.

'Tis worth our consideration a little, to examine how much these hypercritics of English poetry differ from the opinion of the Greek and Latin judges of antiquity; from the Italians and French, who have succeeded them; and, indeed, from the general taste and approbation of all ages. Heroic Poetry, which they condemn, has ever been esteemed, and ever will be, the greatest work of human nature: in that rank has Aristotle placed it; and Longinus is so full of the like expressions, that he abundantly confirms the other's testimony. Horace as plainly delivers his opinion, and particularly praises Homer in these verses—

> Trojani Belli scriptorem, maxime Lolli,
> Dum tu declamas Romæ, Præneste relegi:
> Qui quid sit pulchrum, quid turpe, quid utile, quid non,
> Plenius ac melius Chrysippo et Crantore dicit.

And in another place, modestly excluding himself from the number of poets, because he only writ odes and satires, he tells you a poet is such an one,

> cui mens divinior, atque os
> Magna sonaturum.

Quotations are superfluous in an established truth; otherwise I could reckon up, amongst the moderns, all the Italian commentators on Aristotle's book of poetry; and, amongst the French, the greatest of this age, Boileau and Rapin; the latter of which is alone sufficient, were all other critics lost, to teach anew the rules of writing. Any man who will seriously consider the nature of an Epic Poem, how it agrees with that of Poetry in general, which is to instruct and to delight, what actions it describes, and what persons they are chiefly whom it informs, will find it a work which indeed is full of difficulty in the attempt, but admirable when it is well performed. I write not this with the least intention to undervalue the other parts of poetry: for Comedy is both excellently instructive, and extremely pleasant; satire lashes vice into reformation, and humour represents folly so as to render it ridiculous. Many of our present writers are eminent in both these kinds; and, particularly, the author of the *Plain Dealer*, whom I am proud to call my friend, has obliged all honest and virtuous men, by one of the most bold, most general, and most useful satires which has ever been presented on the English theatre. I do not dispute the preference of Tragedy; let every man enjoy his taste: but 'tis unjust that they, who have not the least notion of heroic writing, should therefore condemn the pleasure which others receive from it, because they cannot comprehend it. Let them please their appetites in eating what they like; but let them not force their dish on all the table. They who would combat general authority with particular opinion, must first establish themselves a reputation of understanding better than other men. Are all the flights of Heroic Poetry to be concluded bombast, unnatural, and mere madness, because they are not affected with their excellencies? It is just as reasonable as to conclude there is no day, because a blind man cannot distinguish of light and colours. Ought they not rather, in modesty, to doubt of their own judgments, when they think this or that expression in Homer, Virgil, Tasso, or Milton's *Paradise* to be too far strained, than positively to conclude that 'tis all fustian, and mere nonsense? 'Tis true, there are limits to be set betwixt the boldness and rashness of a poet; but he must understand those limits who pretends to judge as well as he who undertakes to write: and he who has no liking to the whole, ought, in reason, to be excluded from censuring of the parts. He must be a lawyer before he mounts the tribunal; and the judicature of one court, too, does not qualify a man to preside in another. He may be an excellent pleader in the Chancery who is not fit to rule the Common Pleas. But I will presume for once to tell them, that the boldest strokes of poetry, when they are managed artfully, are those which most delight the reader.

Virgil and Horace, the severest writers of the severest age, have made frequent use of the hardest metaphors, and of the strongest hyperboles; and in this case the best authority is the best argument; for generally to have pleased, and through all ages, must bear the force of universal tradition. And if you would appeal from thence to right reason, you will gain no more by it in effect, than, first, to set up your reason against those authors; and, secondly, against all those who have admired them. You must prove why that ought not to have pleased, which has pleased the most learned, and the most judicious;

and, to be thought knowing, you must first put the fool upon all mankind. If you can enter more deeply than they have done into the causes and resorts of that which moves pleasure in a reader, the field is open, you may be heard: but those springs of human nature are not so easily discovered by every superficial judge: it requires Philosophy, as well as Poetry, to sound the depth of all the passions; what they are in themselves, and how they are to be provoked: and in this science the best poets have excelled. Aristotle raised the fabric of his *Poetry* from observation of those things in which Euripides, Sophocles, and Æschylus pleased: he considered how they raised the passions, and thence has drawn rules for our imitation. From hence have sprung the tropes and figures, for which they wanted a name, who first practised them, and succeeded in them. Thus I grant you that the knowledge of nature was the original rule; and that all poets ought to study her, as well as Aristotle and Horace, her interpreters. But then this also undeniably follows, that those things which delight all ages, must have been an imitation of Nature; which is all I contend. Therefore is Rhetoric made an art; therefore the names of so many tropes and figures were invented; because it was observed they had such and such effect upon the audience. Therefore catachreses and hyperboles have found their place amongst them; not that they were to be avoided, but to be used judiciously, and placed in poetry, as heightenings and shadows are in painting, to make the figure bolder, and cause it to stand off to sight.

> Nec retia cervis
> Ulla dolum meditantur

says Virgil in his Eclogues: and speaking of Leander, in his Georgics,

> Nocte natat cæca, serus freta, quem super ingens
> Porta tonat coeli, et scopulis illisa reclamant
> Æquora.

In both of these, you see, he fears not to give voice and thought to things inanimate.

Will you arraign your master, Horace, for his hardness of expression, when he describes the death of Cleopatra, and says she did *asperos tractare serpentes, ut atrum corpore combiberet venenum*, because the body, in that action, performs what is proper to the mouth?

As for hyperboles, I will neither quote Lucan, nor Statius, men of an unbounded imagination, but who often wanted the poise of judgment. The divine Virgil was not liable to that exception; and yet he describes Polyphemus thus—

> Graditurque per aequor
> Jam medium; necdum fluctus latera ardua tinxit.

In imitation of this place, our admirable Cowley thus paints Goliath—

> The valley, now, this monster seem'd to fill;
> And we, methought, look'd up to him from our hill:

where the two words, *seemed* and *methought,* have mollified the figure; and yet if they had not been there, the fright of the Israelites might have excused their belief of the giant's stature.

In the eighth of the Æneids, Virgil paints the swiftness of Camilla thus:

> Illa vel intactæ segetis per summa volaret
> Gramina, nec teneras cursu læsisset aristas;
> Vel mare per medium, fluctu suspensa tumenti,
> Ferret iter, celeres nec tingeret æquore plantas.

You are not obliged, as in History, to a literal belief of what the poet says; but you are pleased with the image, without being cozened by the fiction.

Yet even in History, Longinus quotes Herodotus on this occasion of hyperboles. The Lacedemonians, says he, at the straits of Thermopylæ, defended themselves to the last extremity; and when their arms failed them, fought it out with their nails and teeth; till at length (the Persians shooting continually upon them) they lay buried under the arrows of their enemies. It is not reasonable (continues the critic) to believe that men could defend themselves with their nails and teeth from an armed multitude; nor that they lay buried under a pile of darts and arrows; and yet there wants not probability for the figure: because the hyperbole seems not to have been made for the sake of the description, but rather to have been produced from the occasion.

'Tis true, the boldness of the figures is to be hidden sometimes by the address of the poet; that they may work their effect upon the mind, without discovering the art which caused it. And therefore they are principally to be used in passion; when we speak more warmly and with more precipitation than at other times: for then, *si vis me flere, dolendum est primum ipsi tibi;* the poet must put on the passion he endeavours to represent: a man in such an occasion is not cool enough, either to reason rightly, or to talk calmly. Aggravations are then in their proper places; interrogations, exclamations, hyperbata, or a disordered connection of discourse, are graceful there, because they are natural. The sum of all depends on what before I hinted, that this boldness of expression is not to be blamed, if it be managed by the coolness and discretion which is necessary to a poet.

Yet before I leave this subject, I cannot but take notice how disingenuous our adversaries appear: all that is dull, insipid, languishing, and without sinews, in a poem, they call an imitation of Nature: they only offend our most equitable judges who think beyond them; and lively images and elocution are never to be forgiven.

What fustian, as they call it, have I heard these gentlemen find out in Mr. Cowley's *Odes!* I acknowledge myself unworthy to defend so excellent an author, neither have I room to do it here; only in general I will say, that nothing can appear more beautiful to me than the strength of those images which they condemn.

Imaging is, in itself, the very height and life of Poetry. It is, as Longinus describes it, a discourse, which, by a kind of enthusiasm, or extraordinary emotion of the soul, makes it seem to us that we behold those things which the poet paints, so as to be pleased with them, and to admire them.

If poetry be imitation, that part of it must needs be best which describes most lively our actions and passions; our virtues and our vices; our follies and our humours: for neither is Comedy without its part of imaging; and they who do it best are certainly the most excellent in their kind. This is too plainly proved to be denied. But how are poetical fictions, how are hippocentaurs and chimeras, or how are angels and immaterial substances to be imaged; which, some of them, are things quite out of nature; others, such whereof we can have no notion? This is the last refuge of our adversaries; and more than any of them have yet had the wit to object against us. The answer is easy to the first part of it: the fiction of some beings which are not in nature (second notions, as the logicians call them) has been founded on the conjunction of two natures, which have a real separate being. So hippocentaurs were imaged by joining the natures of a man and horse together; as Lucretius tells us, who has used this word of *image* oftener than any of the poets—

Nam certe ex vivo centauri non fit imago,
Nulla fuit quoniam talis natura animai:
Verum ubi equi atque hominis, casu, convenit imago,
Hærescit facile extemplo, etc.

The same reason may also be alleged for chimeras and the rest. And poets may be allowed the like liberty for describing things which really exist not, if they are founded on popular belief. Of this nature are fairies, pigmies, and the extraordinary effects of magic; for 'tis still an imitation, though of other men's fancies: and thus are Shakspeare's *Tempest*, his *Midsummer Night's Dream*, and Ben Jonson's *Masque of Witches* to be defended. For immaterial substances, we are authorised by Scripture in their description: and herein the text accommodates itself to vulgar apprehension, in giving angels the likeness of beautiful young men. Thus, after the pagan divinity, has Homer drawn his gods with human faces: and thus we have notions of things above us, by describing them like other beings more within our knowledge.

I wish I could produce any one example of excellent imaging in all this poem. Perhaps I cannot; but that which comes nearest it is in these four lines, which have been sufficiently canvassed by my well-natured censors—

> Seraph and cherub, careless of their charge,
> And wanton, in full ease now live at large:
> Unguarded leave the passes of the sky,
> And all dissolved in hallelujahs lie.

I have heard (says one of them) of anchovies dissolved in sauce; but never of an angel in hallelujahs. A mighty witticism! (if you will pardon a new word), but there is some difference between a laugher and a critic. He might have burlesqued Virgil too, from whom I took the image: *Invadunt urbem, somno vinoque sepultam.* A city's being buried, is just as proper on occasion, as an angel's being dissolved in ease, and songs of triumph. Mr. Cowley lies as open, too, in many places—

> Where their vast courts the mother waters keep, etc.

For if the mass of waters be the mothers, then their daughters, the little streams, are bound, in all good manners, to make courtesy to them, and ask them blessing. How easy 'tis to turn into ridicule the best descriptions, when once a man is in the humour of laughing, till he wheezes at his own dull jest! But an image, which is strongly and beautifully set before the eyes of the reader, will still be poetry when the merry fit is over, and last when the other is forgotten.

I promised to say somewhat of Poetic Licence, but have in part anticipated my discourse already. Poetic Licence I take to be the liberty which poets have assumed to themselves, in all ages, of speaking things in verse, which are beyond the severity of prose. 'Tis that particular character which distinguishes and sets the bounds betwixt *oratio soluta* and poetry. This, as to what regards the thought or imagination of a poet, consists in fiction: but then those thoughts must be expressed; and here arise two other branches of it; for if this licence be included in a single word, it admits of tropes; if in a sentence or proposition, of figures; both which are of a much larger extent, and more forcibly to be used in verse than prose. This is that birthright which is derived to us from our great forefathers, even from Homer down to Ben; and they who would deny it to us, in plain terms, the fox's quarrel to the grapes—they cannot reach it.

How far these liberties are to be extended, I will not presume to determine here, since Horace does not. But it is certain that they are to be varied, according to the language and age in which an author writes. That which would be allowed to a Grecian poet, Martial tells you, would not be suffered in a Roman. And 'tis evident that the English does more nearly follow the strictness of the latter than the freedoms of the former. Connection of epithets, or the conjunction of two words in one, are frequent and elegant in the Greek, which yet Sir Philip Sidney, and the translator of Du Bartas, have unluckily attempted in the English; though this, I confess, is not so proper an instance of poetic licence as it is of variety of idiom in languages.

Horace a little explains himself on this subject of *Licentia Poetica,* in these verses—

> Pictoribus atque Poetis
> Quidlibet audendi semper fuit æqua potestas: . . .
> Sed non, ut placidis coeant immitia, non ut
> Serpentes avibus geminentur, tigribus hædi.

He would have a poem of a piece; not to begin with one thing and end with another: he restrains it so far that thoughts of an unlike nature ought not to be joined together. That were indeed to make a chaos. He taxed not Homer, nor the divine Virgil, for interesting their gods in the wars of Troy and Italy; neither, had he now lived, would he have taxed Milton, as our false critics have presumed to do, for his choice of a supernatural argument; but he would have blamed my author, who was a Christian, had he introduced into his poem heathen deities, as Tasso is condemned by Rapin on the like occasion; and as Camoens, the author of the *Lusiads,* ought to be censured by all his readers, when he brings in Bacchus and Christ into the same adventure of his fable.

From that which has been said, it may be collected, that the definition of Wit (which has been so often attempted, and ever unsuccessfully by many poets) is only this: that it is a propriety of thoughts and words; or, in other terms, thoughts and words elegantly adapted to the subject. If our critics will join issue on this definition, that we may *convenire in alique tertio ;* if they will take it as a granted principle, it will be easy to put an end to this dispute. No man will disagree from another's judgment concerning the dignity of style in Heroic Poetry; but all reasonable men will conclude it necessary, that sublime subjects ought to be adorned with the sublimest, and consequently often with the most figurative expressions. In the meantime I will not run into their fault of imposing my opinions on other men, any more than I would my writings on their taste: I have only laid down, and that superficially enough, my present thoughts; and shall be glad to be taught better by those who pretend to reform our Poetry.

ANTONY AND CLEOPATRA AND THE ART OF TRAGEDY

PREFACE TO "ALL FOR LOVE; OR, THE WORLD WELL LOST" (1678)

THE death of Antony and Cleopatra is a subject which has been treated by the greatest wits of our nation, after Shakspeare; and by all so variously, that their example has given me the confidence to try myself in this bow of Ulysses amongst the crowd of suitors; and, withal, to take my own measures, in aiming at the mark. I doubt not but the same motive has prevailed with all of us in this attempt; I mean the excellency of the moral: for the chief persons represented were famous patterns of unlawful love; and their end accordingly was unfortunate. All reasonable men have long since concluded, that the hero of the poem ought not to be a character of perfect virtue, for then he could not, without injustice, be made unhappy; nor yet altogether wicked, because he could not then be pitied. I have therefore steered the middle course; and have drawn the character of Antony as favourably as Plutarch, Appian, and Dion Cassius would give me leave; the like I have observed in Cleopatra. That which is wanting to work up the pity to a greater height, was not afforded me by the story; for the crimes of love, which they both committed, were not occasioned by any necessity, or fatal ignorance, but were wholly voluntary; since our passions are, or ought to be, within our power. The fabric of the play is regular enough, as to the inferior parts of it; and the Unities of Time, Place, and Action, more exactly observed than perhaps the English theatre requires. Particularly, the action is so much one that it is the only one of the kind without episode, or underplot; every scene in the tragedy conducing to the main design, and every act concluding with a turn of it. The greatest error in the contrivance seems to be in the person of Octavia; for, though I might use the privilege of a poet to introduce her into Alexandria, yet I had not enough considered, that the compassion she moved to herself and

118

children was destructive to that which I reserved for Antony and Cleopatra; whose mutual love being founded upon vice must lessen the favour of the audience to them, when virtue and innocence were oppressed by it. And, though I justified Antony in some measure, by making Octavia's departure to proceed wholly from herself; yet the force of the first machine still remained; and the dividing of pity, like the cutting of a river into many channels, abated the strength of the natural stream. But this is an objection which none of my critics have urged against me; and therefore I might have let it pass, if I could have resolved to have been partial of myself. The fault my enemies have found are rather cavils concerning little and not essential decencies; which a master of the ceremonies may decide betwixt us. The French poets, I confess, are strict observers of these punctilios: they would not, for example, have suffered Cleopatra and Octavia to have met; or, if they had met, there must have only passed betwixt them some cold civilities, but no eagerness of repartee, for fear of offending against the greatness of their characters, and the modesty of their sex. This objection I foresaw, and at the same time contemned; for I judged it both natural and probable that Octavia, proud of her new-gained conquest, would search out Cleopatra to triumph over her; and that Cleopatra, thus attacked, was not of a spirit to shun the encounter: and 'tis not unlikely that two exasperated rivals should use such satire as I have put into their mouths; for, after all, though the one were a Roman, and the other a queen, they were both women. 'Tis true, some actions, though natural, are not fit to be represented; and broad obscenities in words ought in good manners to be avoided: expressions therefore are a modest clothing of our thoughts, as breeches and petticoats are of our bodies. If I have kept myself within the bounds of modesty, all beyond it is but nicety and affectation; which is no more but modesty depraved into a vice. They betray themselves who are too quick of apprehension in such cases, and leave all reasonable men to imagine worse of them than of the poet.

Honest Montaigne goes yet further: *Nous ne sommes que ceremonie ; la ceremonie nous emporte, et laissons la substance des choses. Nous nous tenons aux branches, et abandonnons le tronc et le corps. Nous avons appris aux dames de rougir, oyans seulement nommer ce qu'elles ne craignent aucunement à faire : nous n'osons appeller à droit nos membres, et ne craignons pas de les employer à toute sorte de debauche. La ceremonie nous defend d'exprimer par paroles les choses licites et naturelles, et nous l'en croyons; la raison nous defend de n'en faire point d'illicites et mauvaises, et personne ne l'en croit.* My comfort is, that by this opinion my enemies are but suckling critics, who would fain be nibbling ere their teeth are come.

Yet in this nicety of manners does the excellency of French poetry consist: their heroes are the most civil people breathing; but their good breeding seldom extends to a word of sense; all their wit is in their ceremony; they want the genius which animates our stage; and therefore 'tis but necessary, when they cannot please, that they should take care not to offend. But as the civilest man in the company is commonly the dullest, so these authors, while they are afraid to make you laugh or cry, out of pure good manners make you sleep. They are so careful not to exasperate a critic that they never leave him any work; so busy with the broom, and make so clean a riddance, that there is little left either for censure or for praise: for no part of a poem is worth our discommending where the whole is insipid; as when we have once tasted of palled wine, we stay not to examine it glass by glass. But while they affect to shine in trifles, they are often careless in essentials. Thus, their Hippolytus is so scrupulous in point of decency that he will rather expose himself to death than accuse his stepmother to his father; and my critics, I am sure, will commend him for it; but we of grosser apprehensions are apt to think that this excess of generosity is not practicable but with fools and madmen. This was good manners with a vengeance; and the audience is like to be much concerned at the misfortunes of this admirable hero: but take Hippolytus out of his poetic fit, and I suppose he would think it a wiser part to set the saddle on the right horse, and choose rather to live with the reputation of a plain-spoken, honest man, than to die with the infamy of an incestuous villain. In the meantime we may take notice that where the poet ought to have preserved the character as it was delivered to us by antiquity, when he should have given us the picture of a rough young man, of the Amazonian strain, a jolly huntsman, and both by his profession and his early rising a mortal enemy to love, he has chosen to give him the turn of gallantry, sent him to travel from Athens to Paris, taught him to make love, and transformed the Hippolytus of Euripides into Monsieur Hippolyte. I should not have troubled myself thus far with French poets, but that I find our *Chedreux* critics wholly form their judgments by them. But for my part, I desire to be tried by the laws of my own country; for it seems unjust to me that the French should prescribe here till they have conquered. Our little sonneteers, who follow them, have too narrow souls to judge of Poetry. Poets themselves are the most proper, though I conclude not the only critics. But still some genius, as universal as Aristotle, shall arise, one who can penetrate into all arts and sciences, without the practice of them, I shall think it reasonable that the judgment of an artificer in his own art should be preferable to the opinion of another man; at least where he is not bribed by interest, or prejudiced by malice. And this, I suppose, is manifest by plain induction: for, first, the crowd cannot be presumed to have more than a gross instinct of what pleases or displeases them: every man will grant me this; but then, by a particular kindness to himself, he draws his own stake first, and will be distinguished from the multitude, of which other men may think him one. But, if I come closer to those who are allowed for witty men, either by the advantage of their quality, or by common fame, and affirm that neither are they qualified to decide sovereignly concerning poetry, I shall yet have a strong party of my opinion; for most of them severally will exclude the rest, either from the number of witty men, or at least of able judges. But here again they are all indulgent to themselves; and every one who believes himself a wit, that is, every man, will pretend at the same time to a right of judging. But to press it yet further, there are many witty men, but few poets; neither have all poets a taste of Tragedy. And this is the rock on which they are daily splitting. Poetry, which is a picture of Nature, must generally please; but 'tis not to be understood that all parts of it must please every man; therefore is not Tragedy to be judged by a witty man, whose taste is only confined to Comedy. Nor is every man, who loves Tragedy, a sufficient judge of it; he must understand the excellencies of it too, or he will only prove a blind admirer, not a critic. From hence it comes that so many satires on poets, and censures of their writings, fly abroad. Men of pleasant conversation (at least esteemed so), and endued with a trifling kind of fancy, perhaps helped out with some smattering of Latin, are ambitious to distinguish themselves from the herd of gentlemen, by their Poetry—

> Rarus enim ferme sensus communis in illa
> Fortuna.

And is not this a wretched affectation, not to be contented

with what fortune has done for them, and sit down quietly with
their estates, but they must call their wits in question, and
needlessly expose their nakedness to public view? Not considering that they are not to expect the same approbation from
sober men, which they have found from their flatterers after the
third bottle. If a little glittering in discourse has passed them
on us for witty men, where was the necessity of undeceiving the
world? Would a man who has an ill title to an estate, but yet
is in possession of it; would he bring it of his own accord to be
tried at Westminster? We who write, if we want the talent,
yet have the excuse that we do it for a poor subsistence; but
what can be urged in their defence, who, not having the vocation
of poverty to scribble, out of mere wantonness take pains to
make themselves ridiculous? Horace was certainly in the right
where he said *that no man is satisfied with his own condition.*
A poet is not pleased because he is not rich; and the rich are
discontented because the poets will not admit them of their
number. Thus the case is hard with writers: if they succeed
not, they must starve; and if they do, some malicious satire is
prepared to level them, for daring to please without their leave.
But while they are so eager to destroy the fame of others, their
ambition is manifest in their concernment; some poem of their
own is to be produced, and the slaves are to be laid flat with
their faces on the ground, that the monarch may appear in the
greater majesty.

Dionysius and Nero had the same longings, but with all their
power they could never bring their business well about. 'Tis
true, they proclaimed themselves poets by sound of trumpet;
and poets they were, upon pain of death to any man who durst
call them otherwise. The audience had a fine time on't, you
may imagine; they sat in bodily fear, and looked as demurely
as they could: for it was a hanging matter to laugh unseasonably;
and the tyrants were suspicious, as they had reason, that their
subjects had 'em in the wind; so, every man, in his own defence,
set as good a face upon the business as he could. 'Twas known
beforehand that the monarchs were to be crowned laureates;
but when the show was over, and an honest man was suffered
to depart quietly, he took out his laughter which he had stifled,
with a firm resolution never more to see an Emperor's play,
though he had been ten years a-making it. In the meantime the
true poets were they who made the best markets, for they had
wit enough to yield the prize with a good grace, and not contend
with him who had thirty legions. They were sure to be rewarded

if they confessed themselves bad writers, and that was some-what better than to be martyrs for their reputation. Lucan's example was enough to teach them manners; and after he was put to death for overcoming Nero, the Emperor carried it with-out dispute for the best poet in his dominions. No man was ambitious of that grinning honour; for if he heard the malicious trumpeter proclaiming his name before his betters, he knew there was but one way with him. Mæcenas took another course, and we know he was more than a great man, for he was witty too: but finding himself far gone in Poetry, which Seneca assures us was not his talent, he thought it his best way to be well with Virgil and with Horace; that at least he might be a poet at the second hand; and we see how happily it has succeeded with him; for his own bad poetry is forgotten, and their panegyrics of him still remain. But they who should be our patrons are for no such expensive ways to fame; they have much of the poetry of Mæcenas, but little of his liberality. They are for persecuting Horace and Virgil, in the persons of their successors; for such is every man who has any part of their soul and fire, though in a less degree. Some of their little zanies yet go further; for they are persecutors even of Horace himself, as far as they are able, by their ignorant and vile imitations of him; by making an unjust use of his authority, and turning his artillery against his friends. But how would he disdain to be copied by such hands! I dare answer for him, he would be more uneasy in their company than he was with Crispinus, their forefather, in the Holy Way; and would no more have allowed them a place amongst the critics, than he would Demetrius the mimic, and Tigellius the buffoon:

> Demetri, teque, Tigelli,
> Discipulorum inter jubeo plorare cathedras.

With what scorn would he look down on such miserable trans-lators, who make doggerel of his Latin, mistake his meaning, misapply his censures, and often contradict their own? He is fixed as a landmark to set out the bounds of poetry—

> Saxum antiquum, ingens,—
> Limes agro positus, litem ut discerneret arvis.

But other arms than theirs, and other sinews are required, to raise the weight of such an author; and when they would toss him against enemies—

> Genua labant, gelidus concrevit frigore sanguis.
> Tum lapis ipse, viri vacuum per inane volutus,
> Nec spatium evasit totum, nec pertulit ictum.

For my part, I would wish no other revenge, either for myself, or the rest of the poets, from this rhyming judge of the twelve-penny gallery, this legitimate son of Sternhold, than that he would subscribe his name to his censure, or (not to tax him beyond his learning) set his mark: for, should he own himself publicly, and come from behind the lion's skin, they whom he condemns would be thankful to him, they whom he praises would choose to be condemned; and the magistrates, whom he has elected, would modestly withdraw from their employment, to avoid the scandal of his nomination. The sharpness of his satire, next to himself, falls most heavily on his friends, and they ought never to forgive him for commending them perpetually the wrong way, and sometimes by contraries. If he have a friend whose hastiness in writing is his greatest fault, Horace would have taught him to have minced the matter, and to have called it readiness of thought, and a flowing fancy; for friendship will allow a man to christen an imperfection by the name of some neighbour's virtue—

> Vellem in amicitia sic erraremus; et isti
> Errori nomen virtus posuisset honestum.

But he would never have allowed him to have called a slow man hasty, or a hasty writer a slow drudge, as Juvenal explains it—

> Canibus pigris, scabieque vetusta
> Laevibus, et siccae lambentibus ora lucernae,
> Nomen erit, Pardus, Tigris, Leo; si quid adhuc est
> Quod fremit in terris violentius.

Yet Lucretius laughs at a foolish lover, even for excusing the imperfections of his mistress—

> Nigra μελίχροος est, immunda et foetida ἄκοσμος
> Balba loqui, non quit, τραυλίζει; muta pudens est, etc.

But to drive it *ad Æthiopem cygnum* is not to be endured. I leave him to interpret this by the benefit of his French version on the other side, and without further considering him than I have the rest of my illiterate censors, whom I have disdained to answer, because they are not qualified for judges. It remains that I acquaint the reader that I have endeavoured in this play to follow the practice of the Ancients, who, as Mr. Rymer has judiciously observed, are and ought to be our masters. Horace likewise gives it for a rule in his Art of Poetry—

> Vos exemplaria Græca
> Nocturna versate manu, versate diurna.

Yet, though their models are regular, they are too little for English tragedy; which requires to be built in a larger compass. I could give an instance in the *Œdipus Tyrannus*, which was the masterpiece of Sophocles; but I reserve it for a more fit occasion, which I hope to have hereafter. (In my style, I have professed to imitate the divine Shakspeare; which that I might perform more freely, I have disencumbered myself from rhyme.) Not that I condemn my former way, but that this is more proper to my present purpose. I hope I need not to explain myself, that I have not copied my author servilely: words and phrases must of necessity receive a change in succeeding ages; but it is almost a miracle that much of his language remains so pure; and that he who began Dramatic Poetry amongst us, untaught by any, and as Ben Jonson tells us, without learning, should by the force of his own genius perform so much, that in a manner he has left no praise for any who come after him. The occasion is fair, and the subject would be pleasant to handle the difference of styles betwixt him and Fletcher, and wherein, and how far they are both to be imitated. But since I must not be over-confident of my own performance after him, it will be prudence in me to be silent. Yet, I hope I may affirm, and without vanity, that, by imitating him, I have excelled myself throughout the play; and particularly, that I prefer the scene betwixt Antony and Ventidius in the first act, to anything which I have written in this kind.

THE GROUNDS OF CRITICISM IN TRAGEDY

THE PREFACE TO "TROILUS AND CRESSIDA" (1679)

THE poet Æschylus was held in the same veneration by the Athenians of after ages as Shakspeare is by us; and Longinus has judged, in favour of him, that he had a noble boldness of expression, and that his imaginations were lofty and heroic; but, on the other side, Quintilian affirms that he was daring to extravagance. 'Tis certain that he affected pompous words, and that his sense too often was obscured by figures; notwithstanding these imperfections, the value of his writings after his decease was such that his countrymen ordained an equal reward to those poets who could alter his plays to be acted on the theatre, with those whose productions were wholly new, and of their own. The case is not the same in England; though the difficulties of altering are greater, and our reverence for Shakspeare much more just, than that of the Grecians for Æschylus. In the age of that poet, the Greek tongue was arrived to its full perfection; they had then amongst them an exact standard of writing and of speaking: the English language is not capable of such a certainty; and we are at present so far from it, that we are wanting in the very foundation of it a perfect grammar. Yet it must be allowed to the present age, that the tongue in general is so much refined since Shakspeare's time that many of his words, and more of his phrases, are scarce intelligible. And of those which we understand, some are ungrammatical, others coarse; and his whole style is so pestered with figurative expressions, that it is as affected as it is obscure. 'Tis true that in his latter plays he had worn off somewhat of the rust; but the tragedy which I have undertaken to correct was in all probability one of his first endeavours on the stage.

The original story was written by one Lollius, a Lombard, in Latin verse, and translated by Chaucer into English; intended, I suppose, a satire on the inconstancy of women: I find nothing of it among the Ancients; not so much as the name Cressida once mentioned. Shakspeare (as I hinted), in the apprenticeship of his writing, modelled it into that play which is now called by the name of *Troilus and Cressida*, but so lamely is it left to us, that it is not divided into acts; which fault I ascribe to the actors who printed it after Shakspeare's death; and that too so carelessly, that a more uncorrect copy I never saw. For the play itself, the author seems to have begun it with some fire; the characters of Pandarus and Thersites are promising enough; but as if he grew weary of his task, after an entrance or two, he lets them fall: and the latter part of the tragedy is nothing but a confusion of drums and trumpets, excursions and alarms. The chief persons, who give name to the tragedy, are left alive; Cressida is false, and is not punished. Yet, after all, because the play was Shakspeare's, and that there appeared in some places of it the admirable genius of the author, I undertook to remove that heap of rubbish under which many excellent thoughts lay wholly buried. Accordingly, I new-modelled the plot, threw out many unnecessary persons, improved those characters which were begun and left unfinished, as Hector, Troilus, Pandarus, and Thersites, and added that of Andromache. After this, I made, with no small trouble, an order and connection of all the scenes; removing them from the places where they were inartificially set; and, though it was impossible to keep them all unbroken, because the scene must be sometimes in the city and sometimes in the camp, yet I have so ordered them that there is a coherence of them with one another, and a dependence on the main design; no leaping from Troy to the Grecian tents, and thence back again, in the same act, but a due proportion of time allowed for every motion. I need not say that I have refined his language, which before was obsolete; but I am willing to acknowledge, that as I have often drawn his English nearer to our times, so I have sometimes conformed my own to his; and consequently, the language is not altogether so pure as it is significant. The scenes of Pandarus and Cressida, of Troilus and Pandarus, of Andromache with Hector and the Trojans in the second act, are wholly new; together with that of Nestor and Ulysses with Thersites, and that of Thersites with Ajax and Achilles. I will not wear my reader with the scenes which are added of Pandarus and the lovers, in the third, and those of Thersites, which are wholly altered; but I cannot omit the last scene in it, which is almost half the act, betwixt Troilus and Hector. The occasion of raising it was hinted to me by Mr. Betterton; the contrivance and working of it was my own.

They who think to do me an injury by saying that it is an imitation of the scene betwixt Brutus and Cassius, do me an honour by supposing I could imitate the incomparable Shakspeare; but let me add, that if Shakspeare's scene, or the faulty copy of it in Amintor and Melantius, had never been, yet Euripides had furnished me with an excellent example in his *Iphigenia*, between Agamemnon and Menelaus; and from thence, indeed, the last turn of it is borrowed. The occasion which Shakspeare, Euripides, and Fletcher have all taken is the same, grounded upon friendship; and the quarrel of two virtuous men, raised by natural degrees to the extremity of passion, is conducted in all three to the declination of the same passion, and concludes with a warm renewing of their friendship. But the particular groundwork which Shakspeare has taken is incomparably the best; because he has not only chosen two of the greatest heroes of their age, but has likewise interested the liberty of Rome, and their own honours, who were the redeemers of it, in this debate. And if he has made Brutus, who was naturally a patient man, to fly into excess at first, let it be remembered in his defence, that, just before, he has received the news of Portia's death; whom the poet, on purpose neglecting a little chronology, supposes to have died before Brutus, only to give him an occasion of being more easily exasperated. Add to this, that the injury he had received from Cassius had long been brooding in his mind; and that a melancholy man, upon consideration of an affront, especially from a friend, would be more eager in his passion than he who had given it, though naturally more choleric. Euripides, whom I have followed, has raised the quarrel betwixt two brothers, who were friends. The foundation of the scene was this: the Grecians were wind-bound at the port of Aulis, and the oracle had said that they could not sail, unless Agamemnon delivered up his daughter to be sacrificed: he refuses; his brother Menelaus urges the public safety; the father defends himself by arguments of natural affection, and hereupon they quarrel. Agamemnon is at last convinced, and promises to deliver up Iphigenia, but so passionately laments his loss, that Menelaus is grieved to have been the occasion of it, and, by a return of kindness, offers to intercede for him with the Grecians, that his daughter might not be sacrificed. But my friend Mr. Rymer has so largely, and with so much judgment, described this scene, in comparing it with that of Melantius and Amintor, that it is superfluous to say more of it; I only named the heads of it, that any reasonable man might judge it was from thence I modelled my scene betwixt Troilus and Hector. I will conclude my reflections on it, with a passage of Longinus, concerning Plato's imitation of Homer: " We ought not to regard a good imitation as a theft, but as a beautiful idea of him who undertakes to imitate, by forming himself on the invention and the work of another man; for he enters into the lists like a new wrestler, to dispute the prize with the former champion. This sort of emulation, says Hesiod, is honourable, Ἀγαθὴ δ' ἔρις ἐστὶ βρότοισιν— when we combat for victory with a hero, and are not without glory even in our overthrow. Those great men, whom we propose to ourselves as patterns of our imitation, serve us as a torch, which is lifted up before us, to enlighten our passage, and often elevate our thoughts as high as the conception we have of our author's genius."

I have been so tedious in three acts, that I shall contract myself in the two last. The beginning scenes of the fourth act are either added or changed wholly by me; the middle of it is Shakspeare altered, and mingled with my own; three or four of the last scenes are altogether new. And the whole fifth act, both the plot and the writing, are my own additions.

But having written so much for imitation of what is excellent, in that part of the Preface which related only to myself, methinks it would neither be unprofitable nor unpleasant to inquire how far we ought to imitate our own poets, Shakspeare and Fletcher, in their tragedies; and this will occasion another inquiry, how those two writers differ between themselves: but since neither of these questions can be solved, unless some measures be first taken by which we may be enabled to judge truly of their writings, I shall endeavour, as briefly as I can, to discover the grounds and reason of all criticism, applying them in this place only to Tragedy. Aristotle with his interpreters, and Horace, and Longinus, are the authors to whom I own my lights; and what part soever of my own plays, or of this, which no mending could make regular, shall fall under the condemnation of such judges, it would be impudence in me to defend. I think it no shame to retract my errors, and am well pleased to suffer in the cause, if the art may be improved at my expense: I therefore proceed to

THE GROUNDS OF CRITICISM IN TRAGEDY

Tragedy is thus defined by Aristotle (omitting what I thought unnecessary in his definition). It is an imitation of one entire, great, and probable action; not told, but represented; which, by moving in us fear and pity, is conducive to the purging of those two passions in our minds. More largely thus: Tragedy describes or paints an action, which action must have all the proprieties above named. First, it must be one or single; that is, it must not be a history of one man's life, suppose of Alexander the Great, or Julius Cæsar, but one single action of theirs. This condemns all Shakspeare's historical plays, which are rather chronicles represented, than tragedies; and all double action of plays. As, to avoid a satire upon others, I will make bold with my own *Marriage à la Mode*, where there are manifestly two actions not depending on one another: but in *Œdipus* there cannot properly be said to be two actions, because the love of Adrastus and Eurydice has a necessary dependence on the principal design into which it is woven. The natural reason of this rule is plain; for two different independent actions distract the attention and concernment of the audience, and consequently destroy the intention of the poet; if his business be to move terror and pity, and one of his actions be comical, the other tragical, the former will divert the people, and utterly make void his greater purpose. Therefore, as in perspective, so in Tragedy, there must be a point of sight in which all the lines terminate; otherwise the eye wanders, and the work is false. This was the practice of the Grecian stage. But Terence made an innovation in the Roman: all his plays have double actions; for it was his custom to translate two Greek comedies, and to weave them into one of his, yet so that both their actions were comical, and one was principal, the other but secondary or subservient. And this has obtained on the English stage, to give us the pleasure of variety.

As the action ought to be one, it ought, as such, to have order in it; that is, to have a natural beginning, a middle, and an end. A natural beginning, says Aristotle, is that which could not necessarily have been placed after another thing; and so of the rest. This consideration will arraign all plays after the new model of Spanish plots, where accident is heaped upon accident, and that which is first might as reasonably be last; an inconvenience not to be remedied, but by making one accident naturally produce another, otherwise it is a farce and not a play. Of this nature is the *Slighted Maid ;* where there is no scene in the first act which might not by as good reason be in the fifth. And if the action ought to be one, the tragedy ought likewise to conclude with the action of it. Thus in *Mustapha*, the play should naturally have ended with the death of Zanger, and not have given us the grace-cup after dinner, of Solyman's divorce from Roxolana.

The following properties of the action are so easy that they need not my explaining. It ought to be great, and to consist of great persons, to distinguish it from Comedy, where the action is trivial, and the persons of inferior rank. The last quality of the action is, that it ought to be probable, as well as admirable and great. 'Tis not necessary that there should be historical truth in it; but always necessary that there should be a likeness of truth, something that is more than barely possible; *probable* being that which succeeds, or happens, oftener than it misses. To invent therefore a probability, and to make it wonderful, is the most difficult undertaking in the art of Poetry; for that which is not wonderful is not great; and that which is not probable will not delight a reasonable audience. This action, thus described, must be represented and not told, to distinguish Dramatic Poetry from Epic: but I hasten to the end or scope of Tragedy, which is, to rectify or purge our passions, fear, and pity.

To instruct delightfully is the general end of all poetry. Philosophy instructs, but it performs its work by precept; which is not delightful, or not so delightful as example. To purge the passions by example is therefore the particular instruction which belongs to Tragedy. Rapin, a judicious critic, has observed from Aristotle, that pride and want of commiseration are the most predominant vices in mankind; therefore, to cure us of these two, the inventors of Tragedy have chosen to work upon two other passions, which are fear and pity. We are wrought to fear by their setting before our eyes some terrible example of misfortune, which happened to persons of the highest quality; for such an action demonstrates to us that no condition is privileged from the turns of fortune; this must of necessity cause terror in us, and consequently abate our pride. But when we see that the most virtuous, as well as the greatest, are not exempt from such misfortunes, that consideration moves pity in us, and insensibly works us to be helpful to, and tender over, the distressed; which is the noblest and most god-like of moral virtues. Here it is observable that it is absolutely necessary to make a man virtuous, if we desire he should be pitied: we lament not, but detest, a wicked man; we are glad when we behold his crimes are punished, and that poetical justice is done upon him. Euripides was censured by the critics of his time for making his chief characters too wicked; for example, Phædra, though she loved her son-in-law with reluctancy, and that it was a curse upon her family for offending Venus, yet was thought too ill a pattern for the stage. Shall we therefore banish all characters of villainy? I confess I am not of that opinion; but it is necessary that the hero of the play be not a villain; that is, the characters, which should move our pity, ought to have virtuous inclinations, and degrees of moral goodness in them. As for a perfect character of virtue, it never was in Nature, and therefore there can be no imitation of it; but there are alloys of frailty to be allowed for the chief persons, yet so that the good which is in them shall outweigh the bad, and consequently leave room for punishment on the one side and pity on the other.

After all, if any one will ask me whether a tragedy cannot be made upon any other grounds than those of exciting pity and terror in us, Bossu, the best of modern critics, answers thus in general: That all excellent arts, and particularly that of poetry, have been invented and brought to perfection by men of a transcendent genius; and that, therefore, they who practise afterwards the same arts are obliged to tread in their footsteps, and to search in their writings the foundation of them; for it is not just that new rules should destroy the authority of the old. But Rapin writes more particularly thus, that no passions in a story are so proper to move our concernment as fear and pity; and that it is from our concernment we receive our pleasure is undoubted; when the soul becomes agitated with fear for one character, or hope for another, then it is that we are pleased in Tragedy, by the interest which we take in their adventures.

Here, therefore, the general answer may be given to the first question, how far we ought to imitate Shakspeare and Fletcher in their plots; namely, that we ought to follow them so far only as they have copied the excellencies of those who invented and brought to perfection Dramatic Poetry; those things only excepted which religion, custom of countries, idioms of languages, etc., have altered in the superstructures, but not in the foundation of the design.

How defective Shakspeare and Fletcher have been in all their plots Mr. Rymer has discovered in his criticisms: neither can we, who follow them, be excused from the same or greater errors; which are the more unpardonable in us because we want their beauties to countervail our faults. The best of their designs, the most approaching to antiquity, and the most conducing to move pity, is the *King and no King*, which, if the farce of

Bessus were thrown away, is of that inferior sort of tragedies which end with a prosperous event. It is probably derived from the story of Œdipus, with the character of Alexander the Great in his extravagances given to Arbaces. The taking of this play, amongst many others, I cannot wholly ascribe to the excellency of the action, for I find it moving when it is read: 'tis true the faults of the plot are so evidently proved that they can no longer be denied. The beauties of it must therefore lie either in the lively touches of the passion, or we must conclude, as I think we may, that even in imperfect plots there are less degrees of Nature, by which some faint emotions of pity and terror are raised in us; as a less engine will raise a less proportion of weight, though not so much as one of Archimedes's making; for nothing can move our nature but by some natural reason which works upon passions. And since we acknowledge the effect there must be something in the cause.

The difference between Shakspeare and Fletcher in their plotting seems to be this; that Shakspeare generally moves more terror and Fletcher more compassion: for the first had a more masculine, a bolder and more fiery genius; the second, a more soft and womanish. In the mechanic beauties of the plot, which are the observation of the three Unities, Time, Place, and Action, they are both deficient; but Shakspeare most. Ben Jonson reformed those errors in his comedies, yet one of Shakspeare's was regular before him; which is *The Merry Wives of Windsor*. For what remains concerning the design you are to be referred to our English critic. That method which he has prescribed to raise it, from mistake, or ignorance of the crime, is certainly the best, though it is not the only; for amongst all the tragedies of Sophocles there is but one, *Œdipus*, which is wholly built after that model.

After the plot, which is the foundation of the play, the next thing to which we ought to apply our judgment is the manners; for now the poet comes to work above ground. The groundwork, indeed, is that which is most necessary, as that upon which depends the firmness of the whole fabric; yet it strikes not the eye so much as the beauties or imperfections of the manners, the thoughts, and the expressions.

The first rule which Bossu prescribes to the writer of an Heroic Poem, and which holds too by the same reason in all Dramatic Poetry, is to make the moral of the work; that is, to lay down to yourself what that precept of morality shall be which you would insinuate into the people; as, namely, Homer's (which

I have copied in my *Conquest of Granada*) was, that union preserves a commonwealth and discord destroys it; Sophocles, in his *Œdipus*, that no man is to be accounted happy before his death. 'Tis the moral that directs the whole action of the play to one centre; and that action or fable is the example built upon the moral, which confirms the truth of it to our experience: when the fable is designed, then, and not before, the persons are to be introduced, with their manners, characters, and passions.

The manners, in a poem, are understood to be those inclinations, whether natural or acquired, which move and carry us to actions, good, bad, or indifferent, in a play; or which incline the persons to such or such actions. I have anticipated part of this discourse already in declaring that a poet ought not to make the manners perfectly good in his best persons; but neither are they to be more wicked in any of his characters than necessity requires. To produce a villain, without other reason than a natural inclination to villainy, is, in Poetry, to produce an effect without a cause; and to make him more a villain than he has just reason to be is to make an effect which is stronger than the cause.

The manners arise from many causes; and are either distinguished by complexion, as choleric and phlegmatic, or by the differences of age or sex, of climates, or quality of the persons, or their present condition. They are likewise to be gathered from the several virtues, vices, or passions, and many other commonplaces, which a poet must be supposed to have learned from Natural Philosophy, Ethics, and History; of all which whosoever is ignorant does not deserve the name of poet.

But as the manners are useful in this art, they may be all comprised under these general heads: first, they must be apparent; that is, in every character of the play some inclinations of the person must appear; and these are shown in the actions and discourse. Secondly, the manners must be suitable, or agreeing to the persons; that is, to the age, sex, dignity, and the other general heads of manners: thus, when a poet has given the dignity of a king to one of his persons, in all his actions and speeches that person must discover majesty, magnanimity, and jealousy of power, because these are suitable to the general manners of a king. The third property of manners is resemblance; and this is founded upon the particular characters of men as we have them delivered to us by relation or history; that is, when a poet has the known character of this or that man before him, he is bound to represent him such, at least not contrary to that which fame has reported him to have been. Thus, it is not a poet's choice to make Ulysses choleric or Achilles patient, because Homer has described 'em quite otherwise. Yet this is a rock on which ignorant writers daily split; and the absurdity is as monstrous as if a painter should draw a coward running from a battle, and tell us it was the picture of Alexander the Great.

The last property of manners is that they be constant and equal, that is, maintained the same through the whole design: thus, when Virgil had once given the name of *pious* to Æneas, he was bound to show him such, in all his words and actions, through the whole poem. All these properties Horace has hinted to a judicious observer: 1. *Notandi sunt tibi mores;* 2. *Aut famam sequere;* 3. *Aut sibi convenientia finge;* 4. *Servetur ad imum, qualis ab incepto processerit, et sibi constet.*

From the manners, the characters of persons are derived; for, indeed, the characters are no other than the inclinations as they appear in the several persons of the poem; a character being thus defined—that which distinguishes one man from another. Not to repeat the same things over again which have been said of the manners, I will only add what is necessary here. A character, or that which distinguishes one man from all others, cannot be supposed to consist of one particular virtue, or vice, or passion only; but 'tis a composition of qualities which are not contrary to one another in the same person; thus, the same man may be liberal and valiant, but not liberal and covetous; so in a comical character, or humour (which is an inclination to this or that particular folly), Falstaff is a liar, and a coward, a glutton, and a buffoon, because all these qualities may agree in the same man; yet it is still to be observed that one virtue, vice, and passion ought to be shown in every man as predominant over all the rest; as covetousness in Crassus, love of his country in Brutus; and the same in characters which are feigned.

The chief character or hero in a tragedy, as I have already shown, ought in prudence to be such a man who has so much more of virtue in him than of vice, that he may be left amiable to the audience, which otherwise cannot have any concernment for his sufferings; and it is on this one character that the pity and terror must be principally, if not wholly, founded: a rule which is extremely necessary, and which none of the critics, that I know, have fully enough discovered to us. For terror and compassion work but weakly when they are divided into

many persons. If Creon had been the chief character in *Œdipus*,
there had neither been terror nor compassion moved, but only
detestation of the man and joy for his punishment; if Adrastus
and Eurydice had been made more appearing characters, then
the pity had been divided and lessened on the part of Œdipus:
but making Œdipus the best and bravest person, and even
Jocasta but an underpart to him, his virtues, and the punishment of his fatal crime, drew both the pity and the terror to
himself.

By what has been said of the manners, it will be easy for
a reasonable man to judge whether the characters be truly or
falsely drawn in a tragedy; for if there be no manners appearing
in the characters, no concernment for the persons can be raised;
no pity or horror can be moved but by vice or virtue; therefore,
without them, no person can have any business in the play.
If the inclinations be obscure, it is a sign the poet is in the dark
and knows not what manner of man he presents to you; and
consequently you can have no idea, or very imperfect, of that
man, nor can judge what resolutions he ought to take or what
words or actions are proper for him. Most comedies made up
of accidents or adventures are liable to fall into this error; and
tragedies with many turns are subject to it; for the manners
can never be evident where the surprises of fortune take up
all the business of the stage; and where the poet is more in pain
to tell you what happened to such a man than what he was.
'Tis one of the excellencies of Shakspeare that the manners
of his persons are generally apparent, and you see their bent and
inclinations. Fletcher comes far short of him in this, as indeed
he does almost in everything: there are but glimmerings of
manners in most of his comedies, which run upon adventures;
and in his tragedies, Rollo, Otto the King and no King, Melantius,
and many others of his best, are but pictures shown you in the
twilight; you know not whether they resemble vice or virtue,
and they are either good, bad, or indifferent, as the present
scene requires it. But of all poets, this commendation is to be
given to Ben Jonson, that the manners even of the most inconsiderable persons in his plays are everywhere apparent.

By considering the second quality of manners, which is, that
they be suitable to the age, quality, country, dignity, etc., of
the character, we may likewise judge whether a poet has followed
nature. In this kind, Sophocles and Euripides have more
excelled among the Greeks than Æschylus, and Terence more
than Plautus among the Romans. Thus, Sophocles gives to

Œdipus the true qualities of a king in both those plays which bear his name; but in the latter, which is the *Œdipus Colonœus*, he lets fall on purpose his tragic style; his hero speaks not in the arbitrary tone, but remembers, in the softness of his complaints, that he is an unfortunate blind old man, that he is banished from his country, and persecuted by his next relations. The present French poets are generally accused that, wheresoever they lay the scene, or in whatsoever age, the manners of their heroes are wholly French. Racine's Bajazet is bred at Constantinople, but his civilities are conveyed to him, by some secret passage, from Versailles into the Seraglio. But our Shakspeare, having ascribed to Henry the Fourth the character of a king and of a father, gives him the perfect manners of each relation, when either he transacts with his son or with his subjects. Fletcher, on the other side, gives neither to Arbaces nor to his king, in the *Maid's Tragedy*, the qualities which are suitable to a monarch; though he may be excused a little in the latter, for the king there is not uppermost in the character; 'tis the lover of Evadne, who is king only in a second consideration; and though he be unjust, and has other faults which shall be nameless, yet he is not the hero of the play. 'Tis true, we find him a lawful prince (though I never heard of any king that was in Rhodes), and therefore Mr. Rymer's criticism stands good, that he should not be shown in so vicious a character. Sophocles has been more judicious in his *Antigona;* for, though he represents in Creon a bloody prince, yet he makes him not a lawful king, but an usurper, and Antigona herself is the heroine of the tragedy: but when Philaster wounds Arethusa and the boy, and Perigot his mistress, in the *Faithful Shepherdess*, both these are contrary to the character of manhood. Nor is *Valentinian* managed much better; for though Fletcher has taken his picture truly, and shown him as he was, an effeminate, voluptuous man, yet he has forgotten that he was an emperor, and has given him none of those royal marks which ought to appear in a lawful successor of the throne. If it be inquired what Fletcher should have done on this occasion—ought he not to have represented Valentinian as he was?—Bossu shall answer this question for me by an instance of the like nature: Mauritius, the Greek emperor, was a prince far surpassing Valentinian, for he was endued with many kingly virtues; he was religious, merciful, and valiant, but withal he was noted of extreme covetousness, a vice which is contrary to the character of a hero or a prince: therefore, says the critic, that emperor was no fit person to be represented in a tragedy, unless his good qualities were only to be shown and his covetousness (which sullied them all) were slurred over by the artifice of the poet. To return once more to Shakspeare; no man ever drew so many characters, or generally distinguished 'em better from one another, excepting only Jonson. I will instance but in one to show the copiousness of his intention; it is that of Caliban, or the monster, in the *Tempest*. He seems there to have created a person which was not in nature, a boldness which, at first sight, would appear intolerable; for he makes him a species of himself, begotten by an incubus on a witch; but this, as I have elsewhere proved, is not wholly beyond the bounds of credibility, at least the vulgar still believe it. We have the separated notions of a spirit and of a witch (and spirits, according to Plato, are vested with a subtle body; according to some of his followers have different sexes); therefore, as from the distinct apprehensions of a horse and of a man imagination has formed a centaur, so from those of an incubus and a sorceress Shakspeare has produced his monster. Whether or no his generation can be defended I leave to philosophy; but of this I am certain, that the poet has most judiciously furnished him with a person, a language, and a character, which will suit him, both by father's and mother's side: he has all the discontents and malice of a witch and of a devil, besides a convenient proportion of the deadly sins; gluttony, sloth, and lust are manifest; the dejectedness of a slave is likewise given him, and the ignorance of one bred up in a desert island. His person is monstrous, and he is the product of unnatural lust; and his language is as hobgoblin as his person; in all things he is distinguished from other mortals. The characters of Fletcher are poor and narrow in comparison of Shakspeare's; I remember not one which is not borrowed from him, unless you will accept that strange mixture of a man in the *King and no King ;* so that in this part Shakspeare is generally worth our imitation, and to imitate Fletcher is but to copy after him who was a copyer.

Under this general head of manners the passions are naturally included as belonging to the characters. I speak not of pity and of terror, which are to be moved in the audience by the plot; but of anger, hatred, love, ambition, jealousy, revenge, etc., as they are shown in this or that person of the play. To describe these naturally, and to move them artfully, is one of the greatest commendations which can be given to a poet: to write pathetically, says Longinus, cannot proceed but from a lofty genius.

A poet must be born with this quality: yet, unless he help himself by an acquired knowledge of the passions, what they are in their own nature, and by what springs they are to be moved, he will be subject either to raise them where they ought not to be raised, or not to raise them by the just degrees of nature, or to amplify them beyond the natural bounds, or not to observe the crises and turns of them in their cooling and decay; all which errors proceed from want of judgment in the poet, and from being unskilled in the principles of moral philosophy. Nothing is more frequent in a fanciful writer than to foil himself by not managing his strength; therefore, as in a wrestler, there is first required some measure of force, a well-knit body and active limbs, without which all instruction would be vain; yet, these being granted, if he want the skill which is necessary to a wrestler he shall make but small advantage of his natural robustuousness: so, in a poet, his inborn vehemence and force of spirit will only run him out of breath the sooner if it be not supported by the help of Art. The roar of passion, indeed, may please an audience, three parts of which are ignorant enough to think all is moving which is noise, and it may stretch the lungs of an ambitious actor who will die upon the spot for a thundering clap; but it will move no other passion than indignation and contempt from judicious men. Longinus, whom I have hitherto followed, continues thus: *If the passions be artfully employed, the discourse becomes vehement and lofty : if otherwise, there is nothing more ridiculous than a great passion out of season :* and to this purpose he animadverts severely upon Æschylus, who writ nothing in cold blood, but was always in a rapture and in fury with his audience: the inspiration was still upon him, he was ever tearing it upon the tripos; or (to run off as madly as he does from one similitude to another) he was always at high-flood of passion, even in the dead ebb and lowest water-mark of the scene. He who would raise the passion of a judicious audience, says a learned critic, must be sure to take his hearers along with him; if they be in a calm, 'tis in vain for him to be in a huff: he must move them by degrees, and kindle with 'em; otherwise he will be in danger of setting his own heap of stubble on fire, and of burning out by himself, without warming the company that stand about him. They who would justify the madness of poetry from the authority of Aristotle have mistaken the text and consequently the interpretation: I imagine it to be false read where he says of poetry that it is Εὐφυοῦς ἢ μανικοῦ, that it had always somewhat in it either of a genius or of a madman. 'Tis more probable that the original ran thus, that poetry was Εὐφυοῦς οὐ μανικοῦ, that it belongs to a witty man, but not to a madman. Thus then the passions, as they are considered simply and in themselves, suffer violence when they are perpetually maintained at the same height; for what melody can be made on that instrument, all whose strings are screwed up at first to their utmost stretch and to the same sound? But this is not the worst: for the characters likewise bear a part in the general calamity if you consider the passions as embodied in them; for it follows of necessity that no man can be distinguished from another by his discourse when every man is ranting, swaggering, and exclaiming with the same excess: as if it were the only business of all the characters to contend with each other for the prize at Billingsgate, or that the scene of the tragedy lay in Bet'lem. Suppose the poet should intend this man to be choleric and that man to be patient, yet when they are confounded in the writing you cannot distinguish them from one another: for the man who was called patient and tame is only so before he speaks; but let his clack be set agoing, and he shall tongue it as impetuously, and as loudly, as the errantest hero in the play. By this means the characters are only distinct in name; but, in reality, all the men and women in the play are the same person. No man should pretend to write who cannot temper his fancy with his judgment: nothing is more dangerous to a raw horseman than a hot-mouthed jade without a curb.

It is necessary therefore for a poet, who would concern an audience by describing of a passion, first to prepare it and not to rush upon it all at once. Ovid has judiciously shown the difference of these two ways in the speeches of Ajax and Ulysses: Ajax, from the very beginning, breaks out into his exclamations, and is swearing by his Maker,—*Agimus, proh Jupiter, inquit.* Ulysses, on the contrary, prepares his audience with all the submissiveness he can practise, and all the calmness of a reasonable man; he found his judges in a tranquillity of spirit, and therefore set out leisurely and softly with 'em, till he had warmed 'em by degrees; and then he began to mend his pace and to draw them along with his own impetuousness: yet so managing his breath that it might not fail him at his need, and reserving his utmost proofs of ability even to the last. The success, you see, was answerable; for the crowd only applauded the speech of Ajax—

Vulgique secutum
Ultima murmur erat:

but the judges awarded the prize, for which they contended, to Ulysses—

Mota manus procerum est; et quid facundia posset
Tum patuit, fortisque viri tulit arma disertus.

The next necessary rule is to put nothing into the discourse which may hinder your moving of the passions. Too many accidents, as I have said, encumber the poet as much as the arms of Saul did David; for the variety of passions which they produce are ever crossing and justling each other out of the way. He who treats of joy and grief together is in a fair way of causing neither of those effects. There is yet another obstacle to be removed, which is pointed wit, and sentences affected out of season; these are nothing of kin to the violence of passion: no man is at leisure to make sentences and similes when his soul is in an agony. I the rather name this fault that it may serve to mind me of my former errors; neither will I spare myself, but give an example of this kind from my *Indian Emperor*. Montezuma, pursued by his enemies and seeking sanctuary, stands parleying without the fort and describing his danger to Cydaria in a simile of six lines—

As on the sands the frighted traveller
Sees the high seas come rolling from afar, etc.

My Indian potentate was well skilled in the sea for an inland prince, and well improved since the first act, when he sent his son to discover it. The image had not been amiss from another man at another time: *sed nunc non erat hisce locus :* he destroyed the concernment which the audience might otherwise have had for him; for they could not think the danger near when he had the leisure to invent a simile.

If Shakspeare be allowed, as I think he must, to have made his characters distinct, it will easily be inferred that he understood the nature of the passions: because it has been proved already that confused passions make undistinguishable characters: yet I cannot deny that he has his failings; but they are not so much in the passions themselves as in his manner of expression: he often obscures his meaning by his words, and sometimes makes it unintelligible. I will not say of so great a poet that he distinguished not the blown puffy style from true sublimity; but I may venture to maintain that the fury of his fancy often transported him beyond the bounds of judg-

F

ment, either in coining of new words and phrases, or racking
words which were in use into the violence of a catachresis.
It is not that I would explode the use of metaphors from passion,
for Longinus thinks 'em necessary to raise it: but to use 'em
at every word, to say nothing without a metaphor, a simile,
an image, or description, is, I doubt, to smell a little too strongly
of the buskin.   I must be forced to give an example of expressing
passion figuratively; but that I may do it with respect to Shakspeare, it shall not be taken from anything of his: 'tis an ex-
clamation against fortune, quoted in his *Hamlet* but written by
some other poet—

> Out, out, thou strumpet, Fortune! all you gods,
> In general synod, take away her power;
> Break all the spokes and felleys from her wheel,
> And bowl the round nave down the hill of Heav'n,
> As low as to the fiends.

And immediately after, speaking of Hecuba, when Priam was
killed before her eyes—

> The mobbled queen
> Threatening the flame, ran up and down
> With bisson rheum; a clout about that head
> Where late the diadem stood; and for a robe,
> About her lank and all o'er-teemed loins,
> A blanket in th' alarm of fear caught up.
> Who this had seen, with tongue in venom steep'd
> 'Gainst Fortune's state would treason have pronounced;
> But if the gods themselves did see her then,
> When she saw Pyrrhus make malicious sport
> In mincing with his sword her husband's limbs,
> The instant burst of clamour that she made
> (Unless things mortal move them not at all)
> Would have made milch the burning eyes of heaven,
> And passion in the gods.

What a pudder is here kept in raising the expression of trifling
thoughts! Would not a man have thought that the poet had
been bound prentice to a wheelwright for his first rant? and
had followed a ragman for the clout and blanket in the second?
Fortune is painted on a wheel, and therefore the writer, in a rage,
will have poetical justice done upon every member of that
engine: after this execution, he bowls the nave down-hill, from
Heaven, to the fiends (an unreasonable long mark, a man would
think); 'tis well there are no solid orbs to stop it in the way,
or no element of fire to consume it: but when it came to the earth
it must be monstrous heavy to break ground as low as the centre.
His making milch the burning eyes of heaven was a pretty
tolerable flight too: and I think no man ever drew milk out

of eyes before him: yet, to make the wonder greater, these eyes were burning. Such a sight indeed were enough to have raised passion in the gods; but to excuse the effects of it, he tells you perhaps they did not see it. Wise men would be glad to find a little sense couched under all these pompous words; for bombast is commonly the delight of that audience which loves poetry but understands it not: and as commonly has been the practice of those writers who, not being able to infuse a natural passion into the mind, have made it their business to ply the ears, and to stun their judges by the noise. But Shakspeare does not often thus; for the passions in his scene between Brutus and Cassius are extremely natural, the thoughts are such as arise from the matter, the expression of 'em not viciously figurative. I cannot leave this subject before I do justice to that divine poet by giving you one of his passionate descriptions: 'tis of Richard the Second when he was deposed and led in triumph through the streets of London by Henry of Bullingbrook: the painting of it is so lively, and the words so moving, that I have scarce read anything comparable to it in any other language. Suppose you have seen already the fortunate usurper passing through the crowd, and followed by the shouts and acclamations of the people; and now behold King Richard entering upon the scene: consider the wretchedness of his condition and his carriage in it; and refrain from pity if you can—

> As in a theatre, the eyes of men,
> After a well-graced actor leaves the stage,
> Are idly bent on him that enters next,
> Thinking his prattle to be tedious:
> Even so, or with much more contempt, men's eyes
> Did scowl on Richard: no man cried, God save him:
> No joyful tongue gave him his welcome home,
> But dust was thrown upon his sacred head,
> Which with such gentle sorrow he shook off,
> His face still combating with tears and smiles
> (The badges of his grief and patience),
> That had not God (for some strong purpose) steel'd
> The hearts of men, they must perforce have melted,
> And barbarism itself have pitied him.

To speak justly of this whole matter: 'tis neither height of thought that is discommended, nor pathetic vehemence, nor any nobleness of expression in its proper place; but 'tis a false measure of all these, something which is like them, and is not them; 'tis the Bristol-stone which appears like a diamond; 'tis an extravagant thought instead of a sublime one;

'tis roaring madness instead of vehemence; and a sound of words instead of sense. If Shakspeare were stripped of all the bombasts in his passions, and dressed in the most vulgar words, we should find the beauties of his thoughts remaining; if his embroideries were burnt down, there would still be silver at the bottom of the melting-pot: but I fear (at least let me fear it for myself) that we, who ape his sounding words, have nothing of his thought, but are all outside; there is not so much as a dwarf within our giant's clothes. Therefore, let not Shakspeare suffer for our sakes; 'tis our fault, who succeed him in an age which is more refined, if we imitate him so ill that we copy his failings only and make a virtue of that in our writings which in his was an imperfection.

For what remains, the excellency of that poet was, as I have said, in the more manly passions; Fletcher's in the softer: Shakspeare writ better betwixt man and man; Fletcher betwixt man and woman: consequently, the one described friendship better; the other love: yet Shakspeare taught Fletcher to write love: and Juliet and Desdemona are originals. 'Tis true the scholar had the softer soul; but the master had the kinder. Friendship is both a virtue and a passion essentially; love is a passion only in its nature, and is not a virtue but by accident: good nature makes friendship; but effeminacy love. Shakspeare had an universal mind, which comprehended all characters and passions; Fletcher a more confined and limited: for though he treated love in perfection, yet honour, ambition, revenge, and generally all the stronger passions, he either touched not, or not masterly. To conclude all, he was a limb of Shakspeare.

I had intended to have proceeded to the last property of manners, which is, that they must be constant, and the characters maintained the same from the beginning to the end; and from thence to have proceeded to the thoughts and expressions suitable to a tragedy: but I will first see how this will relish with the age. It is, I confess, but cursorily written; yet the judgment, which is given here, is generally founded upon experience; but because many men are shocked at the name of rules, as if they were a kind of magisterial prescription upon poets, I will conclude with the words of Rapin, in his *Reflections* on Aristotles' work *of Poetry* : " If the rules be well considered, we shall find them to be made only to reduce Nature into method, to trace her step by step, and not to suffer the least mark of her to escape us: 'tis only by these that probability in fiction is maintained, which is the soul of poetry. They are founded upon good sense, and sound reason, rather than on authority; for though Aristotle and Horace are produced, yet no man must argue that what they write is true, because they writ it; but 'tis evident, by the ridiculous mistakes and gross absurdities which have been made by those poets who have taken their fancy only for their guide, that if this fancy be not regulated, it is a mere caprice, and utterly incapable to produce a reasonable and judicious poem."

OVID AND THE ART OF TRANSLATION

PREFACE TO THE "TRANSLATIONS FROM OVID'S
EPISTLES" (1680)

THE life of Ovid being already written in our language, before
the translation of his *Metamorphoses*, I will not presume so far
upon myself to think I can add anything to Mr. Sandys his
undertaking. The English reader may there be satisfied that
he flourished in the reign of Augustus Cæsar; that he was
extracted from an ancient family of Roman knights; that he
was born to the inheritance of a splendid fortune; that he was
designed to the study of the Law, and had made considerable
progress in it, before he quitted that profession for this of
Poetry, to which he was more naturally formed. The cause of
his banishment is unknown; because he was himself unwilling
further to provoke the Emperor, by ascribing it to any other
reason than what was pretended by Augustus, which was, the
lasciviousness of his *Elegies* and his *Art of Love*. 'Tis true, they
are not to be excused in the severity of manners, as being able to
corrupt a larger Empire, if there were any, than that of Rome;
yet this may be said in behalf of Ovid, that no man has ever
treated the passion of love with so much delicacy of thought,
and of expression, or searched into the nature of it more philo-
sophically than he. And the Emperor who condemned him had
as little reason as another man to punish that fault with so much
severity, if at least he were the author of a certain epigram,
which is ascribed to him, relating to the cause of the first civil
war betwixt himself and Mark Anthony the Triumvir, which is
more fulsome than any passage I have met with in our poet. To
pass by the naked familiarity of his expressions to Horace, which
are cited in that author's life, I need only mention one notorious
act of his, in taking Livia to his bed, when she was not only
married, but with child by her husband then living. But deeds,
it seems, may be justified by arbitrary power, when words are
questioned in a poet. There is another guess of the gram-

146

marians, as far from truth as the first from reason; they will have him banished for some favours, which they say he received from Julia, the daughter of Augustus, whom they think he celebrates under the name of Corinna in his *Elegies*. But he who will observe the verses which are made to that mistress, may gather from the whole contexture of them, that Corinna was not a woman of the highest quality. If Julia were then married to Agrippa, why should our poet make his petition to Isis for her safe delivery, and afterwards condole her miscarriage; which, for aught he knew, might be by her own husband? Or indeed how durst he be so bold to make the least discovery of such a crime, which was no less than capital, especially committed against a person of Agrippa's rank? Or if it were before her marriage, he would surely have been more discreet than to have published an accident which must have been fatal to them both. But what most confirms me against this opinion is, that Ovid himself complains that the true person of Corinna was found out by the fame of his verses to her; which if it had been Julia, he durst not have owned; and besides, an immediate punishment must have followed. He seems himself more truly to have touched at the cause of his exile in those obscure verses:—

> Cur aliquid vidi? cur noxia lumina feci?
> Cur imprudenti cognita culpa mihi est?
> Inscius Actæron vidit sine veste Dianam,
> Præda fuit canibus non minus ille suis.

Namely, that he had either seen, or was conscious to somewhat, which had procured him his disgrace. But neither am I satisfied, that this was the incest of the Emperor with his own daughter: for Augustus was of a nature too vindicative to have contented himself with so small a revenge, or so unsafe to himself, as that of simple banishment, and would certainly have secured his crimes from public notice, by the death of him who was witness to them. Neither have historians given us any sight into such an action of this Emperor: nor would he (the greatest politician of his time), in all probability, have managed his crimes with so little secrecy, as not to shun the observation of any man. It seems more probable that Ovid was either the confidant of some other passion, or that he had stumbled, by some inadvertency, upon the privacies of Livia, and seen her in a bath: for the words *sine veste Dianam*, agree better with Livia, who had the fame of chastity, than with either of the Julias, who were both noted of incontinency. The first verses which were made by him in his youth, and recited publicly, according to the custom, were, as he himself assures us, to Corinna: his banishment happened not till the age of fifty; from which it may be deduced, with probability enough, that the love of Corinna did not occasion it: nay, he tells us plainly that his offence was that of error only, not of wickedness; and in the same paper of verses also, that the cause was notoriously known at Rome, though it be left so obscure to after ages.

But to leave conjectures on a subject so uncertain, and to write somewhat more authentic of this poet. That he frequented the court of Augustus, and was well received in it, is most undoubted: all his poems bear the character of a court, and appear to be written, as the French call it, *cavalièrement :* add to this, that the titles of many of his *Elegies*, and more of his *Letters* in his banishment, are addressed to persons well known to us, even at this distance, to have been considerable in that court.

Nor was his acquaintance less with the famous poets of his age than with the noblemen and ladies. He tells you himself, in a particular account of his own life, that Macer, Horace, Tibullus, Propertius, and many others of them, were his familiar friends, and that some of them communicated their writings to him; but that he had only seen Virgil.

If the imitation of Nature be the business of a poet, I know no author who can justly be compared with ours, especially in the description of the passions. And to prove this, I shall need no other judges than the generality of his readers: for, all passions being inborn with us, we are almost equally judges when we are concerned in the representation of them. Now I will appeal to any man, who has read this poet, whether he finds not the natural emotion of the same passion in himself, which the poet describes in his feigned persons? His thoughts, which are the pictures and results of those passions, are generally such as naturally arise from those disorderly motions of our spirits. Yet, not to speak too partially in his behalf, I will confess that the copiousness of his wit was such that he often writ too pointedly for his subject, and made his persons speak more eloquently than the violence of their passion would admit: so that he is frequently witty out of season; leaving the imitation of Nature, and the cooler dictates of his judgment, for the false applause of Fancy. Yet he seems to have found out this imperfection in his riper age; for why else should he complain that his *Metamorphoses* was left unfinished? Nothing sure can be added to the wit of that poem, or of the rest; but many things ought to have been retrenched, which I suppose would have been the business of his age, if his misfortunes had not come too fast upon him. But take him uncorrected, as he is transmitted to us, and it must be acknowledged, in spite of his Dutch friends, the commentators, even of Julius Scaliger himself, that Seneca's censure will stand good against him; *Nescivit quod bene cessit relinquere :* he never knew how to give over, when he had done well; but, continually varying the same sense an hundred ways, and taking up in another place what he had more than enough inculcated before, he sometimes cloys his readers, instead of satisfying them; and gives occasion to his translators, who dare not cover him, to blush at the nakedness of their father. This, then, is the alloy of Ovid's writings, which is sufficiently recompensed by his other excellencies; nay, this very fault is not without its beauties; for the most severe censor cannot but be pleased with the prodigality of his wit, though at the same time he could have wished that the master of it had been a better manager. Everything which he does becomes him, and if sometimes he appears too gay, yet there is a secret gracefulness of youth which accompanies his writings, though the staidness and sobriety of age be wanting. In the most material part, which is the conduct, 'tis certain that he seldom has miscarried: for if his *Elegies* be compared with those of Tibullus and Propertius, his contemporaries, it will be found that those poets seldom designed before they writ; and though the language of Tibullus be more polished, and the learning of Propertius, especially in his Fourth Book, more set out to ostentation; yet their common practice was to look no further before them than the next line; whence it will inevitably follow that they can drive to no certain point, but ramble from one subject to another, and conclude with somewhat which is not of a piece with their beginning:—

> Purpureus late qui splendeat, unus et alter
> Assuitur pannus . . .

as Horace says; though the verses are golden, they are but patched into the garment. But our Poet has always the goal in his eye, which directs him in his race; some beautiful design, which he first establishes, and then contrives the means which will naturally conduct it to his end. This will be evident to judicious readers in this work of his *Epistles*, of which somewhat, at least in general, will be expected.

The title of them in our late editions is *Epistolæ Heroidum*, the Letters of the *Heroines*. But Heinsius has judged more truly

that the inscription of our author was barely *Epistles;* which
he concludes from his cited verses, where Ovid asserts this work
as his own invention, and not borrowed from the Greeks, whom
(as the masters of their learning) the Romans usually did
imitate. But it appears not from his writings that any of
the Grecians ever touched upon this way, which our poet therefore justly has vindicated to himself. I quarrel not at the word
Heroidum, because it is used by Ovid in his *Art of Love*—

Jupiter ad veteres supplex *Heroidas* ibat.

But sure he could not be guilty of such an oversight, to call his
work by the name of *Heroines,* when there are divers men, or
heroes, as namely Paris, Leander, and Acontius, joined in it.
Except Sabinus, who writ some answers to Ovid's *Letters,*

(Quam celer e toto rediit meus orbe Sabinus)

I remember not any of the Romans who have treated this subject, save only Propertius, and that but once, in his Epistle of
Arethusa to Lycotas, which is written so near the style of Ovid
that it seems to be but an imitation; and therefore ought not
to defraud our poet of the glory of his invention.

Concerning this work of the *Epistles,* I shall content myself to
observe these few particulars: first, that they are generally
granted to be the most perfect pieces of Ovid, and that the style
of them is tenderly passionate and courtly; two properties well
agreeing with the persons, which were heroines, and lovers.
Yet where the characters were lower, as in Œnone and Hero,
he has kept close to Nature, in drawing his images after a
country life, though perhaps he has Romanised his Grecian
dames too much, and made them speak, sometimes, as if they
had been born in the city of Rome, and under the Empire of
Augustus. There seems to be no great variety in the particular
subjects which he has chosen; most of the *Epistles* being written
from ladies, who were forsaken by their lovers: which is the
reason that many of the same thoughts come back upon us in
divers letters: but of the general character of women, which is
modesty, he has taken a most becoming care; for his amorous
expressions go no further than virtue may allow, and therefore
may be read, as he intended them, by matrons without a blush.

Thus much concerning the Poet, whom you find translated
by divers hands, that you may at least have that variety in the
English which the subject denied to the author of the Latin: it
remains that I should say somewhat of Poetical Translations in

general, and give my opinion (with submission to better judgments) which way of version seems to be the most proper.

All translation, I suppose, may be reduced to these three heads.

First, that of metaphrase, or turning an author word by word, and line by line, from one language into another. Thus, or near this manner, was Horace his *Art of Poetry* translated by Ben Jonson. The second way is that of paraphrase, or translation with latitude, where the author is kept in view by the translator, so as never to be lost, but his words are not so strictly followed as his sense; and that too is admitted to be amplified, but not altered. Such is Mr. Waller's translation of Virgil's Fourth *Æneid*. The third way is that of imitation, where the translator (if now he has not lost that name) assumes the liberty not only to vary from the words and sense, but to forsake them both as he sees occasion; and taking only some general hints from the original, to run division on the groundwork, as he pleases. Such is Mr. Cowley's practice in turning two Odes of Pindar, and one of Horace, into English.

Concerning the first of these methods, our master Horace has given us this caution:

> Nec verbum verbo curabis reddere, fidus
> Interpres . . .
>
> Nor word for word too faithfully translate;

as the Earl of Roscommon has excellently rendered it. Too faithfully is, indeed, pedantically: 'tis a faith like that which proceeds from superstition, blind and zealous. Take it in the expression of Sir John Denham to Sir Richard Fanshaw, on his version of the *Pastor Fido* :—

> That servile path thou nobly dost decline,
> Of tracing word by word, and line by line:
> A new and nobler way thou dost pursue,
> To make translations and translators too:
> They but preserve the ashes, thou the flame,
> True to his sense, but truer to his fame.

'Tis almost impossible to translate verbally, and well, at the same time; for the Latin (a most severe and compendious language) often expresses that in one word which either the barbarity or the narrowness of modern tongues cannot supply in more. 'Tis frequent, also, that the conceit is couched in some expression which will be lost in English:—

> Atque iidem venti vela fidemque ferent.

What poet of our nation is so happy as to express this thought literally in English, and to strike wit, or almost sense, out of it?

In short, the verbal copier is encumbered with so many difficulties at once, that he can never disentangle himself from all. He is to consider, at the same time, the thought of his author, and his words, and to find out the counterpart to each in another language; and, besides this, he is to confine himself to the compass of numbers, and the slavery of rhyme. 'Tis much like dancing on ropes with fettered legs: a man may shun a fall by using caution; but the gracefulness of motion is not to be expected: and when we have said the best of it, 'tis but a foolish task; for no sober man would put himself into a danger for the applause of escaping without breaking his neck. We see Ben Jonson could not avoid obscurity in his literal translation of Horace, attempted in the same compass of lines: nay, Horace himself could scarce have done it to a Greek poet:—

> Brevis esse laboro, obscurus fio:

either perspicuity or gracefulness will frequently be wanting. Horace has indeed avoided both these rocks in his translation of the three first lines of Homer's *Odysseis*, which he has contracted into two:—

> Dic mihi musa virum captæ post tempora Trojæ,
> Qui mores hominum multorum vidit, et urbes.
>
> Muse, speak the man, who, since the siege of Troy,
> So many towns, such change of manners saw.
>
> EARL OF ROSCOMMON.

But then the sufferings of Ulysses, which are a considerable part of that sentence, are omitted:—

> Ὅς μάλα πολλὰ πλάγχθη.

The consideration of these difficulties, in a servile, literal translation, not long since made two of our famous wits, Sir John Denham and Mr. Cowley, to contrive another way of turning authors into our tongue, called, by the latter of them, imitation. As they were friends, I suppose they communicated their thoughts on this subject to each other; and therefore their reasons for it are little different, though the practice of one is much more moderate. I take imitation of an author, in their sense, to be an endeavour of a later poet to write like one who has written before him, on the same subject; that is, not to translate his words, or be confined to his sense, but only to set him as a pattern, and to write as he supposes that author would have done, had he lived in our age, and in our country. Yet I dare not say that either of them have carried this libertine way of rendering authors (as Mr. Cowley calls it) so far as my definition reaches; for in the *Pindaric Odes*, the customs and ceremonies of ancient Greece are still preserved. But I know not what mischief may arise hereafter from the example of such an innovation, when writers of unequal parts to him shall imitate so bold an undertaking. To add and to diminish what we please, which is the way avowed by him, ought only to be granted to Mr. Cowley, and that too only in his translation of Pindar; because he alone was able to make him amends, by giving him better of his own, whenever he refused his author's thoughts. Pindar is generally known to be a dark writer, to want connection (I mean as to our understanding), to soar out of sight, and leave his reader at a gaze. So wild and ungovernable a poet cannot be translated literally; his genius is too strong to bear a chair, and Samson-like he shakes it off. A genius so elevated and unconfined as Mr. Cowley's was but necessary to make Pindar speak English, and that was to be performed by no other way than imitation. But if Virgil, or Ovid, or any regular intelligible authors, be thus used, 'tis no longer to be called their work, when neither the thoughts nor words are drawn from the original; but instead of them there is something new produced, which is almost the creation of another hand. By this way, 'tis true, somewhat that is excellent may be invented, perhaps more excellent than the first design; though Virgil must be still excepted, when that *perhaps* takes place. Yet he who is inquisitive to know an author's thoughts will be disappointed in his expectation; and 'tis not always that a man will be contented to have a present made him, when he expects the payment of a debt. To state it fairly; imitation of an author is the most advantageous way for a translator to show himself, but the greatest wrong which can be done to the memory and reputation of the dead. Sir John Denham (who advised more liberty than he took himself) gives his reason for his innovation, in his admirable Preface before the translation of the Second *Æneid*: *Poetry is of so subtile a spirit, that, in pouring out of one language into another, it will all evaporate ; and, if a new spirit be not added in the transfusion, there will remain nothing but a* caput mortuum. I confess this argument holds good against a literal translation; but who defends it? Imitation and verbal version are, in my opinion, the two extremes which ought to be avoided; and therefore, when I have proposed the mean betwixt them, it will be seen how far his argument will reach.

No man is capable of translating poetry who, besides a genius to that art, is not a master both of his author's language, and of his own; nor must we understand the language only of the poet, but his particular turn of thoughts and expression, which are the characters that distinguish, and, as it were, individuate him from all other writers. When we are come thus far, 'tis time to look into ourselves, to conform our genius to his, to give his thought either the same turn, if our tongue will bear it, or, if not, to vary but the dress, not to alter or destroy the substance. The like care must be taken of the more outward ornaments, the words. When they appear (which is but seldom) literally graceful, it were an injury to the author that they should be changed. But since every language is so full of its own proprieties, that what is beautiful in one is often barbarous, nay sometimes nonsense, in another, it would be unreasonable to limit a translator to the narrow compass of his author's words: 'tis enough if he choose out some expression which does not vitiate the sense. I suppose he may stretch his chain to such a latitude; but by innovation of thoughts, methinks he breaks it. By this means the spirit of an author may be transfused, and yet not lost: and thus 'tis plain, that the reason alleged by Sir John Denham has no farther force than to expression; for thought, if it be translated truly, cannot be lost in another language; but the words that convey it to our apprehension (which are the image and ornament of that thought) may be so ill chosen as to make it appear in an unhandsome dress, and rob it of its native lustre. There is, therefore, a liberty to be allowed for the expression; neither is it necessary that words and lines should be confined to the measure of their original. The sense of an author, generally speaking, is to be sacred and inviolable. If the fancy of Ovid be luxuriant, 'tis his character to be so; and if I retrench it, he is no longer Ovid. It will be replied that he receives advantage by this lopping of his superfluous branches; but I rejoin that a translator has no such right. When a painter copies from the life, I suppose he has no privilege to alter features and lineaments, under pretence that his picture will look better: perhaps the face which he has drawn would be more exact, if the eyes or nose were altered; but 'tis his business to make it resemble the original. In two cases only there may a seeming difficulty arise; that is, if the thought be notoriously trivial or dishonest; but the same answer will serve for both, that then they ought not to be translated:—

Et quæ
Desperes tractata nitescere posse, relinquas.

Thus I have ventured to give my opinion on this subject against the authority of two great men, but I hope without offence to either of their memories; for I both loved them living, and reverence them now they are dead. But if, after what I have urged, it be thought by better judges that the praise of a translation consists in adding new beauties to the piece, thereby to recompense the loss which it sustains by change of language, I shall be willing to be taught better, and to recant. In the meantime it seems to me that the true reason why we have so few versions which are tolerable, is not from the too close pursuing of the author's sense, but because there are so few who have all the talents which are requisite for translation, and that there is so little praise and so small encouragement for so considerable a part of learning.

To apply, in short, what has been said to this present work, the reader will here find most of the Translations with some little latitude or variation from the author's sense. That of *Œnone to Paris* is in Mr. Cowley's way of imitation only. I was desired to say that the author, who is of the fair sex, understood not Latin. But if she does not, I am afraid she has given us occasion to be ashamed who do.

For my own part, I am ready to acknowledge that I have transgressed the rules which I have given; and taken more liberty than a just translation will allow. But so many gentlemen whose wit and learning are well known being joined in it, I doubt not but that their excellencies will make you ample satisfaction for my errors.

NATURE AND DRAMATIC ART

TO THE RIGHT HONOURABLE

JOHN, LORD HAUGHTON

Epistle Dedicatory to " The Spanish Friar ; or, the Double Discovery" (1681)

MY LORD,—When I first designed this play, I found, or thought I found, somewhat so moving in the serious part of it, and so pleasant in the comic, as might deserve a more than ordinary care in both; accordingly, I used the best of my endeavour, in the management of two plots, so very different from each other, that it was not perhaps the talent of every writer to have made them of a piece. Neither have I attempted other plays of the same nature, in my opinion, with the same judgment, though with like success. And though many poets may suspect themselves for the fondness and partiality of parents to their youngest children, yet I hope I may stand exempted from this rule, because I know myself too well to be ever satisfied with my own conceptions, which have seldom reached to those ideas that I had within me; and consequently, I presume I may have liberty to judge when I write more or less pardonably, as an ordinary marksman may know certainly when he shoots less wide at what he aims. Besides, the care and pains I have bestowed on this, beyond my other tragi-comedies, may reasonably make the world conclude that either I can do nothing tolerably, or that this poem is not much amiss. Few good pictures have been finished at one sitting; neither can a true just play, which is to bear the test of ages, be produced at a heat, or by the force of fancy, without the maturity of judgment. For my own part, I have both so just a diffidence of myself, and so great a reverence for my audience, that I dare venture nothing without a strict examination; and am as much ashamed to put a loose indigested play upon the public, as I should be to offer brass money in a payment; for though it should be taken (as it is too often on the stage), yet it will be found in the second telling; and a judicious reader will discover, in his closet, that trashy stuff, whose glittering deceived him in the action. I have often heard the stationer sighing in his shop, and wishing for those hands to take off his melancholy bargain which clapped its performance on the stage. In a play-house, everything contributes to impose upon the judgment; the lights, the scenes, the habits, and, above all, the grace of action, which is commonly the best where there is the most need of it, surprise the audience, and cast a mist upon their understandings; not unlike the cunning of a juggler, who is always staring us in the face, and overwhelming us with gibberish, only that he may gain the opportunity of making the cleaner conveyance of his trick. But these false beauties of the stage are no more lasting than a rainbow; when the actor ceases to shine upon them, when he gilds them no longer with his reflection, they vanish in a twinkling. I have sometimes wondered, in the reading, what was become of those glaring colours which amazed me in *Bussy D'Amboys* upon the theatre; but when I had taken up what I supposed a fallen star, I found I had been cozened with a jelly; nothing but a cold, dull mass, which glittered no longer than it was shooting; a dwarfish thought, dressed up in gigantic words, repetition in abundance, looseness of expression, and gross hyperboles; the sense of one line expanded prodigiously into ten; and, to sum up all, uncorrect English, and a hideous mingle of false poetry and true nonsense; or, at best, a scantling of wit, which lay gasping for life, and groaning beneath a heap of rubbish. A famous modern poet used to sacrifice every year a Statius to Virgil's *Manes;* and I have indignation enough to burn a *D'Amboys* annually to the memory of Jonson. But now, My Lord, I am sensible, perhaps too late, that I have gone too far: for, I remember some verses of my own, *Maximin* and *Almanzor*, which cry vengeance upon me for their extravagance, and which I wish heartily in the same fire with Statius and Chapman. All I can say for those passages, which are, I hope, not many, is, that I knew they were bad enough to please, even when I writ them; but I repent of them amongst my sins; and if any of their fellows intrude by chance into my present writings, I draw a stroke over all those Delilahs of the theatre; and am resolved I will settle myself no reputation by the applause of fools. 'Tis not that I am mortified to all ambition, but I scorn as much to take it from half-witted judges, as I should to raise an estate by cheating of bubbles. Neither do I discommend the lofty style in Tragedy, which is naturally pompous and magnificent; but nothing is truly sublime that is not just and proper. If the Ancients had judged by the same measures which a common reader takes, they had concluded Statius to have written higher than Virgil, for,

> Quæ superimposito moles geminata Colosso

carries a more thundering kind of sound than

> Tityre tu patulæ recubans sub tegmine fagi:

yet Virgil had all the majesty of a lawful prince, and Statius only the blustering of a tyrant. But when men affect a virtue which they cannot easily reach, they fall into a vice which bears the nearest resemblance to it. Thus an injudicious poet who aims at loftiness runs easily into the swelling puffy style, because it looks like greatness. I remember, when I was a boy, I thought inimitable Spenser a mean poet in comparison of Sylvester's *Dubartas*, and was rapt into an ecstasy when I read these lines:—

> Now when the Winter's keener breath began
> To chrystallise the Baltic Ocean;
> To glaze the Lakes, to bridle up the Floods,
> And periwig with Snow the bald-pate Woods.

I am much deceived if this be not abominable fustian, that is, thoughts and words ill-sorted, and without the least relation to each other; yet I dare not answer for an audience, that they would not clap it on the stage: so little value there is to be given to the common cry, that nothing but madness can please madmen, and a poet must be of a piece with the spectators to gain a reputation with them. But as in a room contrived for state, the height of the roof should bear a proportion to the area; so, in the heightenings of Poetry, the strength and vehemence of figures should be suited to the occasion, the subject, and the persons. All beyond this is monstrous: 'tis out of Nature, 'tis an excrescence, and not a living part of Poetry. I had not said thus much if some young gallants who pretend to criticism had not told me that this tragi-comedy wanted the dignity of style; but as a man who is charged with a crime of which he thinks himself innocent is apt to be too eager in his own defence, so perhaps I have vindicated my play with more partiality than I ought, or than such a trifle can deserve. Yet, whatever beauties it may want, 'tis free at least from the grossness of those faults I mentioned: what credit it has gained upon the stage I value no further than in reference to my profit, and the satisfaction I had in seeing it represented with all the justness and gracefulness of action. But, as 'tis my interest to please my audience, so 'tis my ambition to be read: that I am sure is the more lasting and the nobler design: for the propriety of thoughts and words, which are the hidden beauties of a play, are but confusedly judged in the vehemence of action: all things are there beheld as in a hasty motion, where the objects only glide before the eye and disappear. The most discerning critic can judge no more of these silent graces in the action than he who rides post through an unknown country can distinguish the situation of places, and the nature of the soil. The purity of phrase, the clearness of conception and expression, the boldness maintained to majesty, the significancy and sound of words, not strained into bombast, but justly elevated; in short, those very words and thoughts, which cannot be changed, but for the worse, must of necessity escape our transient view upon the theatre; and yet without all these a play may take. For if either the story move us, or the actor help the lameness of it with his performance, or now and then a glittering beam of wit or passion strike through the obscurity of the poem, any of these are sufficient to effect a present liking, but not to fix a lasting admiration; for nothing but truth can long continue; and time is the surest judge of truth. I am not vain enough to think I have left no faults in this, which that touchstone will not discover; neither indeed is it possible to avoid them in a play of this nature. There are evidently two actions in it; but it will be clear to any judicious man, that with half the pains I could have raised a play from either of them; for this time I satisfied my own humour, which was to tack two plays together; and to break a rule for the pleasure of variety. The truth is, the audience are grown weary of continued melancholy scenes; and I dare venture to prophesy that few tragedies except those in verse shall succeed in this age if they are not lightened with a course of mirth. For the feast is too dull and solemn without the fiddles. But how difficult a task this is will soon be tried; for a several genius is required to either way; and, without both of 'em, a man, in my opinion, is but half a poet for the stage. Neither is it so trivial an undertaking to make a tragedy end happily; for 'tis more difficult to save than 'tis to kill. The dagger and the cup of poison are always in a readiness; but to bring the action to the last extremity, and then by probable means to recover all, will require the art and judgment of a writer, and cost him many a pang in the performance.

And now, My Lord, I must confess, that what I have written looks more like a preface than a dedication; and truly it was thus far my design, that I might entertain you with somewhat in my own art which might be more worthy of a noble mind than the stale exploded trick of fulsome panegyrics. 'Tis difficult to write justly on anything, but almost impossible in praise. I shall therefore waive so nice a subject; and only tell you, that, in recommending a Protestant play to a Protestant patron, as I do myself an honour, so I do your noble family a right, who have been always eminent in the support and favour of our religion and liberties. And if the promises of your youth, your education at home, and your experience abroad, deceive me not, the principles you have embraced are such as will no way degenerate from your ancestors, but refresh their memory in the minds of all true Englishmen, and renew their lustre in your person; which, My Lord, is not more the wish than it is the constant expectation of your Lordship's

Most obedient,
faithful Servant,
JOHN DRYDEN.

PREFACE TO SYLVÆ

OR

THE SECOND PART OF "POETICAL MISCELLANIES"
(1685)

FOR this last half year I have been troubled with the disease
(as I may call it) of translation; the cold prose fits of it, which are
always the most tedious with me, were spent in the *History of
the League*: the hot, which succeeded them, in this volume of
Verse Miscellanies. The truth is, I fancied to myself a kind
of ease in the change of the paroxysm; never suspecting but
that the humour would have wasted itself in two or three
Pastorals of Theocritus, and as many *Odes* of Horace. But
finding, or at least thinking I found, something that was more
pleasing in them than my ordinary productions, I encouraged
myself to renew my old acquaintance with Lucretius and Virgil;
and immediately fixed upon some parts of them, which had most
affected me in the reading. These were my natural impulses
for the undertaking. But there was an accidental motive
which was full as forcible, and God forgive him who was the
occasion of it. It was my Lord Roscommon's *Essay on Translated Verse* which made me uneasy till I tried whether or no
I was capable of following his rules, and of reducing the specu-
lation into practice. For many a fair precept in poetry is, like
a seeming demonstration in the mathematics, very specious
in the diagram, but failing in the mechanic operation. I think
I have generally observed his instructions; I am sure my reason
is sufficiently convinced both of their truth and usefulness;
which, in other words, is to confess no less a vanity than to
pretend that I have at least in some places made examples to
his rules. Yet withal, I must acknowledge that I have many
times exceeded my commission; for I have both added and
omitted, and even sometimes very boldly made such expositions
of my authors, as no Dutch commentator will forgive me.
Perhaps, in such particular passages, I have thought that I
discovered some beauty yet undiscovered by those pedants,
which none but a poet could have found. Where I have taken

away some of their expressions, and cut them shorter, it may possibly be on this consideration, that what was beautiful in the Greek or Latin would not appear so shining in the English: and where I have enlarged them, I desire the false critics would not always think that those thoughts are wholly mine, but that either they are secretly in the poet, or may be fairly deduced from him; or at least, if both those considerations should fail, that my own is of a piece with his, and that if he were living, and an Englishman, they are such as he would probably have written.

For, after all, a translator is to make his author appear as charming as possibly he can, provided he maintains his character, and makes him not unlike himself. Translation is a kind of drawing after the life; where every one will acknowledge there is a double sort of likeness, a good one and a bad. 'Tis one thing to draw the outlines true, the features like, the proportions exact, the colouring itself perhaps tolerable; and another thing to make all these graceful, by the posture, the shadowings, and, chiefly, by the spirit which animates the whole. I cannot, without some indignation, look on an ill copy of an excellent original; much less can I behold with patience Virgil, Homer, and some others, whose beauties I have been endeavouring all my life to imitate, so abused, as I may say, to their faces, by a botching interpreter. What English readers, unacquainted with Greek or Latin, will believe me, or any other man, when we commend those authors, and confess we derive all that is pardonable in us from their fountains, if they take those to be the same poets whom our Oglebys have translated? But I dare assure them, that a good poet is no more like himself in a dull translation than his carcass would be to his living body. There are many who understand Greek and Latin, and yet are ignorant of their mother-tongue. The proprieties and delicacies of the English are known to few; 'tis impossible even for a good wit to understand and practise them, without the help of a liberal education, long reading, and digesting of those few good authors we have amongst us, the knowledge of men and manners, the freedom of habitudes and conversation with the best company of both sexes; and, in short, without wearing off the rust which he contracted while he was laying in a stock of learning. Thus difficult it is to understand the purity of English, and critically to discern not only good writers from bad, and a proper style from a corrupt, but also to distinguish that which is pure in a good author from that which is vicious and corrupt in him.

And for want of all these requisites, or the greatest part of them, most of our ingenious young men take up some cried-up English poet for their model, adore him, and imitate him, as they think, without knowing wherein he is defective, where he is boyish and trifling, wherein either his thoughts are improper to his subject, or his expressions unworthy of his thoughts, or the turn of both is unharmonious. Thus it appears necessary that a man should be a nice critic in his mother-tongue before he attempts to translate a foreign language. Neither is it sufficient that he be able to judge of words and style, but he must be a master of them too; he must perfectly understand his author's tongue and absolutely command his own. So that to be a thorough translator he must be a thorough poet. Neither is it enough to give his author's sense in good English, in poetical expressions, and in musical numbers; for though all these are exceeding difficult to perform, there yet remains an harder task; and 'tis a secret of which few translators have sufficiently thought. I have already hinted a word or two concerning it; that is, the maintaining the character of an author, which distinguishes him from all others, and makes him appear that individual poet whom you would interpret. For example, not only the thoughts, but the style and versification of Virgil and Ovid are very different: yet I see, even in our best poets who have translated some parts of them, that they have confounded their several talents, and, by endeavouring only at the sweetness and harmony of numbers, have made them both so much alike that, if I did not know the originals, I should never be able to judge by the copies which was Virgil and which was Ovid. It was objected against a late noble painter that he drew many graceful pictures, but few of them were like. And this happened to him because he always studied himself more than those who sat to him. In such translators I can easily distinguish the hand which performed the work, but I cannot distinguish their poet from another. Suppose two authors are equally sweet, yet there is a great distinction to be made in sweetness, as in that of sugar and that of honey. I can make the difference more plain by giving you (if it be worth knowing) my own method of proceeding in my translations out of four several poets in this volume; Virgil, Theocritus, Lucretius, and Horace. In each of these, before I undertook them, I considered the genius and distinguishing character of my author. I looked on Virgil as a succinct and grave majestic writer; one who weighed not only every thought, but every word and syllable;

who was still aiming to crowd his sense into as narrow a compass as possibly he could; for which reason he is so very figurative that he requires (I may almost say) a grammar apart to construe him. His verse is everywhere sounding the very thing in your ears whose sense it bears, yet the numbers are perpetually varied to increase the delight of the reader; so that the same sounds are never repeated twice together. On the contrary, Ovid and Claudian, though they write in styles differing from each other, yet have each of them but one sort of music in their verses. All the versification and little variety of Claudian is included within the compass of four or five lines, and then he begins again in the same tenor; perpetually closing his sense at the end of a verse, and that verse commonly which they call golden, or two substantives and two adjectives, with a verb betwixt them to keep the peace. Ovid, with all his sweetness, has as little variety of numbers and sound as he: he is always, as it were, upon the hand-gallop, and his verse runs upon carpet-ground. He avoids, like the other, all synalœphas, or cutting off one vowel when it comes before another in the following word; so that, minding only smoothness, he wants both variety and majesty. But to return to Virgil: though he is smooth where smoothness is required, yet he is so far from affecting it that he seems rather to disdain it; frequently makes use of synalœphas, and concludes his sense in the middle of his verse. He is everywhere above conceits of epigrammatic wit and gross hyperboles; he maintains majesty in the midst of plainness; he shines, but glares not; and is stately without ambition, which is the vice of Lucan. I drew my definition of poetical wit from my particular consideration of him: for propriety of thoughts and words are only to be found in him; and where they are proper they will be delightful. Pleasure follows of necessity as the effect does the cause, and therefore is not to be put into the definition. This exact propriety of Virgil I particularly regarded as a great part of his character; but must confess, to my shame, that I have not been able to translate any part of him so well as to make him appear wholly like himself. For where the original is close no version can reach it in the same compass. Hannibal Caro's, in the Italian, is the nearest, the most poetical, and the most sonorous of any translation of the *Æneids;* yet, though he takes the advantage of blank verse, he commonly allows two lines for one of Virgil, and does not always hit his sense. Tasso tells us, in his letters, that Sperone Speroni, a great Italian wit, who was his contemporary, observed of Virgil and Tully, that the Latin orator endeavoured to imitate the copiousness of Homer, the Greek poet; and that the Latin poet made it his business to reach the conciseness of Demosthenes, the Greek orator. Virgil therefore, being so very sparing of his words, and leaving so much to be imagined by the reader, can never be translated as he ought in any modern tongue. To make him copious is to alter his character; and to translate him line for line is impossible, because the Latin is naturally a more succinct language than either the Italian, Spanish, French, or even than the English, which, by reason of its monosyllables, is far the most compendious of them. Virgil is much the closest of any Roman poet, and the Latin hexameter has more feet than the English heroic.

Besides all this, an author has the choice of his own thoughts and words, which a translator has not; he is confined by the sense of the inventor to those expressions which are the nearest to it: so that Virgil, studying brevity, and having the command of his own language, could bring those words into a narrow compass, which a translator cannot render without circumlocutions. In short, they who have called him the torture of grammarians, might also have called him the plague of translators; for he seems to have studied not to be translated. I own that, endeavouring to turn his *Nisus and Euryalus* as close as I was able, I have performed that episode too literally; that giving more scope to *Mezentius and Lausus*, that version, which has more of the majesty of Virgil, has less of his conciseness; and all that I can promise for myself is only that I have done both better than Ogleby, and perhaps as well as Caro; so that, methinks, I come like a malefactor, to make a speech upon the gallows, and to warn all other poets, by my sad example, from the sacrilege of translating Virgil. Yet, by considering him so carefully as I did before my attempt, I have made some faint resemblance of him; and had I taken more time, might possibly have succeeded better; but never so well as to have satisfied myself.

He who excels all other poets in his own language, were it possible to do him right, must appear above them in our tongue, which, as my Lord Roscommon justly observes, approaches nearest to the Roman in its majesty; nearest indeed, but with a vast interval betwixt them. There is an inimitable grace in Virgil's words, and in them principally consists that beauty which gives so unexpressible a pleasure to him who best understands their force. This diction of his, I must once again say, is never to be copied; and, since it cannot, he will appear but lame in the best translation. The turns of his verse, his breakings, his propriety, his numbers, and his gravity, I have as far imitated as the poverty of our language and the hastiness of my performance would allow. I may seem sometimes to have varied from his sense; but I think the greatest variations may be fairly deduced from him; and where I leave his commentators, it may be I understand him better: at least I writ without consulting them in many places. But two particular lines in *Mezentius and Lausus* I cannot so easily excuse. They are indeed remotely allied to Virgil's sense, but they are too like the trifling tenderness of Ovid, and were printed before I had considered them enough to alter them. The first of them I have forgotten, and cannot easily retrieve, because the copy is at the press. The second is this:

> When Lausus died, I was already slain.

This appears pretty enough at first sight; but I am convinced, for many reasons, that the expression is too bold; that Virgil would not have said it, though Ovid would. The reader may pardon it, if he please, for the freeness of the confession; and instead of that, and the former, admit these two lines, which are more according to the author—

> Nor ask I life, nor fought with that design;
> As I had used my fortune, use thou thine.

Having with much ado got clear of Virgil, I have, in the next place, to consider the genius of Lucretius, whom I have translated more happily in those parts of him which I undertook. If he was not of the best age of Roman poetry, he was at least of that which preceded it; and he himself refined it to that degree of perfection, both in the language and the thoughts, that he left an easy task to Virgil; who, as he succeeded him in time, so he copied his excellencies; for the method of the *Georgics* is plainly derived from him. Lucretius had chosen a subject naturally crabbed; he therefore adorned it with poetical descriptions, and precepts of morality, in the beginning and ending of his books; which you see Virgil has imitated with great success in those four books, which, in my opinion, are more perfect in their kind than even his divine *Æneids*. The turn of his verse he has likewise followed in those places which Lucretius has most laboured, and some of his very lines he has transplanted into his own works without much variation. If I am not mistaken, the distinguishing character of Lucretius (I mean of his soul and genius) is a certain kind of noble pride and positive assertion of his opinions. He is everywhere confident of his own reason, and assuming an absolute command, not only over his vulgar reader, but even his patron Memmius. For he is always bidding him attend as if he had the rod over him, and using a magisterial authority while he instructs him. From his time to ours, I know none so like him as our poet and philosopher of Malmesbury. This is that perpetual dictatorship which is exercised by Lucretius; who, though often in the wrong, yet seems to deal *bonâ fide* with his reader, and tells him nothing but what he thinks; in which plain sincerity, I believe, he differs from our Hobbes, who could not but be convinced, or at least doubt, of some eternal truths which he had opposed. But for Lucretius, he seems to disdain all manner of replies, and is so confident of his cause that he is beforehand with his antagonists; urging for them whatever he imagined they could say, and leaving them, as he supposes, without an objection for the future. All this, too, with so much scorn and indignation as if he were assured of the triumph before he entered into the lists. From this sublime and daring genius of his, it must of necessity come to pass that his thoughts must be masculine, full of argumentation, and that sufficiently warm. From the same fiery temper proceeds the loftiness of his expressions and the perpetual torrent of his verse, where the barrenness of his subject does not too much constrain the quickness of his fancy. For there is no doubt to be made but that he could have been everywhere as poetical as he is in his descriptions, and in the moral part of his philosophy, if he had not aimed more to instruct in his System of Nature than to delight. But he was bent upon making Memmius a materialist, and teaching him to defy an invisible power: in short, he was so much an atheist that he forgot sometimes to be a poet. These are the considerations which I had of that author before I attempted to translate some parts of him. And accordingly I laid by my natural diffidence and scepticism for a while to take up that dogmatical way of his, which, as I said, is so much his character as to make him that individual poet. As for his opinions concerning the mortality of the soul, they are so absurd that I cannot, if I would, believe them. I think a future state demonstrable even by natural arguments; at least to take away rewards and punishments is only a pleasing prospect to a man who resolves beforehand not to live morally. But on the other side, the thought of being nothing after death is a burden unsupportable to a virtuous man, even though a heathen. We naturally aim at happiness, and cannot bear to have it confined to the shortness of our present being, especially when we consider that virtue is generally unhappy in this world, and vice fortunate. So that 'tis hope of futurity alone that makes this life tolerable, in expectation of a better. Who would not commit all the excesses to which he is prompted by his natural inclinations if he may do them with security while he is alive and be incapable of punishment after he is dead? If he be cunning and secret enough to avoid the laws, there is no band of morality to restrain him: for fame and reputation are weak ties; many men have not the least sense of them; powerful men are only awed by them as they conduce to their interest, and that not always when a passion is predominant; and no man will be contained within the bounds of duty when he may safely transgress them. These are my thoughts abstractedly, and without entering into the notions of our Christian faith, which is the proper business of divines.

But there are other arguments in this poem (which I have turned into English) not belonging to the mortality of the soul which are strong enough to a reasonable man to make him less in love with life and consequently in less apprehensions of death. Such as are the natural satiety proceeding from a perpetual enjoyment of the same things; the inconveniencies of old age, which make him incapable of corporeal pleasures; the decay of understanding and memory, which render him contemptible and useless to others. These, and many other reasons, so pathetically urged, so beautifully expressed, so adorned with examples, and so admirably raised by the *prosopopœia* of Nature, who is brought in speaking to her children with so much authority and vigour, deserve the pains I have taken with them, which I hope have not been unsuccessful, or unworthy of my author: at least I must take the liberty to own that I was pleased with my own endeavours, which but rarely happens to me; and that I am not dissatisfied upon the review of anything I have done in this author.

It is true, there is something, and that of some moment, to be objected against my Englishing the *Nature of Love*, from the fourth book of Lucretius; and I can less easily answer why I translated it than why I thus translated it. The objection arises from the obscenity of the subject, which is aggravated by the too lively and alluring delicacy of the verses. In the first place, without the least formality of an excuse, I own it pleased me; and let my enemies make the worst they can of this confession. I am not yet so secure from that passion but that I want my author's antidotes against it. He has given the truest and most philosophical account, both of the disease and remedy, which I ever found in any author; for which reasons I translated him. But it will be asked why I turned him into this luscious English, for I will not give it a worse word. Instead of an answer, I would ask again of my supercilious adversaries whether I am not bound, when I translate an author, to do him all the right I can, and to translate him to the best advantage? If, to mince his meaning, which I am satisfied was honest and instructive, I had either omitted some part of what he said, or taken from the strength of his expression, I certainly had wronged him; and that freeness of thought and words being thus cashiered in my hands he had no longer been Lucretius. If nothing of this kind be to be read, physicians must not study nature, anatomies must not be seen, and somewhat I could say of particular passages in books which, to avoid profaneness, I do not name. But the intention qualifies the act; and both mine and my author's were to instruct, as well as please. 'Tis most certain that barefaced bawdry is the poorest pretence to wit imaginable. If I should say otherwise, I should have two great authorities against me: the one is the *Essay on Poetry*, which I publicly valued before I knew the author of it, and with the commendation of which my Lord Roscommon so happily begins his *Essay on Translated Verse;* the other is no less than our admired Cowley, who says the same thing in other words; for, in his *Ode concerning Wit*, he writes thus of it:—

> Much less can that have any place,
> At which a virgin hides her face;
> Such dross the fire must purge away; 'tis just
> The author blush, there where the reader must.

Here indeed Mr. Cowley goes further than the *Essay:* for he asserts plainly that obscenity has no place in wit; the other only says 'tis a poor pretence to it, or an ill sort of wit, which has nothing more to support it than barefaced ribaldry; which is both unmannerly in itself and fulsome to the reader. But neither of these will reach my case: for, in the first place, I am only the translator, not the inventor; so that the heaviest part of the censure falls upon Lucretius before it reaches me: in the next place, neither he nor I have used the grossest words, but the cleanliest metaphors we could find to palliate the broadness of the meaning; and, to conclude, have carried the poetical part no further than the philosophical exacted.

There is one mistake of mine which I will not lay to the printer's charge, who has enough to answer for in false pointings; it is in the word *viper ;* I would have the verse run thus—

> The scorpion, love, must on the wound be bruised.

There are a sort of blundering, half-witted people who make a great deal of noise about a verbal slip; though Horace would instruct them better in true criticism—

> non ego paucis
> Offendar maculis, quas aut incuria fudit,
> Aut humana parum cavit natura.

True judgment in Poetry, like that in Painting, takes a view of the whole together, whether it be good or not; and where the beauties are more than the faults, concludes for the poet against the little judge; 'tis a sign that malice is hard driven, when 'tis forced to lay hold on a word or syllable; to arraign a man is one thing, and to cavil at him is another. In the midst of an ill-natured generation of scribblers, there is always justice enough left in mankind to protect good writers: and they too are obliged, both by humanity and interest, to espouse each other's cause against false critics, who are the common enemies. This last consideration puts me in mind of what I owe to the ingenious and learned translator of Lucretius. I have not here designed to rob him of any part of that commendation which he has so justly acquired by the whole author, whose fragments only fall to my portion. What I have now performed is no more than I intended above twenty years ago. The ways of our translation are very different. He follows him more closely than I have done, which became an interpreter of the whole poem: I take more liberty, because it best suited with my design, which was to make him as pleasing as I could. He had been too voluminous had he used my method in so long a work; and I had certainly taken his had I made it my business to translate the whole. The preference, then, is justly his; and I join with Mr. Evelyn in the confession of it, with this additional advantage to him, that his reputation is already established in this poet; mine is to make its fortune in the world. If I have been any-where obscure, in following our common author, or if Lucretius himself is to be condemned, I refer myself to his excellent annotations, which I have often read, and always with some new pleasure.

My Preface begins already to swell upon me, and looks as if I were afraid of my reader, by so tedious a bespeaking of him; and yet I have Horace and Theocritus upon my hands; but the Greek gentleman shall quickly be dispatched, because I have more business with the Roman.

That which distinguishes Theocritus from all other poets, both Greek and Latin, and which raises him even above Virgil in his *Eclogues,* is the inimitable tenderness of his passions, and the natural expression of them in words so becoming of a pastoral. A simplicity shines through all he writes: he shows his art and learning by disguising both. His shepherds never rise above their country education in their complaints of love: there is the same difference betwixt him and Virgil as there is betwixt Tasso's *Aminta* and the *Pastor Fido* of Guarini. Virgil's shepherds are too well read in the philosophy of Epicurus and of Plato, and Guarini's seem to have been bred in courts; but Theocritus and Tasso have taken theirs from cottages and plains. It was said of Tasso, in relation to his similitudes, *mai esce del bosco :* that he never departed from the woods; that is, all his comparisons were taken from the country. The same may be said of our Theocritus: he is softer than Ovid; he touches the passions more delicately, and performs all this out of his own fond, without diving into the arts and sciences for a supply. Even his Doric dialect has an incomparable sweetness in its clownishness, like a fair shepherdess in her country russet, talking in a Yorkshire tone. This was impossible for Virgil to imitate; because the severity of the Roman language denied him that advantage. Spenser has endeavoured it in his *Shepherd's Calendar;* but neither will it succeed in English; for which reason I forbore to attempt it. For Theocritus writ to Sicilians, who spoke that dialect; and I direct this part of my translations to our ladies, who neither understand, nor will take pleasure in such homely expressions. I proceed to Horace.

Take him in parts, and he is chiefly to be considered in his three different talents, as he was a critic, a satirist, and a writer of odes. His morals are uniform, and run through all of them; for let his Dutch commentators say what they will, his philosophy was Epicurean; and he made use of Gods and Providence only to serve a turn in Poetry. But since neither his Criticisms, which are the most instructive of any that are written in this art, nor his Satires, which are incomparably beyond Juvenal's (if to laugh and rally is to be preferred to railing and declaiming), are no part of my present undertaking, I confine myself wholly to his Odes. These are also of several sorts: some of them are panegyrical, others moral, the rest jovial, or (if I may so call them) Bacchanalian. As difficult as he makes it, and as indeed it is, to imitate Pindar, yet, in his most elevated flights, and in the sudden changes of his subject with almost imperceptible connections, that Theban poet is his master. But Horace is of the more bounded fancy, and confines himself strictly to one sort of verse, or stanza, in every Ode. That which will distinguish his style from all other poets is the elegance of his words and the numerousness of his verse; there is nothing so delicately turned in all the Roman language. There appears in every part of his diction, or (to speak English) in all his expressions, a kind of noble and bold purity. His words are chosen with as much exactness as Virgil's; but there seems to be a greater spirit in them. There is a secret happiness attends his choice, which in Petronius is called *curiosa felicitas*, and which I suppose he had from the *feliciter audere* of Horace himself. But the most distinguishing part of all his character seems to me to be his briskness, his jollity, and his good humour; and those I have chiefly endeavoured to copy; his other excellencies, I confess, are above my imitation. One Ode, which infinitely pleased me in the reading, I have attempted to translate in Pindaric verse: 'tis that which is inscribed to the present Earl of Rochester, to whom I have particular obligations which this small testimony of my gratitude can never pay. 'Tis his darling in the Latin, and I have taken some pains to make it my masterpiece in English: for which reason I took this kind of verse, which allows more latitude than any other. Every one knows it was introduced into our language, in this age, by the happy genius of Mr. Cowley. The seeming easiness of it has made it spread; but it has not been considered enough, to be so well cultivated. It languishes in almost every hand but his, and some very few whom (to keep the rest in countenance) I do not name. He, indeed, has brought it as near perfection as was possible in so short a time. But if I may be allowed to speak my mind modestly, and without injury to his sacred ashes, somewhat of the purity of English, somewhat of more equal thoughts, somewhat of sweetness in the numbers, in one word, somewhat of a finer turn and more lyrical verse, is yet wanting. As for the soul of it, which consists in the warmth and vigour of fancy, the masterly figures, and the copiousness of imagination, he has excelled all others in this kind. Yet if the kind itself be capable of more perfection, though rather in the ornamental parts of it than the essential, what rules of morality or respect have I broken, in naming the defects, that they may hereafter be amended? Imitation is a nice point, and there are few poets who deserve to be models in all they write. Milton's *Paradise Lost* is admirable; but am I therefore bound to maintain that there are no flats amongst his elevations, when 'tis evident he creeps along sometimes for above an hundred lines together? Cannot I admire the height of his invention, and the strength of his expression, without defending his antiquated words, and the perpetual harshness of their sound? It is as much commendation as a man can bear, to own him excellent; all beyond it is idolatry. Since Pindar was the prince of lyric poets, let me have leave to say that, in imitating him, our numbers should, for the most part, be lyrical: for variety, or rather where the majesty of thought requires it, they may be stretched to the English heroic of five feet, and to the French Alexandrine of six. But the ear must preside and direct the judgment to the choice of numbers: without the nicety of this, the harmony of Pindaric verse can never be complete; the cadency of one line must be a rule to that of the next; and the sound of the former must slide gently into that which follows, without leaping from one extreme into another. It must be done like the shadowings of a picture, which fall by degrees into a darker colour. I shall be glad, if I have so explained myself as to be understood; but if I have not, *quod nequeo dicere, et sentio tantum*, must be my excuse.

There remains much more to be said on this subject; but, to avoid envy, I will be silent. What I have said is the general opinion of the best judges, and in a manner has been forced from me, by seeing a noble sort of poetry so happily restored by one man, and so grossly copied by almost all the rest. A musical ear, and a great genius, if another Mr. Cowley could arise in another age, may bring it to perfection. In the meantime,

> fungar vice cotis, acutum
> Reddere quæ ferrum valet, expers ipsa secandi.

I hope it will not be expected from me that I should say anything of my fellow undertakers in this Miscellany. Some of them are too nearly related to me to be commended without suspicion of partiality; others I am sure need it not; and the rest I have not perused.

To conclude, I am sensible that I have written this too hastily and too loosely; I fear I have been tedious, and, which is worse,

G

it comes out from the first draught, and uncorrected. This I grant is no excuse; for it may be reasonably urged, why did he not write with more leisure, or if he had it not (which was certainly my case), why did he attempt to write on so nice a subject? The objection is unanswerable; but, in part of recompense, let me assure the reader that, in hasty productions, he is sure to meet with an author's present sense, which cooler thoughts would possibly have disguised. There is undoubtedly more of spirit, though not of judgment, in these uncorrect essays; and consequently, though my hazard be the greater, yet the reader's pleasure is not the less.

JOHN DRYDEN.

MUSICAL DRAMA

THE PREFACE TO "ALBION AND ALBANIUS," AN OPERA
(1685)

IF Wit has truly been defined, "a propriety of thoughts and words," then that definition will extend to all sorts of Poetry: and, among the rest, to this present entertainment of an opera. Propriety of thought is that fancy which arises naturally from the subject, or which the poet adapts to it. Propriety of words is the clothing of those thoughts with such expressions as are naturally proper to them; and from both these, if they are judiciously performed, the delight of poetry results. An opera is a poetical tale, or fiction, represented by vocal and instrumental music, adorned with scenes, machines, and dancing. The supposed persons of this musical drama are generally supernatural, as gods, and goddesses, and heroes, which at least are descended from them, and are in due time to be adopted into their number. The subject, therefore, being extended beyond the limits of human nature, admits of that sort of marvellous and surprising conduct which is rejected in other plays. Human impossibilities are to be received as they are in faith; because, where gods are introduced, a supreme power is to be understood, and second causes are out of doors. Yet propriety is to be observed even here. The gods are all to manage their peculiar provinces; and what was attributed by the heathens to one power ought not to be performed by any other. Phœbus must foretell, Mercury must charm with his caduceus, and Juno must reconcile the quarrels of the marriage-bed. To conclude, they must all act according to their distinct and peculiar characters. If the persons represented were to speak upon the stage, it would follow, of necessity, that the expressions should be lofty, figurative, and majestical, but the nature of an opera denies the frequent use of these poetical ornaments; for vocal music, though it often admits a loftiness of sound, yet always exacts an harmonious sweetness; or, to distinguish yet more justly, the recitative part of the opera requires a more masculine beauty of expression and sound; the other, which, for want of a proper

English word, I must call the *songish part*, must abound in the softness and variety of numbers; its principal intention being to please hearing rather than to gratify the understanding. It appears, indeed, preposterous at first sight, that rhyme, on any consideration, should take place of reason; but, in order to resolve the problem, this fundamental proposition must be settled, that the first inventors of any art or science, provided they have brought it to perfection, are, in reason, to give laws to it; and, according to their model, all after-undertakers are to build. Thus, in Epic Poetry, no man ought to dispute the authority of Homer, who gave the first being to that master-piece of art, and endued it with that form of perfection in all its parts that nothing was wanting to its excellency. Virgil there-fore, and those very few who have succeeded him, endeavoured not to introduce, or innovate, anything in a design already perfected, but imitated the plan of the inventor; and are only so far true heroic poets as they have built on the foundations of Homer. Thus, Pindar, the author of those Odes which are so admirably restored by Mr. Cowley in our language, ought for ever to be the standard of them; and we are bound, according to the practice of Horace and Mr. Cowley, to copy him. Now, to apply this axiom to our present purpose, whosoever undertakes the writing of an opera (which is a modern invention, though built indeed on the foundation of ethnic worship), is obliged to imitate the design of the Italians, who have not yet invented, but brought to perfection, this sort of dramatic musical enter-tainment. I have not been able, by any search, to get any light, either of the time when it began, or of the first author. But I have probable reasons, which induce me to believe that some Italians, having curiously observed the gallantries of the Spanish Moors, at their *zambras*, or royal feasts, where music, songs, and dancing were in perfection, together with their machines, which are usual at their *sortijas*, or running at the ring, and other solemnities, may possibly have refined upon those Moresque divertisements, and produced this delightful entertainment, by leaving out the warlike part of the carousels, and forming a poetical design for the use of the machines, the songs, and dances. But however it began (for this is only conjectural), we know that, for some centuries, the knowledge of Music has flourished principally in Italy, the mother of learning and of arts; that Poetry and Painting have been there restored and so cultivated by Italian masters that all Europe has been enriched out of their treasury; and the other parts of it, in relation to those delightful arts, are still as much provincial to Italy as they were in the time of the Roman empire. Their first operas seem to have been intended for the celebration of the marriages of their princes, or for the magnificence of some general time of joy; accordingly, the expenses of them were from the purse of the sovereign, or of the republic, as they are still practised at Venice, Rome, and at other places, at their carnivals. Savoy and Florence have often used them in their courts, at the weddings of their dukes; and at Turin particularly, was performed the *Pastor Fido*, written by the famous Guarini, which is a pastoral opera made to solemnise the marriage of a Duke of Savoy. The prologue of it has given the design to all the French; which is a compliment to the sovereign power by some god or goddess; so that it looks no less than a kind of embassy from heaven to earth. I said in the beginning of this preface that the persons represented in operas are generally gods, goddesses, and heroes descended from them, who are supposed to be their peculiar care; which hinders not but that meaner persons may sometimes gracefully be introduced, especially if they have relation to those first times, which poets call the Golden Age; wherein, by reason of their innocence, those happy mortals were supposed to have had a more familiar intercourse with superior beings; and therefore shepherds might reasonably be admitted, as of all callings the most innocent, the most happy, and who by reason of the spare time they had, in their almost idle employment, had most leisure to make verses, and to be in love; without somewhat of which passion no opera can possibly subsist.

It is almost needless to speak anything of that noble language in which this musical drama was first invented and performed. All who are conversant in the Italian cannot but observe that it is the softest, the sweetest, the most harmonious, not only of any modern tongue, but even beyond any of the learned. It seems indeed to have been invented for the sake of Poetry and Music; the vowels are so abounding in all words, especially in terminations of them, that, excepting some few monosyllables, the whole language ends in them. Then the pronunciation is so manly, and so sonorous, that their very speaking has more of music in it than Dutch poetry and song. It has withal derived so much copiousness and eloquence from the Greek and Latin, in the composition of words and the formation of them, that if, after all, we must call it barbarous, 'tis the most beautiful and most learned of any barbarism in modern tongues; and we may at least as justly praise it, as Pyrrhus did the Roman discipline and martial order, that it was of barbarians (for so the Greeks called all other nations), but had nothing in it of barbarity. This language has in a manner been refined and purified from the Gothic ever since the time of Dante, which is above four hundred years ago; and the French, who now cast a longing eye to their country, are not less ambitious to possess their elegance in Poetry and Music; in both which they labour at impossibilities. 'Tis true, indeed, they have reformed their tongue, and brought both their prose and poetry to a standard; the sweetness, as well as the purity, is much improved, by throwing off the unnecessary consonants, which made their spelling tedious, and their pronunciation harsh: but, after all, as nothing can be improved beyond its own *species*, or farther than its original nature will allow; as an ill voice, though ever so thoroughly instructed in the rules of music, can never be brought to sing harmoniously, nor many an honest critic ever arrive to be a good poet; so neither can the natural harshness of the French, or their perpetual ill accent, be ever refined into perfect harmony like the Italian. The English has yet more natural disadvantages than the French; our original Teutonic, consisting most in monosyllables, and those encumbered with consonants, cannot possibly be freed from those inconveniences. The rest of our words, which are derived from the Latin chiefly, and the French, with some small sprinklings of Greek, Italian, and Spanish, are some relief in Poetry, and help us to soften our uncouth numbers; which, together with our English genius, incomparably beyond the trifling of the French, in all the nobler parts of verse, will justly give us the pre-eminence. But, on the other hand, the effeminacy of our pronunciation (a defect common to us and to the Danes), and our scarcity of female rhymes, have left the advantage of musical composition for songs, though not for recitative, to our neighbours.

Through these difficulties I have made a shift to struggle in my part of the performance of this opera; which, as mean as it is, deserves at least a pardon, because it has attempted a discovery beyond any former undertaker of our nation; only remember, that if there be no North-East Passage to be found, the fault is in Nature, and not in me; or, as Ben Jonson tells us in *The Alchymist*, when projection had failed, and the glasses were all broken, there was enough, however, in the bottoms of them to cure the itch; so I may thus far be positive, that if I have not succeeded as I desire, yet there is somewhat still remaining to satisfy the curiosity, or itch of sight and hearing.

Yet I have no great reason to despair; for I may, without vanity, own some advantages which are not common to every writer; such as are the knowledge of the Italian and French language, and the being conversant with some of their best performances in this kind; which have furnished me with such variety of measures, as have given the composer, Monsieur Grabut, what occasions he could wish to show his extraordinary talent in diversifying the recitative, the lyrical part, and the chorus; in all which, not to attribute anything to my own opinion, the best judges, and those too of the best quality, who have honoured his rehearsals with their presence, have no less commended the happiness of his genius than his skill. And let me have the liberty to add one thing, that he has so exactly expressed my sense in all places where I intended to move the passions that he seems to have entered into my thoughts and to have been the poet as well as the composer. This I say, not to flatter him, but to do him right; because amongst some English musicians, and their scholars, who are sure to judge after them, the imputation of being a Frenchman is enough to make a party who maliciously endeavour to decry him. But the knowledge of Latin and Italian poets, both which he possesses, besides his skill in music, and his being acquainted with all the performances of the French operas, adding to these the good sense to which he is born, have raised him to a degree above any man who shall pretend to be his rival upon our stage. When any of our countrymen excel him, I shall be glad, for the sake of old England, to be shown my error; in the meantime, let virtue be commended, though in the person of a stranger.

If I thought it convenient I could here discover some rules which I have given to myself in the writing of an opera in general, and of this opera in particular; but I consider that the effect would only be to have my own performance measured by the laws I gave; and, consequently, to set up some little judges, who, not understanding thoroughly, would be sure to fall upon the faults and not to acknowledge any of the beauties; an hard measure, which I have often found from false critics. Here, therefore, if they will criticise, they shall do it out of their own fond; but let them first be assured that their ears are nice; for there is neither writing nor judgment on this subject without that good quality. 'Tis no easy matter, in our language, to make words so smooth, and numbers so harmonious, that they shall almost set themselves. And yet there are rules for this in Nature, and as great a certainty of quantity in our syllables, as either in the Greek or Latin: but let poets and judges understand those first, and then let them begin to study English. When they have chawed a while upon these preliminaries, it may be they will scarce adventure to tax me with want of thought and elevation of fancy in this work; for they will soon be satisfied that those are not of the nature of this sort of writing. The necessity of double rhymes, and ordering of the words and numbers for the sweetness of the voice, are the main hinges on which an opera must move; and both of these are without the compass of any art to teach another to perform, unless Nature, in the first place, has done her part by enduing the poet with that nicety of hearing that the discord of sounds in words shall as much offend him as a seventh in music would a good composer. I have therefore no need to make excuses for meanness of thought in many places: the Italians, with all the advantages of their language, are continually forced upon it, or, rather, affect it. The chief secret is the choice of words; and, by this choice, I do not here mean elegancy of expression, but propriety of sound, to be varied according to the nature of the subject. Perhaps a time may come when I may treat of this more largely, out of some observations which I have made from Homer and Virgil, who, amongst all the poets, only understood the art of numbers, and of that which was properly called *rhythmus* by the ancients.

The same reasons which depress thought in an opera have a stronger effect upon the words, especially in our language; for there is no maintaining the purity of English in short measures, where the rhyme returns so quick, and is so often female, or double rhyme, which is not natural to our tongue, because it consists too much of monosyllables, and those, too, most commonly clogged with consonants; for which reason I am often forced to coin new words, revive some that are antiquated, and botch others; as if I had not served out my time in poetry, but was bound apprentice to some doggrel rhymer, who makes songs to tunes and sings them for a livelihood. It is true, I have not been often put to this drudgery; but where I have, the words will sufficiently show that I was then a slave to the composition, which I will never be again: it is my part to invent, and the musician's to humour that invention. I may be counselled, and will always follow my friend's advice where I find it reasonable, but will never part with the power of the militia.

I am now to acquaint my reader with somewhat more particular concerning this opera, after having begged his pardon for so long a preface to so short a work. It was originally intended only for a prologue to a play of the nature of *The Tempest;* which is a tragedy mixed with opera, or a drama, written in blank verse, adorned with scenes, machines, songs, and dances, so that the fable of it is all spoken and acted by the best of the comedians; the other part of the entertainment to be performed by the same singers and dancers who were introduced in this present opera. It cannot properly be called a play, because the action of it is supposed to be conducted sometimes by supernatural means or magic; nor an opera, because the story of it is not sung. But more of this at its proper time. But some intervening accidents having hitherto deferred the performance of the main design, I proposed to the actors to turn the intended prologue into an entertainment by itself, as you now see it, by adding two acts more to what I had already written. The subject of it is wholly allegorical; and the allegory itself so very obvious that it will no sooner be read than understood. It is divided, according to the plain and natural method of every action, into three parts. For even Aristotle himself is contented to say simply that in all actions there is a beginning, a middle, and an end; after which model all the Spanish plays are built.

The descriptions of the scenes and other decorations of the stage I had from Mr. Betterton, who has spared neither for industry, nor cost, to make this entertainment perfect, nor for invention of the ornaments to beautify it.

To conclude, though the enemies of the composer are not few, and that there is a party formed against him of his own profession, I hope, and am persuaded, that this prejudice will turn in the end to his advantage. For the greatest part of an audience is always uninterested, though seldom knowing; and if the music be well composed and well performed, they who find themselves pleased will be so wise as not to be imposed upon and fooled out of their satisfaction. The newness of the undertaking is all the hazard. When operas were first set up in France they were not followed over eagerly; but they gained daily upon their hearers, till they grew to that height of reputation which they now enjoy. The English, I confess, are not altogether so musical as the French; and yet they have been pleased already with *The Tempest,* and some pieces that followed, which were neither much better written nor so well composed as this. If it finds encouragement, I dare promise myself to mend my hand by making a more pleasing fable. In the meantime, every loyal Englishman cannot but be satisfied with the moral of this, which so plainly represents the double restoration of his Sacred Majesty.

POSTSCRIPT

This Preface being wholly written before the death of my late Royal Master (*quem semper acerbum, semper honoratum, sic di voluistis habebo*) I have now lately reviewed it, as supposing I should find many notions in it that would require correction on cooler thoughts. After four months lying by me, I looked on it as no longer mine, because I had wholly forgotten it; but I confess with some satisfaction, and perhaps a little vanity, that I found myself entertained by it; my own judgment was new to me, and pleased me when I looked on it as another man's. I see no opinion that I would retract or alter, unless it be that possibly the Italians went not so far as Spain for the invention of their operas. They might have it in their own country; and that by gathering up the shipwrecks of the Athenian and Roman theatres, which we know were adorned with scenes, music, dances, and machines, especially the Grecian. But of this the learned Monsieur Vossius, who has made our nation his second country, is the best and perhaps the only judge now living. As for the opera itself, it was all composed, and was just ready to have been performed, when he, in honour of whom it was principally made, was taken from us.

He had been pleased twice or thrice to command that it should be practised before him, especially the first and third acts of it; and publicly declared, more than once, that the composition and choruses were more just and more beautiful than any he had heard in England. How nice an ear he had in music is sufficiently known; his praise therefore has established the reputation of it above censure, and made it in manner sacred. 'Tis therefore humbly and religiously dedicated to his memory.

It might reasonably have been expected that his death must have changed the whole fabric of the opera, or at least a great part of it. But the design of it originally was so happy that it needed no alteration, properly so called; for the addition of twenty or thirty lines in the apotheosis of Albion has made it entirely of a piece. This was the only way which could have been invented to save it from botched ending; and it fell luckily into my imagination; as if there were a kind of fatality even in the most trivial things concerning the succession: a change was made, and not for the worse, without the least confusion or disturbance; and those very causes, which seemed to threaten us with troubles, conspired to produce our lasting happiness.

RHYME AND BLANK VERSE

TO THE RIGHT HONOURABLE

ROGER, EARL OF ORRERY

*Epistle Dedicatory of "The Rival Ladies": A Tragi-
Comedy* (1694)

My Lord,—This worthless present was designed you long
before it was a play; when it was only a confused mass of
thoughts, tumbling over one another in the dark; when the fancy
was yet in its first work, moving the sleeping images of things
towards the light, there to be distinguished, and then either chosen
or rejected by the judgment; it was yours, my Lord, before I
could call it mine. And, I confess, in that first tumult of my
thoughts, there appeared a disorderly kind of beauty in some
of them, which gave me hope something worthy my Lord of
Orrery might be drawn from them: but I was then in that
eagerness of imagination which, by overpleasing fanciful men,
flatters them into the danger of writing; so that, when I had
moulded it into that shape it now bears, I looked with such
disgust upon it that the censures of our severest critics are
charitable to what I thought (and still think) of it myself: 'tis
so far from me to believe this perfect that I am apt to conclude
our best plays are scarcely so. For the stage being the representation of the world, and the actions in it, how can it be
imagined that the picture of human life can be more exact than
life itself is? He may be allowed sometimes to err who undertakes to move so many characters and humours as are requisite
in a play in those narrow channels which are proper to each of
them; to conduct his imaginary persons through so many
various intrigues and chances as the labouring audience shall
think them lost under every billow; and then at length to work
them so naturally out of their distresses that when the whole
plot is laid open the spectators may rest satisfied that every
cause was powerful enough to produce the effect it had; and
that the whole chain of them was with such due order linked
together that the first accident would naturally beget the
second, till they all rendered the conclusion necessary.

These difficulties, my Lord, may reasonably excuse the errors of my undertaking; but for this confidence of my dedication, I have an argument which is too advantageous for me not to publish it to the world. 'Tis the kindness your Lordship has continually shown to all my writings. You have been pleased, my Lord, they should sometimes cross the Irish seas to kiss your hands; which passage (contrary to the experience of others) I have found the least dangerous in the world. Your favour has shone upon me at a remote distance without the least knowledge of my person; and (like the influence of the heavenly bodies) you have done good without knowing to whom you did it. 'Tis this virtue in your lordship which emboldens me to this attempt; for, did I not consider you as my patron, I have little reason to desire you for my judge; and should appear with as much awe before you in the reading, as I had when the full theatre sat upon the action. For who could so severely judge of faults as he who has given testimony he commits none? Your excellent poems having afforded that knowledge of it to the world, that your enemies are ready to upbraid you with it, as a crime for a man of business to write so well. Neither durst I have justified your lordship in it, if examples of it had not been in the world before you; if Xenophon had not written a romance, and a certain Roman, called Augustus Caesar, a tragedy and epigrams. But their writing was the entertainment of their pleasure; yours is only a diversion of your pain. The Muses have seldom employed your thoughts but when some violent fit of the gout has snatched you from affairs of state; and like the priestess of Apollo, you never come to deliver his oracles but unwillingly and in torment. So that we are obliged to your lordship's misery for our delight: you treat us with the cruel pleasure of a Turkish triumph, where those who cut and wound their bodies sing songs of victory as they pass, and divert others with their own sufferings. Other men endure their diseases; your Lordship only can enjoy them. Plotting and writing in this kind are certainly more troublesome employments than many which signify more, and are of greater moment in the world: the fancy, memory, and judgment are then extended (like so many limbs) upon the rack; all of them reaching with their utmost stress at Nature; a thing so almost infinite and boundless as can never fully be comprehended but where the images of all things are always present. Yet I wonder not your Lordship succeeds so well in this attempt; the knowledge of men is your daily practice in the world; to work and bend their stubborn minds, which go not all after the same grain, but each of them so particular a way, that the same common humours, in several persons, must be wrought upon by several means. Thus, my Lord, your sickness is but the imitation of your health; the Poet but subordinate to the Statesman in you; you still govern men with the same address, and manage business with the same prudence; allowing it here (as in the world) the due increase and growth, till it comes to the just height; and then turning it when it is fully ripe, and Nature calls out, as it were, to be delivered. With this only advantage of ease to you in your poetry, that you have fortune here at your command; with which wisdom does often unsuccessfully struggle in the world. Here is no chance which you have not foreseen; all your heroes are more than your subjects, they are your creatures; and though they seem to move freely in all the sallies of their passions, yet you make destinies for them which they cannot shun. They are moved (if I may dare to say so) like the rational creatures of the Almighty Poet, who walk at liberty in their own opinion because their fetters are invisible; when, indeed, the prison of their will is the more sure for being large; and instead of an absolute power over their actions, they have only a wretched desire of doing that which they cannot choose but do.

I have dwelt, my Lord, thus long upon your writing, not because you deserve not greater and more noble commendations, but because I am not equally able to express them in other subjects. Like an ill swimmer, I have willingly stayed long in my own depth; and though I am eager of performing more, yet am loth to venture out beyond my knowledge: for beyond your poetry, my Lord, all is ocean to me. To speak of you as a soldier, or a statesman, were only to betray my own ignorance; and I could hope no better success from it than that miserable rhetorician had who solemnly declaimed before Hannibal of the conduct of armies and the art of war. I can only say, in general, that the souls of other men shine out at little crannies; they understand some one thing, perhaps, to admiration, while they are darkened on all the other parts; but your Lordship's soul is an entire globe of light, breaking out on every side; and, if I have only discovered one beam of it, 'tis not that the light falls unequally, but because the body, which receives it, is of unequal parts.

The acknowledgment of which is a fair occasion offered me to retire from the consideration of your Lordship to that of myself. I here present you, my Lord, with that in print which you had the goodness not to dislike upon the stage; and account it happy to have met you here in England; it being, at best, like small wines, to be drunk out upon the place, and has not body enough to endure the sea. I know not whether I have been so careful of the plot and language as I ought; but, for the latter, I have endeavoured to write English, as near as I could distinguish it from the tongue of pedants and that of affected travellers. Only I am sorry that (speaking so noble a language as we do) we have not a more certain measure of it, as they have in France, where they have an academy erected for that purpose, and endowed with large privileges by the present king. I wish we might at length leave to borrow words from other nations, which is now a wantonness in us, not a necessity; but so long as some affect to speak them there will not want others who will have the boldness to write them.

But I fear lest, defending the received words, I shall be accused for following the new way; I mean, of writing scenes in verse. Though, to speak properly, 'tis not so much a new way amongst us, as an old way new revived; for many years before Shakspeare's plays was the tragedy of Queen *Gorboduc*, in English verse, written by that famous Lord Buckhurst, afterwards Earl of Dorset, and progenitor to that excellent person who (as he inherits his soul and title) I wish may inherit his good fortune. But supposing our countrymen had not received this writing till of late, shall we oppose ourselves to the most polished and civilised nations of Europe? Shall we, with the same singularity, oppose the world in this as most of us do in pronouncing Latin? Or do we desire that the brand which Barclay has (I hope unjustly) laid upon the English should still continue? *Angli suos ac sua omnia impensè mirantur ; cæteras nationes despectui habent.* All the Spanish and Italian tragedies I have yet seen are writ in rhyme. For the French, I do not name them, because it is the fate of our countrymen to admit little of theirs among us but the basest of their men, the extravagancies of their fashions, and the frippery of their merchandise. Shakspeare (who, with some errors not to be avoided in that age, had undoubtedly a larger soul of poesy than ever any of our nation) was the first who, to shun the pains of continual rhyming, invented that kind of writing which we call blank verse, but the French, more properly, *prose mesurée ;* into which the English tongue so naturally slides that, in writing prose, it is hardly to be avoided. And, therefore, I admire some men should perpetually stumble in a way so easy, and inverting the order of their words, constantly close their lines with verbs, which though commended sometimes in writing Latin, yet we were whipt at Westminster if we used it twice together. I know some, who, if they were to write in blank verse, *Sir, I ask your pardon*, would think it sounded more heroically to write, *Sir, I your pardon ask*. I should judge him to have little command of English whom the necessity of a rhyme should force often upon this rock; though sometimes it cannot easily be avoided; and indeed this is the only inconvenience with which rhyme can be charged. This is that which makes them say rhyme is not natural, it being only so, when the poet either makes a vicious choice of words, or places them, for rhyme sake, so unnaturally as no man would in ordinary speaking; but when 'tis so judiciously ordered, that the first word in the verse seems to beget the second, and that the next, till that becomes the last word in the line, which, in the negligence of prose, would be so; it must then be granted, rhyme has all the advantages of prose, besides its own. But the excellence and dignity of it were never fully known till Mr. Waller taught it; he first made writing easily an art; first showed us to conclude the sense most commonly in distichs, which, in the verse of those before him, runs on for so many lines together that the reader is out of breath to overtake it. This sweetness of Mr. Waller's lyric poesy was afterwards followed in the epic by Sir John Denham, in his *Cooper's Hill*, a poem which your Lordship knows for the majesty of the style, is, and ever will be, the exact standard of good writing. But if we owe the invention of it to Mr. Waller, we are acknowledging for the noblest use of it to Sir William D'Avenant, who at once brought it upon the stage, and made it perfect, in the *Siege of Rhodes*.

The advantages which rhyme has over blank verse are so many that it were lost time to name them. Sir Philip Sidney, in his *Defence of Poesy*, gives us one, which, in my opinion, is not the least considerable; I mean the help it brings to memory, which rhyme so knits up, by the affinity of sounds, that, by remembering the last word in one line, we often call to mind both the verses. Then, in the quickness of reparties (which in discoursive scenes fall very often), it has so particular a grace, and is so aptly suited to them, that the sudden smartness of the answer, and the sweetness of the rhyme, set off the beauty of each other. But that benefit which I consider most in it, because I have not seldom found it, is, that it bounds and circumscribes the fancy. For imagination in a poet is a faculty so wild and lawless that, like an high-ranging spaniel, it must have clogs tied to it, lest it outrun the judgment. The great easiness of blank verse renders the poet too luxuriant; he is tempted to say many things which might better be omitted, or at least shut up in fewer words; but when the difficulty of artful rhyming is interposed, where the poet commonly confines his sense to his couplet, and must contrive that sense into such words that the rhyme shall naturally follow them, not they the rhyme; the fancy then gives leisure to the judgment to come in, which, seeing so heavy a tax imposed, is ready to cut off all unnecessary expenses. This last consideration has already answered an objection which some have made, that rhyme is only an embroidery of sense, to make that which is ordinary in itself pass for excellent with less examination. But certainly, that which most regulates the fancy, and gives the judgment its busiest employment, is like to bring forth the richest and clearest thoughts. The poet examines that most which he produceth with the greatest leisure, and which he knows must pass the severest test of the audience, because they are aptest to have it ever in their memory; as the stomach makes the best concoction when it strictly embraces the nourishment, and takes account of every little particle as it passes through. But as the best medicines may lose their virtue by being ill applied, so is it with verse, if a fit subject be not chosen for it. Neither must the argument alone, but the characters and persons, be great and noble; otherwise (as Scaliger says of Claudian) the poet will be *ignobiliore materiâ depressus*. The scenes which in my opinion most commend it are those of argumentation and discourse, on the result of which the doing or not doing some considerable action should depend.

But, my Lord, though I have more to say upon this subject, yet I must remember it is your Lordship to whom I speak; who have much better commended this way by your writing in it than I can do by writing for it. Where my reasons cannot prevail, I am sure your Lordship's example must. Your rhetoric has gained my cause; at least the greatest part of my design has already succeeded to my wish, which was to interest so noble a person in the quarrel, and withal to testify to the world how happy I esteem myself in the honour of being,

My Lord,
Your Lordship's most humble,
and most obedient Servant,
JOHN DRIDEN.

THE PROPER WIT OF POETRY

An Account of the ensuing Poem, "Annus Mirabilis":
the Year of Wonders, 1666, in a Letter to the
Honourable Sir Robert Howard

Sir,—I am so many ways obliged to you, and so little able to
return your favours, that, like those who owe too much, I can
only live by getting farther into your debt. You have not only
been careful of my fortune, which was the effect of your nobleness, but you have been solicitous of my reputation, which is that
of your kindness. It is not long since I gave you the trouble of
perusing a play for me, and now, instead of an acknowledgment,
I have given you a greater, in the correction of a poem. But
since you are to bear this persecution, I will at least give you
the encouragement of a martyr,—you could never suffer in a
nobler cause. For I have chosen the most heroic subject which
any poet could desire: I have taken upon me to describe the
motives, the beginning, progress, and successes, of a most just
and necessary war; in it, the care, management, and prudence
of our King; the conduct and valour of a Royal Admiral, and
of two incomparable Generals; the invincible courage of our
captains and seamen, and three glorious victories, the result of
all. After this, I have in the Fire, the most deplorable, but
withal the greatest argument that can be imagined; the destruction being so swift, so sudden, so vast and miserable, as
nothing can parallel in story. The former part of this Poem,
relating to the war, is but a due expiation for my not serving
my King and country in it. All gentlemen are almost obliged
to it; and I know no reason we should give that advantage to
the commonalty of England, to be foremost in brave actions,
which the noblesse of France would never suffer in their
peasants. I should not have written this but to a person who
has been ever forward to appear in all employments whither
his honour and generosity have called him. The latter part
of my Poem, which describes the Fire, I owe, first, to the piety
and fatherly affection of our Monarch to his suffering subjects;
and, in the second place, to the courage, loyalty, and mag-

nanimity of the City; both which were so conspicuous, that I have wanted words to celebrate them as they deserve. I have called my poem *historical*, not *epic*, though both the actions and actors are as much heroic as any poem can contain. But since the action is not properly one, nor that accomplished in the last successes, I have judged it too bold a title for a few stanzas, which are little more in number than a single *Iliad*, or the longest of the *Æneids*. For this reason (I mean not of length, but broken action, tied too severely to the laws of history), I am apt to agree with those who rank Lucan rather among historians in verse than epic poets; in whose room, if I am not deceived, Silius Italicus, though a worse writer, may more justly be admitted. I have chosen to write my poem in quatrains, or stanzas of four in alternate rhyme, because I have ever judged them more noble, and of greater dignity, both for the sound and number, than any other verse in use amongst us; in which I am sure I have your approbation. The learned languages have certainly a great advantage of us, in not being tied to the slavery of any rhyme; and were less constrained in the quantity of every syllable, which they might vary with spondees or dactyls, besides so many other helps of grammatical figures, for the lengthening or abbreviation of them, than the modern are in the close of that one syllable, which often confines, and more often corrupts, the sense of all the rest. But in this necessity of our rhymes, I have always found the couplet verse most easy (though not so proper for this occasion), for there the work is sooner at an end, every two lines concluding the labour of the poet; but in quatrains he is to carry it farther on, and not only so, but to bear along in his head the troublesome sense of four lines together. For those who write correctly in this kind must needs acknowledge that the last line of the stanza is to be considered in the composition of the first. Neither can we give ourselves the liberty of making any part of a verse for the sake of rhyme, or concluding with a word which is not current English, or using the variety of female rhymes, all which our fathers practised; and for the female rhymes, they are still in use amongst other nations; with the Italian in every line, with the Spaniard promiscuously, with the French alternately, as those who have read the *Alaric*, the *Pucelle*, or any of their later poems, will agree with me. And besides this, they write in Alexandrines, or verses of six feet; such as, amongst us, is the old translation of Homer by Chapman: all which, by lengthening of their chain, makes the sphere of their activity the larger.

I have dwelt too long upon the choice of my stanza, which you may remember is much better defended in the preface to *Gondibert;* and therefore I will hasten to acquaint you with my endeavours in the writing.   In general I will only say I have never yet seen the description of any naval fight in the proper terms which are used at sea; and if there be any such, in another language, as that of Lucan in the third of his *Pharsalia*, yet I could not prevail myself of it in the English; the terms of art in every tongue bearing more of the idiom of it than any other words.   We hear indeed among our poets of the thundering of guns, the smoke, the disorder, and the slaughter, but all these are common notions.   And certainly, as those who, in a logical dispute, keep in general terms, would hide a fallacy; so those, who do it in any poetical description, would veil their ignorance:—

> Descriptas servare vices, operumque colores,
> Cur ego, si nequeo ignoroque, poeta salutor?

For my own part, if I had little knowledge of the sea, yet I have thought it no shame to learn; and if I have made some few mistakes, it is only, as you can bear me witness, because I have wanted opportunity to correct them; the whole poem being first written, and now sent you from a place, where I have not so much as the converse of any seaman.   Yet though the trouble I had in writing it was great, it was more than recompensed by the pleasure; I found myself so warm in celebrating the praises of military men, two such especially as the Prince and General, that it is no wonder if they inspired me with thoughts above my ordinary level.   And I am well satisfied that, as they are incomparably the best subject I ever had, excepting only the Royal Family, so also that this I have written of them is much better than what I have performed on any other.   I have been forced to help out other arguments, but this has been bountiful to me; they have been low and barren of praise, and I have exalted them and made them fruitful; but here — *Omnia sponte sua reddit justissima tellus.* I have had a large, a fair, and a pleasant field; so fertile that, without my cultivating, it has given me two harvests in a summer, and in both oppressed the reaper.   All other greatness in subjects is only counterfeit; it will not endure the test of danger; the greatness of arms is only real.   Other greatness burdens a nation with its weight; this supports it with its strength.   And as it is the happiness of the age, so it is the peculiar goodness of the best of Kings, that we may praise his subjects without offending him. Doubtless it proceeds from a just confidence of his own virtue, which the lustre of no other can be so great as to darken in him; for the good or the valiant are never safely praised under a bad or a degenerate Prince.

But to return from this digression to a farther account of my poem; I must crave leave to tell you that, as I have endeavoured to adorn it with noble thoughts, so much more to express those thoughts with elocution. The composition of all poems is, or ought to be, of wit; and wit in the poet, or *Wit writing* (if you will give me leave to use a school-distinction), is no other than the faculty of imagination in the writer, which, like a nimble spaniel, beats over and ranges through the field of memory, till it springs the quarry it hunted after; or, without metaphor, which searches over all the memory for the species or ideas of those things which it designs to represent. *Wit written* is that which is well defined, the happy result of thought or product of imagination. But to proceed from wit, in the general notion of it, to the proper wit of an Heroic or Historical Poem, I judge it chiefly to consist in the delightful imagining of persons, actions, passions, or things. 'Tis not the jerk or sting of an epigram, nor the seeming contradiction of a poor antithesis (the delight of an ill-judging audience in a play of rhyme), nor the jingle of a more poor paronomasia; neither is it so much the morality of a grave sentence, affected by Lucan, but more sparingly used by Virgil; but it is some lively and apt description, dressed in such colours of speech that it sets before your eyes the absent object as perfectly and more delightfully than nature. So then the first happiness of the poet's imagination is properly invention, or finding of the thought; the second is fancy, or the variation, deriving, or moulding, of that thought, as the judgment represents it proper to the subject; the third is elocution, or the art of clothing and adorning that thought, so found and varied, in apt, significant, and sounding words: the quickness of the imagination is seen in the invention, the fertility in the fancy, and the accuracy in the expression. For the two first of these Ovid is famous amongst the poets; for the latter, Virgil. Ovid images more often the movements and affections of the mind, either combating between two contrary passions or extremely discomposed by one. His words therefore are the least part of his care; for he pictures nature in disorder, with which the study and choice of words is inconsistent. This is the proper wit of dialogue or discourse, and consequently of the Drama, where all that is said is supposed to be the effect of sudden thought; which, though it excludes not the quickness of wit in repartees, yet admits not a too curious election of words, too frequent allusions, or use of tropes, or, in fine, anything that shows remoteness of thought or labour in the writer. On the other side, Virgil speaks not so often to us in the person of another, like Ovid, but in his own: he relates almost all things as from himself, and thereby gains more liberty than the other to express his thoughts with all the graces of elocution, to write more figuratively, and to confess as well the labour as the force of his imagination. Though he describes his *Dido* well and naturally in the violence of her passions, yet he must yield in that to the *Myrrha*, the *Byblis*, the *Althœa*, of Ovid; for, as great an admirer of him as I am, I must acknowledge that if I see not more of their souls than I see of Dido's, at least I have a greater concernment for them: and that convinces me that Ovid has touched those tender strokes more delicately than Virgil could. But when action or persons are to be described, when any such image is to be set before us, how bold, how masterly, are the strokes of Virgil! We see the objects he presents us with in their native figures, in their proper motions; but so we see them as our own eyes could never have beheld them so beautiful in themselves. We see the soul of the poet, like that universal one of which he speaks, informing and moving through all his pictures—

> Totamque infusa per artus
> Mens agitat molem, et magno se corpore miscet:

we behold him embellishing his images, as he makes Venus breathing beauty upon her son Æneas—

> lumenque juventæ
> Purpureum, et lætos oculis afflarat honores
> Quale manus addunt ebori decus, aut ubi flavo
> Argentum, Pariusve lapis, circumdatur auro.

See his *Tempest*, his *Funeral Sports*, his *Combat of Turnus and Æneas :* and in his *Georgics*, which I esteem the divinest part of all his writings, the *Plague*, the *Country*, the *Battle of Bulls*, the labour of the *Bees*, and those many other excellent images of Nature, most of which are neither great in themselves nor have any natural ornament to bear them up; but the words wherewith he describes them are so excellent that it might be well applied to him which was said by Ovid, *Materiam superabat opus :* the very sound of his words have often somewhat that is connatural to the subject; and while we read him, we sit, as in a play, beholding the scenes of what he represents. To perform this, he made frequent use of tropes, which you know change the nature of a known word by applying it to some other signification; and this is it which Horace means in his *Epistle to the Pisos*—

> Dixeris egregie, notum si callida verbum
> Reddiderit junctura novum.

But I am sensible I have presumed too far to entertain you with a rude discourse of that art, which you both know so well and put into practice with so much happiness. Yet before I leave Virgil, I must own the vanity to tell you, and by you the world, that he has been my master in this poem. I have followed him everywhere, I know not with what success, but I am sure with diligence enough; my images are many of them copied from him, and the rest are imitations of him. My expressions also are as near as the idioms of the two languages would admit of in translation. And this, Sir, I have done with that boldness, for which I will stand accomptable to any of our little critics, who perhaps are not better acquainted with him than I am. Upon your first perusal of this poem you have taken notice of some words which I have innovated (if it be too bold for me to say refined) upon his Latin; which, as I offer not to introduce into English prose, so I hope they are neither improper, nor altogether unelegant in verse; and in this Horace will again defend me—

> Et nova, fictaque nuper, habebunt verba fidem, si
> Græco fonte cadant, parce detorta.

The inference is exceeding plain; for, if a Roman poet might have liberty to coin a word, supposing only that it was derived from the Greek, was put into a Latin termination, and that he used this liberty but seldom, and with modesty; how much more justly may I challenge that privilege to do it with the same pre-requisites, from the best and most judicious of Latin writers? In some places, where either the fancy or the words were his, or any other's, I have noted it in the margin, that I might not seem a plagiary; in others I have neglected it, to avoid as well tediousness as the affectation of doing it too often. Such descriptions or images, well wrought, which I promise not for mine, are, as I have said, the adequate delight of Heroic Poesy; for they beget admiration, which is its proper object; as the images of the Burlesque, which is contrary to this, by the same reason beget laughter: for the one shows nature beautified, as in the picture of a fair woman which we all admire; the other shows her deformed, as in that of a Lazar, or of a fool with distorted face and antic gestures, at which we cannot forbear to laugh because it is a deviation from Nature. But though the same images serve equally for the epic poesy and for the historic and panegyric, which are branches of it, yet a several sort of sculpture is to be used in them: if some of them are to be like those of Juvenal, *stantes in curribus Aemiliani*, heroes drawn in their triumphal chariots and in their full proportion; others are to be like that of Virgil, *spirantia mollius æra* : there is somewhat more of softness and tenderness to be shown in them. You will soon find I write not this without concern. Some, who have seen a paper of verses which I wrote last year to her Highness the Duchess, have accused them of that only thing I could defend in them. They said I did *humi serpere*—that I wanted not only height of fancy, but dignity of words, to set it off. I might well answer with that of Horace, *Nunc non erat his locus ;* I knew I addressed them to a lady, and accordingly I affected the softness of expression, and the smoothness of measure, rather than the height of thought; and in what I did endeavour it is no vanity to say I have succeeded. I detest arrogance; but there is some difference betwixt that and a just defence. But I will not farther bribe your candour or the reader's. I leave them to speak for me; and, if they can, to make out that character, not pretending to a greater, which I have given them.

. . . .

And now, Sir, 'tis time I should relieve you from the tedious length of this account. You have better and more profitable employment for your hours, and I wrong the public to detain you longer. In conclusion, I must leave my poem to you with all its faults, which I hope to find fewer in the printing by your emendations. I know you are not of the number of those of whom the younger Pliny speaks; *Nec sunt parum multi, qui carpere amicos suos judicium vocant :* I am rather too secure of you on that side. Your candour in pardoning my errors may make you more remiss in correcting them; if you will not withal consider that they come into the world with your approbation, and through your hands. I beg from you the greatest favour you can confer upon an absent person, since I repose upon your management what is dearest to me, my fame and reputation; and therefore I hope it will stir you up to make my poem fairer by many of your blots; if not, you know the story of the gamester who married the rich man's daughter, and when her father denied the portion, christened all the children by his sirname, that if, in conclusion, they must beg, they should do so by one name as well as by the other. But, since the reproach of my faults will light on you, 'tis but reason I should do you that justice to the readers, to let them know that, if there be anything tolerable in this poem, they owe the argument to your choice, the writing to your encouragement, the correction to your judgment, and the care of it to your friendship, to which he must ever acknowledge himself to owe all things, who is,

Sir,

The most obedient, and most

faithful of your Servants,

John Dryden.

From Charlton, *in* Wiltshire,
November 10, 1666.

EXAMEN POETICUM

DEDICATION OF THE THIRD PART OF MISCELLANY POEMS[1] TO
THE RIGHT HONOURABLE MY LORD RADCLIFFE

MY LORD,—These Miscellany Poems are by many titles yours.
The first they claim from your acceptance of my promise to
present them to you before some of them were yet in being.
The rest are derived from your own merit, the exactness of your
judgment in Poetry, and the candour of your nature, easy to
forgive some trivial faults when they come accompanied with
countervailing beauties. But, after all, though these are your
equitable claims to a dedication from other poets, yet I must
acknowledge a bribe in the case, which is your particular liking
of my verses. 'Tis a vanity common to all writers to overvalue
their own productions; and 'tis better for me to own this failing
in myself than the world to do it for me. For what other reason
have I spent my life in so unprofitable a study? why am I grown
old in seeking so barren a reward as fame? The same parts and
application which have made me a poet might have raised me
to any honours of the gown, which are often given to men of as
little learning and less honesty than myself. No Government
has ever been, or ever can be, wherein timeservers and blockheads will not be uppermost. The persons are only changed, but
the same jugglings in State, the same hypocrisy in religion, the
same self-interest and mismanagement, will remain for ever.
Blood and money will be lavished in all ages only for the pre-
ferment of new faces with old consciences. There is too often
a jaundice in the eyes of great men; they see not those whom
they raise in the same colours with other men. All whom they
affect look golden to them, when the gilding is only in their own
distempered sight. These considerations have given me a kind
of contempt for those who have risen by unworthy ways. I am
not ashamed to be little when I see them so infamously great;
neither do I know why the name of poet should be dishonourable
to me, if I am truly one, as I hope I am; for I will never do anything that shall dishonour it. The notions of morality are known

to all men; none can pretend ignorance of those ideas which are inborn in mankind; and if I see one thing, and practise the contrary, I must be disingenuous not to acknowledge a clear truth, and base to act against the light of my own conscience. For the reputation of my honesty, no man can question it who has any of his own; for that of my poetry, it shall either stand by its own merit or fall for want of it. Ill writers are usually the sharpest censors; for they, as the best poet and the best patron said,

> When in the full perfection of decay,
> Turn vinegar, and come again in play.

Thus the corruption of a poet is the generation of a critic; I mean of a critic in the general acceptation of this age; for formerly they were quite another species of men. They were defenders of poets and commentators on their works; to illustrate obscure beauties; to place some passages in a better light; to redeem others from malicious interpretations; to help out an author's modesty, who is not ostentatious of his wit; and, in short, to shield him from the ill-nature of those fellows, who were then called *Zoili* and *Momi*, and now take upon themselves the venerable name of censors. But neither Zoilus, nor he who endeavoured to defame Virgil, were ever adopted into the name of critics by the Ancients; what their reputation was then we know; and their successors in this age deserve no better. Are our auxiliary forces turned our enemies? are they, who at best are but wits of the second order, and whose only credit amongst readers is what they obtained by being subservient to the fame of writers, are these become rebels of slaves and usurpers of subjects? or, to speak in the most honourable terms of them, are they from our seconds become principals against us? Does the ivy undermine the oak which supports its weakness? What labour would it cost them to put in a better line than the worst of those which they expunge in a true poet? Petronius, the greatest wit perhaps of all the Romans, yet when his envy prevailed upon his judgment to fall on Lucan, he fell himself in his attempt; he performed worse in his *Essay of the Civil War* than the author of the *Pharsalia ;* and, avoiding his errors, has made greater of his own. Julius Scaliger would needs turn down Homer, and abdicate him after the possession of three thousand years: has he succeeded in his attempt? He has indeed shown us some of those imperfections in him which are incident to humankind; but who had not rather be that Homer than this Scaliger? You see the same hypercritic when he endeavours to mend the beginning of Claudian (a faulty poet and living in a barbarous age), yet how short he comes of him, and substitutes such verses of his own as deserve the ferula. What a censure has he made of Lucan, that " he rather seems to bark than sing "! Would any but a dog have made so snarling a comparison? one would have thought he had learned Latin as late as they tell us he did Greek. Yet he came off with a *pace tuâ*, " by your good leave, Lucan "; he called him not by those outrageous names, of *fool*, *booby*, and *blockhead* : he had somewhat more of good manners than his successors, as he had much more of knowledge. We have two sorts of those gentlemen in our nation; some of them, proceeding with a seeming moderation and pretence of respect to the dramatic writers of the last age, only scorn and vilify the present poets to set up their predecessors. But this is only in appearance; for their real design is nothing less than to do honour to any man besides themselves. Horace took notice of such men in his age—

Non ingeniis favet ille sepultis,
Nostra sed impugnat; nos nostraque lividus odit.

'Tis not with an ultimate intention to pay reverence to the *Manes* of Shakspeare, Fletcher, and Ben Jonson that they commend their writings, but to throw dirt on the writers of this age: their declaration is one thing and their practice is another. By a seeming veneration to our fathers, they would thrust out us, their lawful issue, and govern us themselves, under a specious pretence of reformation. If they could compass their intent, what would wit and learning get by such a change? If we are bad poets, they are worse; and when any of their woful pieces come abroad, the difference is so great betwixt them and good writers that there need no criticisms on our part to decide it. When they describe the writers of this age they draw such monstrous figures of them as resemble none of us; our pretended pictures are so unlike that 'tis evident we never sat to them: they are all grotesque; the products of their wild imaginations, things out of nature; so far from being copied from us, that they resemble nothing that ever was or ever can be. But there is another sort of insects, more venomous than the former; those who manifestly aim at the destruction of our poetical church and state; who allow nothing to their countrymen, either of this or of the former age. These attack the living by raking up the ashes of the dead; well knowing that if they can subvert their original title to the stage, we who claim under them must fall of course. Peace be to the venerable shades of Shakspeare and Ben Jonson! none of the living will presume to have any competition with them; as they were our predecessors, so they were our masters. We trail our plays under them; but as at the funerals of a Turkish emperor, our ensigns are furled or dragged upon the ground in honour to the dead, so we may lawfully advance our own afterwards to show that we succeed; if less in dignity, yet on the same foot and title, which we think too we can maintain against the insolence of our own Janizaries. If I am the man, as I have reason to believe, who am seemingly courted and secretly undermined, I think I shall be able to defend myself when I am openly attacked, and to show, besides, that the Greek writers only gave us the rudiments of a stage which they never finished; that many of the tragedies in the former age amongst us were without comparison beyond those of Sophocles and Euripides. But at present I have neither the leisure, nor the means, for such an undertaking. 'Tis ill going to law for an estate with him who is in possession of it, and enjoys the present profits to feed his cause. But the *quantum mutatus* may be remembered in due time. In the meanwhile, I leave the world to judge who gave the provocation.

This, my Lord, is, I confess, a long digression from *Miscellany Poems* to *Modern Tragedies ;* but I have the ordinary excuse of an injured man, who will be telling his tale unseasonably to his betters; though, at the same time, I am certain you are so good a friend as to take a concern in all things which belong to one who so truly honours you. And besides, being yourself a critic of the genuine sort, who have read the best authors in their own languages, who perfectly distinguish of their several merits, and in general prefer them to the Moderns, yet, I know, you judge for the English tragedies against Greek and Latin, as well as against the French, Italian, and Spanish, of these latter ages. Indeed, there is a vast difference betwixt arguing like Perrault in behalf of the French poets against Homer and Virgil, and betwixt giving the English poets their undoubted due of excelling Æschylus, Euripides, and Sophocles. For if we, or our greater fathers, have not yet brought the drama to an absolute perfection, yet at least we have carried it much further than those ancient Greeks; who, beginning from a chorus, could never totally exclude it, as we have done; who find it an unprofitable encumbrance, without any necessity of entertaining it amongst us, and without the possibility of establishing it here, unless it were supported by a public charge. Neither can we accept of those Lay-Bishops, as some call them, who, under pretence of reforming the stage, would intrude themselves upon us as our superiors; being indeed incompetent judges of what is manners, what religion, and, least of all, what is poetry and good sense. I can tell them, in behalf of all my fellows, that when they come to exercise a jurisdiction over us they shall have the stage to themselves, as they have the laurel. As little can I grant that the French dramatic writers excel the English. Our authors as far surpass them in genius as our soldiers excel theirs in courage. 'Tis true, in conduct they surpass us either way; yet that proceeds not so much from their greater knowledge, as from the difference of tastes in the two nations. They content themselves with a thin design, without episodes, and managed by few persons. Our audience will not be pleased but with variety of accidents, an underplot, and many actors. They follow the ancients too servilely in the mechanic rules, and we assume too much licence to ourselves, in keeping them only in view at too great a distance. But if our audience had their tastes, our poets could more easily comply with them than the French writers could come up to the sublimity of our thoughts or to the difficult variety of our designs. However it be, I dare establish it for a rule of practice on the stage, that we are bound to please those whom we pretend to entertain; and that at any price, religion and good manners only excepted. And I care not much if I give this handle to our bad illiterate poetasters, for the defence of their *scriptions*, as they call them. There is a sort of merit in delighting the spectators, which is a name more proper for them than that of auditors; or else Horace is in the wrong when he commends Lucilius for it. But these common-places I mean to treat at greater leisure; in the meantime submitting that little I have said to your Lordship's approbation, or your censure, and choosing rather to entertain you this way, as you are a judge of writing, than to oppress your modesty with other commendations; which, though they are your due, yet would not be equally received in this satirical and censorious age. That which cannot, without injury, be denied to you is the easiness of your conversation, far from affectation or pride; not denying even to enemies their just praises. And this, if I would dwell on any theme of this nature, is no vulgar commendation to your Lordship. Without flattery, my Lord, you have it in your nature to be a patron and encourager of good poets; but your fortune has not yet put into your hands the opportunity of expressing it. What you will be hereafter may be more than guessed by what you are at present. You maintain the character of a nobleman, without that haughtiness which generally attends too many of the nobility; and when you converse with gentlemen, you forget not that you have been of their order. You are married to the daughter of a King, who, amongst her other high perfections, has derived from him a charming behaviour, a winning goodness, and a majestic person. The Muses and the Graces are the ornaments of your family; while the Muse sings, the Grace accompanies her voice: even the servants of the Muses have sometimes had the happiness to hear her, and to receive their inspirations from her.

I will not give myself the liberty of going further; for 'tis so sweet to wander in a pleasing way, that I should never arrive at my journey's end. To keep myself from being belated in my letter, and tiring your attention, I must return to the place where I was setting out. I humbly dedicate to your Lordship my own labours in this *Miscellany;* at the same time not arrogating to myself the privilege of inscribing to you the works of others who are joined with me in this undertaking, over which I can pretend no right. Your Lady and you have done me the favour to hear me read my translations of Ovid; and you both seemed not to be displeased with them. Whether it be the partiality of an old man to his youngest child I know not; but they appear to me the best of all my endeavours in this kind. Perhaps this poet is more easy to be translated than some others whom I have lately attempted; perhaps, too, he was more according to my genius. He is certainly more palatable to the reader than any of the Roman wits, though some of them are more lofty, some more instructive, and others more correct. He had learning enough to make him equal to the best; but, as his verse came easily, he wanted the toil of application to amend it. He is often luxuriant both in his fancy and expressions, and, as it has lately been observed, not always natural. If wit be pleasantry, he has it to excess; but if it be propriety, Lucretius, Horace, and, above all, Virgil, are his superiors. I have said so much of him already in my Preface to his *Heroical Epistles* that there remains little to be added in this place. For my own part, I have endeavoured to copy his character, what I could, in this translation—even, perhaps, further than I should have done—to his very faults. Mr. Chapman, in his *Translation of Homer,* professes to have done it somewhat paraphrastically, and that on set purpose; his opinion being that a good poet is to be translated in that manner. I remember not the reason which he gives for it; but I suppose it is for fear of omitting any of his excellencies. Sure I am, that if it be a fault, 'tis much more pardonable than that of those who run into the other extreme of a literal and close translation, where the poet is confined so straitly to his author's words that he wants elbow-room to express his elegancies. He leaves him obscure; he leaves him prose where he found him verse; and no better than thus has Ovid been served by the so-much-admired Sandys. This is at least the idea which I have remaining of his translation; for I never read him since I was a boy. They who take him upon content, from the praises which their fathers gave him, may inform their judgment by reading him again, and see (if they understand the original) what is become of Ovid's poetry in his version; whether it be not all, or the greatest part of it, evaporated. But this proceeded from the wrong judgment of the age in which he lived. They neither knew good verse, nor loved it; they were scholars, 'tis true, but they were pedants; and for a just reward of their pedantic pains, all their translations want to be translated into English.

If I flatter not myself, or if my friends have not flattered me, I have given my author's sense for the most part truly; for to mistake sometimes is incident to all men; and not to follow the Dutch commentators always may be forgiven to a man who thinks them, in the general, heavy gross-witted fellows fit only to gloss on their own dull poets. But I leave a further satire on their wit till I have a better opportunity to show how much I love and honour them. I have likewise attempted to restore Ovid to his native sweetness, easiness, and smoothness; and to give my poetry a kind of cadence and, as we call it, a run of verse, as like the original as the English can come up to the Latin. As he seldom uses any synalœphas, so I have endeavoured to avoid them as often as I could. I have likewise given him his own turns, both on the words and on the thought; which I cannot say are inimitable, because I have copied them, and so may others, if they use the same diligence; but certainly they are wonderfully graceful in this poet. Since I have named the synalœpha, which is the cutting off one vowel immediately before another, I will give an example of it from Chapman's *Homer*, which lies before me, for the benefit of those who understand not the Latin *prosodia*. 'Tis in the first line of the argument to the first *Iliad*—

Apollo's priest to th' Argive fleet doth bring, etc.

There we see he makes it not *the Argive*, but *th' Argive*, to shun
the shock of the two vowels immediately following each other.
But in his second argument, in the same page, he gives a bad
example of the quite contrary kind—

> *Alpha* the pray'r of Chryses sings:
> The army's plague, the strife of kings.

In these words, *the army's*, *the* ending with a vowel, and *army's*
beginning with another vowel, without cutting off the first,
which by it had been *th' army's*, there remains a most horrible ill-
sounding gap betwixt those words.   I cannot say that I have
everywhere observed the rule of the synalœpha in my translation;
but wheresoever I have not, 'tis a fault in sound.   The French
and the Italians have made it an inviolable precept in their
versification;   therein following the severe example of the Latin
poets.   Our countrymen have not yet reformed their poetry so
far, but content themselves with following the licentious practice
of the Greeks;   who, though they sometimes use synalœphas,
yet make no difficulty, very often, to sound one vowel upon
another;   as Homer does, in the very first line of *Alpha*—

> Μῆνιν ἄειδε, θεά, Πηληϊάδεω 'Αχιλῆος

It is true, indeed, that in the second line, in these words, μυρί'
'Αχαιοῖς and ἄλγε' ἔθηκε, the synalœpha, in revenge, is twice
observed.   But it becomes us, for the sake of euphony, rather
Musas colere severiores, with the Romans, than to give into the
looseness of the Grecians.

I have tired myself, and have been summoned by the press to
send away this *Dedication ;* otherwise I had exposed some other
faults, which are daily committed by our English poets;   which,
with care and observation, might be amended.   For, after all,
our language is both copious, significant, and majestical, and
might be reduced into a more harmonious sound.   But for want
of public encouragement, in this Iron Age, we are so far from
making any progress in the improvement of our tongue, that
in few years we shall speak and write as barbarously as our
neighbours.

Notwithstanding my haste, I cannot forbear to tell your Lordship that there are two fragments of Homer translated in this
Miscellany ; one by Mr. Congreve (whom I cannot mention
without the honour which is due to his excellent parts, and that
entire affection which I bear him) and the other by myself.   Both
the subjects are pathetical;   and I am sure my friend has added

to the tenderness which he found in the original, and without flattery, surpassed his author. Yet I must needs say this in reference to Homer, that he is much more capable of exciting the manly passions than those of grief and pity. To cause admiration is, indeed, the proper and adequate design of an Epic Poem; and in that he has excelled even Virgil. Yet, without presuming to arraign our master, I may venture to affirm that he is somewhat too talkative, and more than somewhat too digressive. This is so manifest that it cannot be denied in that little parcel which I have translated, perhaps too literally: there Andromache, in the midst of her concernment and fright for Hector, runs off her bias to tell him a story of her pedigree, and of the lamentable death of her father, her mother, and her seven brothers. The devil was in Hector if he knew not all this matter as well as she who told it him; for she had been his bedfellow for many years together: and if he knew it, then it must be confessed that Homer, in this long digression, has rather given us his own character than that of the fair lady whom he paints. His dear friends the commentators, who never fail him at a pinch, will needs excuse him by making the present sorrow of Andromache to occasion the remembrance of all the past; but others think that she had enough to do with that grief which now oppressed her without running for assistance to her family. Virgil, I am confident, would have omitted such a work of supererogation. But Virgil had the gift of expressing much in little, and sometimes in silence; for, though he yielded much to Homer in invention, he more excelled him in his admirable judgment. He drew the passion of Dido for Æneas in the most lively and most natural colours that are imaginable. Homer was ambitious enough of moving pity, for he has attempted twice on the same subject of Hector's death; first, when Priam and Hecuba beheld his corpse, which was dragged after the chariot of Achilles; and then in the lamentation which was made over him when his body was redeemed by Priam; and the same persons again bewail his death with a chorus of others to help the cry. But if this last excite compassion in you, as I doubt not but it will, you are more obliged to the translator than the poet; for Homer, as I observed before, can move rage better than he can pity. He stirs up the irascible appetite, as our philosophers call it; he provokes to murder, and the destruction of God's images; he forms and equips those ungodly man-killers, whom we poets, when we flatter them, call heroes; a race of men who can never enjoy quiet in themselves till they have taken it

H

from all the world. This is Homer's commendation; and, such as it is, the lovers of peace, or at least of more moderate heroism, will never envy him. But let Homer and Virgil contend for the prize of honour betwixt themselves; I am satisfied they will never have a third concurrent. I wish Mr. Congreve had the leisure to translate him, and the world the good nature and justice to encourage him in that noble design, of which he is more capable than any man I know. The Earl of Mulgrave and Mr. Waller, two of the best judges of our age, have assured me that they could never read over the translation of Chapman without incredible pleasure and extreme transport. This admiration of theirs must needs proceed from the author himself; for the translator has thrown him down as low as harsh numbers, improper English, and a monstrous length of verse could carry him. What then would he appear in the harmonious version of one of the best writers, living in a much better age than was the last? I mean for versification, and the art of numbers; for in the drama we have not arrived to the pitch of Shakspeare and Ben Jonson. But here, my Lord, I am forced to break off abruptly, without endeavouring at a compliment in the close. This *Miscellany* is, without dispute, one of the best of the kind which has hitherto been extant in our tongue. At least, as Sir Samuel Tuke has said before me, a modest man may praise what is not his own. My fellows have no need of any protection; but I humbly recommend my part of it, as much as it deserves, to your patronage and acceptance, and all the rest to your forgiveness.

I am,

My Lord,

Your Lordship's most obedient servant,

JOHN DRYDEN.

VIRGIL AND THE ÆNEID

DEDICATION OF THE ÆNEIS
TO THE
MOST HONOURABLE JOHN,
LORD MARQUIS OF NORMANBY, EARL OF MULGRAVE, ETC., AND
KNIGHT OF THE MOST NOBLE ORDER OF THE GARTER [1]

A HEROIC POEM, truly such, is undoubtedly the greatest work
which the soul of man is capable to perform. The design of it is
to form the mind to heroic virtue by example; 'tis conveyed in
verse that it may delight while it instructs. The action of it is
always one, entire, and great. The least and most trivial
episodes, or under-actions, which are interwoven in it are parts
either necessary or convenient to carry on the main design;
either so necessary that, without them, the poem must be imperfect, or so convenient that no others can be imagined more
suitable to the place in which they are. There is nothing to be
left void in a firm building; even the cavities ought not to be
filled with rubbish which is of a perishable kind, destructive
to the strength, but with brick or stone, though of less pieces,
yet of the same nature, and fitted to the crannies. Even the
least portions of them must be of the epic kind: all things must
be grave, majestical, and sublime, nothing of a foreign nature,
like the trifling novels which Ariosto, and others, have inserted
in their poems; by which the reader is misled into another sort
of pleasure, opposite to that which is designed in an epic poem.
One raises the soul, and hardens it to virtue; the other softens
it again, and unbends it into vice. One conduces to the poet's
aim, the completing of his work, which he is driving on, labouring and hastening in every line; the other slackens his pace,
diverts him from his way, and locks him up like a knight-errant
in an enchanted castle, when he should be pursuing his first
adventure. Statius, as Bossu has well observed, was ambitious
of trying his strength with his master Virgil, as Virgil had before
tried his with Homer. The Grecian gave the two Romans an

[1] Published in 1697.

example in the games which were celebrated at the funerals of Patroclus. Virgil imitated the invention of Homer, but changed the sports. But both the Greek and Latin poets took their occasions from the subject; though, to confess the truth, they were both ornamental, or, at best, convenient parts of it, rather than of necessity arising from it. Statius, who, through his whole poem, is noted for want of conduct and judgment, instead of staying, as he might have done, for the death of Capaneus, Hippomedon, Tydeus, or some other of his seven champions (who are heroes all alike), or more properly for the tragical end of the two brothers, whose exequies the next successor had leisure to perform when the siege was raised, and in the interval betwixt the poet's first action and his second—went out of his way, as it were on prepense malice, to commit a fault. For he took his opportunity to kill a royal infant by the means of a serpent (that author of all evil), to make way for those funeral honours which he intended for him. Now, if this innocent had been of any relation to his *Thebais ;* if he had either furthered or hindered the taking of the town; the poet might have found some sorry excuse at least for detaining the reader from the promised siege. I can think of nothing to plead for him but what I verily believe he thought himself, which was, that as the funerals of Anchises were solemnised in Sicily, so those of Archemorus should be celebrated in Candy. For the last was an island, and a better than the first, because Jove was born there. On these terms, this Capaneus of a poet engaged his two immortal predecessors; and his success was answerable to his enterprise.

If this economy must be observed in the minutest parts of an epic poem, which, to a common reader, seems to be detached from the body, and almost independent of it; what soul, though sent into the world with great advantages of Nature, cultivated with the liberal arts and sciences, conversant with histories of the dead, and enriched with observations on the living, can be sufficient to inform the whole body of so great a work? I touch here but transiently, without any strict method, on some few of those many rules of imitating nature which Aristotle drew from Homer's *Iliads* and *Odysseys*, and which he fitted to the drama; furnishing himself also with observations from the practice of the theatre, when it flourished under Æschylus, Euripides, and Sophocles. For the original of the stage was from the Epic Poem. Narration, doubtless, preceded acting, and gave laws to it: what at first was told artfully, was, in process of time, represented gracefully to the sight and hearing. Those episodes of Homer, which were proper for the stage, the poets amplified each into an action; out of his limbs they formed their bodies; what he had contracted they enlarged; out of one Hercules were made infinity of pigmies, yet all endued with human souls; for from him, their great creator, they have each of them the *divinæ particulam auræ*. They flowed from him at first, and are at last resolved into him. Nor were they only animated by him, but their measure and symmetry was owing to him. His one, entire, and great action was copied by them according to the proportions of the drama. If he finished his orb within the years, it sufficed to teach them, that their action being less, and being also less diversified with incidents, their orb, of consequence, must be circumscribed in a less compass, which they reduced within the limits either of a natural or an artificial day; so that, as he taught them to amplify what he had shortened, by the same rule, applied the contrary way, he taught them to shorten what he had amplified. Tragedy is the miniature of human life; an epic poem is the draught at length. Here, my Lord, I must contract also; for, before I was aware, I was almost running into a long digression, to prove that there is no such absolute necessity that the time of a stage action should so strictly be confined to twenty-four hours as never to exceed them, for which Aristotle contends, and the Grecian stage has practised. Some longer space, on some occasions, I think, may be allowed, especially for the English theatre, which requires more variety of incidents than the French. Corneille himself, after long practice, was inclined to think that the time allotted by the Ancients was too short to raise and finish a great action: and better a mechanic rule were stretched or broken, than a great beauty were omitted. To raise, and afterwards to calm the passions—to purge the soul from pride, by the examples of human miseries, which befall the greatest—in few words, to expel arrogance, and introduce compassion, are the great effects of tragedy. Great, I must confess, if they were altogether as true as they are pompous. But are habits to be introduced at three hours' warning? are radical diseases so suddenly removed? A mountebank may promise such a cure, but a skilful physician will not undertake it. An epic is not in so much haste: it works leisurely; the changes which it makes are slow; but the cure is likely to be more perfect. The effects of tragedy, as I said, are too violent to be lasting. If it be answered that, for this reason, tragedies are often to be seen, and the dose to be repeated, this is tacitly to confess that there is more virtue in one heroic poem than in many tragedies. A man is humbled one day, and his pride returns the next. Chymical medicines are observed to relieve oftener than to cure: for 'tis the nature of spirits to make swift impressions, but not deep. Galenical decoctions, to which I may properly compare an epic poem, have more of body in them; they work by their substance and their weight. It is one reason of Aristotle's to prove that Tragedy is the more noble, because it turns in a shorter compass; the whole action being circumscribed within the space of four-and-twenty hours. He might prove as well that a mushroom is to be preferred before a peach, because it shoots up in the compass of a night. A chariot may be driven round the pillar in less space than a large machine, because the bulk is not so great. Is the Moon a more noble planet than Saturn, because she makes her revolution in less than thirty days, and he in little less than thirty years? Both their orbs are in proportion to their several magnitudes; and consequently the quickness or slowness of their motion, and the time of their circumvolutions, is no argument of the greater or less perfection. And, besides what virtue is there in a tragedy which is not contained in an epic poem, where pride is humbled, virtue rewarded, and vice punished; and those more amply treated than the narrowness of the drama can admit? The shining quality of an epic hero, his magnanimity, his constancy, his patience, his piety, or whatever characteristical virtue his poet gives him, raises first our admiration; we are naturally prone to imitate what we admire; and frequent acts produce a habit. If the hero's chief quality be vicious, as, for example, the choler and obstinate desire of vengeance in Achilles, yet the moral is instructive: and, besides, we are informed in the very proposition of the *Iliads*, that this anger was pernicious; that it brought a thousand ills on the Grecian camp. The courage of Achilles is proposed to imitation, not his pride and disobedience to his general, nor his brutal cruelty to his dead enemy, nor the selling of his body to his father. We abhor these actions while we read them; and what we abhor we never imitate. The poet only shows them, like rocks or quicksands, to be shunned.

By this example, the critics have concluded that it is not necessary the manners of the hero should be virtuous. They are poetically good, if they are of a piece: though where a character of perfect virtue is set before us, it is more lovely; for there the whole hero is to be imitated. This is the Æneas of our author; this is that idea of perfection in an epic poem which painters and statuaries have only in their minds, and which no hands are able to express. These are the beauties of a god in a human body. When the picture of Achilles is drawn in tragedy, he is taken with those warts, and moles, and hard features by those who represent him on the stage, or he is no more Achilles; for his creator, Homer, has so described him. Yet even thus he appears a perfect hero, though an imperfect character of virtue. Horace paints him after Homer, and delivers him to be copied on the stage with all those imperfections. Therefore they are either not faults in a heroic poem, or faults common to the drama. After all, on the whole merits of the cause, it must be acknowledged that the Epic Poem is more for the manners, and Tragedy for the passions. The passions, as I have said, are violent; and acute distempers require medicines of a strong and speedy operation. Ill habits of the mind are like chronical diseases, to be corrected by degrees, and cured by alternatives; wherein, though purges are sometimes necessary, yet diet, good air, and moderate exercise have the greatest part. The matter being thus stated, it will appear that both sorts of poetry are of use for their proper ends. The stage is more active; the Epic Poem works at greater leisure, yet is active too, when need requires; for dialogue is imitated by the drama from the more active parts of it. One puts off a fit, like the quinquina, and relieves us only for a time; the other roots out the distemper, and gives a healthful habit. The sun enlightens and cheers us, dispels fogs, and warms the ground with his daily beams; but the corn is sowed, increases, is ripened, and is reaped for use in process of time, and in its proper season. I proceed from the greatness of the action to the dignity of the actors; I mean to the persons employed in both poems. There likewise Tragedy will be seen to borrow from the Epopee; and that which borrows is always of less dignity, because it has not of its own. A subject, it is true, may lend to his sovereign; but the act of borrowing makes the king inferior, because he wants, and the subject supplies. And suppose the persons of the drama wholly fabulous, or of the poet's invention, yet Heroic Poetry gave him the examples of that invention, because it was first and Homer the common father of the stage. I know not of any one advantage which Tragedy can boast above Heroic Poetry, but that it is represented to the view, as well as read, and instructs in the closet, as well as on the theatre. This is an uncontended excellence, and a chief branch of its prerogative; yet I may be allowed to say, without partiality, that herein the actors share the poet's praise. Your Lordship knows some modern tragedies which are beautiful on the stage, and yet I am confident you would not read them. Tryphon the stationer complains they are seldom asked for in his shop. The poet who flourished in the scene is damned in the *ruelle ;* nay more, he is not esteemed a good poet by those who see and hear his extravagances with delight. They are a sort of stately fustian, and lofty childishness. Nothing but Nature can give a sincere pleasure; where that is not imitated, 'tis grotesque painting; the fine woman ends in a fish's tail.

I might also add that many things, which not only please, but are real beauties in the reading, would appear absurd upon the stage; and those not only the *speciosa miracula*, as Horace calls them, of transformations, of Scylla, Antiphates and the Læstrygons, which cannot be represented even in operas; but the prowess of Achilles or Æneas would appear ridiculous in our dwarf heroes of the theatre. We can believe they routed armies in Homer or in Virgil; but *ne Hercules contra duos* in the drama. I forbear to instance in many things, which the stage cannot, or ought not to represent; for I have said already more than I intended on this subject, and should fear it might be turned against me, that I plead for the pre-eminence of Epic Poetry because I have taken some pains in translating Virgil, if this were the first time that I had delivered my opinion in this dispute. But I have more than once already maintained the rights of my two masters against their rivals of the scene, even while I wrote tragedies myself, and had no thoughts of this present undertaking. I submit my opinion to your judgment, who are better qualified than any man I know to decide this controversy. You come, my Lord, instructed in the cause, and needed not that I should open it. Your *Essay of Poetry*, which was published without a name, and of which I was not honoured with the confidence, I read over and over with much delight, and as much instruction, and, without flattering you, or making myself more moral than I am, not without some envy. I was loath to be informed how an epic poem should be written, or how a tragedy should be contrived and managed, in better verse, and with more judgment, than I could teach others. A native of Parnassus, and bred up in the studies of its fandumental laws, may receive new lights from his contemporaries; but it is a grudging kind of praise which he gives his benefactors. He is more obliged than he is willing to acknowledge; there is a tincture of malice in his commendations. For where I own I am taught, I confess my want of knowledge. A judge upon the bench may, out of good nature, or at least interest, encourage the pleadings of a puny counsellor; but he does not willingly commend his brother serjeant at the bar, especially when he controuls his law, and exposes that ignorance which is made sacred by his place. I gave the unknown author his due commendation, I must confess; but who can answer for me and for the rest of the poets who heard me read the poem, whether we should not have been better pleased to have seen our own names at the bottom of the title-page? Perhaps we commended it the more, that we might seem to be above the censure. We are naturally displeased with an unknown critic, as the ladies are with a lampooner, because we are bitten in the dark, and know not where to fasten our revenge. But great excellencies will work their way through all sorts of opposition. I applauded rather out of decency than affection; and was ambitious, as some yet can witness, to be acquainted with a man with whom I had the honour to converse, and that almost daily, for so many years together. Heaven knows, if I have heartily forgiven you this deceit. You extorted a praise which I should willingly have given had I known you. Nothing had been more easy than to commend a patron of long standing. The world would join with me, if the encomiums were just; and, if unjust, would excuse a grateful flatterer. But to come anonymous upon me, and force me to commend you against my interest, was not altogether so fair, give me leave to say, as it was politic. For, by concealing your quality, you might clearly understand how your work succeeded, and that the general approbation was given to your merit, not your titles. Thus, like Apelles, you stood unseen behind your own Venus, and received the praises of the passing multitude; the work was commended, not the author; and I doubt not, this was one of the most pleasing adventures of your life.

I have detained your Lordship longer than I intended in this dispute of preference betwixt the Epic Poem and the Drama, and yet have not formally answered any of the arguments which are brought by Aristotle on the other side, and set in the fairest light by Dacier. But I suppose, without looking on the book, I may have touched on some of the objections; for, in this address to your Lordship, I design not a Treatise of Heroic Poetry, but write in a loose epistolary way, somewhat tending to that subject, after the example of Horace, in his *First Epistle* of the Second Book to *Augustus Cæsar*, and in that to the Piso's, which we call his *Art of Poetry;* in both of which he observes no method that I can trace, whatever Scaliger the father, or Heinsius, may have seen, or rather think they had seen. I have taken up, laid down, and resumed as often as I pleased, the same subject; and this loose proceeding I shall use through all this prefatory Dedication. Yet all this while I have been sailing with some side-wind or other toward the point I proposed in the beginning, the greatness and excellency of a Heroic Poem, with some of the difficulties which attend that work. The comparison, therefore, which I made betwixt the Epopee and the Tragedy was not altogether a digression; for 'tis concluded on all hands that they are both the masterpieces of human wit.

In the meantime, I may be bold to draw this corollary from what has been already said, that the file of heroic poets is very short; all are not such who have assumed that lofty title in ancient or modern ages, or have been so esteemed by their partial and ignorant admirers.

There have been but one great *Ilias* and one *Æneis* in so many ages. The next, but the next with a long interval betwixt, was the *Jerusalem*: I mean not so much in distance of time as in excellency. After these three are entered, some Lord Chamberlain should be appointed, some critic of authority should be set before the door, to keep out a crowd of little poets, who press for admission, and are not of quality. Mævius would be deafening your Lordship's ears with his

Fortunam Priami cantabo, et nobile bellum;

mere fustian, as Horace would tell you from behind, without pressing forward, and more smoke than fire. Pulci, Boiardo, and Ariosto, would cry out, "make room for the Italian poets, the descendants of Virgil in a right line:" Father Le Moine, with his *Saint Louis*, and Scudery with his *Alaric*, for a godly king and a Gothic conqueror; and Chapelain would take it ill that his *Maid* should be refused a place with Helen and Lavinia. Spenser has a better plea for his *Fairy Queen*, had his action been finished, or had been one. And Milton, if the Devil had not been his hero, instead of Adam; if the giant had not foiled the knight, and driven him out of his stronghold, to wander through the world with his lady errant; and if there had not been more machining persons than human in his poem. After these, the rest of our English poets shall not be mentioned. I have that honour for them which I ought to have; but, if they are worthies, they are not to be ranked amongst the three whom I have named, and who are established in their reputation.

Before I quitted the comparison betwixt Epic Poetry and Tragedy, I should have acquainted my judge with one advantage of the former over the latter, which I now casually remember out of the preface of Segrais before his translation of the *Æneis*, or out of Bossu, no matter which: *the style of the Heroic Poem is, and ought to be, more lofty than that of the drama.* The critic is certainly in the right for the reason already urged; the work of Tragedy is on the passions and in dialogue; both of them abhor strong metaphors, in which the Epopee delights. A poet cannot speak too plainly on the stage: for *volat irrevocabile verbum;* the sense is lost if it be not taken flying. But what we read alone we have leisure to digest; there an author may beautify his sense by the boldness of his expression, which if we understand not fully at the first, we may dwell upon it till we find the secret force and excellence. That which cures the manners by alterative physics, as I said before, must proceed by insensible degrees; but that which purges the passions must do its business all at once, or wholly fail of its effect, at least in the present operation, and without repeated doses. We must beat the iron while it is hot, but we may polish it at leisure. Thus, my Lord, you pay the fine of my forgetfulness; and yet the merits of both causes are where they were, and undecided, till you declare whether it be more for the benefit of mankind to have their manners in general corrected or their pride and hard-heartedness removed.

I must now come closer to my present business, and not think of making more invasive wars abroad, when, like Hannibal, I am called back to the defence of my own country. Virgil is attacked by many enemies; he has a whole confederacy against him; and I must endeavour to defend him as well as I am able. But their principal objections being against his moral, the duration or length of time taken up in the action of the poem, and what they have to urge against the manners of his hero, I shall omit the rest as mere cavils of grammarians; at the worst, but casual slips of a great man's pen, or inconsiderable faults of an admirable poem, which the author had not leisure to review before his death. Macrobius has answered what the ancients could urge against him; and some things I have lately read in Tanneguy le Fèvre, Valois, and another whom I name not, which are scarce worth answering. They begin with the moral of his poem, which I have elsewhere confessed, and still must own, not to be so noble as that of Homer. But let both be fairly stated; and, without contradicting my first opinion,

I can show that Virgil's was as useful to the Romans of his age as Homer's was to the Grecians of his, in what time soever he may be supposed to have lived and flourished. Homer's moral was to urge the necessity of union and of a good understanding betwixt confederate states and princes engaged in a war with a mighty monarch; as also of discipline in an army, and obedience in the several chiefs to the supreme commander of the joint forces. To inculcate this, he sets forth the ruinous effects of discord in the camp of those allies, occasioned by the quarrel betwixt the general and one of the next in office under him. Agamemnon gives the provocation and Achilles resents the injury. Both parties are faulty in the quarrel and accordingly they are both punished: the aggressor is forced to sue for peace to his inferior on dishonourable conditions: the deserter refuses the satisfaction offered, and his obstinacy costs him his best friend. This works the natural effect of choler, and turns his rage against him by whom he was last affronted, and most sensibly. The greater anger expels the less; but his character is still preserved. In the meantime, the Grecian army receives loss on loss, and is half destroyed by a pestilence into the bargain:—

Quidquid delirant reges, plectuntur Achivi.

As the poet, in the first part of the example, had shown the bad effects of discord, so, after the reconcilement, he gives the good effects of unity; for Hector is slain and then Troy must fall. By this it is probable that Homer lived when the Persian Monarchy was grown formidable to the Grecians, and that the joint endeavours of his countrymen were little enough to preserve their common freedom from an encroaching enemy. Such was his moral, which all critics have allowed to be more noble than that of Virgil, though not adapted to the times in which the Roman poet lived. Had Virgil flourished in the age of Ennius, and addressed to Scipio, he had probably taken the same moral, or some other not unlike it: for then the Romans were in as much danger from the Carthaginian commonwealth as the Grecians were from the Persian monarchy. But we are to consider him as writing his poem in a time when the old form of government was subverted, and a new one just established by Octavius Cæsar, in effect by force of arms, but seemingly by the consent of the Roman people. The Commonwealth had received a deadly wound in the former civil wars betwixt Marius and Sylla. The commons, while the first prevailed, had almost shaken off the yoke of the nobility; and Marius and

Cinna, like the captains of the mob, under the specious pretence of the public good, and of doing justice on the oppressors of their liberty, revenged themselves, without form of law, on their private enemies. Sylla, in his turn, proscribed the heads of the adverse party: he too had nothing but liberty and reformation in his mouth (for the cause of religion is but a modern motive to rebellion, invented by the Christian priesthood, refining on the heathen); Sylla, to be sure, meant no more good to the Roman people than Marius before him, whatever he declared; but sacrificed the lives, and took the estates, of all his enemies to gratify those who brought him into power. Such was the reformation of the government by both parties. The Senate and the Commons were the two bases on which it stood; and the two champions of either faction, each destroyed the foundations of the other side; so the fabric, of consequence, must fall betwixt them, and tyranny must be built upon their ruins. This comes of altering fundamental laws and constitutions; like him, who, being in good health, lodged himself in a physician's house and was over-persuaded by his landlord to take physic (of which he died) for the benefit of his doctor. *Stavo ben* (was written on his monument), *ma, per star meglio, sto qui*.

After the death of those two usurpers, the Commonwealth seemed to recover and held up its head for a little time. But it was all the while in a deep consumption, which is a flattering disease. Pompey, Crassus, and Cæsar had found the sweets of arbitrary power; and, each being a check to the other's growth, struck up a false friendship amongst themselves and divided the government betwixt them, which none of them was able to assume alone. These were the public-spirited men of their age; that is, patriots for their own interest. The Commonwealth looked with a florid countenance in their management, spread in bulk, and all the while was wasting in the vitals. Not to trouble your Lordship with the repetition of what you know: after the death of Crassus, Pompey found himself outwitted by Cæsar, broke with him, overpowered him in the Senate, and caused many unjust decrees to pass against him. Cæsar, thus injured, and unable to resist the faction of the nobles which was now uppermost (for he was a Marian), had recourse to arms; and his cause was just against Pompey, but not against his country, whose constitution ought to have been sacred of him, and never to have been violated on the account of any private wrong. But he prevailed; and Heaven declaring for him, he became a providential monarch under the title of perpetual dictator. He being murdered by his own son, whom I neither dare commend nor can justly blame (though Dante, in his *Inferno*, has put him and Cassius, and Judas Iscariot betwixt them, into the great Devil's mouth), the Commonwealth popped up its head for the third time, under Brutus and Cassius, and then sunk for ever.

Thus the Roman people were grossly gulled twice or thrice over and as often enslaved in one century, and under the same pretence of reformation. At last the two battles of Philippi gave the decisive stroke against liberty; and, not long after, the Commonwealth was turned into a Monarchy by the conduct and good fortune of Augustus. 'Tis true that the despotic power could not have fallen into better hands than those of the first and second Cæsar. Your Lordship well knows what obligations Virgil had to the latter of them: he saw, besides, that the Commonwealth was lost without resource; the heads of it destroyed; the Senate, new moulded, grown degenerate, and either bought off or thrusting their own necks into the yoke out of fear of being forced. Yet I may safely affirm for our great author (as men of good sense are generally honest), that he was still of republic principles in his heart.

Secretosque pios, his dantem jura Catonem.

I think I need use no other argument to justify my opinion than that of this one line, taken from the Eighth Book of the *Æneis*. If he had not well studied his patron's temper, it might have ruined him with another prince. But Augustus was not discontented, at least that we can find, that Cato was placed, by his own poet, in Elysium, and there giving laws to the holy souls who deserved to be separated from the vulgar sort of good spirits; for his conscience could not but whisper to the arbitrary Monarch that the Kings of Rome were at first elective and governed not without a Senate; that Romulus was no hereditary prince; and though, after his death, he received divine honours for the good he did on earth, yet he was but a god of their own making; that the last Tarquin was expelled justly for overt acts of tryanny and maladministration; for such are the conditions of an elective kingdom: and I meddle not with others, being, for my own opinion, of Montaigne's principles, that an honest man ought to be contented with that form of government, and with those fundamental constitutions of it, which he received from his ancestors, and under which himself was born; though at the same time he confessed freely that, if he could have chosen his place of birth, it should have been at Venice; which, for many reasons, I dislike, and am better pleased to have been born an Englishman.

But, to return from my long rambling: I say, that Virgil having maturely weighed the condition of the times in which he lived; that an entire liberty was not to be retrieved; that the present settlement had the prospect of a long continuance in the same family, or those adopted into it; that he held his paternal estate from the bounty of the conqueror, by whom he was likewise enriched, esteemed, and cherished; that this conqueror, though of a bad kind, was the very best of it; that the arts of peace flourished under him; that all men might be happy if they would be quiet; that, now he was in possession of the whole, yet he shared a great part of his authority with the Senate; that he would be chosen into the ancient offices of the Commonwealth, and ruled by the power which he derived from them; and prorogued his government from time to time, still, as it were, threatening to dismiss himself from public cares, which he exercised more for the common good than for any delight he took in greatness; these things, I say, being considered by the poet, he concluded it to be the interest of his country to be so governed; to infuse an awful respect into the people towards such a prince; by that respect to confirm their obedience to him, and by that obedience to make them happy. This was the moral of his divine poem; honest in the poet; honourable to the emperor, whom he derives from a divine extraction; and reflecting part of that honour on the Roman people, whom he derives also from the Trojans; and not only profitable, but necessary, to the present age, and likely to be such to their posterity. That it was the received opinion that the Romans were descended from the Trojans, and Julius Cæsar from Iulus the son of Æneas, was enough for Virgil; though perhaps he thought not so himself, or that Æneas ever was in Italy; which Bochartus manifestly proves. And Homer, where he says that Jupiter hated the house of Priam, and was resolved to transfer the kingdom to the family of Æneas, yet mentions nothing of his leading a colony into a foreign country and settling there. But that the Romans valued themselves on their Trojan ancestry is so undoubted a truth that I need not prove it. Even the seals which we have remaining of Julius Cæsar, which we know to be antique, have the star of Venus over them (though they were all graven after his death), as a note that he was deified. I doubt not but it was one reason why Augustus should be so passionately concerned for the preservation of the *Æneis*, which its author had condemned to be burnt, as an imperfect poem, by his last will and testament, because it did him a real service, as well as an honour; that a work should not be lost where his divine original was celebrated in verse which had the character of immortality stamped upon it.

Neither were the great Roman families, which flourished in his time, less obliged by him than the Emperor. Your Lordship knows with what address he makes mention of them, as captains of ships or leaders in the war; and even some of Italian extraction are not forgotten. These are the single stars which are sprinkled through the *Æneis*: but there are whole constellations of them in the Fifth Book. And I could not but take notice, when I translated it, of some favourite families to which he gives the victory and awards the prizes, in the person of his hero, at the funeral games which were celebrated in honour of Anchises. I insist not on their names; but am pleased to find the Memmii amongst them, derived from Mnestheus, because Lucretius dedicates to one of that family, a branch of which destroyed Corinth. I likewise either found or formed an image to myself of the contrary kind; that those who lost the prizes were such as had disobliged the poet, or were in disgrace with Augustus, or enemies to Mæcenas; and this was the poetical revenge he took: for *genus irritabile vatum*, as Horace says. When a poet is thoroughly provoked, he will do himself justice, however dear it cost him; *animamque in vulnere ponit*. I think these are not bare imaginations of my own, though I find no trace of them in the commentators; but one poet may judge of another by himself. The vengeance we defer is not forgotten. I hinted before that the whole Roman people were obliged by Virgil in deriving them from Troy, an ancestry which they affected. We and the French are of the same humour: they would be thought to descend from a son, I think, of Hector; and we would have our Britain both named and planted by a descendant of Æneas. Spenser favours this opinion what he can. His Prince Arthur, or whoever he intends by him, is a Trojan. Thus the hero of Homer was a Grecian, of Virgil a Roman, of Tasso an Italian.

I have transgressed my bounds, and gone further than the moral led me. But if your Lordship is not tired, I am safe enough.

Thus far, I think, my author is defended. But, as Augustus

is still shadowed in the person of Æneas, of which I shall say
more when I come to the manners which the poet gives his
hero, I must prepare that subject by showing how dexterously
he managed both the prince and people, so as to displease
neither and to do good to both; which is the part of a wise
and an honest man, and proves that it is possible for a courtier
not to be a knave. I shall continue still to speak my thoughts
like a free-born subject, as I am; though such things, perhaps,
as no Dutch commentator could, and I am sure no Frenchman
durst. I have already told your Lordship my opinion of Virgil,
that he was no arbitrary man. Obliged he was to his master
for his bounty; and he repays him with good counsel, how to
behave himself in his new monarchy, so as to gain the affections
of his subjects and deserve to be called the Father of his Country.
From this consideration it is that he chose, for the ground-work
of his poem, one empire destroyed and another raised from the
ruins of it. This was just the parallel. Æneas could not
pretend to be Priam's heir in a lineal succession; for Anchises,
the hero's father, was only of the second branch of the royal
family; and Helenus, a son of Priam, was yet surviving, and
might lawfully claim before him. It may be Virgil mentions
him on that account. Neither has he forgotten Priamus, in the
fifth of his *Æneis*, the son of Polites, youngest son to Priam,
who was slain by Pyrrhus, in the Second Book. Æneas had
only married Creusa, Priam's daughter, and by her could have
no title while any of the male issue were remaining. In this
case, the poet gave him the next title, which is that of an
elective king. The remaining Trojans chose him to lead them
forth and settle them in some foreign country. Ilioneus, in
his speech to Dido, calls him expressly by the name of king.
Our poet, who all this while had Augustus in his eye, had no
desire he should seem to succeed by any right of inheritance
derived from Julius Cæsar (such a title being but one degree
removed from conquest), for what was introduced by force, by
force may be removed. 'Twas better for the people that they
should give than he should take; since that gift was indeed
no more at bottom than a trust. Virgil gives us an example
of this in the person of Mezentius: he governed arbitrarily;
he was expelled, and came to the deserved end of all tyrants.
Our author shows us another sort of kingship in the person of
Latinus: he was descended from Saturn, and, as I remember,
in the third degree. He is described a just and gracious prince,
solicitous for the welfare of his people, always consulting with

his Senate to promote the common good. We find him at the head of them, when he enters into the council-hall, speaking first, but still demanding their advice, and steering by it, as far as the iniquity of the times would suffer him. And this is the proper character of a king by inheritance, who is born a Father of his Country. Æneas, though he married the heiress of the crown, yet claimed no title to it during the life of his father-in-law. *Pater arma Latinus habeto*, etc., are Virgil's words. As for himself, he was contented to take care of his country gods, who were not those of Latium; wherein our divine author seems to relate to the after-practice of the Romans, which was to adopt the gods of those they conquered, or received as members of their commonwealth. Yet, withal, he plainly touches at the office of the high-priesthood, with which Augustus was invested, and which made his person more sacred and inviolable than even the tribunitial power. It was not therefore for nothing that the most judicious of all poets made that office vacant by the death of Panthus in the Second Book of the *Æneis* for his hero to succeed in it, and consequently for Augustus to enjoy. I know not that any of the commentators have taken notice of that passage. If they have not, I am sure they ought; and if they have, I am not indebted to them for the observation. The words of Virgil are very plain:—

> Sacra, suosque tibi commendat Troja penates.

As for Augustus, or his uncle Julius, claiming by descent from Æneas, that title is already out of doors. Æneas succeeded not, but was elected. Troy was fore-doomed to fall for ever:—

> Postquam res Asiæ Priamique evertere gentem
> Immeritam visum superis.—Æneis iii. line 1.

Augustus, 'tis true, had once resolved to rebuild that city, and there to make the seat of empire: but Horace writes an ode on purpose to deter him from that thought; declaring the place to be accursed, and that the gods would as often destroy it as it should be raised. Hereupon the emperor laid aside a project so ungrateful to the Roman people. But by this, my Lord, we may conclude that he had still his pedigree in his head, and had an itch of being thought a divine king, if his poets had not given him better counsel.

I will pass by many less material objections, for want of room to answer them: what follows next is of great importance, if the critics can make out their charge; for 'tis levelled at the manners which our poet gives his hero, and which are the same which were eminently seen in his Augustus. Those manners were, piety to the gods and a dutiful affection to his father, love to his relations, care of his people, courage and conduct in the wars, gratitude to those who had obliged him, and justice in general to mankind.

Piety, as your Lordship sees, takes place of all, as the chief part of his character; and the word in Latin is more full than it can possibly be expressed in any modern language: for there it comprehends not only devotion to the gods, but filial love, and tender affection to relations of all sorts. As instances of this, the deities of Troy, and his own Penates, are made the companions of his flight: they appear to him in his voyage, and advise him; and at last he replaces them in Italy, their native country. For his father, he takes him on his back: he leads his little son: his wife follows him; but, losing his footsteps through fear or ignorance, he goes back into the midst of his enemies to find her, and leaves not his pursuit until her ghost appears to forbid his further search. I will say nothing of his duty to his father while he lived, his sorrow for his death, of the games instituted in honour of his memory, or seeking him, by his command, even after his death, in the Elysian fields. I will not mention his tenderness for his son, which everywhere is visible—of his raising a tomb for Polydorus, the obsequies for Misenus, his pious remembrance of Deiphobus, the funerals of his nurse, his grief for Pallas, and his revenge taken on his murderer, whom otherwise, by his natural compassion, he had forgiven: and then the poem had been left imperfect; for we could have had no certain prospect of his happiness, while the last obstacle to it was removed. Of the other parts which compose his character, as a king or as a general, I need say nothing; the whole *Æneis* is one continued instance of some one or other of them; and where I find anything of them taxed, it shall suffice me, as briefly as I can, to vindicate my divine master to your Lordship, and by you to the reader. But herein Segrais, in his admirable preface to his translation of the *Æneis*, as the author of the Dauphin's *Virgil* justly calls it, has prevented me. Him I follow, and what I borrow from him, am ready to acknowledge to him. For, impartially speaking, the French are as much better critics than the English, as they are worse poets. Thus we generally allow, that they better understand the management of a war than our islanders; but we know we are superior to them in the day of battle. They value themselves on their generals, we on our soldiers. But this is not the proper place to decide that question, if they make it one. I shall say perhaps as much of other nations, and their poets, excepting only Tasso; and hope to make my assertion good, which is but doing justice to my country; part of which honour will reflect on your Lordship, whose thoughts are always just; your numbers harmonious, your words chosen, your expressions strong and manly, your verse flowing, and your turns as happy as they are easy. If you would set us more copies, your example would make all precepts needless. In the meantime, that little you have written is owned, and that particularly by the poets (who are a nation not over lavish of praise to their contemporaries), as a principal ornament of our language; but the sweetest essences are always confined in the smallest glasses.

When I speak of your Lordship, 'tis never a digression, and therefore I need beg no pardon for it; but take up Segrais where I left him, and shall use him less often than I have occasion for him; for his preface is a perfect piece of criticism, full and clear, and digested into an exact method; mine is loose, and, as I intended it, epistolary. Yet I dwell on many things which he durst not touch; for 'tis dangerous to offend an arbitrary master; and every patron who has the power of Augustus has not his clemency. In short, my Lord, I would not translate him, because I would bring you somewhat of my own. His notes and observations on every book are of the same excellency; and, for the same reason, I omit the greater part.

He takes notice that Virgil is arraigned for placing piety before valour, and making that piety the chief character of his hero. I have said already from Bossu, that a poet is not obliged to make his hero a virtuous man; therefore, neither Homer nor Tasso are to be blamed for giving what predominant quality they pleased to their first character. But Virgil, who designed to form a perfect prince, and would insinuate that Augustus, whom he calls Æneas in his poem, was truly such, found himself obliged to make him without blemish, thoroughly virtuous; and a thorough virtue both begins and ends in piety. Tasso, without question, observed this before me, and therefore split his hero in two: he gave Godfrey piety, and Rinaldo fortitude, for their chief qualities or manners. Homer, who had chosen another moral, makes both Agamemnon and Achilles vicious; for his design was to instruct in virtue, by showing the deformity of vice. I avoid repetition of what I have said above. What follows is translated literally from Segrais.

" Virgil had considered that the greatest virtues of Augustus consisted in the perfect art of governing his people; which caused him to reign for more than forty years in great felicity. He considered that his emperor was valiant, civil, popular, eloquent, politic, and religious; he has given all these qualities to Æneas. But, knowing that piety alone comprehends the whole duty of man towards the gods, towards his country and towards his relation, he judged that this ought to be his first character, whom he would set for a pattern of perfection. In reality, they who believe that the praises which arise from valour are superior to those which proceed from any other virtues, have not considered (as they ought) that valour, destitute of other virtues, cannot render a man worthy of any true esteem. That quality, which signifies no more than an intrepid courage, may be separated from many others which are good, and accompanied with many which are ill. A man may be very valiant, and yet impious and vicious. But the same cannot be said of piety, which excludes all ill qualities, and comprehends even valour itself, with all other qualities which are good. Can we, for example, give the praise of valour to a man who should see his gods profaned, and should want the courage to defend them? to a man who should abandon his father, or desert his king, in his last necessity? "

Thus far Segrais, in giving the preference to piety before valour. I will now follow him where he considers this valour, or intrepid courage, singly in itself; and this also Virgil gives to his Æneas, and that in the heroical degree.

Having first concluded that our poet did for the best in taking the first character of his hero from that essential virtue on which the rest depend, he proceeds to tell us that in the ten years' war of Troy he was considered as the second champion of his country, allowing Hector the first place; and this, even by the confession of Homer, who took all occasions of setting up his own countrymen the Grecians, and of undervaluing the Trojan chiefs. But Virgil (whom Segrais forgot to cite) makes Diomede give him a higher character for strength and courage. His testimony is this, in the Eleventh Book:—

> Stetimus tela aspera contra,
> Contulimusque manus: experto credite, quantus
> In clypeum assurgat, quo turbine torqueat hastam.
> Si duo præterea tales Idæa tulisset
> Terra viros, ultro Inachias venisset ad urbes
> Dardanus, et versis lugeret Græcia fatis.
> Quicquid apud duræ cessatum est mænia Trojæ,
> Hectoris Æneæque manu victoria Graium

Hæsit, et in decumum vestigia rettulit annum.
Ambo animis, ambo insignes præstantibus armis:
Hic pietate prior . . .

I give not here my translation of these verses, though I think
I have not ill succeeded in them, because your Lordship is so
great a master of the original, that I have no reason to desire
you should see Virgil and me so near together; but you may
please, my Lord, to take notice, that the Latin author refines
upon the Greek, and insinuates that Homer had done his hero
wrong in giving the advantage of the duel to his own countryman; though Diomedes was manifestly the second champion of
the Grecians; and Ulysses preferred him before Ajax, when he
chose him for the companion of his nightly expedition; for he
had a headpiece of his own, and wanted only the fortitude of
another to bring him off with safety, and that he might compass
his design with honour.

The French translator thus proceeds: "They, who accuse
Æneas for want of courage, either understand not Virgil or
have read him slightly; otherwise they would not raise an
objection so easily to be answered." Hereupon he gives so
many instances of the hero's valour, that to repeat them after
him would tire your Lordship, and put me to the unnecessary
trouble of transcribing the greatest part of the three last Æneids.
In short, more could not be expected from an Amadis, a Sir
Lancelot, or the whole Round Table, than he performs. *Proxima
quæque metit gladio* is the perfect account of a knight-errant.
"If it be replied," continues Segrais, "that it was not difficult
for him to undertake and achieve such hardy enterprises, because
he wore enchanted arms; that accusation, in the first place,
must fall on Homer ere it can reach Virgil." Achilles was as
well provided with them as Æneas, though he was invulnerable
without them. And Ariosto, the two Tassos, Bernardo, and
Torquato, even our own Spenser, in a word, all modern poets,
have copied Homer as well as Virgil: he is neither the first nor
last, but in the midst of them; and therefore is safe, if they are
so. "Who knows," says Segrais, "but that his fated armour was
only an allegorical defence, and signified no more than that he
was under the peculiar protection of the gods?—born, as the
astrologers will tell us out of Virgil (who was well versed in the
Chaldean mysteries), under the favourable influence of Jupiter,
Venus, and the Sun." But I insist not on this, because I know
you believe not there is such an art; though not only Horace
and Persius, but Augustus himself, thought otherwise. But, in

defence of Virgil, I dare positively say, that he has been more cautious in this particular than either his predecessor, or his descendants: for Æneas was actually wounded, in the Twelfth of the *Æneis;* though he had the same God-smith to forge his arms as had Achilles. It seems he was no warluck, as the Scots commonly call such men, who, they say, are iron-free, or lead-free. Yet, after this experiment, that his arms were not impenetrable, when he was cured indeed by his mother's help, because he was that day to conclude the war by the death of Turnus, the poet durst not carry the miracle too far, and restore him wholly to his former vigour: he was still too weak to overtake his enemy; yet we see with what courage he attacks Turnus, when he faces and renews the combat. I need say no more; for Virgil defends himself without needing my assistance, and proves his hero truly to deserve that name. He was not then a second-rate champion, as they would have him, who thinks fortitude the first virtue in a hero. But, being beaten from this hold, they will not yet allow him to be valiant, because he wept more often, as they think, than well becomes a man of courage.

In the first place, if tears are arguments of cowardice, what shall I say of Homer's hero? Shall Achilles pass for timorous because he wept, and wept on less occasions than Æneas? Herein Virgil must be granted to have excelled his master. For once both heroes are described lamenting their lost loves: Briseis was taken away by force from the Grecians; Creusa was lost for ever to her husband. But Achilles went roaring along the salt sea-shore, and, like a booby, was complaining to his mother when he should have revenged his injury by arms. Æneas took a nobler course; for, having secured his father and his son, he repeated all his former dangers, to have found his wife, if she had been above ground. And here your Lordship may observe the address of Virgil; it was not for nothing that this passage was related with all these tender circumstances. Æneas told it; Dido heard it. That he had been so affectionate a husband was no ill argument to the coming dowager, that he might prove as kind to her. Virgil has a thousand secret beauties, though I have not leisure to remark them.

Segrais, on this subject of a hero shedding tears, observes, that historians commend Alexander for weeping when he read the mighty actions of Achilles; and Julius Cæsar is likewise praised, when, out of the same noble envy, he wept at the victories of Alexander. But, if we observe more closely, we shall find that

the tears of Æneas were always on a laudable occasion. Thus
he weeps out of compassion and tenderness of nature, when, in
the temple of Carthage, he beholds the pictures of his friends
who sacrificed their lives in defence of their country. He
deplores the lamentable end of his pilot Palinurus, the untimely
death of young Pallas his confederate, and the rest, which I omit.
Yet, even for these tears, his wretched critics dare condemn him.
They make Æneas little better than a kind of St. Swithin hero,
always raining. One of these censors is bold enough to argue
him of cowardice, when, in the beginning of the First Book, he
not only weeps, but trembles, at an approaching storm—

> Extemplo Æneæ solvuntur frigore membra:
> Ingemit; et duplices tendens ad sidera palmas, etc.

But to this I have answered formerly, that his fear was not for
himself but for his people. And what can give a sovereign a
better commendation, or recommend a hero more to the affection
of the reader? They were threatened with a tempest, and he
wept; he was promised Italy, and therefore he prayed for the
accomplishment of that promise. All this in the beginning of a
storm; therefore he showed the more early piety, and the quicker
sense of compassion. Thus much I have urged elsewhere in
the defence of Virgil; and, since, I have been informed by Mr.
Moyle, a young gentleman whom I can never sufficiently commend that the Ancients accounted drowning an accursed
death; so that, if we grant him to have been afraid, he had just
occasion for that fear, both in relation to himself and to his
subjects. I think our adversaries can carry this argument no
further, unless they tell us that he ought to have had more confidence in the promise of the gods; but how was he assured
that he had understood their oracles aright? Helenus might be
mistaken; Phœbus might speak doubtfully, even his mother
might flatter him, that he might prosecute his voyage, which if
it succeeded happily, he should be the founder of an empire;
for, that she herself was doubtful of his fortune, is apparent by
the address she made to Jupiter on his behalf, to which the god
makes answer in these words—

> Parce metu, Cytherea: manent immota tuorum
> Fata tibi, etc.—

notwithstanding which, the goddess, though comforted, was not
assured; for, even after this, through the course of the whole
Æneis, she still apprehends the interest which Juno might wake
with Jupiter against her son. For it was a moot point in heaven,

whether he could alter Fate or not. And indeed some passages
in Virgil would make us suspect that he was of opinion Jupiter
might defer Fate, though he could not alter it; for, in the latter
end of the Tenth Book, he introduces Juno begging for the life
of Turnus, and flattering her husband with the power of changing
destiny: *Tua, qui potes, orsa reflectas!* To which he graciously
answers—

> Si mora præsentis leti, tempusque caduco
> Oratur juveni, meque hoc ita ponere sentis,
> Tolle fuga Turnum, atque instantibus eripe fatis.
> Hactenus indulsisse vacat. Sin altior istis
> Sub precibus venia ulla latet, totumque moveri
> Mutarive putas bellum, spes pascis inanes.

But, that he could not alter those decrees, the king of gods
himself confesses, in the book above cited, when he comforts
Hercules for the death of Pallas, who had invoked his aid, before
he threw his lance at Turnus—

> Trojæ sub mænibus altis,
> Tot nati cecidere deum; quin occidit una
> Sarpedon, mea progenies. Etiam sua Turnum
> Fata manent, metasque dati pervenit ad ævi.

Where he plainly acknowledges that he could not save his own
son, or prevent the death which he foresaw. Of his power to
defer the blow, I once occasionally discoursed with that excellent
person Sr Robert Howard, who is better conversant than any
man that I know in the doctrine of the Stoics; and he set me
right, from the concurrent testimony of philosophers and poets,
that Jupiter could not retard the effect of Fate, even for a
moment. For, when I cited Virgil, as favouring the contrary
opinion in that verse,

> Tolle fuga Turnum, atque instantibus eripe fatis,

he replied, and, I think, with exact judgment, that, when
Jupiter gave Juno leave to withdraw Turnus from the present
danger, it was because he certainly foreknew that his fatal hour
was not come; that it was in Destiny for Juno at that time to
save him; and that he himself obeyed Destiny in giving her
that leave.

I need say no more in justification of our hero's courage, and
am much deceived if he ever be attacked on this side of his character again. But he is arraigned with more show of reason by
the ladies, who will make a numerous party against him, for
being false to love in forsaking Dido. And I cannot much
blame them; for, to say the truth, it is an ill precedent for their

gallants to follow. Yet, if I can bring him off with flying colours, they may learn experience at her cost, and, for her sake, avoid a cave, as the worst shelter they can choose from a shower of rain, especially when they have a lover in their company.

In the first place, Segrais observes with much acuteness that they who blame Æneas for his insensibility of love when he left Carthage, contradict their former accusation of him for being always crying, compassionate, and effeminately sensible of those misfortunes which befell others. They give him two contrary characters; but Virgil makes him of a piece, always grateful, always tender-hearted. But they are impudent enough to discharge themselves of this blunder, by laying the contradiction at Virgil's door. He, say they, has shown his hero with these inconsistent characters, acknowledging and ungrateful, compassionate and hardhearted, but, at the bottom, fickle, and self-interested. For Dido had not only received his weather-beaten troops before she saw him, and given them her protection, but had also offered them an equal share in her dominion—

> Vultis et his mecum pariter considere regnis?
> Urbem quam statuo, vestra est.

This was an obligement never to be forgotten; and the more to be considered, because antecedent to her love. That passion, 'tis true, produced the usual effects, of generosity, gallantry, and care to please; and thither we refer them. But when she had made all these advances it was still in his power to have refused them; after the intrigue of the cave (call it marriage, or enjoyment only), he was no longer free to take or leave; he had accepted the favour, and was obliged to be constant, if he would be grateful.

My Lord, I have set this argument in the best light I can, that the ladies may not think I write booty; and perhaps it may happen to me, as it did to Dr. Cudworth, who has raised such strong objections against the being of a God and Providence, that many think he has not answered them. You may please at least to hear the adverse party. Segrais pleads for Virgil that no less than an absolute command from Jupiter could excuse this insensibility of the hero, and this abrupt departure, which looks so like extreme ingratitude. But, at the same time, he does wisely to remember you that Virgil had made piety the first character of Æneas; and this being allowed, as I am afraid it must, he was obliged, antecedent to all other considerations, to search an asylum for his Gods in

Italy; for those very Gods, I say, who had promised to his race the universal empire. Could a pious man dispense with the commands of Jupiter to satisfy his passion? or take it in the strongest sense, to comply with the obligations of his gratitude? Religion, 'tis true, must have moral honesty for its ground-work or we shall be apt to suspect its truth; but an immediate revelation dispenses with all duties of morality. All casuists agree that theft is a breach of the moral law; yet, if I might presume to mingle things sacred with profane, the Israelites only spoiled the Egyptians, not robbed them; because the propriety was transferred by a revelation to their law-giver. I confess Dido was a very infidel in this point; for she would not believe, as Virgil makes her say, that ever Jupiter would send Mercury on such an immoral errand. But this needs no answer, at least no more than Virgil gives it:—

> Fata obstant; placidasque viri Deus obstruit aures.

This notwithstanding, as Segrais confesses, he might have shown a little more sensibility when he left her; for that had been according to his character.

But let Virgil answer for himself. He still loved her, and struggled with his inclinations to obey the Gods—

> Curam sub corde premebat,
> Multa gemens, magnoque animum labefactus amore.

Upon the whole matter, and humanly speaking, I doubt there was a fault somewhere; and Jupiter is better able to bear the blame than either Virgil or Æneas. The poet, it seems, had found it out, and therefore brings the deserting hero and the forsaken lady to meet together in the lower regions, where he excuses himself when 'tis too late; and accordingly she will take no satisfaction, nor so much as hear him. Now Segrais is forced to abandon his defence, and excuses his author by saying that the *Æneis* is an imperfect work, and that death prevented the divine poet from reviewing it; and for that reason he had condemned it to the fire; though, at the same time, his two translators must acknowledge that the Sixth Book is the most correct of the whole *Æneis*. Oh, how convenient is a machine sometimes in a heroic poem! This of Mercury is plainly one; and Virgil was constrained to use it here, or the honesty of his hero would be ill-defended. And the fair sex, however, if they had the deserter in their power, would certainly have shown him no more mercy than the Bacchanals did Orpheus: for if too much constancy may be a fault sometimes, then want of constancy, and ingratitude after the last favour, is a crime that never will be forgiven. But of machines more in their proper place, where I shall show with how much judgment they have been used by Virgil; and, in the meantime, pass to another article of his defence, on the present subject; where, if I cannot clear the hero, I hope at least to bring off the poet; for here I must divide their causes. Let Æneas trust to his machine, which will only help to break his fall; but the address is incomparable. Plato, who borrowed so much from Homer, and yet concluded for the banishment of all poets, would at least have rewarded Virgil before he sent him into exile. But I go further, and say, that he ought to be acquitted, and deserved, beside, the bounty of Augustus and the gratitude of the Roman people. If, after this, the ladies will stand out, let them remember that the jury is not all agreed; for Octavia was of his party, and was of the first quality in Rome; she was present at the reading of the Sixth Æneid: and we know not that she condemned Æneas; but we are sure she presented the poet for his admirable elegy on her son Marcellus.

But let us consider the secret reasons which Virgil had for thus framing this noble episode, wherein the whole passion of love is more exactly described than in any other poet. Love was the theme of his Fourth Book; and, though it is the shortest of the whole *Æneis*, yet there he has given its beginning, its progress, its traverses, and its conclusion; and had exhausted so entirely this subject that he could resume it but very slightly in the eight ensuing books.

She was warmed with the graceful appearance of the hero; she smothered those sparkles out of decency; but conversation blew them up into a flame. Then she was forced to make a confident of her whom she best might trust, her own sister, who approves the passion and thereby augments it; then succeeds her public owning it; and, after that, the consummation. Of Venus and Juno, Jupiter and Mercury, I say nothing; for they were all machining work; but, possession having cooled his love, as it increased hers, she soon perceived the change, or at least grew suspicious of a change; this suspicion soon turned to jealousy, and jealousy to rage; then she disdains and threatens, and again is humble, and entreats, and, nothing availing, despairs, curses, and at last becomes her own executioner. See here the whole process of that passion, to which nothing can be added. I dare go no further, lest I should lose the connection of my discourse.

To love our native country, and to study its benefit and its glory, to be interested in its concerns, is natural to all men, and is indeed our common duty. A poet makes a further step; for endeavouring to do honour to it, 'tis allowable in him even to be partial in its cause, for he is not tied to truth or fettered by the laws of history. Homer and Tasso are justly praised for choosing their heroes out of Greece and Italy; Virgil indeed made his a Trojan; but it was to derive the Romans and his own Augustus from him. But all the three poets are manifestly partial to their heroes in favour of their country; for Dares Phrygius reports of Hector that he was slain cowardly; Æneas, according to the best account, slew not Mezentius, but was slain by him; and the chronicles of Italy tell us little of that Rinaldo d'Este who conquers Jerusalem in Tasso. He might be a champion of the Church; but we know not that he was so much as present at the siege. To apply this to Virgil, he thought himself engaged in honour to espouse the cause and quarrel of his country against Carthage. He knew he could not please the Romans better, or oblige them more to patronise his poem, than by disgracing the foundress of that city. He shows her ungrateful to the memory of her first husband, doting on a stranger; enjoyed, and afterwards forsaken, by him. This was the original, says he, or the immortal hatred betwixt the two rival nations. 'Tis true, he colours the falsehood of Æneas by an express command from Jupiter to forsake the queen who had obliged him; but he knew the Romans were to be his readers; and them he bribed, perhaps at the expense of his hero's honesty; but he gained his cause, however, as pleading before corrupt judges. They were content to see their founder false to love; for still he had the advantage of the amour; it was their enemy whom he forsook; and she might have forsaken him if he had not got the start of her; she had already forgotten her vows to her Sichæus; and *varium et mutabile semper femina* is the sharpest satire, in the fewest words, that ever was made on womankind; for both the adjectives are neuter, and *animal* must be understood to make them grammar. Virgil does well to put those words into the mouth of Mercury. *If a God had not spoken them, neither durst he have written them, nor I translated them.* Yet the deity was forced to come twice on the same errand; and the second time, as much a hero as Æneas was, he frighted him. It seems he feared not Jupiter so much as Dido; for your Lordship may observe that, as much intent as he was upon his voyage, yet he still delayed it till the messenger was obliged to tell him plainly that, if he weighed not anchor in the night, the queen would be with him in the morning. *Notumque furens quid femina possit;* she was injured; she was revengeful; she was powerful. The poet had likewise before hinted that her people were naturally perfidious; for he gives their character in their queen, and makes a proverb of *Punica fides* many ages before it was invented.

Thus, I hope, my Lord, that I have made good my promise, and justified the poet, whatever becomes of the false knight. And sure a poet is as much privileged to lie as an ambassador for the honour and interest of his country; at least as Sir Henry Wotton has defined.

This naturally leads me to the defence of the famous anachronism in making Æneas and Dido contemporaries; for it is certain that the hero lived almost two hundred years before the building of Carthage. One who imitates Boccalini says that Virgil was accused before Apollo for this error. The God soon found that he was not able to defend his favourite by reason; for the case was clear: he therefore gave this middle sentence, that anything might be allowed to his son Virgil on the account of his other merits; that, being a monarch, he had a dispensing power, and pardoned him. But, that this special act of grace might never be drawn into example, or pleaded by his puny successors in justification of their ignorance, he decreed for the future no poet should presume to make a lady die for love two hundred years before her birth. To moralise this story, Virgil is the Apollo who has this dispensing power. His great judgment made the laws of poetry; but he never made himself a slave to them; chronology, at best, is but a cobweb-law, and he broke through it with his weight. They who will imitate him wisely, must choose, as he did, an obscure and a remote era, where they may invent at pleasure and not be easily contradicted. Neither he, nor the Romans, had ever read the Bible, by which only his false computation of times can be made out against him. This Segrais says in his defence, and proves it from his learned friend Bochartus, whose letter on this subject he has printed at the end of the Fourth Æneid, to which I refer your Lordship and the reader. Yet the credit of Virgil was so great that he made this fable of his own invention pass for an authentic history, or at least as credible as anything in Homer. Ovid takes it up after him, even in the same age, and makes an ancient heroine of Virgil's new-created Dido; dictates a letter for her, just before her death, to the ungrateful fugitive; and, very unluckily for himself, is for measuring a sword with a man so much superior in force to him on the same subject. I think I may be judge of this, because I have translated both. The famous author of the *Art of Love* has nothing of his own; he borrows all from a greater master in his own profession; and, which is worse, improves nothing which he finds. Nature fails him; and, being forced to his old shift, he has recourse to witticism. This passes indeed with his soft admirers, and gives him the preference to Virgil in their esteem. But let them like for themselves and not prescribe to others: for our author needs not their admiration.

The motives that induced Virgil to coin this fable I have showed already; and have also begun to show that he might make this anachronism by superseding the mechanic rules of poetry, for the same reason that a monarch may dispense with or suspend his own laws when he finds it necessary so to do, especially if those laws are not altogether fundamental. Nothing is to be called a fault in poetry, says Aristotle, but what is against the art; therefore a man may be an admirable poet without being an exact chronologer. Shall we dare, continues Segrais, to condemn Virgil for having made a fiction against the order of time, when we commend Ovid and other poets, who have made many of their fictions against the order of Nature? For what else are the splendid miracles of the *Metamorphoses*? Yet these are beautiful as they are related, and have also deep learning and instructive mythologies couched under them: but to give, as Virgil does in this episode, the original cause of the long wars betwixt Rome and Carthage, to draw truth out of fiction after so probable a manner, with so much beauty, and so much for the honour of his country, was proper only to the divine wit of Maro; and Tasso, in one of his *Discourses*, admires him for this particularly. 'Tis not lawful, indeed, to contradict a point of history which is known to all the world, as, for example, to make Hannibal and Scipio contemporaries with Alexander; but, in the dark recesses of antiquity, a great poet may and ought to feign such things as he finds not there, if they can be brought to embellish that subject which he treats. On the other side, the pains and diligence of ill poets is but thrown away when they want the genius to invent and feign agreeably. But, if the fictions be delightful (which they always are, if they be natural), if they be of a piece; if the beginning, the middle, and the end be in their due places, and artfully united to each other, such works can never fail of their deserved success. And such is Virgil's episode of Dido and Æneas; where the sourest critic must acknowledge that if he had deprived his *Æneis* of so great an ornament, because he found no traces of it in antiquity, he had avoided their unjust censure, but had wanted one of the greatest beauties of his poem. I shall say more of this in the next article of their charge against him, which is want of invention. In the meantime, I may affirm, in honour of this episode, that it is not only now esteemed the most pleasing entertainment of the *Æneis*, but was so accounted in his own age, and before it was mellowed into that reputation which time has given it; for which I need produce no other testimony than that of Ovid, his contemporary:

> Nec pars ulla magis legitur de corpore toto,
> Quam non legitimo fœdere junctus amor.

Where, by the way, you may observe, my Lord, that Ovid in those words, *Non legitimo fœdere junctus amor*, will by no means allow it to be a lawful marriage betwixt Dido and Æneas. He was in banishment when he wrote those verses, which I cite from his letter to Augustus: "You, Sir," says he, "have sent me into exile for writing my *Art of Love* and my wanton *Elegies;* yet your own poet was happy in your good graces, though he brought Dido and Æneas into a cave, and left them there not over honestly together. May I be so bold to ask your Majesty, is it a greater fault to teach the art of unlawful love than to show it in the action?" But was Ovid, the court-poet, so bad a courtier as to find no other plea to excuse himself than by a plain accusation of his master? Virgil confessed it was a lawful marriage betwixt the lovers, that Juno, the Goddess of Matrimony, had ratified it by her presence; for it was her business to bring matters to that issue. That the ceremonies were short we may believe; for Dido was not only amorous, but a widow. Mercury himself, though employed on a quite contrary errand, yet owns it a marriage by an *innuendo : pulchramque uxorius urbem Exstruis.* He calls Æneas not only a husband, but upbraids him for being a fond husband, as the word *uxorius* implies. Now mark a little, if your Lordship pleases, why Virgil is so much concerned to make this marriage (for he seems to be the father of the bride himself, and to give her to the bridegroom): it was to make way for the divorce which he intended afterwards; for he was a finer flatterer than Ovid; and I more than conjecture that he had in his eye the divorce which not long before had passed betwixt the Emperor and Scribonia. He drew this dimple in the cheek of Æneas to prove Augustus of the same family by so remarkable a feature in the same place. Thus, as we say in our homespun English proverb, he killed two birds with one stone; pleased the Emperor, by giving him the resemblance of his ancestor, and gave him such a resemblance as was not scandalous in that age. For to leave one wife and take another was but a matter of gallantry at that time of day among the Romans. *Neque hæc in fœdera veni* is the very excuse which Æneas makes when he leaves his lady: "I made no such bargain with you at our marriage, to live always drudging on at Carthage: my business was Italy; and I never made a secret of it. If I took my pleasure, had not you your share of it? I leave you free, at my departure, to comfort yourself with the next stranger who happens to be shipwrecked on your coast. Be as kind a hostess as you have been to me; and you can never fail of another husband. In the meantime, I call the Gods to witness that I leave your shore unwillingly; for though Juno made the marriage, yet Jupiter commands me to forsake you." This is the effect of what he saith, when it is dishonoured out of Latin verse into English prose. If the poet argued not aright, we must pardon him for a poor blind heathen, who knew no better morals.

I have detained your Lordship longer than I intended on this objection; which would indeed weigh something in a spiritual court, but I am not to defend our poet there. The next, I think, is but a cavil, though the cry is great against him, and hath continued from the time of Macrobius to this present age. I hinted it before. They lay no less than want of invention to his charge—a capital crime, I must acknowledge; for a poet is a maker, as the word signifies; and he who cannot make, that is, invent, has his name for nothing. That which makes this accusation look so strange at the first sight is that he has borrowed so many things from Homer, Apollonius Rhodius, and others who preceded him. But, in the first place, if invention is to be taken in so strict a sense that the matter of a poem must be wholly new, and that in all its parts, then Scaliger has made out, says Segrais, that the history of Troy was no more the invention of Homer than of Virgil. There was not an old woman, or almost a child, but had it in their mouths before the Greek poet or his friends digested it into this admirable order in which we read it. At this rate, as Solomon hath told us, there is nothing new beneath the sun. Who then can pass for an inventor, if Homer, as well as Virgil, must be deprived of that glory? Is Versailles the less a new building, because the architect of that palace hath imitated others which were built before it? Walls, doors, and windows, apartments, offices, rooms of convenience and magnificence are in all great houses. So descriptions, figures, fables, and the rest, must be in all heroic poems; they are the common materials of poetry, furnished from the magazine of nature; every poet hath as much right to them, as every man hath to air or water.

> Quid prohibetis aquas? Usus communis aquarum est.

But the argument of the work, that is to say, its principal action, the economy and disposition of it; these are the things which distinguish copies from originals. The poet who borrows nothing from others is yet to be born; he and the Jews' Messias will come together. There are parts of the *Æneis* which resemble some parts both of the *Ilias* and of the *Odysseis;* as, for example, Æneas descended into Hell, and Ulysses had been there before him; Æneas loved Dido, and Ulysses loved Calypso; in few words, Virgil hath imitated Homer's *Odysseis* in his first six books, and, in his six last, the *Ilias*. But from hence can we infer that the two poets write the same history? Is there no invention in some other parts of Virgil's *Æneis?* The disposition of so many various matters, is not that his own? From what book of Homer had Virgil his episode of Nisus and Euryalus, of Mezentius and Lausus? From whence did he borrow his design of bringing Æneas into Italy? of establishing the Roman Empire on the foundations of a Trojan colony? to say nothing of the honour he did his patron, not only in his descent from Venus, but in making him so like her in his best features, that the Goddess might have mistaken Augustus for her son. He had indeed the story from common fame, as Homer had his from the Egyptian priestess. *Æneadum genetrix* was no more unknown to Lucretius than to him. But Lucretius taught him not to form his hero, to give him piety or valour for his manners, and both in so eminent a degree that, having done what was possible for man to save his king and country, his mother was forced to appear to him and restrain his fury, which hurried him to death in their revenge. But the poet made his piety more successful; he brought off his father and his son; and his Gods witnessed to his devotion, by putting themselves under his protection, to be replaced by him in their promised Italy. Neither the invention nor the conduct of this great action were owing to Homer, or any other poet. 'Tis one thing to copy, and another thing to imitate from Nature. The copier is that servile imitator to whom Horace gives no better a name than that of animal; he will not so much as allow him to be a man. Raphael imitated Nature; they who copy one of Raphael's pieces imitate but him; for his work is their original. They translate him as I do Virgil; and fall as short of him as I of Virgil. There is a kind of invention in the imitation of Raphael; for, though the thing was in Nature, yet the idea of it was his own. Ulysses travelled; so did Æneas: but neither of them were the first travellers; for Cain went into the land of Nod before they were born: and neither of the poets ever heard of such a man. If Ulysses had been killed at Troy, yet Æneas must have gone to sea, or he could never have arrived in Italy. But the designs of the two poets were as different as the courses of their heroes; one went home, and the other sought a home. To return to my first similitude: suppose Apelles and Raphael had each of them painted a burning Troy, might not the modern painter have succeeded as well as the ancient, though neither of them had seen the town on fire? For the draughts of both were taken from the ideas which they had of Nature. Cities had been burnt before either of them were in being. But, to close the simile as I begun it, they would not have designed after the same manner. Apelles would have distinguished Pyrrhus from the rest of all the Grecians, and showed him forcing his entrance into Priam's palace; there he had set him in the fairest light and given him the chief place of all his figures; because he was a Grecian, and he would do honour to his country. Raphael, who was an Italian, and descended from the Trojans, would have made Æneas the hero of his piece; and perhaps not with his father on his back, his son in one hand, his bundle of gods in the other, and his wife following (for an act of piety is not half so graceful in a picture as an act of courage): he would rather have drawn him killing Androgeos, or some other, hand to hand; and the blaze of the fires should have darted full upon his face, to make him conspicuous amongst his Trojans. This, I think, is a just comparison betwixt the two poets, in the conduct of their several designs. Virgil cannot be said to copy Homer; the Grecian had only the advantage of writing first. If it be urged that I have granted a resemblance in some parts, yet therein Virgil has excelled him. For what are the tears of Calypso for being left, to the fury and death of Dido? Where is there the whole process of her passion and all its violent effects to be found, in the languishing episode of the *Odysseis*? If this be to copy, let the critics show us the same disposition, features, or colouring, in their original. The like may be said of the Descent to Hell, which was not of Homer's invention neither; he had it from the story of Orpheus and Eurydice. But to what end did Ulysses make that journey? Æneas undertook it by the express commandment of his father's ghost; there he was to show him all the succeeding heroes of his race, and, next to Romulus (mark, if you please, the address of Virgil), his own patron, Augustus Cæsar. Anchises was likewise to instruct him how to manage the Italian war, and how to conclude it with his honour; that is, in other words, to lay the foundations of that Empire which Augustus was to govern. This is the noble invention of our author; but it has been copied by so many sign-post daubers, that now 'tis grown fulsome, rather by their want of skill, than by the commonness.

In the last place, I may safely grant that, by reading Homer, Virgil was taught to imitate his invention; that is, to imitate like him; which is no more than if a painter studied Raphael that he might learn to design after his manner. And thus I might imitate Virgil if I were capable of writing an heroic poem, and yet the invention be my own: but I should endeavour to avoid a servile copying. I would not give the same story under other names, with the same characters, in the same order, and with the same sequel, for every common reader to find me out at the first sight for a plagiary, and cry: "This I read before in Virgil, in a better language, and in better verse: this is like Merry Andrew on the low rope, copying lubberly the same tricks which his master is so dexterously performing on the high."

I will trouble your Lordship but with one objection more, which I know not whether I found in Le Fèvre or Valois; but I am sure I have read it in another French critic, whom I will not name, because I think it is not much for his reputation. Virgil, in the heat of action—suppose, for example, in describing the fury of his hero in a battle, when he is endeavouring to raise our concernments to the highest pitch—turns short on the sudden into some similitude which diverts say they, your attention from the main subject, and misspends it on some trivial image. He pours cold water into the cauldron, when his business is to make it boil.

This accusation is general against all who would be thought heroic poets; but I think it touches Virgil less than any. He is too great a master of his art to make a blot which may so easily be hit. Similitudes, as I have said, are not for tragedy, which

is all violent, and where the passions are in a perpetual ferment;
for there they deaden where they should animate; they are not
of the nature of dialogue, unless in comedy: a metaphor is
almost all the stage can suffer, which is a kind of similitude
comprehended in a word. But this figure has a contrary effect
in heroic poetry; there it is employed to raise the admiration,
which is its proper business; and admiration is not of so violent
a nature as fear or hope, compassion or horror, or any concernment we can have for such or such a person on the stage. Not
but I confess that similitudes and descriptions, when drawn
into an unreasonable length, must needs nauseate the reader.
Once, I remember, and but once, Virgil makes a similitude of
fourteen lines; and his description of Fame is about the same
number. He is blamed for both; and I doubt not but he would
have contracted them had he lived to reviewed his work;
but faults are no precedents. This I have observed of his
similitudes in general, that they are not placed, as our un-
observing critics tell us, in the heat of any action, but commonly
in its declining. When he has warmed us in his description as
much as possible he can, then, lest that warmth should languish,
he renews it by some apt similitude, which illustrates his subject,
and yet palls not his audience. I need give your Lordship but
one example of this kind, and leave the rest to your observation,
when next you review the whole *Æneis* in the original, un-
blemished by my rude translation. 'Tis in the First Book,
where the poet describes Neptune composing the ocean, on
which Æolus had raised a tempest without his permission. He
had already chidden the rebellious winds for obeying the commands of their usurping master; he had warned them from the
seas; he had beaten down the billows with his mace, dispelled
the clouds, restored the sunshine, while Triton and Cymothoë
were heaving the ships from off the quicksands, before the poet
would offer at a similitude for illustration:—

> Ac, veluti magno in populo cum sæpe coorta est
> Seditio, sævitque animis ignobile vulgus,
> Jamque faces et saxa volant; furor arma ministrat;
> Tum, pietate gravem ac meritis si forte virum quem
> Conspexere, silent, arrectisque auribus adstant;
> Ille regit dictis animos, et pectora mulcet;
> Sic cunctus pelagi cecidit fragor, æquora postquam
> Prospiciens genitor, cæloque invectus aperto,
> Flectit equos, curruque volans dat lora secundo.

This is the first similitude which Virgil makes in this poem,
and one of the longest in the whole; for which reason I the

rather cite it. While the storm was in its fury, any allusion had been improper; for the poet could have compared it to nothing more impetuous than itself; consequently he could have made no illustration. If he could have illustrated, it had been an ambitious ornament out of season, and would have diverted our concernment: *nunc non erat hisce locus;* and therefore he deferred it to its proper place.

These are the criticisms of most moment which have been made against the *Æneis* by the Ancients or Moderns. As for the particular exceptions against this or that passage, Macrobius and Pontanus have answered them already. If I desired to appear more learned than I am, it had been as easy for me to have taken their objections and solutions as it is for a country parson to take the expositions of the fathers out of Junius and Tremellius, or not to have named the authors from whence I had them; for so Ruæus, otherwise a most judicious commentator on Virgil's works, has used Pontanus, his greatest benefactor; of whom he is very silent; and I do not remember that he once cites him.

What follows next is no objection; for that implies a fault: and it had been none in Virgil, if he had extended the time of his action beyond a year. At least Aristotle has set no precise limits to it. Homer's, we know, was within two months: Tasso, I am sure, exceeds not a summer; and, if I examined him, perhaps he might be reduced into a much less compass. Bossu leaves it doubtful whether Virgil's action were within the year, or took up some months beyond it. Indeed, the whole dispute is of no more concernment to the common reader than it is to a ploughman, whether February this year had 28 or 29 days in it. But, for the satisfaction of the more curious (of which number I am sure your Lordship is one), I will translate what I think convenient out of Segrais, whom perhaps you have not read; for he has made it highly probable that the action of the *Æneis* began in the spring, and was not extended beyond the autumn. And we have known campaigns that have begun sooner, and have ended later.

Ronsard, and the rest whom Segrais names, who are of opinion that the action of this poem takes up almost a year and half, ground their calculation thus. Anchises died in Sicily at the end of winter or beginning of the spring. Æneas, immediately after the interment of his father, puts to sea for Italy. He is surprised by the tempest described in the beginning of the First Book; and there it is that the scene of the poem opens, and where the action must commence. He is driven by this storm on the coasts of Afric; he stays at Carthage all that summer, and almost all the winter following, sets sail again for Italy just before the beginning of the spring, meets with contrary winds, and makes Sicily the second time. This part of the action completes the year. Then he celebrates the anniversary of his father's funerals, and shortly after arrives at Cumes; and from thence his time is taken up in his first treaty with Latinus, the overture of the war, the siege of his camp by Turnus, his going for succours to relieve it, his return, the raising of the siege by the first battle, the twelve days' truce, the second battle, the assault of Laurentum, and the single fight with Turnus; all which, they say, cannot take up less than four or five months more; by which account we cannot suppose the entire action to be contained in a much less compass than a year and half.

Segrais reckons another way; and his computation is not condemned by the learned Ruæus, who compiled and published the commentaries on our poet which we call the *Dauphin's Virgil*.

He allows the time of year when Anchises died to be in the latter end of winter, or the beginning of the spring: he acknowledges that, when Æneas is first seen at sea afterwards, and is driven by the tempest on the coast of Afric, is the time when the action is naturally to begin: he confesses, further, that Æneas left Carthage in the latter end of winter; for Dido tells him in express terms, as an argument for his longer stay,

Quinetiam hiberno moliris sidere classem.

But, whereas Ronsard's followers suppose that, when Æneas had buried his father, he set sail immediately for Italy (though the tempest drove him on the coast of Carthage), Segrais will by no means allow that supposition, but thinks it much more probable that he remained in Sicily till the midst of July, or the beginning of August; at which time he places the first appearance of his hero on the sea; and there opens the action of the poem. From which beginning, to the death of Turnus, which concludes the action, there need not be supposed above ten months of intermediate time; for, arriving at Carthage in the latter end of summer, staying there the winter following, departing thence in the very beginning of the spring, making a short abode in Sicily the second time, landing in Italy, and making the war, may be reasonably judged the business but of ten [1] months. To this the Ronsardians reply, that, having

[1] "three," ed. 1697.

been for seven years before in quest of Italy, and having no
more to do in Sicily than to inter his father—after that office was
performed, what remained for him, but, without delay, to
pursue his first adventure? To which Segrais answers, that the
obsequies of his father, according to the rites of the Greeks and
Romans, would detain him for many days; that a longer time
must be taken up in the refitting of his ships after so tedious a
voyage, and in refreshing his weather-beaten soldiers on a
friendly coast. These indeed are but suppositions on both
sides; yet those of Segrais seem better grounded: for the feast of
Dido, when she entertained Æneas first, has the appearance
of a summer's night, which seems already almost ended when
he begins his story; therefore the love was made in autumn:
the hunting followed properly when the heats of that scorching
country were declining; the winter was passed in jollity, as the
season and their love required; and he left her in the latter end
of winter, as is already proved. This opinion is fortified by the
arrival of Æneas at the mouth of Tiber; which marks the season
of the spring; that season being perfectly described by the singing of the birds saluting the dawn, and by the beauty of the
place, which the poet seems to have painted expressly in the
Seventh Æneid—

> Aurora in roseis fulgebat lutea bigis,
> Cum venti posuere. . . .
>   Variæ, circumque supraque,
> Assuetæ ripis volucres, et fluminis alveo,
> Æthera mulcebant cantu.

The remainder of the action required but three months more:
for, when Æneas went for succour to the Tuscans, he found their
army in a readiness to march, and wanting only a commander:
so that, according to this calculation, the *Æneis* takes not up
above a year complete, and may be comprehended in less
compass.

This, amongst other circumstances treated more at large by
Segrais, agrees with the rising of Orion, which caused the tempest
described in the beginning of the First Book. By some passages
in the *Pastorals*, but more particularly in the *Georgics*, our poet
is found to be an exact astronomer, according to the knowledge
of that age. Now Ilioneus (whom Virgil twice employs in
embassies, as the best speaker of the Trojans) attributes that
tempest to Orion, in his speech to Dido—

> Cum, subito assurgens fluctu, nimbosus Orion.—

He must mean either the heliacal or achronical rising of that sign. The heliacal rising of a constellation is when it comes from under the rays of the sun, and begins to appear before daylight; the achronical rising, on the contrary, is when it appears at the close of day, and in opposition to the sun's diurnal course.

The heliacal rising of Orion is at present computed to be about the sixth of July; and about that time it is that he either causes or presages tempests on the seas.

Segrais has observed further, that, when Anna counsels Dido to stay Æneas during the winter, she speaks also of Orion—

> Dum pelago desævit hiems, et aquosus Orion.

If therefore Ilioneus, according to our supposition, understand the heliacal rising of Orion, Anna must mean the achronical, which the different epithets given to that constellation seem to manifest. Ilioneus calls him *nimbosus;* Anna, *aquosus.* He is tempestuous in the summer, when he rises heliacally, and rainy in the winter, when he rises achronically. Your Lordship will pardon me for the frequent repetition of these cant words, which I could not avoid in this abbreviation of Segrais who, I think, deserves no little commendation in this new criticism.

I have yet a word or two to say of Virgil's machines, from my own observation of them. He has imitated those of Homer, but not copied them. It was established, long before this time, in the Roman religion as well as in the Greek, that there were Gods; and both nations, for the most part, worshipped the same Deities; as did also the Trojans, from whom the Romans, I suppose, would rather be thought to derive the rites of their religion, than from the Grecians; because they thought themselves descended from them. Each of those Gods had his proper office, and the chief of them their particular attendants. Thus Jupiter had in propriety Ganymede and Mercury, and Juno had Iris. It was then not for Virgil to create new ministers: he must take what he found in his religion. It cannot therefore be said that he borrowed them from Homer, any more than Apollo, Diana, and the rest, whom he uses as he finds occasion for them, as the Grecian poet did; but he invents the occasions for which he uses them. Venus, after the destruction of Troy, had gained Neptune entirely to her party; therefore we find him busy in the beginning of the *Æneis* to calm the tempest raised by Æolus, and afterwards conducting the Trojan fleet to

Cumes in safety, with the loss only of their pilot, for whom he bargains. I name those two examples amongst a hundred which I omit to prove that Virgil, generally speaking, employed his machines in performing those things which might possibly have been done without them. What more frequent than a storm at sea upon the rising of Orion? What wonder, if, amongst so many ships, there should one be overset, which was commanded by Orontes, though half the winds had not been there which Æolus employed? Might not Palinurus, without a miracle, fall asleep and drop into the sea, having been over-wearied with watching, and secure of a quiet passage by his observation of the skies? At least Æneas, who knew nothing of the machine of Somnus, takes it plainly in this sense—

> O nimium cælo et pelago confise sereno,
> Nudus in ignota, Palinure, jacebis arena.

But machines sometimes are specious things to amuse the reader and give a colour of probability to things otherwise incredible. And besides it soothed the vanity of the Romans to find the Gods so visibly concerned in all the actions of their predecessors. We, who are better taught by our religion, yet own every wonderful accident, which befalls us for the best, to be brought to pass by some special providence of Almighty God and by the care of guardian Angels: and from hence I might infer that no heroic poem can be writ on the Epicurean principles. Which I could easily demonstrate, if there were need to prove it, or I had leisure.

When Venus opens the eyes of her son Æneas to behold the Gods who combated against Troy in that fatal night when it was surprised, we share the pleasure of that glorious vision (which Tasso has not ill copied in the sacking of Jerusalem): but the Greeks had done their business, though neither Neptune, Juno, nor Pallas had given them their divine assistance. The most crude machine which Virgil uses is in the episode of Camilla, where Opis, by the command of her mistress, kills Aruns. The next is in the Twelfth Æneid, where Venus cures her son Æneas. But in the last of these the poet was driven to a necessity; for Turnus was to be slain that very day; and Æneas, wounded as he was, could not have engaged him in single combat unless his hurt had been miraculously healed. And the poet had considered that the dittany which she brought from Crete could not have wrought so speedy an effect without the juice of ambrosia which she mingled with it. After all, that his machine might not seem too violent, we see the hero limping after Turnus. The wound was skinned; but the strength of his thigh was not restored. But what reason had our author to wound Æneas at so critical a time? and how came the cuisses to be worse tempered than the rest of his armour, which was all wrought by Vulcan and his journeymen? These difficulties are not easily to be solved without confessing that Virgil had not life enough to correct his work; though he had reviewed it and found those errors which he resolved to mend: but, being prevented by death, and not willing to leave an imperfect work behind him, he ordained, by his last testament, that his *Æneis* should be burned. As for the death of Aruns, who was shot by a goddess, the machine was not altogether so outrageous as the wounding Mars and Venus by the sword of Diomede. Two divinities, one would have thought, might have pleaded their prerogative of impassibility, or at least not to have been wounded by any mortal hand; beside that the ἰχὼρ, which they shed, was so very like our common blood that it was not to be distinguished from it, but only by the name and colour. As for what Horace says in his *Art of Poetry*, that no machines are to be used unless on some extraordinary occasion—

Nec deus intersit, nisi dignus vindice nodus—

that rule is to be applied to the theatre, of which he is then speaking; and means no more than this, that when the knot of the play is to be untied, and no other way is left for making the discovery, then, and not otherwise, let a God descend upon a rope and clear the business to the audience: but this has no relation to the machines which are used in an epic poem.

In the last place, for the *Dira*, or flying pest, which, flapping on the shield of Turnus, and fluttering about his head, disheartened him in the duel, and presaged to him his approaching death, I might have placed it more properly amongst the objections: for the critics, who lay want of courage to the charge of Virgil's hero, quote this passage as a main proof of their assertion. They say our author had not only secured him before the duel, but also, in the beginning of it, had given him the advantage in impenetrable arms and in his sword; for that of Turnus was not his own, which was forged by Vulcan for his father, but a weapon which he had snatched in haste, and by mistake, belonging to his charioteer Metiscus; that, after all this, Jupiter, who was partial to the Trojan and distrustful of the event, though he had hung the balance, and given it a jog of his hand to weigh

down Turnus thought convenient to give the Fates a collateral
security by sending the screech-owl to discourage him. For
which they quote these words of Virgil—

> Non me tua turbida virtus
> Terret, ait: di me terrent, et Jupiter hostis.

In answer to which, I say, that this machine is one of those
which the poet uses only for ornament, and not out of necessity.
Nothing can be more beautiful or more poetical than his description of the three *Diræ*, or the setting of the balance, which our
Milton has borrowed from him, but employed to a different end:
for, first, he makes God Almighty set the scales for St. Michael
and Satan, when he knew no combat was to follow; then he
makes the good angel's scale descend, and the Devil's mount,
quite contrary to Virgil, if I have translated the three verses
according to my author's sense—

> Jupiter ipse duas æquato examine lances
> Sustinet; et fata imponit diversa duorum;
> Quem damnet labor, et quo vergat pondere letum—

for I have taken these words, *quem damnet labor*, in the sense
which Virgil gives them in another place—*damnabis tu quoque
votis*—to signify a prosperous event. Yet I dare not condemn
so great a genius as Milton: for I am much mistaken if he alludes
not to the text in Daniel, where Belshazzar was put into the
balance and found too light. This is digression; and I return
to my subject. I said above, that these two machines of the
balance and the *Diræ* were only ornamental, and that the success
of the duel had been the same without them: for, when Æneas
and Turnus stood fronting each other before the altar, Turnus
looked dejected, and his colour faded in his face, as if he desponded
of the victory before the fight; and not only he, but all his
party when the strength of the two champions was judged by
the proportion of their limbs, concluded it was *impar pugna*,
and that their chief was over-matched: whereupon Juturna (who
was of the same opinion) took this opportunity to break the
treaty and renew the war. Juno herself had plainly told the
nymph beforehand that her brother was to fight—

> Imparibus fatis, nec dis nec viribus æquis;

so that there was no need of an apparition to fright Turnus: he
had the presage within himself of his impending destiny. The
Diræ only served to confirm him in his first opinion, that it was

his destiny to die in the ensuing combat; and in this sense are those words of Virgil's to be taken—

> Non me tua turbida virtus
> Terret, ait: di me terrent, et Jupiter hostis.

I doubt not but the adverb *solum* is to be understood; "'Tis not your valour only that gives me this concernment; but I find also, by this portent, that Jupiter is my enemy." For Turnus fled before, when his first sword was broken, till his sister supplied him with a better; which indeed he could not use, because Æneas kept him at a distance with his spear. I wonder Ruæus saw not this where he charges his author so unjustly for giving Turnus a second sword to no purpose. How could he fasten a blow, or make a thrust, when he was not suffered to approach? Besides, the chief errand of the *Dira* was to warn Juturna from the field; for she could have brought the chariot again when she saw her brother worsted in the duel. I might further add, that Æneas was so eager of the fight that he left the city, now almost in his possession, to decide his quarrel with Turnus by the sword; whereas Turnus had manifestly declined the combat, and suffered his sister to convey him as far from the reach of his enemy as she could. I say, not only suffered her, but consented to it; for 'tis plain he knew her, by these words—

> O soror, et dudum agnovi, cum prima per artem
> Fœdera turbasti, teque hæc in bella dedisti;
> Et nunc necquicquam fallis dea. . . .

I have dwelt so long on this subject that I must contract what I have to say in reference to my translation, unless I would swell my preface into a volume, and make it formidable to your lordship, when you see so many pages yet behind. And indeed what I have already written, either in justification or praise of Virgil, is against myself, for presuming to copy, in my coarse English, the thoughts and beautiful expressions of this inimitable poet, who flourished in an age when his language was brought to its last perfection, for which it was particularly owing to him and Horace. I will give your Lordship my opinion that those two friends had consulted each other's judgment wherein they should endeavour to excel; and they seem to have pitched on propriety of thought, elegance of words, and harmony of numbers. According to this model, Horace writ his *Odes* and *Epdeso :* for his *Satires* and *Epistles*, being intended wholly for instruction, required another style—

> Ornari res ipsa negat, contenta doceri:

and therefore, as he himself professes, are *sermoni propiora*, nearer prose than verse. But Virgil, who never attempted the lyric verse, is everywhere elegant, sweet, and flowing in his hexameters. His words are not only chosen, but the places in which he ranks them for the sound. He who removes them from the station wherein their master set them spoils the harmony. What he says of the Sibyl's prophecies may be as properly applied to every word of his: they must be read in order as they lie; the least breath discomposes them and somewhat of their divinity is lost. I cannot boast that I have been thus exact in my verses; but I have endeavoured to follow the example of my master, and am the first Englishman, perhaps, who made it his design to copy him in his numbers, his choice of words, and his placing them for the sweetness of the sound. On this last consideration I have shunned the *cæsura* as much as possibly I could: for, wherever that is used, it gives a roughness to the verse; of which we can have little need in a language which is overstocked with consonants. Such is not the Latin, where the vowels and consonants are mixed in proportion to each other: yet Virgil judged the vowels to have somewhat of an over-balance, and therefore tempers their sweetness with *cæsuras*. Such difference there is in tongues that the same figure, which roughens one, gives majesty to another: and that was it which Virgil studied in his verses. Ovid uses it but rarely; and hence it is that his versification cannot so properly be called sweet as luscious. The Italians are forced upon it once or twice in every line, because they have a redundancy of vowels in their language. Their metal is so soft that it will not coin without alloy to harden it. On the other side, for the reason already named, 'tis all we can do to give sufficient sweetness to our language: we must not only choose our words for elegance, but for sound; to perform which, a mastery in the language is required; the poet must have a magazine of words, and have the art to manage his few vowels to the best advantage, that they may go the further. He must also know the nature of the vowels, which are more sonorous, and which more soft and sweet, and so dispose them as his present occasions require: all which, and a thousand secrets of versification beside, he may learn from Virgil if he will take him for his guide. If he be above Virgil, and is resolved to follow his own *verve* (as the French call it), the proverb will fall heavily upon him: *Who teaches himself has a fool for his master.*

Virgil employed eleven years upon his *Æneis;* yet he left it, as he thought himself, imperfect; which when I seriously consider, I wish that, instead of three years, which I have spent in the translation of his works, I had four years more allowed me to correct my errors, that I might make my version somewhat more tolerable than it is. For a poet cannot have too great a reverence for his readers if he expects his labours should survive him. Yet I will neither plead my age nor sickness in excuse of the faults which I have made: that I wanted time is all that I have to say, for some of my subscribers grew so clamorous that I could no longer defer the publication. I hope, from the candour of your Lordship, and your often experienced goodness to me, that, if the faults are not too many, you will take allowances with Horace—

> si plura nitent in carmine, non ego paucis
> Offendar maculis, quas aut incuria fudit,
> Aut humana parum cavit natura.—

You may please also to observe that there is not, to the best of my remembrance, one vowel gaping on another for want of a *cæsura* in this whole poem: but, where a vowel ends a word, the next begins either with a consonant or what is its equivalent; for our *W* and *H* aspirate, and our diphthongs, are plainly such. The greatest latitude I take is in the letter *Y* when it concludes a word and the first syllable of the next begins with a vowel. Neither need I have called this a latitude, which is only an explanation of this general rule, that no vowel can be cut off before another when we cannot sink the pronunciation of it; as *he*, *she*, *me*, *I*, etc. Virgil thinks it sometimes a beauty to imitate the licence of the Greeks, and leave two vowels opening on each other, as in that verse of the Third *Pastoral*—

> Et succus pecori, et lac subducitur agnis.

But *nobis non licet esse tam disertis*, at least if we study to refine our numbers. I have long had by me the materials of an English *Prosodia*, containing all the mechanical rules of versification, wherein I have treated, with some exactness, of the feet, the quantities, and the pauses. The French and Italians know nothing of the two first; at least their best poets have not practised them. As for the pauses, Malherbe first brought them into France within this last century; and we see how they adorn their Alexandrines. But as Virgil propounds a riddle, which he leaves unsolved—

> Dic, quibus in terris, inscripti nomina regum
> Nascantur flores, et Phyllida solus habeto—

so I will give your Lordship another, and leave the exposition of it to your acute judgment. I am sure there are few who make verses have observed the sweetness of these two lines in *Cooper's Hill*—

> Though deep, yet clear; though gentle, yet not dull
> Strong without rage; without o'erflowing, full.

And there are yet fewer who can find the reason of that sweetness. I have given it to some of my friends in conversation; and they have allowed the criticism to be just. But, since the evil of false quantities is difficult to be cured in any modern language; since the French and the Italians, as well as we, are yet ignorant what feet are to be used in Heroic Poetry; since I have not strictly observed those rules myself which I can teach others; since I pretend to no dictatorship among my fellow-poets; since, if I should instruct some of them to make well-running verses, they want genius to give them strength as well as sweetness; and, above all, since your Lordship has advised me not to publish that little which I know, I look on your counsel as your command, which I shall observe inviolably, till you shall please to revoke it, and leave me at liberty to make my thoughts public. In the meantime, that I may arrogate nothing to myself, I must acknowledge that Virgil in Latin, and Spenser in English, have been my masters. Spenser has also given me the boldness to make use sometimes of his Alexandrine line, which we call, though improperly, the Pindaric, because Mr. Cowley has often employed it in his *Odes*. It adds a certain majesty to the verse when it is used with judgment, and stops the sense from overflowing into another line. Formerly the French, like us, and the Italians, had but five feet, or ten syllables, in their heroic verse; but, since Ronsard's time as I suppose, they found their tongue too weak to support their epic poetry without the addition of another foot. That indeed has given it somewhat of the run and measure of a trimeter; but it runs with more activity than strength: their language is not strung with sinews like our English; it has the nimbleness of a greyhound, but not the bulk and body of a mastiff. Our men and our verses overbear them by their weight; and *Pondere, non numero*, is the British motto. The French have set up purity for the standard of their language; and a masculine vigour is that of ours. Like their tongue is the genius of their poets, light and trifling in comparison of the English; more proper for sonnets, madrigals, and elegies than heroic poetry.

The turn on thoughts and words is their chief talent; but the Epic Poem is too stately to receive those little ornaments. The painters draw their nymphs in thin and airy habits; but the weight of gold and of embroideries is reserved for queens and goddesses. Virgil is never frequent in those turns, like Ovid, but much more sparing of them in his *Æneis* than in his *Pastorals* and *Georgics*.

> Ignoscenda quidem, scirent si ignoscere manes.

That turn is beautiful indeed; but he employs it in the story of Orpheus and Eurydice, not in his great poem. I have used that licence in his *Æneis* sometimes; but I own it as my fault. 'Twas given to those who understand no better. 'Tis like Ovid's

> Semivirumque bovem, semibovemque virum.

The poet found it before his critics, but it was a darling sin, which he would not be persuaded to reform. The want of genius, of which I have accused the French, is laid to their charge by one of their own great authors, though I have forgotten his name and where I read it. If rewards could make good poets, their great master has not been wanting on his part in his bountiful encouragements: for he is wise enough to imitate Augustus if he had a Maro. The triumvir and proscriber had descended to us in a more hideous form than they now appear, if the Emperor had not taken care to make friends of him and Horace. I confess the banishment of Ovid was a blot in his escutcheon: yet he was only banished; and who knows but his crime was capital, and then his exile was a favour? Ariosto, who, with all his faults, must be acknowledged a great poet, has put these words into the mouth of an Evangelist: but whether they will pass for gospel now I cannot tell.

> Non fu si santo ni benigno Augusto,
> Come la tuba di Virgilio suona;
> L'haver havuto in poesia buon gusto,
> La proscrittione iniqua gli perdona.

But Heroic Poetry is not of the growth of France, as it might be of England, if it were cultivated. Spenser wanted only to have read the rules of Bossu; for no man was ever born with a greater genius, or had more knowledge to support it. But the performance of the French is not equal to their skill; and hitherto we have wanted skill to perform better. Segrais, whose preface is so wonderfully good, yet is wholly destitute of elevation, though his version is much better than that of the two brothers, or any of the rest who have attempted Virgil. Hannibal Caro is a great name amongst the Italians; yet his translation of the *Æneis* is most scandalously mean, though he has taken the advantage of writing in blank verse, and freed himself from the shackles of modern rhyme, if it be modern; for Le Clerc has told us lately, and I believe has made it out, that David's Psalms were written in as arrant rhyme as they are translated. Now, if a Muse cannot run when she is unfettered, it is a sign she has but little speed. I will not make a digression here, though I am strangely tempted to it; but will only say that he who can write well in rhyme may write better in blank verse. Rhyme is certainly a constraint even to the best poets, and those who make it with most ease; though perhaps I have as little reason to complain of that hardship as any man, excepting Quarles and Withers. What it adds to sweetness, it takes away from sense; and he who loses the least by it may be called a gainer. It often makes us swerve from an author's meaning; as, if a mark be set up for an archer at a great distance, let him aim as exactly as he can, the least wind will take his arrow, and divert it from the white. I return to our Italian translator of the *Æneis*. He is a foot-poet, he lacqueys by the side of Virgil at the best, but never mounts behind him. Doctor Morelli, who is no mean critic in our poetry, and therefore may be presumed to be a better in his own language, has confirmed me in this opinion by his judgment, and thinks, withal, that he has often mistaken his master's sense. I would say so, if I durst, but am afraid I have committed the same fault more often, and more grossly; for I have forsaken Ruæus (whom generally I follow) in many places, and made expositions of my own in some, quite contrary to him; of which I will give but two examples, because they are so near each other in the Tenth Æneid.

Sorti Pater æquus utrique:

Pallas says it to Turnus just before they fight. Ruæus thinks that the word *Pater* is to be referred to Evander, the father of Pallas. But how could he imagine that it was the same thing to Evander, if his son were slain, or if he overcame? The poet certainly intended Jupiter, the common father of mankind; who, as Pallas hoped, would stand an impartial spectator of the combat, and not be more favourable to Turnus than to him. The second is not long after it, and both before the duel is begun. They are the words of Jupiter, who comforts Hercules for the death of Pallas, which was immediately to ensue, and which Hercules could not hinder (though the young hero had addressed his prayers to him for his assistance) because the Gods cannot control Destiny.   The verse follows:—

> Sic ait; atque oculos Rutulorum rejicit arvis,—

which the same Ruæus thus construes: Jupiter, after he had said this, immediately turns his eyes to the Rutulian fields, and beholds the duel.   I have given this place another exposition: that he turned his eyes from the field of combat that he might not behold a sight so unpleasing to him.   The word *rejicit*, I know, will admit of both senses; but Jupiter, having confessed that he could not alter Fate, and being grieved he could not, in consideration of Hercules, it seems to me that he should avert his eyes rather than take pleasure in the spectacle.   But of this I am not so confident as the other, though I think I have followed Virgil's sense.

What I have said, though it has the face of arrogance, yet is intended for the honour of my country; and therefore I will boldly own that this English translation has more of Virgil's spirit in it than either the French or the Italian.   Some of our countrymen have translated episodes and other parts of Virgil with great success; as particularly your Lordship, whose version of *Orpheus and Eurydice* is eminently good.   Amongst the dead authors, the *Silenus* of my Lord Roscommon cannot be too much commended.   I say nothing of Sir John Denham, Mr. Waller, and Mr. Cowley; 'tis the utmost of my ambition to be thought their equal, or not to be much inferior to them, and some others of the living.   But 'tis one thing to take pains on a fragment and translate it perfectly; and another thing to have the weight of a whole author on my shoulders.   They who believe the burthen light, let them attempt the Fourth, Sixth, or Eighth *Pastoral;* the First or Fourth *Georgic;* and, amongst the *Æneids*, the Fourth, the Fifth, the Seventh, the Ninth, the Tenth, the Eleventh, or the Twelfth; for in these I think I have succeeded best.

Long before I undertook this work, I was no stranger to the original.   I had also studied Virgil's design, his disposition of it, his manners, his judicious management of the figures, the sober retrenchments of his sense, which always leaves somewhat to gratify our imagination, on which it may enlarge at pleasure; but, above all, the elegance of his expressions, and the harmony of his numbers.   For, as I have said in a former dissertation, the words are in Poetry what the colours are in Painting; if the design be good and the draught be true, the colouring is the first beauty that strikes the eye. Spenser and Milton are the nearest in English to Virgil and Horace in the Latin; and I have endeavoured to form my style by imitating their masters. I will further own to you, my Lord, that my chief ambition is to please those readers who have discernment enough to prefer Virgil before any other poet in the Latin tongue. Such spirits as he desired to please, such would I choose for my judges, and would stand or fall by them alone. Segrais has distinguished the readers of poetry, according to their capacity of judging, into three classes (he might have said the same of writers too, if he had pleased): in the lowest form he places those whom he calls *les petits esprits;* such things as are our upper-gallery audience in a playhouse, who like nothing but the husk and rind of wit; prefer a quibble, a conceit, an epigram, before solid sense and elegant expression. These are mob readers: if Virgil and Martial stood for Parliament-men, we know already who would carry it. But, though they make the greatest appearance in the field, and cry the loudest, the best on't is, they are but a sort of French Huguenots, or Dutch boors, brought over in herds, but not naturalised; who have not land of two pounds *per annum* in Parnassus, and therefore are not privileged to poll. Their authors are of the same level, fit to represent them on a mountebank's stage, or to be masters of the ceremonies in a bear-garden. Yet these are they who have the most admirers. But it often happens, to their mortification, that, as their readers improve their stock of sense (as they may by reading better books, and by conversation with men of judgment), they soon forsake them: and when the torrent from the mountain falls no more, the swelling writer is reduced into his shallow bed, like the Mançanares at Madrid with scarce water to moisten his own pebbles. There are a middle sort of readers (as we hold there is a middle state of souls), such as have a further insight than the former, yet have not the capacity of judging right; for I speak not of those who are bribed by a party, and know better, if they were not corrupted; but I mean a company of warm young men, who are not yet arrived so far as to discern the difference betwixt fustian, or ostentatious sentences, and the true sublime. These are above liking Martial, or Owen's Epigrams, but they would certainly set Virgil below Statius or Lucan. I need not say their poets are of the same taste with their admirers. They affect greatness in all they write; but 'tis a bladdered greatness, like that of the vain man whom Seneca describes; an ill habit of body, full of humours, and swelled with dropsy. Even these too desert their authors, as their judgment ripens. The young gentlemen themselves are commonly misled by their pedagogue at school, their tutor at the university, or their governor in their travels: and many of those three sorts are the most positive blockheads in the world. How many of those flatulent writers have I known, who have sunk in their reputation, after seven or eight editions of their works; for indeed they are poets only for young men. They had great success at their first appearance; but, not being of God (as a wit said formerly), they could not stand.

I have already named two sorts of judges; but Virgil wrote for neither of them: and, by his example, I am not ambitious of pleasing the lowest or the middle form of readers.

He chose to please the most judicious: souls of the highest rank, and truest understanding. These are few in number; but whoever is so happy as to gain their approbation can never lose it, because they never give it blindly. Then they have a certain magnetism in their judgment which attracts others to their sense. Every day they gain some new proselyte, and in time become the Church. For this reason, a well-weighed judicious poem, which at its first appearance gains no more upon the world than to be just received, and rather not blamed than much applauded, insinuates itself by insensible degrees into the liking of the reader: the more he studies it the more it grows upon him; every time he takes it up he discovers some new graces in it. And whereas poems which are produced by the vigour of imagination only have a gloss upon them at the first which time wears off, the works of judgment are like the diamond; the more they are polished, the more lustre they receive. Such is the difference betwixt Virgil's *Æneis* and Marini's *Adone*. And, if I may be allowed to change the metaphor, I would say, that Virgil is like the Fame which he describes—

Mobilitate viget, viresque acquirit eundo.

Such a sort of reputation is my aim, though in a far inferior degree, according to my motto in the title-page: *Sequiturque patrem non passibus æquis :* and therefore I appeal to the highest court of judicature, like that of the peers, of which your Lordship is so great an ornament.

Without this ambition, which I own, of desiring to please

the *judices natos*, I could never have been able to have done anything at this age, when the fire of poetry is commonly extinguished in other men. Yet Virgil has given me the example of Entellus for my encouragement: when he was well heated, the younger champion could not stand before him. And we find the elder contended not for the gift but for the honour: *nec dona moror*. For Dampier has informed us, in his *Voyages*, that the air of the country which produces gold is never wholesome.

I had long since considered that the way to please the best judges is not to translate a poet literally, and Virgil least of any other: for, his peculiar beauty lying in his choice of words, I am excluded from it by the narrow compass of our heroic verse, unless I would make use of monosyllables only, and those clogged with consonants, which are the dead weight of our mother-tongue. 'Tis possible, I confess, though it rarely happens, that a verse of monosyllables may sound harmoniously; and some examples of it I have seen. My first line of the *Æneis* is not harsh—

> Arms, and the Man I sing, who forc'd by Fate, etc.

But a much better instance may be given from the last line of Manilius, made English by our learned and judicious Mr. Creech—

> Nor could the World have borne so fierce a Flame—

where the many liquid consonants are placed so artfully that they give a pleasing sound to the words, though they are all of one syllable.

'Tis true, I have been sometimes forced upon it in other places of this work: but I never did it out of choice; I was either in haste, or Virgil gave me no occasion for the ornament of words; for it seldom happens but a monosyllable line turns verse to prose; and even that prose is rugged and unharmonious. Philarchus, I remember, taxes Balzac for placing twenty mono-syllables in file, without one dissyllable betwixt them. The way I have taken is not so strait as metaphrase, nor so loose as paraphrase: some things too I have omitted, and sometimes have added of my own. Yet the omissions, I hope, are but of circumstances, and such as would have no grace in English; and the additions, I also hope, are easily deduced from Virgil's sense. They will seem (at least I have the vanity to think so), not stuck into him, but growing out of him. He studies brevity more than any other poet: but he had the advantage of a language wherein much may be comprehended in a little space.

We, and all the modern tongues, have more articles and pronouns, besides signs of tenses and cases, and other barbarities on which our speech is built by the faults of our forefathers. The Romans founded theirs upon the Greek: and the Greeks, we know, were labouring many hundred years upon their language, before they brought it to perfection. They rejected all those signs, and cut off as many articles as they could spare; comprehending in one word what we are constrained to express in two; which is one reason why we cannot write so concisely as they have done. The word *pater*, for example, signifies not only *a* father, but *your* father, *my* father, *his* or *her* father, all included in a word.

This inconvenience is common to all modern tongues; and this alone constrains us to employ more words than the ancients needed. But having before observed that Virgil endeavours to be short, and at the same time elegant, I pursue the excellence and forsake the brevity: for there he is like ambergris, a rich perfume, but of so close and glutinous a body, that it must be opened with inferior scents of musk or civet, or the sweetness will not be drawn out into another language.

On the whole matter, I thought fit to steer betwixt the two extremes of paraphrase and literal translation; to keep as near my author as I could, without losing all his graces, the most eminent of which are in the beauty of his words; and those words, I must add, are always figurative. Such of these as would retain their elegance in our tongue, I have endeavoured to graff on it; but most of them are of necessity to be lost, because they will not shine in any but their own. Virgil has sometimes two of them in a line; but the scantiness of our heroic verse is not capable of receiving more than one; and that too must expiate for many others which have none. Such is the difference of the languages, or such my want of skill in choosing words. Yet I may presume to say, and I hope with as much reason as the French translator, that, taking all the materials of this divine author, I have endeavoured to make Virgil speak such English as he would himself have spoken, if he had been born in England, and in this present age. I acknowledge, with Segrais, that I have not succeeded in this attempt according to my desire: yet I shall not be wholly without praise, if in some sort I may be allowed to have copied the clearness, the purity, the easiness, and the magnificence of his style. But I shall have occasion to speak further on this subject before I end the Preface.

When I mentioned the Pindaric line, I should have added that I take another licence in my verses: for I frequently make use of triplet rhymes, and for the same reason, because they bound the sense. And therefore I generally join these two licences together, and make the last verse of the triplet a Pindaric: for, besides the majesty which it gives, it confines the sense within the barriers of three lines, which would languish if it were lengthened into four. Spenser is my example for both these privileges of English verses, and Chapman has followed him in his translation of Homer. Mr. Cowley has given into them after both, and all succeeding writers after him. I regard them now as the *Magna Charta* of heroic poetry, and am too much an Englishman to lose what my ancestors have gained for me. Let the French and Italians value themselves on their regularity; strength and elevation are our standard. I said before, and I repeat it, that the affected purity of the French has unsinewed their heroic verse. The language of an epic poem is almost wholly figurative: yet they are so fearful of a metaphor, that no example of Virgil can encourage them to be bold with safety. Sure they might warm themselves by that sprightly blaze, without approaching it so close as to singe their wings; they may come as near it as their master. Not that I would discourage that purity of diction in which he excels all other poets. But he knows how far to extend his franchises, and advances to the verge, without venturing a foot beyond it. On the other side, without being injurious to the memory of our English Pindar, I will presume to say that his metaphors are sometimes too violent, and his language is not always pure. But at the same time I must excuse him, for through the iniquity of the times he was forced to travel, at an age when, instead of learning foreign languages, he should have studied the beauties of his mother-tongue, which, like all other speeches is to be cultivated early, or we shall never write it with any kind of elegance. Thus, by gaining abroad, he lost at home; like the painter in the *Arcadia*, who, going to see a skirmish, had his arms lopped off, and returned, says Sir Philip Sidney, well instructed how to draw a battle, but without a hand to perform his work.

There is another thing in which I have presumed to deviate from him and Spenser. They both make hemistichs (or half verses) breaking off in the middle of a line. I confess there are not many such in the *Fairy Queen;* and even those few might be occasioned by his unhappy choice of so long a stanza. Mr.

Cowley had found out that no kind of staff is proper for a heroic poem, as being all too lyrical: yet, though he wrote in couplets, where rhyme is freer from constraint, he frequently affects half verses; of which we find not one in Homer, and I think not in any of the Greek poets, or the Latin, excepting only Virgil; and there is no question but he thought he had Virgil's authority for that licence. But I am confident our poet never meant to leave him, or any other, such a precedent: and I ground my opinion on these two reasons: first, we find no example of a hemistich in any of his Pastorals or Georgics; for he had given the last finishing strokes to both these poems: but his *Æneis* he left so incorrect, at least so short of that perfection at which he aimed, that we know how hard a sentence he passed upon it: and, in the second place, I reasonably presume that he intended to have filled up all those hemistichs, because in one of them we find the sense imperfect—

> Quem tibi jam Troja,

which some foolish grammarian has ended for him with a half line of nonsense—

> peperit fumante Creusa:

for Ascanius must have been born some years before the burning of that city; which I need not prove. On the other side, we find also, that he himself filled up one line in the Sixth Æneid, the enthusiasm seizing him while he was reading to Augustus—

> Misenum, Æolidem, quo non præstantior alter
> Ære ciere viros

to which he added, in that transport, *Martemque accendere cantu :* and never was any line more nobly finished; for the reasons which I have given in the *Book of Painting*. On these considerations I have shunned hemistichs; not being willing to imitate Virgil to a fault, like Alexander's courtiers, who affected to hold their necks awry, because he could not help it. I am confident your Lordship is by this time of my opinion, and that you will look on those half lines hereafter as the imperfect products of a hasty Muse; like the frogs and serpents in the Nile; part of them kindled into life, and part a lump of unformed unanimated mud.

I am sensible that many of my whole verses are as imperfect as those halves, for want of time to digest them better: but give me leave to make the excuse of Boccace, who, when he was upbraided that some of his novels had not the spirit of the rest, returned this answer, that Charlemain, who made the Paladins, was never able to raise an army of them. The leaders may be heroes, but the multitude must consist of common men.

I am also bound to tell your Lordship, in my own defence, that, from the beginning of the First Georgic to the end of the last Æneid, I found the difficulty of translation growing on me in every succeeding book. For Virgil, above all poets, had a stock, which I may call almost inexhaustible, of figurative, elegant, and sounding words: I, who inherit but a small portion of his genius, and write in a language so much inferior to the Latin, have found it very painful to vary phrases, when the same sense returns upon me. Even he himself, whether out of necessity or choice, has often expressed the same thing in the same words, and often repeated two or three whole verses which he had used before. Words are not so easily coined as money; and yet we see that the credit not only of banks but of exchequers cracks when little comes in and much goes out. Virgil called upon me in every line for some new word: and I paid so long, that I was almost bankrupt; so that the latter end must needs be more burdensome than the beginning or the middle; and consequently the Twelfth Æneid cost me double the time of the First and Second. What had become of me if Virgil had taxed me with another book? I had certainly been reduced to pay the public in hammered money, for want of milled; that is, in the same old words which I had used before: and the receivers must have been forced to have taken anything, where there was so little to be had.

Besides this difficulty (with which I have struggled, and made a shift to pass it over), there is one remaining, which is insuperable to all translators. We are bound to our author's sense, though with the latitudes already mentioned; for I think it not so sacred as that one iota must not be added or diminished on pain of an anathema. But slaves we are, and labour on another man's plantation; we dress the vineyard, but the vine is the owner's: if the soil be sometimes barren, then we are sure of being scourged: if it be fruitful, and our care succeeds, we are not thanked; for the proud reader will only say, the poor drudge has done his duty. But this is nothing to what follows; for, being obliged to make his sense intelligible, we are forced to untune our own verses, that we may give his meaning to the reader. He who invents is master of his thoughts and words: he can turn and vary them as he pleases, till he renders them harmonious; but the wretched translator has no such privilege:

for, being tied to the thoughts, he must make what music he can in the expression; and, for this reason, it cannot always be so sweet as that of the original. There is a beauty of sound, as Segrais has observed, in some Latin words, which is wholly lost in any modern language. He instances in that *mollis amaracus*, on which Venus lays Cupid, in the First Æneid. If I should translate it *sweet marjoram*, as the word signifies, the reader would think I had mistaken Virgil: for those village words, as I may call them, give us a mean idea of the thing; but the sound of the Latin is so much more pleasing, by the just mixture of the vowels with the consonants, that it raises our fancies to conceive somewhat more noble than a common herb, and to spread roses under him, and strew lilies over him; a bed not unworthy the grandson of the goddess.

If I cannot copy his harmonious numbers, how shall I imitate his noble flights, where his thoughts and words are equally sublime? *Quem*

> quisquis studet æmulari,
> cæratis ope Dædalea
> Nititur pennis, vitreo daturus
> Nomina ponto.

What modern language, or what poet, can express the majestic beauty of this one verse, amongst a thousand others?

> Aude, hospes, contemnere opes, et te quoque dignum
> Finge deo.

For my part, I am lost in the admiration of it: I contemn the world when I think on it, and myself when I translate it.

Lay by Virgil, I beseech your Lordship, and all my better sort of judges, when you take up my version; and it will appear a passable beauty when the original Muse is absent. But, like Spenser's false Florimel made of snow, it melts and vanishes when the true one comes in sight. I will not excuse, but justify myself, for one pretended crime, with which I am liable to be charged by false critics, not only in this translation, but in many of my original poems; that I latinise too much. 'Tis true that, when I find an English word significant and sounding, I neither borrow from the Latin nor any other language; but, when I want at home, I must seek abroad.

If sounding words are not of our growth and manufacture, who shall hinder me to import them from a foreign country? I carry not out the treasure of the nation, which is never to return; but what I bring from Italy I spend in England: here it remains and here it circulates; for, if the coin be good, it will pass from one hand to another. I trade both with the living and the dead for the enrichment of our native language. We have enough in England to supply our necessity; but, if we will have things of magnificence and splendour, we must get them by commerce. Poetry requires ornament; and that is not to be had from our old Teuton monosyllables: therefore, if I find any elegant word in a classic author, I propose it to be naturalised by using it myself; and, if the public approves of it, the bill passes. But every man cannot distinguish between pedantry and poetry: every man, therefore, is not fit to innovate. Upon the whole matter, a poet must first be certain that the word he would introduce is beautiful in the Latin, and is to consider, in the next place, whether it will agree with the English idiom: after this, he ought to take the opinion of judicious friends, such as are learned in both languages: and, lastly, since no man is infallible, let him use this licence very sparingly; for if too many foreign words are poured in upon us, it looks as if they were designed not to assist the natives, but to conquer them.

I am now drawing towards a conclusion, and suspect your Lordship is very glad of it. But permit me first to own what helps I have had in this undertaking. The late Earl of Lauderdale, sent me over his new translation of the *Æneis*, which he had ended before I engaged in the same design. Neither did I then intend it: but, some proposals being afterwards made me by my bookseller, I desired his Lordship's leave that I might accept them, which he freely granted; and I have his letter yet to show for that permission. He resolved to have printed his work; which he might have done two years before I could publish mine; and had performed it if death had not prevented him. But, having his manuscript in my hands, I consulted it as often as I doubted of my author's sense; for no man understood Virgil better than that learned nobleman. His friends, I hear, have yet another and more correct copy of that translation by them, which, had they pleased to have given the public, the judges must have been convinced that I have not flattered him. Besides this help, which was not inconsiderable, Mr. Congreve has done me the favour to review the *Æneis*, and compare my version with the original. I shall never be ashamed to own that this excellent young man has showed me many faults, which I have endeavoured to correct. 'Tis true, he might have easily found more, and then my translation had been more perfect.

Two other worthy friends of mine, who desire to have their names concealed, seeing me straitened in my time, took pity on me, and gave me the *Life of Virgil*, the two Prefaces to the Pastorals and the Georgics, and all the arguments in prose to the whole translation; which, perhaps, has caused a report that the two first poems are not mine. If it had been true that I had taken their verses for my own, I might have gloried in their aid, and, like Terence, have fathered[1] the opinion that Scipio and Lælius joined with me. But the same style being continued through the whole, and the same laws of versification observed, are proofs sufficient that this is one man's work: and your Lordship is too well acquainted with my manner to doubt that any part of it is another's.

That your Lordship may see I was in earnest when I promised to hasten to an end, I will not give the reasons why I writ not always in the proper terms of navigation, land-service, or in the cant of any profession. I will only say that Virgil has avoided those proprieties, because he writ not to mariners, soldiers, astronomers, gardeners, peasants, etc., but to all in general, and in particular to men and ladies of the first quality, who have been better bred than to be too nicely knowing in the terms. In such cases, it is enough for a poet to write so plainly that he may be understood by his readers, to avoid impropriety, and not affect to be thought learned in all things.

I have omitted the four preliminary lines of the First Æneid, because I think them inferior to any four others in the whole poem, and consequently believe they are not Virgil's. There is too great a gap betwixt the adjective *vicina* in the second line, and the substantive *arva* in the latter end of the third, which keeps his meaning in obscurity too long, and is contrary to the clearness of his style.

Ut quamvis avido

is too ambitious an ornament to be his; and

Gratum opus agricolis,

are all words unnecessary, and independent of what he had said before.

Horrentia Martis

Arma

is worse than any of the rest. *Horrentia* is such a flat epithet as Tully would have given us in his verses. It is a mere filler, to

[1] farther'd, ed. 1697.

stop a vacancy in the hexameter, and connect the preface to the work of Virgil. Our author seems to sound a charge, and begins like the clangour of a trumpet—

> Arma, virumque cano, Trojæ qui primus ab oris

scarce a word without an *r* and the vowels, for the greater part, sonorous. The preface began with *Ille ego*, which he was constrained to patch up in the fourth line with *at nunc*, to make the sense cohere; and, if both those words are not notorious botches, I am much deceived, though the French translator thinks otherwise. For my own part, I am rather of the opinion that they were added by Tucca and Varius than retrenched.

I know it may be answered, by such as think Virgil the author of the four lines, that he asserts his title to the *Æneis* in the beginning of his work, as he did to the two former in the last lines of the Fourth Georgic. I will not reply otherwise to this, than by desiring them to compare these four lines with the four others, which we know are his, because no poet but he alone could write them. If they cannot distinguish creeping from flying, let them lay down Virgil, and take up Ovid *de Ponto*, in his stead. My master needed not the assistance of that preliminary poet to prove his claim. His own majestic mien discovers him to be the king amidst a thousand courtiers. It was a superfluous office; and, therefore, I would not set those verses in the front of Virgil, but have rejected them to my own preface.

> I, who before, with Shepherds in the Groves,
> Sung to my oaten Pipe, their rural Loves,
> And, issuing thence, compell'd the neighbouring Field
> A plenteous Crop of rising Corn to yield,
> Manur'd the Glebe, and stock'd the fruitful Plain,
> (A Poem grateful to the greedy Swain), etc.

If there be not a tolerable line in all these six, the prefacer gave me no occasion to write better. This is a just apology in this place; but I have done great wrong to Virgil in the whole translation: want of time, the inferiority of our language, the inconvenience of rhyme, and all the other excuses I have made, may alleviate my fault, but cannot justify the boldness of my undertaking. What avails it me to acknowledge freely that I have not been able to do him right in any line? For even my own confession makes against me; and it will always be returned upon me, "Why then did you attempt it?" To which no other answer can be made than that I have done him less injury than any of his former libellers.

What they called his picture had been drawn at length, so many times, by the daubers of almost all nations, and still so unlike him that I snatched up the pencil with disdain; being satisfied beforehand that I could make some small resemblance of him, though I must be content with a worse likeness. A Sixth Pastoral, a Pharmaceutria, a single Orpheus, and some other features, have been exactly taken: but those holiday authors writ for pleasure; and only showed us what they could have done if they would have taken pains to perform the whole.

Be pleased, my Lord, to accept, with your wonted goodness, this unworthy present which I make you. I have taken off one trouble from you, of defending it, by acknowledging its imperfections: and, though some part of them are covered in the verse (as Erichthonius rode always in a chariot to hide his lameness), such of them as cannot be concealed, you will please to connive at, though, in the strictness of your judgment, you cannot pardon. If Homer was allowed to nod sometimes in so long a work, it will be no wonder if I often fall asleep. You took my *Aureng-zebe* into your protection, with all his faults: and I hope here cannot be so many, because I translate an author who gives me such examples of correctness. What my jury may be, I know not; but it is good for a criminal to plead before a favourable judge: if I had said partial, would your Lordship have forgiven me? or will you give me leave to acquaint the world that I have many times been obliged to your bounty since the Revolution? Though I never was reduced to beg a charity, nor ever had the impudence to ask one, either of your Lordship or your noble kinsman the Earl of Dorset, much less of any other, yet, when I least expected it, you have both remembered me: so inherent it is in your family not to forget an old servant. It looks rather like ingratitude on my part, that, where I have been so often obliged, I have appeared so seldom to return my thanks, and where I was also so sure of being well received. Somewhat of laziness was in the case, and somewhat too of modesty, but nothing of disrespect or of unthankfulness. I will not say that your Lordship has encouraged me to this presumption, lest, if my labours meet with no success in public, I may expose your judgment to be censured. As for my own enemies, I shall never think them worth an answer; and, if your Lordship has any, they will not dare to arraign you for want of knowledge in this art till they can produce somewhat better of their own than your *Essay on Poetry*. 'Twas on this consideration that I have drawn out my

Preface to so great a length. Had I not addressed to a poet
and a critic of the first magnitude, I had myself been taxed for
want of judgment, and shamed my patron for want of understanding. But neither will you, my Lord, so soon be tired as
any other, because the discourse is on your art; neither will the
learned reader think it tedious, because it is *ad Clerum*. At
least, when he begins to be weary, the church doors are open.
That I may pursue the allegory with a short prayer after a long
sermon:

May you live happily and long, for the service of your country,
the encouragement of good letters, and the ornament of Poetry;
which cannot be wished more earnestly by any man, than by

> Your Lordship's most humble,
> Most obliged, and most obedient Servant,
> JOHN DRYDEN.

II

POSTSCRIPT TO THE READER

WHAT Virgil wrote in the vigour of his age, in plenty and at
ease, I have undertaken to translate in my declining years;
struggling with wants, oppressed with sickness, curbed in my
genius, liable to be misconstrued in all I write; and my judges,
if they are not very equitable, already prejudiced against me,
by the lying character which has been given them of my morals.
Yet steady to my principles, and not dispirited with my afflic-
tions, I have, by the blessing of God on my endeavours, overcome all difficulties, and, in some measure, acquitted myself of
the debt which I owed the public when I undertook this work.
In the first place, therefore, I thankfully acknowledge to the
Almighty Power the assistance He has given me in the beginning, the prosecution, and conclusion of my present studies,
which are more happily performed than I could have promised
to myself, when I laboured under such discouragements. For
what I have done, imperfect as it is for want of health and
leisure to correct it, will be judged in after-ages, and possibly
in the present, to be no dishonour to my native country, whose
language and poetry would be more esteemed abroad if they
were better understood. Somewhat (give me leave to say)
I have added to both of them in the choice of words, and har-

mony of numbers, which were wanting, especially the last, in all our poets, even in those who, being endued with genius, yet have not cultivated their mother-tongue with sufficient care; or, relying on the beauty of their thoughts, have judged the ornament of words, and sweetness of sound, unnecessary. One is for raking in Chaucer (our English Ennius) for antiquated words, which are never to be revived, but when sound or significancy is wanting in the present language. But many of his deserve not this redemption, any more than the crowds of men who daily die, or are slain for sixpence in a battle, merit to be restored to life if a wish could revive them. Others have no ear for verse, nor choice of words, nor distinction of thoughts; but mingle farthings with their gold to make up the sum. Here is a field of satire opened to me: but, since the Revolution, I have wholly renounced that talent. For who would give physic to the great, when he is uncalled?—to do his patient no good, and endanger himself for his prescription? Neither am I ignorant, but I may justly be condemned for many of those faults of which I have too liberally arraigned others.

Cynthius aurem
Vellit, et admonuit.

'Tis enough for me if the Government will let me pass unquestioned. In the meantime, I am obliged, in gratitude, to return my thanks to many of them, who have not only distinguished me from others of the same party, by a particular exception of grace, but, without considering the man, have been bountiful to the poet: have encouraged Virgil to speak such English as I could teach him, and rewarded his interpreter for the pains he has taken in bringing him over into Britain, by defraying the charges of his voyage. Even Cerberus, when he had received the sop, permitted Æneas to pass freely to Elysium. Had it been offered me, and I had refused it, yet still some gratitude is due to such who were willing to oblige me; but how much more to those from whom I have received the favours which they have offered to one of a different persuasion! Amongst whom I cannot omit naming the Earls of Derby and of Peterborough. To the first of these I have not the honour to be known; and therefore his liberality was as much unexpected as it was undeserved. The present Earl of Peterborough has been pleased long since to accept the tenders of my service: his favours are so frequent to me, that I receive them almost by prescription. No difference of interests or opinion has been able to withdraw his protection from me; and I might justly be condemned for the most unthankful of mankind, if I did not always preserve for him a most profound respect and inviolable gratitude. I must also add, that, if the last Æneid shine amongst its fellows, 'tis owing to the commands of Sir William Trumball, one of the principal Secretaries of State, who recommended it, as his favourite, to my care; and for his sake particularly, I have made it mine. For who would confess weariness, when he enjoined a fresh labour? I could not but invoke the assistance of a Muse for this last office.

> Extremum hunc, Arethusa
> Negat quis carmina Gallo?

Neither am I to forget the noble present which was made me by Gilbert Dolben, Esq., the worthy son of the late Archbishop of York, who, when I began this work, enriched me with all the several editions of Virgil, and all the commentaries of those editions in Latin; amongst which, I could not but prefer the Dauphin's, as the last, the shortest, and the most judicious. Fabrini I had also sent me from Italy; but either he understands Virgil very imperfectly, or I have no knowledge of my author.

Being invited by that worthy gentleman, Sir William Bowyer, to Denham Court, I translated the First Georgic at his house, and the greatest part of the last Æneid. A more friendly entertainment no man ever found. No wonder, therefore, if both those versions surpass the rest, and own the satisfaction I received in his converse, with whom I had the honour to be bred in Cambridge, and in the same college. The Seventh Æneid was made English at Burleigh, the magnificent abode of the Earl of Exeter. In a village belonging to his family I was born; and under his roof I endeavoured to make that Æneid appear in English with as much lustre as I could; though my author has not given the finishing strokes either to it or to the Eleventh, as I perhaps could prove in both, if I durst presume to criticise my master.

By a letter from William Walsh, of Abberley, Esq. (who has so long honoured me with his friendship, and who, without flattery, is the best critic of our nation), I have been informed, that his Grace the Duke of Shrewsbury has procured a printed copy of the Pastorals, Georgics, and first six Æneids, from my bookseller, and has read them in the country, together with my friend. This noble person having been pleased to give them a commendation, which I presume not to insert, has made me

vain enough to boast of so great a favour, and to think I have
succeeded beyond my hopes; the character of his excellent
judgment, the acuteness of his wit, and his general knowledge
of good letters, being known as well to all the world, as the
sweetness of his disposition, his humanity, his easiness of access,
and desire of obliging those who stand in need of his protection,
are known to all who have approached him, and to me in particular, who have formerly had the honour of his conversation.
Whoever has given the world the translation of part of the
Third Georgic, which he calls *The Power of Love,* has put me to
sufficient pains to make my own not inferior to his; as my
Lord Roscommon's *Silenus* had formerly given me the same
trouble. The most ingenious Mr. Addison of Oxford has also
been as troublesome to me as the other two, and on the same
account. After his *Bees,* my latter swarm is scarcely worth the
hiving. Mr. Cowley's *Praise of a Country Life* is excellent, but
is rather an imitation of Virgil than a version. That I have
recovered, in some measure, the health which I had lost by too
much application to this work, is owing, next to God's mercy,
to the skill and care of Dr. Guibbons and Dr. Hobbs, the two
ornaments of their profession, whom I can only pay by this
acknowledgment. The whole Faculty has always been ready
to oblige me; and the only one of them, who endeavoured to
defame me, had it not in his power. I desire pardon from my
readers for saying so much in relation to myself which concerns
not them; and, with my acknowledgments to all my subscribers,
have only to add, that the few notes which follow are *par
manière d'acquit,* because I had obliged myself by articles to do
somewhat of that kind. These scattering observations are
rather guesses at my author's meaning in some passages, than
proofs that so he meant. The unlearned may have recourse
to any poetical dictionary in English for the names of persons,
places, or fables, which the learned need not: but that little
which I say is either new or necessary; and the first of these
qualifications never fails to invite a reader, if not to please
him.

ON TRANSLATING THE POETS

PREFACE TO " FABLES ANCIENT AND MODERN, TRANSLATED
INTO VERSE FROM HOMER, OVID, BOCCACE, AND CHAUCER "

'TIS with a poet, as with a man who designs to build, and is
very exact, as he supposes, in casting up the cost beforehand;
but, generally speaking, he is mistaken in his account, and
reckons short of the expense he first intended. He alters his
mind as the work proceeds, and will have this or that convenience
more, of which he had not thought when he began. So has it
happened to me; I have built a house where I intended but a
lodge; yet with better success than a certain nobleman, who,
beginning with a dog-kennel, never lived to finish the palace
he had contrived.

From translating the first of Homer's Iliads (which I
intended as an essay to the whole work), I proceeded to the translation of the Twelfth Book of Ovid's *Metamorphoses*, because
it contains, among other things, the causes, the beginning, and
ending, of the Trojan war. Here I ought in reason to have
stopped; but the speeches of Ajax and Ulysses lying next in my
way, I could not balk 'em. When I had compassed them, I was
so taken with the former part of the Fifteenth Book (which is
the masterpiece of the whole *Metamorphoses*), that I enjoined
myself the pleasing task of rendering it into English. And now
I found, by the number of my verses, that they began to swell
into a little volume, which gave me an occasion of looking backward on some beauties of my author in his former books: here
occurred to me the *Hunting of the Boar, Cinyras and Myrrha*,
the good-natured story of *Baucis and Philemon*, with the rest,
which I hope I have translated closely enough, and given them
the same turn of verse which they had in the original; and this,
I may say, without vanity, is not the talent of every poet. He
who has arrived the nearest to it is the ingenious and learned
Sandys, the best versifier of the former age; if I may properly
call it by that name, which was the former part of this concluding century. For Spenser and Fairfax both flourished in
the reign of Queen Elizabeth; great masters in our language,

and who saw much further into the beauties of our numbers than those who immediately followed them. Milton was the poetical son of Spenser, and Mr. Waller of Fairfax; for we have our lineal descents and clans as well as other families. Spenser more than once insinuates that the soul of Chaucer was transfused into his body; and that he was begotten by him two hundred years after his decease. Milton has acknowledged to me that Spenser was his original; and many besides myself have heard our famous Waller own that he derived the harmony of his numbers from *Godfrey of Bulloign,* which was turned into English by Mr. Fairfax.

But to return: having done with Ovid for this time, it came into my mind that our old English poet, Chaucer, in many things resembled him, and that with no disadvantage on the side of the modern author, as I shall endeavour to prove when I compare them; and as I am, and always have been, studious to promote the honour of my native country, so I soon resolved to put their merits to the trial, by turning some of the *Canterbury Tales* into our language, as it is now refined; for by this means, both the poets being set in the same light, and dressed in the same English habit, story to be compared with story, a certain judgment may be made betwixt them by the reader, without obtruding my opinion on him. Or, if I seem partial to my countryman and predecessor in the laurel, the friends of antiquity are not few; and, besides many of the learned, Ovid has almost all the beaux, and the whole fair sex, his declared patrons. Perhaps I have assumed somewhat more to myself than they allow me, because I have adventured to sum up the evidence; but the readers are the jury, and their privilege remains entire, to decide according to the merits of the cause; or, if they please, to bring it to another hearing before some other court. In the meantime, to follow the thread of my discourse (as thoughts, according to Mr. Hobbes, have always some connection), so from Chaucer I was led to think on Boccace, who was not only his contemporary, but also pursued the same studies; wrote novels in prose, and many works in verse; particularly is said to have invented the octave rhyme, or stanza of eight lines, which ever since has been maintained by the practice of all Italian writers who are, or at least assume the title of heroic poets. He and Chaucer, among other things, had this in common, that they refined their mother-tongues; but with this difference, that Dante had begun to file their language, at least in verse, before the time of Boccace, who likewise received no

little help from his master Petrarch; but the reformation of
their prose was wholly owing to Boccace himself, who is yet the
standard of purity in the Italian tongue, though many of his
phrases are become obsolete, as in process of time it must needs
happen. Chaucer (as you have formerly been told by our
learned Mr. Rymer) first adorned and amplified our barren
tongue from the Provençal, which was then the most polished
of all the modern languages; but this subject has been copiously
treated by that great critic, who deserves no little commendation from us his countrymen. For these reasons of time, and
resemblance of genius, in Chaucer and Boccace, I resolved to
join them in my present work; to which I have added some
original papers of my own, which whether they are equal or
inferior to my other poems, an author is the most improper
judge; and therefore I leave them wholly to the mercy of the
reader. I will hope the best, that they will not be condemned;
but if they should, I have the excuse of an old gentleman, who,
mounting on horseback before some ladies, when I was present,
got up somewhat heavily, but desired of the fair spectators that
they would count fourscore and eight before they judged him.
By the mercy of God, I am already come within twenty years
of his number; a cripple in my limbs, but what decays are
in my mind, the reader must determine. I think myself as
vigorous as ever in the faculties of my soul, excepting only my
memory, which is not impaired to any great degree; and if I lose
not more of it, I have no great reason to complain. What
judgment I had increases rather than diminishes; and thoughts,
such as they are, come crowding in so fast upon me that my
only difficulty is to choose or to reject, to run them into verse,
or to give them the other harmony of prose: I have so long
studied and practised both that they are grown into a habit,
and become familiar to me. In short, though I may lawfully
plead some part of the old gentleman's excuse, yet I will reserve
it till I think I have greater need, and ask no grains of allowance
for the faults of this my present work but those which are given
of course to human frailty. I will not trouble my reader with
the shortness of time in which I writ it, or the several intervals
of sickness. They who think too well of their own performances are apt to boast in their prefaces how little time their
works have cost them, and what other business of more importance interfered; but the reader will be as apt to ask the
question, why they allowed not a longer time to make their
works more perfect? and why they had so despicable an opinion

of their judges as to thrust their indigested stuff upon them, as if they deserved no better?

With this account of my present undertaking, I conclude the first part of this discourse: in the second part, as at a second sitting, though I alter not the draught, I must touch the same features over again, and change the dead-colouring of the whole. In general I will only say that I have written nothing which savours of immorality or profaneness; at least, I am not conscious to myself of any such intention. If there happen to be found an irreverent expression, or a thought too wanton, they are crept into my verses through my inadvertency: if the searchers find any in the cargo, let them be staved or forfeited, like counterbanded goods; at least, let their authors be answerable for them, as being but imported merchandise, and not of my own manufacture. On the other side, I have endeavoured to choose such fables, both ancient and modern, as contain in each of them some instructive moral; which I could prove by induction, but the way is tedious, and they leap foremost into sight, without the reader's trouble of looking after them. I wish I could affirm, with a safe conscience, that I had taken the same care in all my former writings; for it must be owned that, supposing verses are never so beautiful or pleasing, yet, if they contain anything which shocks religion or good manners, they are at best what Horace says of good numbers without good sense, *Versus inopes rerum, nugæque canoræ.* Thus far, I hope, I am right in court, without renouncing to my other right of self-defence, where I have been wrongfully accused, and my sense wire-drawn into blasphemy or bawdry, as it has often been by a religious lawyer, in a late pleading against the stage; in which he mixes truth with falsehood, and has not forgotten the old rule of calumniating strongly, that something may remain.

I resume the third of my discourse with the first of my translations, which was the first Iliad of Homer. If it shall please God to give me longer life, and moderate health, my intentions are to translate the whole *Ilias;* provided still that I meet with those encouragements from the public which may enable me to proceed in my undertaking with some cheerfulness. And this I dare assure the world beforehand, that I have found, by trial, Homer a more pleasing task than Virgil, though I say not the translation will be less laborious; for the Grecian is more according to my genius than the Latin poet. In the works of the two authors we may read their manners, and natural inclinations, which are wholly different. Virgil was of a quiet, sedate temper; Homer was violent, impetuous, and full of fire. The chief talent of Virgil was propriety of thoughts, and ornament of words: Homer was rapid in his thoughts, and took all the liberties, both of numbers and of expressions, which his language, and the age in which he lived, allowed him. Homer's invention was more copious, Virgil's more confined; so that if Homer had not led the way, it was not in Virgil to have begun heroic poetry; for nothing can be more evident than that the Roman poem is but the second part of the *Ilias ;* a continuation of the same story, and the persons already formed. The manners of Æneas are those of Hector, superadded to those which Homer gave him. The adventures of Ulysses in the *Odysseis* are imitated in the first Six Books of Virgil's *Æneis ;* and though the accidents are not the same (which would have argued him of a servile copying, and total barrenness of invention), yet the seas were the same in which both the heroes wandered; and Dido cannot be denied to be the poetical daughter of Calypso. The six latter Books of Virgil's poem are the four-and-twenty *Iliads* contracted; a quarrel occasioned by a lady, a single combat, battles fought, and a town besieged. I say not this in derogation to Virgil, neither do I contradict anything which I have formerly said in his just praise; for his episodes are almost wholly of his own invention, and the form which he has given to the telling makes the tale his own, even though the original story had been the same. But this proves, however, that Homer taught Virgil to design; and if invention be the first virtue of an epic poet, then the Latin poem can only be allowed the second place. Mr. Hobbes, in the preface to his own bald translation of the *Ilias* (studying poetry as he did mathematics, when it was too late), Mr. Hobbes, I say, begins the praise of Homer where he should have ended it. He tells us that the first beauty of an epic poem consists in diction; that is, in the choice of words, and harmony of numbers. Now the words are the colouring of the work, which, in the order of nature, is last to be considered. The design, the disposition, the manners, and the thoughts are all before it: where any of those are wanting or imperfect, so much wants or is imperfect in the imitation of human life, which is in the very definition of a poem. Words, indeed, like glaring colours, are the first beauties that arise and strike the sight; but, if the draught be false or lame, the figures ill disposed, the manners obscure or inconsistent, or the thoughts unnatural, then the finest colours are but daubing, and the piece is a beautiful monster at the best. Neither Virgil nor Homer were deficient in any of the former beauties; but in this last, which is expression, the Roman poet is at least equal to the Grecian, as I have said elsewhere: supplying the poverty of his language by his musical ear, and by his diligence.

But to return: our two great poets being so different in their tempers, one choleric and sanguine, the other phlegmatic and melancholic; that which makes them excel in their several ways is, that each of them has followed his own natural inclination, as well in forming the design as in the execution of it. The very heroes show their authors: Achilles is hot, impatient, revengeful—

> Impiger, iracundus, inexorabilis, acer, etc.,

Æneas patient, considerate, careful of his people, and merciful to his enemies; ever submissive to the will of heaven—

> quo fata trahunt retrahuntque, sequamur.

I could please myself with enlarging on this subject, but am forced to defer it to a fitter time. From all I have said, I will only draw this inference, that the action of Homer, being more full of vigour than that of Virgil, according to the temper of the writer, is of consequence more pleasing to the reader. One warms you by degrees; the other sets you on fire all at once, and never intermits his heat. 'Tis the same difference which Longinus makes betwixt the effects of eloquence in Demosthenes and Tully; one persuades, the other commands. You never cool while you read Homer, even not in the Second Book (a graceful flattery to his countrymen); but he hastens from the ships, and concludes not that book till he has made you an amends by the violent playing of a new machine. From thence he hurries on his action with variety of events, and ends it in less compass than two months. This vehemence of his, I confess, is more suitable to my temper; and, therefore, I have translated his First Book with greater pleasure than any part of Virgil; but it was not a pleasure without pains. The continual agitations of the spirits must needs be a weakening of any constitution, especially in age; and many pauses are required for refreshment betwixt the heats; the *Iliad* of itself being a third part longer than all Virgil's works together.

This is what I thought needful in this place to say of Homer. I proceed to Ovid and Chaucer; considering the former only in relation to the latter. With Ovid ended the golden age of the

Roman tongue; from Chaucer the purity of the English tongue began. The manners of the poets were not unlike. Both of them were well-bred, well-natured, amorous, and libertine, at least in their writings; it may be also in their lives. Their studies were the same, philosophy and philology. Both of them were knowing in astronomy; of which Ovid's books of the *Roman Feasts*, and Chaucer's *Treatise of the Astrolabe*, are sufficient witnesses. But Chaucer was likewise an astrologer, as were Virgil, Horace, Persius, and Manilius. Both writ with wonderful facility and clearness; neither were great inventors: for Ovid only copied the Grecian fables, and most of Chaucer's stories were taken from his Italian contemporaries, or their predecessors. Boccace his *Decameron* was first published, and from thence our Englishman has borrowed many of his *Canterbury Tales* : yet that of *Palamon and Arcite* was written, in all probability, by some Italian wit, in a former age, as I shall prove hereafter. The tale of *Grizild* was the invention of Petrarch; by him sent to Boccace, from whom it came to Chaucer. *Troilus and Cressida* was also written by a Lombard author, but much amplified by our English translator, as well as beautified; the genius of our countrymen, in general, being rather to improve an invention than to invent themselves, as is evident not only in our poetry, but in many of our manufactures. I find I have anticipated already, and taken up from Boccace before I come to him: but there is so much less behind; and I am of the temper of most kings, who love to be in debt, are all for present money, no matter how they pay it afterwards: besides, the nature of a preface is rambling, never wholly out of the way, nor in it. This I have learned from the practice of honest Montaigne, and return at my pleasure to Ovid and Chaucer, of whom I have little more to say.

Both of them built on the inventions of other men; yet since Chaucer had something of his own, as *The Wife of Bath's Tale, The Cock and the Fox*, which I have translated, and some others, I may justly give our countryman the precedence in that part; since I can remember nothing of Ovid which was wholly his. Both of them understood the manners; under which name I comprehend the passions, and in a larger sense, the descriptions of persons, and their very habits. For an example, I see Baucis and Philemon as perfectly before me as if some ancient painter had drawn them; and all the Pilgrims in the *Canterbury Tales*, their humours, their features, and the very dress, as distinctly as if I had supped with them at the *Tabard* in Southwark. Yet even there, too, the figures of Chaucer are much more lively, and set in a better light; which though I have not time to prove, yet I appeal to the reader, and am sure he will clear me from partiality. The thoughts and words remain to be considered, in the comparison of the two poets, and I have saved myself one-half of the labour, by owning that Ovid lived when the Roman tongue was in its meridian, Chaucer in the dawning of our language; therefore, that part of the comparison stands not on an equal foot, any more than the diction of Ennius and Ovid, or of Chaucer and our present English. The words are given up, as a post not to be defended in our poet, because he wanted the modern art of fortifying. The thoughts remain to be considered; and they are to be measured only by their propriety; that is, as they flow more or less naturally from the persons described, on such and such occasions. The vulgar judges, which are nine parts in ten of all nations, who call conceits and jingles wit, who see Ovid full of them, and Chaucer altogether without them, will think me little less than mad for preferring the Englishman to the Roman. Yet, with their leave, I must presume to say that the things they admire are only glittering trifles, and so far from being witty, that in a serious poem they are nauseous, because they are unnatural. Would any man, who is ready to die for love, describe his passion like Narcissus? Would he think of *inopem me copia fecit*, and a dozen more of such expressions, poured on the neck of one another, and signifying all the same thing? If this were wit, was this a time to be witty, when the poor wretch was in the agony of death? This is just John Littlewit, in *Bartholomew Fair*, who had a conceit (as he tells you) left him in his misery; a miserable conceit. On these occasions the poet should endeavour to raise pity; but, instead of this, Ovid is tickling you to laugh. Virgil never made use of such machines when he was moving you to commiserate the death of Dido: he would not destroy what he was building. Chaucer makes Arcite violent in his love, and unjust in the pursuit of it; yet, when he came to die, he made him think more reasonably: he repents not of his love, for that had altered his character; but acknowledges the injustice of his proceedings, and resigns Emilia to Palamon. What would Ovid have done on this occasion? He would certainly have made Arcite witty on his deathbed; he had complained he was further off from possession, by being so near, and a thousand such boyisms, which Chaucer rejected as below the dignity of the subject. They who think otherwise would, by the same reason, prefer

Lucan and Ovid to Homer and Virgil, and Martial to all four of them. As for the turn of words, in which Ovid particularly excels all poets, they are sometimes a fault, and sometimes a beauty, as they are used properly or improperly; but in strong passions always to be shunned, because passions are serious, and will admit no playing. The French have a high value for them; and, I confess, they are often what they call delicate, when they are introduced with judgment; but Chaucer writ with more simplicity, and followed Nature more closely than to use them. I have thus far, to the best of my knowledge, been an upright judge betwixt the parties in competition, not meddling with the design nor the disposition of it; because the design was not their own; and in the disposing of it they were equal. It remains that I say somewhat of Chaucer in particular.

In the first place, as he is the father of English poetry, so I hold him in the same degree of veneration as the Grecians held Homer, or the Romans Virgil. He is a perpetual fountain of good sense; learn'd in all sciences; and, therefore, speaks properly on all subjects. As he knew what to say, so he knows also when to leave off; a continence which is practised by few writers, and scarcely by any of the ancients, excepting Virgil and Horace. One of our late great poets is sunk in his reputation, because he could never forgive any conceit which came in his way; but swept like a drag-net, great and small. There was plenty enough, but the dishes were ill sorted; whole pyramids of sweetmeats for boys and women but little of solid meat for men. All this proceeded not from any want of knowledge, but of judgment. Neither did he want that in discerning the beauties and faults of other poets, but only indulged himself in the luxury of writing; and perhaps knew it was a fault, but hoped the reader would not find it. For this reason, though he must always be thought a great poet, he is no longer esteemed a good writer; and for ten impressions, which his works have had in so many successive years, yet at present a hundred books are scarcely purchased once a twelvemonth; for, as my last Lord Rochester said, though somewhat profanely, *Not being of God, he could not stand.*

Chaucer followed Nature everywhere, but was never so bold to go beyond her; and there is a great difference of being *poeta* and *nimis poeta*, if we may believe Catullus, as much as betwixt a modest behaviour and affectation. The verse of Chaucer, I confess, is not harmonious to us; but 'tis like the eloquence of one whom Tacitus commends, it was *auribus istius temporis aecommodata :* they who lived with him, and some time after him, thought it musical; and it continues so, even in our judgment, if compared with the numbers of Lidgate and Gower, his contemporaries: there is the rude sweetness of a Scotch tune in it, which is natural and pleasing, though not perfect. 'Tis true, I cannot go so far as he who published the last edition of him; for he would make us believe the fault is in our ears, and that there were really ten syllables in a verse where we find but nine: but this opinion is not worth confuting; 'tis so gross and obvious an error, that common sense (which is a rule in everything but matters of Faith and Revelation) must convince the reader that equality of numbers, in every verse which we call *heroic,* was either not known, or not always practised, in Chaucer's age. It were an easy matter to produce some thousands of his verses, which are lame for want of half a foot, and sometimes a whole one, and which no pronunciation can make otherwise. We can only say, that he lived in the infancy of our poetry, and that nothing is brought to perfection at the first. We must be children before we grow men. There was an Ennius, and in process of time a Lucilius, and a Lucretius, before Virgil and Horace; even after Chaucer there was a Spenser, a Harrington, a Fairfax, before Waller and Denham were in being; and our numbers were in their nonage till these last appeared. I need say little of his parentage, life, and fortunes; they are to be found at large in all the editions of his works. He was employed abroad, and favoured, by Edward the Third, Richard the Second, and Henry the Fourth, and was poet, as I suppose, to all three of them. In Richard's time, I doubt, he was a little dipt in the rebellion of the Commons; and being brother-in-law to John of Ghant, it was no wonder if he followed the fortunes of that family; and was well with Henry the Fourth when he had deposed his predecessor. Neither is it to be admired, that Henry, who was a wise as well as a valiant prince, who claimed by succession, and was sensible that his title was not sound, but was rightfully in Mortimer, who had married the heir of York; it was not to be admired, I say, if that great politician should be pleased to have the greatest wit of those times in his interests, and to be the trumpet of his praises. Augustus had given him the example, by the advice of Mæcenas, who recommended Virgil and Horace to him; whose praises helped to make him popular while he was alive, and after his death have made him precious to posterity. As for the religion of our poet, he seems to have some little bias towards the opinions of Wicliffe, **after**

John of Ghant his patron; somewhat of which appears in the tale of *Piers Plowman*: yet I cannot blame him for inveighing so sharply against the vices of the clergy in his age: their pride, their ambition, their pomp, their avarice, their worldly interest, deserved the lashes which he gave them, both in that, and in most of his *Canterbury Tales*. Neither has his contemporary Boccace spared them: yet both those poets lived in much esteem with good and holy men in orders; for the scandal which is given by particular priests reflects not on the sacred function. Chaucer's *Monk*, his *Canon*, and his *Friar*, took not from the character of his *Good Parson*. A satirical poet is the check of the laymen on bad priests. We are only to take care that we involve not the innocent with the guilty in the same condemnation. The good cannot be too much honoured, nor the bad too coarsely used, for the corruption of the best becomes the worst. When a clergyman is whipped, his gown is first taken off, by which the dignity of his order is secured. If he be wrongfully accused, he has his action of slander; and 'tis at the poet's peril if he transgress the law. But they will tell us that all kind of satire, though never so well deserved by particular priests, yet brings the whole order into contempt. Is then the peerage of England anything dishonoured when a peer suffers for his treason? If he be libelled, or any way defamed, he has his *scandalum magnatum* to punish the offender. They who use this kind of argument seem to be conscious to themselves of somewhat which has deserved the poet's lash, and are less concerned for their public capacity than for their private; at least there is pride at the bottom of their reasoning. If the faults of men in orders are only to be judged among themselves, they are all in some sort parties; for, since they say the honour of their order is concerned in every member of it, how can we be sure that they will be impartial judges? How far I may be allowed to speak my opinion in this case, I know not; but I am sure a dispute of this nature caused mischief in abundance betwixt a King of England and an Archbishop of Canterbury; one standing up for the laws of his land, and the other for the honour (as he called it) of God's Church; which ended in the murder of the prelate, and in the whipping of his Majesty from post to pillar for his penance. The learned and ingenious Dr. Drake has saved me the labour of inquiring into the esteem and reverence which the priests have had of old; and I would rather extend than diminish any part of it: yet I must needs say that when a priest provokes me without any occasion given him, I have no reason, unless it be the charity of a Christian, to forgive him: *prior læsit* is justification sufficient in the civil law. If I answer him in his own language, self-defence, I am sure must be allowed me; and if I carry it further, even to a sharp recrimination, somewhat may be indulged to human frailty. Yet my resentment has not wrought so far but that I have followed Chaucer in his character of a holy man, and have enlarged on that subject with some pleasure; reserving to myself the right, if I shall think fit hereafter, to describe another sort of priests, such as are more easily to be found than the Good Parson; such as have given the last blow to Christianity in this age, by a practice so contrary to their doctrine. But this will keep cold till another time. In the meanwhile, I take up Chaucer where I left him.

He must have been a man of a most wonderful comprehensive nature, because, as it has been truly observed of him, he has taken into the compass of his *Canterbury Tales* the various manners and humours (as we now call them) of the whole English nation in his age. Not a single character has escaped him. All his pilgrims are severally distinguished from each other; and not only in their inclinations, but in their very physiognomies and persons. Baptista Porta could not have described their natures better, than by the marks which the poet gives them. The matter and manner of their tales, and of their telling, are so suited to their different educations, humours, and callings, that each of them would be improper in any other mouth. Even the grave and serious characters are distinguished by their several sorts of gravity: their discourses are such as belong to their age, their calling, and their breeding; such as are becoming of them, and of them only. Some of his persons are vicious, and some virtuous; some are unlearn'd, or (as Chaucer calls them) lewd, and some are learn'd. Even the ribaldry of the low characters is different: the Reeve, the Miller, and the Cook, are several men, and distinguished from each other as much as the mincing Lady-Prioress and the broad-speaking, gap-toothed Wife of Bath. But enough of this; there is such a variety of game springing up before me that I am distracted in my choice, and know not which to follow. 'Tis sufficient to say, according to the proverb, that *here is God's plenty*. We have our forefathers and great-grand-dames all before us, as they were in Chaucer's days: their general characters are still remaining in mankind, and even in England, though they are called by other names than those of Monks, and Friars, and Canons, and Lady Abbesses, and Nuns; for mankind is ever the same, and nothing lost out of Nature, though everything is altered. May I have leave to do myself the justice (since my enemies will do me none, and are so far from granting me to be a good poet, that they will not allow me so much as to be a Christian, or a moral man), may I have leave, I say, to inform my reader that I have confined my choice to such tales of Chaucer as savour nothing of immodesty. If I had desired more to please than to instruct, the *Reeve*, the *Miller*, the *Shipman*, the *Merchant*, the *Sumner*, and, above all, the *Wife of Bath*, in the Prologue to her *Tale*, would have procured me as many friends and readers as there are beaux and ladies of pleasure in the town. But I will no more offend against good manners: I am sensible as I ought to be of the scandal I have given by my loose writings; and make what reparation I am able, by this public acknowledgment. If anything of this nature, or of profaneness be crept into these poems, I am so far from defending it that I disown it. *Totum hoc indictum volo.* Chaucer makes another manner of apology for his broad speaking, and Boccace makes the like; but I will follow neither of them. Our countryman, in the end of his *Characters*, before the *Canterbury Tales*, thus excuses the ribaldry, which is very gross in many of his novels—

> But firste, I pray you, of your courtesy,
> That ye ne arrete it not my villany,
> Though that I plainly speak in this mattere,
> To tellen you her words, and eke her chere:
> Ne though I speak her words properly,
> For this ye knowen as well as I,
> Who shall tellen a tale after a man,
> He mote rehearse as nye as ever he can:
> Everich word of it ben in his charge,
> All speke he, never so rudely, ne large:
> Or else he mote tellen his tale untrue,
> Or feine things, or find words new:
> He may not spare, altho he were his brother,
> He mote as wel say o word as another.
> Crist spake himself ful broad in holy Writ,
> And well I wote no villany is it,
> Eke Plato saith, who so can him rede,
> The words mote been cousin to the dede.

Yet if a man should have inquired of Boccace or of Chaucer what need they had of introducing such characters, where obscene words were proper in their mouths, but very indecent to be heard; I know not what answer they could have made; for that reason, such tales shall be left untold by me. You have here a specimen of Chaucer's language, which is so obsolete,

that his sense is scarce to be understood; and you have likewise more than one example of his unequal numbers, which were
mentioned before. Yet many of his verses consist of ten
syllables, and the words not much behind our present English:
as for example, these two lines, in the description of the
Carpenter's young wife—

> Wincing she was, as is a jolly colt,
> Long as a mast, and upright as a bolt.

I have almost done with Chaucer, when I have answered
some objections relating to my present work. I find some
people are offended that I have turned these tales into modern
English; because they think them unworthy of my pains, and
look on Chaucer as a dry, old-fashioned wit, not worth reviving.
I have often heard the late Earl of Leicester say that Mr.
Cowley himself was of that opinion; who, having read him over
at my Lord's request, declared he had no taste of him. I dare
not advance my opinion against the judgment of so great an
author; but I think it fair, however, to leave the decision to the
public. Mr. Cowley was too modest to set up for a dictator;
and being shocked perhaps with his old style, never examined
into the depth of his good sense. Chaucer, I confess, is a rough
diamond, and must first be polished ere he shines. I deny not
likewise, that, living in our early days of poetry, he writes not
always of a piece; but sometimes mingles trivial things with
those of greater moment. Sometimes also, though not often,
he runs riot, like Ovid, and knows not when he has said enough.
But there are more great wits besides Chaucer, whose fault is
their excess of conceits, and those ill sorted. An author is not
to write all he can, but only all he ought. Having observed
this redundancy in Chaucer (as it is an easy matter for a man
of ordinary parts to find a fault in one of greater), I have not
tied myself to a literal translation; but have often omitted
what I judged unnecessary, or not of dignity enough to appear
in the company of better thoughts. I have presumed further,
in some places, and added somewhat of my own where I thought
my author was deficient, and had not given his thoughts their
true lustre, for want of words in the beginning of our language.
And to this I was the more emboldened, because (if I may be
permitted to say it of myself) I found I had a soul congenial to
his, and that I had been conversant in the same studies. Another
poet, in another age, may take the same liberty with my writings; if at least they live long enough to deserve correction. It

was also necessary sometimes to restore the sense of Chaucer, which was lost or mangled in the errors of the press. Let this example suffice at present: in the story of *Palamon and Arcite*, where the temple of Diana is described, you find these verses in all the editions of our author:—

> There saw I Danè turned unto a tree,
> I mean not the goddess Diane,
> But Venus daughter, which that hight Danè.

Which, after a little consideration, I knew was to be reformed into this sense, that *Daphne*, the daughter of Peneus, was turned into a tree. I durst not make thus bold with Ovid, lest some future Milbourne should arise and say I varied from my author because I understood him not.

But there are other judges who think I ought not to have translated Chaucer into English, out of a quite contrary notion: they suppose there is a certain veneration due to his old language, and that it is little less than profanation and sacrilege to alter it. They are farther of opinion, that somewhat of his good sense will suffer in this transfusion, and much of the beauty of his thoughts will infallibly be lost, which appear with more grace in their old habit. Of this opinion was that excellent person, whom I mentioned, the late Earl of Leicester, who valued Chaucer as much as Mr. Cowley despised him. My Lord dissuaded me from this attempt (for I was thinking of it some years before his death) and his authority prevailed so far with me, as to defer my undertaking while he lived, in deference to him: yet my reason was not convinced with what he urged against it. If the first end of a writer be to be understood, then, as his language grows obsolete, his thoughts must grow obscure—

> Multa renascentur, quæ nunc cecidere; cadentque
> Quæ nunc sunt in honore vocabula, si volet usus,
> Quem penes arbitrium est et jus et norma loquendi.

When an ancient word, for its sound and significancy, deserves to be revived, I have that reasonable veneration for antiquity to restore it. All beyond this is superstition. Words are not like landmarks, so sacred as never to be removed; customs are changed, and even statutes are silently repealed, when the reason ceases for which they were enacted. As for the other part of the argument, that his thoughts will lose of their original beauty by the innovation of words; in the first place, not only their beauty, but their being is lost, where they are no longer understood, which is the present case. I grant that something must be lost in all transfusion, that is, in all translations; but the sense will remain, which would otherwise be lost, or at least be maimed, when it is scarce intelligible, and that but to a few. How few are there who can read Chaucer so as to understand him perfectly? And if imperfectly, then with less profit, and no pleasure. It is not for the use of some old Saxon friends that I have taken these pains with him: let them neglect my version, because they have no need of it. I made it for their sakes, who understand sense and poetry as well as they, when that poetry and sense is put into words which they understand. I will go farther, and dare to add, that what beauties I lose in some places, I give to others which had them not originally: but in this I may be partial to myself; let the reader judge, and I submit to his decision. Yet I think I have just occasion to complain of them, who because they understand Chaucer, would deprive the greater part of their countrymen of the same advantage, and hoard him up, as misers do their grandam gold, only to look on it themselves, and hinder others from making use of it. In sum, I seriously protest, that no man ever had, or can have, a greater veneration for Chaucer than myself. I have translated some part of his works, only that I might perpetuate his memory, or at least refresh it, amongst my countrymen. If I have altered him anywhere for the better, I must at the same time acknowledge that I could have done nothing without him. *Facile est inventis addere* is no great commendation; and I am not so vain to think I have deserved a greater. I will conclude what I have to say of him singly, with this one remark: A lady of my acquaintance, who keeps a kind of correspondence with some authors of the fair sex in France, has been informed by them that Mademoiselle de Scudery, who is as old as Sibyl, and inspired like her by the same God of Poetry, is at this time translating Chaucer into modern French. From which I gather that he has been formerly translated into the old Provençal; for how she should come to understand old English, I know not. But the matter of fact being true, it makes me think that there is something in it like fatality; that, after certain periods of time, the fame and memory of great Wits should be renewed, as Chaucer is both in France and England. If this be wholly chance, 'tis extraordinary; and I dare not call it more, for fear of being taxed with superstition.

Boccace comes last to be considered, who, living in the same age with Chaucer, had the same genius, and followed the same studies. Both writ novels, and each of them cultivated his mother tongue. But the greatest resemblance of our two modern authors being in their familiar style and pleasing way of relating comical adventures, I may pass it over, because I have translated nothing from Boccace of that nature. In the serious part of poetry, the advantage is wholly on Chaucer's side, for though the Englishman has borrowed many tales from the Italian, yet it appears that those of Boccace were not generally of his own making, but taken from authors of former ages, and by him only modelled; so that what there was of invention, in either of them, may be judged equal. But Chaucer has refined on Boccace, and has mended the stories, which he has borrowed, in his way of telling; though prose allows more liberty of thought, and the expression is more easy when unconfined by numbers. Our countryman carries weight, and yet wins the race at disadvantage. I desire not the reader should take my word; and, therefore, I will set two of their discourses, on the same subject, in the same light, for every man to judge betwixt them. I translated Chaucer first, and, amongst the rest, pitched on *The Wife of Bath's Tale ;* not daring, as I have said, to adventure on her Prologue, because 'tis too licentious. There Chaucer introduces an old woman, of mean parentage, whom a youthful knight, of noble blood, was forced to marry, and consequently loathed her. The crone being in bed with him on the wedding-night, and finding his aversion, endeavours to win his affection by reason, and speaks a good word for herself (as who could blame her?) in hopes to mollify the sullen bridegroom. She takes her topics from the benefits of poverty, the advantages of old age and ugliness, the vanity of youth, and the silly pride of ancestry and titles, without inherent virtue, which is the true nobility. When I had closed Chaucer, I returned to Ovid, and translated some more of his fables; and, by this time, had so far forgotten *The Wife of Bath's Tale,* that, when I took up Boccace, unawares I fell on the same argument, of preferring virtue to nobility of blood and titles, in the story of *Sigismonda ;* which I had certainly avoided, for the resemblance of the two discourses, if my memory had not failed me. Let the reader weigh them both; and, if he thinks me partial to Chaucer, 'tis in him to right Boccace.

I prefer, in our countryman, far above all his other stories, the noble poem of *Palamon and Arcite,* which is of the epic kind, and perhaps not much inferior to the *Ilias,* or the *Æneis.* The story is more pleasing than either of them, the manners as perfect, the diction as poetical, the learning as deep and various, and the disposition full as artful: only it concludes a greater length of time, as taking up seven years at least; but Aristotle has left undecided the duration of the action; which yet is easily reduced into the compass of a year, by a narration of what preceded the return of Palamon to Athens. I had thought, for the honour of our narration, and more particularly for his, whose laurel, though unworthy, I have worn after him, that this story was of English growth, and Chaucer's own: but I was undeceived by Boccace; for, casually looking on the end of his seventh *Giornata*, I found Dioneo (under which name he shadows himself), and Fiametta (who represents his mistress, the natural daughter of Robert, King of Naples), of whom these words are spoken: *Dioneo e Fiametta gran pezza cantarono insieme d'Arcita, e di Palemone;* by which it appears that this story was written before the time of Boccace; but the name of its author being wholly lost, Chaucer is now become an original; and I question not but the poem has received many beauties, by passing through his noble hands. Besides this tale, there is another of his own invention, after the manner of the Provençals, called *The Flower and the Leaf*, with which I was so particularly pleased, both for the invention and the moral, that I cannot hinder myself from recommending it to the reader.

As a corollary to this preface, in which I have done justice to others, I owe somewhat to myself; not that I think it worth my time to enter the lists with one M——, and one B——, but barely to take notice that such men there are, who have written scurrilously against me, without any provocation. M——, who is in orders, pretends, amongst the rest, this quarrel to me, that I have fallen foul on priesthood: if I have, I am only to ask pardon of good priests, and am afraid his part of the reparation will come to little. Let him be satisfied that he shall not be able to force himself upon me for an adversary. I contemn him too much to enter into competition with him. His own translations of Virgil have answered his criticisms on mine. If (as they say, he has declared in print) he prefers the version of Ogilby to mine, the world has made him the same compliment; for 'tis agreed, on all hands, that he writes even below Ogilby. That, you will say, is not easily to be done; but what cannot M—— bring about? I am satisfied, however, that, while he and I live together, I shall not be thought the worst poet of the age. It looks as if I had desired him underhand to write so ill against me; but upon my honest word I have not bribed him to do me this service, and am wholly guiltless of his pamphlet. 'Tis true, I should be glad if I could persuade him to continue his good offices, and write such another critique on anything of mine; for I find, by experience, he has a great stroke with the reader, when he condemns any of my poems, to make the world have a better opinion of them. He has taken some pains with my poetry; but nobody will be persuaded to take the same with his. If I had taken to the Church, as he affirms, but which was never in my thoughts, I should have had more sense, if not more grace, than to have turned myself out of my benefice, by writing libels on my parishioners. But his account of my manners and my principles are of a piece with his cavils and his poetry; and so I have done with him for ever.

As for the City Bard, or Knight Physician, I hear his quarrel to me is, that I was the author of *Absalom and Achitophel*, which, he thinks, is a little hard on his fanatic patrons in London.

But I will deal the more civilly with his two poems, because nothing ill is to be spoken of the dead; and therefore peace be to the *Manes* of his *Arthurs*. I will only say, that it was not for this noble Knight that I drew the plan of an epic poem on *King Arthur*, in my preface to the translation of *Juvenal*. The Guardian Angels of kingdoms were machines too ponderous for him to manage; and therefore he rejected them, as Dares did the whirl-bats of Eryx when they were thrown before him by Entellus: yet from that preface, he plainly took his hint; for he began immediately upon the story, though he had the baseness not to acknowledge his benefactor, but instead of it, to traduce me in a libel.

I shall say the less of Mr. Collier, because in many things he has taxed me justly; and I have pleaded guilty to all thoughts and expressions of mine, which can be truly argued of obscenity, profaneness, or immorality, and retract them. If he be my enemy, let him triumph; if he be my friend, as I have given him no personal occasion to be otherwise, he will be glad of my repentance. It becomes me not to draw my pen in the defence of a bad cause, when I have so often drawn it for a good one. Yet it were not difficult to prove that in many places he has perverted my meaning by his glosses, and interpreted my words into blasphemy and bawdry, of which they were not guilty. Besides that, he is too much given to horse-play in his raillery, and comes to battle like a dictator from the plough. I will not say, *the zeal of God's house has eaten him up;* but I am sure it has devoured some part of his good manners and civility. It might also be doubted whether it were altogether zeal which prompted him to this rough manner of proceeding; perhaps it became not one of his function to rake into the rubbish of ancient and modern plays: a divine might have employed his pains to better purpose than in the nastiness of Plautus and Aristophanes, whose examples, as they excuse not me, so it might be possibly supposed that he read them not without some pleasure. They who have written commentaries on those poets, or on Horace, Juvenal, and Martial, have explained some vices, which, without their interpretation, had been unknown to modern times. Neither has he judged impartially betwixt the former age and us. There is more bawdry in one play of Fletcher's, called *The Custom of the Country*, than in all ours together. Yet this has been often acted on the stage, in my remembrance. Are the times so much more reformed now than they were five-and-twenty years ago? If they are, I congratulate the amendment of our morals. But I am not to prejudice the cause of my fellow poets, though I abandon my own defence: they have some of them answered for themselves; and neither they nor I can think Mr. Collier so formidable an enemy, that we should shun him. He has lost ground, at the latter end of the day, by pursuing his point too far, liked the Prince of Condé, at the battle of Senneph: from immoral plays to no plays, *ab abusu ad usum, non valet consequentia.* But, being a party, I am not to erect myself into a judge. As for the rest of those who have written against me, they are such scoundrels that they deserve not the least notice to be taken of them. B—— and M—— are only distinguished from the crowd by being remembered to their infamy:—

> Demetri, teque, Tigelli
> Discipulorum inter jubeo plorare cathedras.

NOTES

ESSAY OF DRAMATIC POESY

Page 1. *The way of writing plays in verse.* Verse here means rhyme.

Pompey. A translation of Corneille's *Mort de Pompée* "by certain persons of honour." It is evident from the reference that Buckhurst was one of these.

P. 2. *the French poet.* This poet has never been identified.

"*As Nature, when she first designs,*" etc. From an address to the king by Sir William Davenant.

P. 3. *to defend my own.* In his dedication to the *Rival Ladies* Dryden had maintained the superiority of rhyme to blank verse. In an edition of his plays the following year Sir Robert Howard defended blank verse. This essay contains Dryden's rejoinder.

P. 5. *that memorable day.* The 3rd June 1665; the day of the great naval battle (see *Annus Mirabilis*) between the English and the Dutch off the Suffolk coast.

P. 7. *two poets.* One of these was probably Robert Wild, author of *Iter Boreale*, in eulogy of General Monk; the other possibly Richard Flecknoe, the writer of much bad verse and a favourite target for Dryden's wit (see the opening lines of *MacFlecknoe*).

Clevelandism. John Cleveland, a cavalier poet, whose writings are full of " clenches " (puns, quibbles), and " catachresis " (the straining of words out of their proper meanings). Two examples of his style are given later in the essay.

P. 15. *Father Ben.* Ben Jonson.

P. 16. *Aristotle indeed divides the integral parts of a play into four.* The division here erroneously ascribed to Aristotle was really made by J. C. Scaliger (1484-1558).

P. 17. *a late writer.* Uncertain; perhaps Howard; perhaps Ménage.

P. 18. *Euripides . . . in one of his tragedies. The Suppliants.*

P. 19. *says the French poet.* Corneille.

P. 21. " *Had Cain been Scot,*" etc. From Cleveland's *Rebel Scot.*

" *For beauty, like white powder,*" etc. From Cleveland's *Rupertismus.*

P. 25. *the Red Bull.* One of the early London theatres which survived the Commonwealth, only to be demolished soon after the Restoration. It was situated in St. John's Street, Clerkenwell, and, according to Malone, was famous " for entertainments adapted to the taste of the lower orders of the people."

P. 26. *plays of Calderon.* There were several adaptations of plays by the famous Spanish dramatist, Calderon de la Barca, on the Restoration stage; the most noteworthy being Sir Samuel Tuke's *Adventures of Five Hours*, referred to farther on in the essay.

P. 27. *Rollo. The Bloody Brother, or Rollo, Duke of Normandy*, by Fletcher.

P. 28. *protatic persons.* Characters appearing in the introductory part of a play, or employed simply to explain the action without being themselves directly connected with it.

P. 31. *The Scornful Lady.* By Beaumont and Fletcher.

P. 33. *The Adventures.* Tuke's *Adventures of Five Hours.* Diego is a comic character in this play.

P. 34. *Cinna, Pompey, Polieucte.* Tragedies by Corneille.
P. 35. *The Maid's Tragedy.* By Beaumont and Fletcher.
The Alchemist, The Silent Woman, The Fox. By Jonson.
P. 37. *extreme severity in his judgment on . . . Shakspeare.* No passage in Jonson bears out this statement. The criticism of Shakspeare's over-facility and occasional carelessness in the *Discoveries*—Jonson's only direct censure of Shakspeare—is certainly not marked by "extreme severity."
P. 38. *Philipin.* The common name for the comic servant, a stock character in French imitations of Spanish comedy.
P. 49. *that person from whom you have borrowed your strongest arguments.* Howard.
P. 52. *Pindaric way.* Irregularly as regards both the length of the lines and the disposition of the rhymes; as in the so-called "Pindaric" odes of Cowley, and in Dryden's *Alexander's Feast.*
The Siege of Rhodes. A play by Davenant, interesting as the first performed on the reopening of the theatres in London after the Commonwealth.
P. 54. *Mustapha.* By Sir Roger Boyle.
Blank verse is acknowledged to be too low for a poem. At this same time Milton was completing his *Paradise Lost.* That he was conscious of making an innovation in using blank verse for it, is shown in his prefatory note.
P. 57. *the Water-poet.* John Taylor, an industrious writer of poor verse, who owed his nickname to the fact that he had been a Thames waterman.

A DEFENCE OF AN ESSAY OF DRAMATIC POESY

P. 60. *The Great Favourite, or The Duke of Lerma.* By Howard. The supercilious tone of Howard's criticisms of Dryden accounts for the pungency of the present rejoinder.
an infant Dimock. The Dimocks (or Dymokes) were hereditary champions of England.
P. 63. *Catiline, Sejanus.* By Jonson.
P. 67. *My Lord L.* According to Malone, John Maitland, then Earl, afterwards Duke, of Lauderdale.
P. 68. *as Homer reports of little Teucer.* *Iliad,* viii. 267

ON COMEDY, FARCE, AND TRAGEDY

P. 81. *Mr. Cowley . . . tells us.* "Rather than all things wit, let there be none" (*Of Wit*).
the liar. Dorante in Corneille's *Le Menteur.*
The Chances, Wit without Money. Comedies by Fletcher.
P. 85. *Most of Shakspeare's plays . . . Cinthio.* Dryden is writing carelessly. Shakspeare's indebtedness to Cinthio is limited to *Othello* and *Measure for Measure.* The Italian tale of "Romeo and Juliet" to which Dryden refers was the work not of Cinthio but of Bandello.

OF HEROIC PLAYS

P. 90. *The oracle of Appius.* *Pharsalia,* v. 86 *ff.*
Erictho. *Pharsalia,* vi. 420 *ff.*
Polydorus. *Æneid,* iii. 22 *ff.*
Enchanted Wood. *Gerusalemme Liberata,* books xiii. and xvi.
the Bower of Bliss. *Faëry Queene,* book ii. canto xii.
P. 91. *Mr. Cowley's verses.*

> "Methinks heroic poesy till now
>   Like some fantastic fairy-land did show;

> Gods, devils, nymphs, witches, and giants' race,
> And all but man, in man's best work had place.
> Thou, like some worthy knight, with sacred arms,
> Dost drive the monsters back and end the charms."

Godfrey. That is, *Gerusalemme Liberata.*

P. 92. *Almanzor.* The hero of *The Conquest of Granada.*
Artaban. In *Cléopatre,* an heroic romance by La Calprenède.

P. 93. *Cyrus.* In *Artamène, ou le Grand Cyrus,* an heroic romance by Mlle. de Scudéry.
Oroondates. In *Cassandre,* another heroic romance by La Calprenède.
Cethegus. In *Catiline.* "To look Cato dead," however, is spoken by Catiline, not by Cethegus.

P. 94. *the late Duke of Guise.* Henri de Lorraine, fifth Duc de Guise (1614-64), who on the overthrow of Masaniello in 1647, marched into Naples with a handful of followers, and was for a short time master of the city.

THE DRAMATIC POETRY OF THE LAST AGE

P. 100. *The preposition at the end . . . in my own writings.* " His *Essay on Dramatic Poesy,* published in 1668, was reprinted sixteen years afterwards, and it is curious to observe the changes which Dryden made in the expression. Malone has carefully noted all these: they show both the care the author took with his own style, and the change which was gradually working in the English language. The Anglicism of terminating a sentence with a preposition is rejected. Thus 'I cannot think so contemptibly of the age I live in,' is exchanged for 'the age in which I live.' 'A deeper expression of belief than the actor can persuade me to' is altered to 'can insinuate into me.'" (Hallam, *Literature of Europe,* part iv. chap. vii.)

P. 104. *a famous Italian.* The reference is uncertain.
P. 105. *Fletcher's Don John.* In *The Chances.* Dryden refers to the revision of the play by the Duke of Buckingham.
the Black Friars. One of the most famous of the early London playhouses. It was built by James Burbage in 1596.
the Apollo. The meeting-room of Ben Jonson's club in the Old Devil Tavern, Temple Bar. His *Leges Conviviales, or Rules for a Tavern Academy,* were engraved in marble over the chimney-piece in this room.

HEROIC POETRY AND HEROIC LEGEND

P. 108. *a Princess.* Mary of Este, second wife of the Duke of York, afterwards James II.
my friend. Nat Lee, the dramatist.
P. 111. *the author of the Plain Dealer.* Wycherley.
P. 112. *Cleopatra. Carminum,* i. 37
P. 113. *Polyphemus. Æneid,* iii. 664
Goliath. Davideis, book iii.
the swiftness of Camilla. In the seventh, not the eighth, *Æneid.*
P. 114. *Lucretius. De Rerum Natura,* iv. 737 *ff.*
P. 115. *Virgil . . . from whom I took the image. Æneid,* ii. 265.
Mr. Cowley. Davideis, book i.
P. 116. *the translator of Du Bartas.* Joshua Sylvester.

ANTONY AND CLEOPATRA AND THE ART OF TRAGEDY

P. 119. *Montaigne. Essais,* ii. 17.
P. 120. *their Hippolytus.* In Racine's *Phèdre,* act v.
Chedreux. Scott explains that "Chedreux was the name of the fashion-

able periwigs of the day, and appears to have been derived from their maker."

P. 123. *that grinning honour.* The phrase is Falstaff's. See 1 *Henry IV.* v. 3.

P. 124. *that rhyming judge of the twopenny gallery.* The reference is to an attack on Dryden in an imitation of Horace entitled *An Allusion to the Tenth Satire of his First Book.* Dryden probably knew that this, though published anonymously, was really the work of the Earl of Rochester; but he chose to ascribe it to one of the " small fry " of literature.

THE GROUNDS OF CRITICISM IN TRAGEDY

P. 126. *Lollius.* Nothing is known of the Lollius to whom Chaucer expresses indebtedness for the ground-work of his poem. According to Lydgate, Boccaccio was actually meant. The matter is still one of controversy among Chaucer students.

P. 128. *Amintor and Melantius.* In *The Maid's Tragedy* by Beaumont and Fletcher.

Iphigenia. The *Iphigenia in Aulis* is referred to.

P. 130. *The Slighted Maid.* A comedy by Sir Robert Stapylton, 1663.

P. 132. *King and No King.* By Beaumont and Fletcher.

P. 138. *that strange mixture of a man.* Bessus.

P. 139. *a learned critic.* Bossu, in *Du Poëme Épique.*

P. 140. *Ovid. Metamorphoses,* xiii. 5.

OVID AND THE ART OF TRANSLATION

P. 150. *translated by divers hands.* The " hands " were those of Dryden himself, Cooper, Rhymer, Settle, Tate, Butler, and Mrs. Behn.

P. 151. *All translations . . . three heads.* The reader interested in the general question of translation should turn to Tytler's *Essay on the Principles of Translation,* published in Everyman's Library.

to run divisions on the ground-work. An old technical phrase, meaning to introduce variations on a musical theme.

P. 155. *the author, who is of the fair sex.* Mrs. Behn.

NATURE AND DRAMATIC ART

P. 157. *Bussy D'Amboys.* A tragedy by George Chapman, 1607.

A famous modern poet. According to Malone, this is an inaccurate recollection of a passage in Strada's *Prolusiones,* in which it is related that Andreas Navagero annually sacrificed a copy of Martial (not Statius) to the manes of Virgil.

PREFACE TO SYLVÆ

P. 161. *History of the League.* Translated in 1684 from the French of Maimbourg.

P. 162. *our Oglebys.* John Ogilby (1600-76), translated Homer and Virgil.

P. 167. *a late noble painter.* Sir Peter Lely (died 1680), who was painter to Charles II., and was famous for his portraits of the beauties of that monarch's court.

P. 169. *Essay on Poetry.* By Lord Mulgrave.

P. 170. *the ingenious and learned translator of Lucretius.* Thomas Creech.

P. 173. *too nearly related to me.* Dryden's eldest son, Charles, then about twenty, was a contributor to *Sylvæ.*

MUSICAL DRAMA

P. 177. *Pastor Fido.* Produced at the marriage of Duke Charles Emanuel in 1585.

P. 178. *Ben Jonson tells us in the Alchymist.* See act iv. scene 3.

P. 181. *Spanish plays.* These were habitually in three acts (*jornadas*).

P. 182. *Monsieur Vossius.* Settled in England in 1670, and, though a scoffer at religion and a man of profligate life, was made a Canon of Windsor by Charles II.

RHYME AND BLANK VERSE

P. 184. *Xenophon . . . a romance.* The *Cyropædeia*, or *Education of Cyrus*, a kind of didactic romance with an historical basis.

Augustus Cæsar, a tragedy. On the subject of Ajax.

P. 186. *Queen Gorboduc.* An example of Dryden's carelessness. Gorboduc was king, not queen, of Britain; and the play in question (the choruses excepted) was written in blank verse.

THE PROPER WIT OF POETRY

P. 189. *a Royal Admiral.* The Duke of York.

two incomparable Generals. Prince Rupert and the Duke of Albemarle—"two such as each seemed worthiest when alone" (*Annus Mirabilis*, stanza 47).

P. 190. *I have chosen to write my poem in quatrains.* Dryden took the quatrain directly from Davenant's *Gondibert*, a poem which enjoyed considerable vogue at the time. The heroic couplet had not yet established itself as the recognised form for all dignified poetry. *Paradise Lost* was published in the year of this essay, but in regard to its use of blank verse see note to p. 54.

female rhymes. Feminine, or double rhymes, like "ever" and "never" in the opening couplet of Keats's *Endymion*.

Alaric. A poem by Georges de Scudéry, brother of the better known Mlle. de Scudéry.

Pucelle. By Jean Chapelain.

the old translation of Homer by Chapman. Dryden is in error in stating this to be in Alexandrines. The *Iliad* is in "fourteeners"—
"For Hector's glory still he stood, and ever went about," etc.
The *Odyssey* is in rhymed iambic pentameters, or heroic couplets.

P. 191. *in the preface to Gondibert.* "I shall say a little why I have chosen my interwoven *Stanza* of four, though I am not obliged to excuse the choice, for numbers in verse must, like distinct kind of Music, be exposed to the uncertain and different taste of several Ears. Yet I may declare, that I believ'd it would be more pleasant to the Reader in a Work of length, to give this respite or pause, between every *Stanza* (having endeavoured that each should contain a period) than to run him out of breath with continued *Couplets*."

EXAMEN POETICUM

P. 198. *the best poet and the best patron.* Lord Dorset, in a poem addressed to Edward Howard on that writer's *British Princes*.

Zoili and Momi. The name of Zoilus the grammarian became a synonym for a captious critic. Momus was the god of ill-tempered mockery.

he who endeavoured to defame Virgil. Virgil had numerous detractors among his contemporaries, notably the poetasters Bavius and Mævius. Possibly Dryden is thinking of one of these; possibly of a certain Carvilius Pictor, who wrote an *Æneidomastix*.

P. 201. *their scriptions.* This passage remains unexplained.

P. 202. *the daughter of a king.* Lord Radcliffe's wife was the daughter of Charles II. and Mary Davies.

Mr. Chapman, in his translation of Homer. In the verses prefixed to his *Iliad* Chapman condemns " word for word traductions."

VIRGIL AND THE ÆNEID

P. 207. *the trifling novels.* The episodical stories numerous in *Orlando Furioso. Novel* then meant a short story (Italian *novella*).

P. 212. *the ruelle.* Originally, the space between the bed and the wall; hence used for a fashionable gathering or literary coterie at a time when fine ladies received visitors while at their toilets.

my two masters. Homer and Virgil.

P. 214. *the Jerusalem.* Tasso's *Gerusalemme Liberata.*

Machinery persons. The supernatural agents, or, in the current technical phraseology of the time, the " machinery," or " machines."

P. 215. *another whom I name not.* Probably St. Évremont, whom Dryden admired, and therefore preferred not to mention in the present context.

P. 223. *the author of the Dauphin's Virgil.* Charles de la Rue (Ruæus), whose edition of Virgil appeared in 1675. See p. 243.

P. 226. *Achilles . . . invulnerable.* " Dryden had forgot, what he must certainly have known, that the fiction of Achilles being invulnerable, bears date long posterior to the days of Homer. In the *Iliad* he is actually wounded " (Scott).

the two Tassos. Torquato Tasso's father, Bernardo, wrote an epic poem on Amadis of Gaul.

P. 234. *an ambassador . . . as Sir Henry Wotton has defined.* Dryden alludes to Wotton's pungent remark: " An ambassador is a honest man sent to lie abroad for the good of his country."

P. 240. *another French critic, whom I will not name.* Probably, St. Évremond again, though Scott suggested Dacier.

P. 246. *which Tasso has not ill copied. Gerusalemme Liberata,* xviii. 92-97.

P. 253. *Ariosto. Orlando Furioso,* xxxv. 26.

P. 254. *the two brothers.* Robert and Antione le Chevalier d'Agneaux.

P. 255. *in a former dissertation. The Parallel of Poetry and Painting.*

P. 257. *as a wit said formerly.* Lord Rochester. See p. 280.

P. 260. *the Pindaric line.* The Alexandrine.

P. 261. *staff.* That is, stave or stanza.

the excuse of Boccace. In the *Conclusione dell' Autore,* or Epilogue to the *Decamerone.*

P. 264. *the late Earl of Lauderdale . . . his new translation of the Æneis.* The translation in question was made by the Earl while living in exile in Paris.

P. 265. *Two other worthy friends of mine.* Dr. Knightly Chetwood wrote the *Life* and the preface to the *Pastorals ;* Addison, the preface to the *Georgics.*

P. 267. *A Sixth Pastoral.* The *Silenus,* translated by Lord Roscommon. See p. 271.

a Pharmaceutria. The eighth Pastoral.

a single Orpheus. The episode of Orpheus, translated by Lord Mulgrave from the fourth *Georgic.*

P. 271. *Whoever has given the world the translation of part of the Third Georgic.* Malone conjectures that this may have been Lord Lansdowne.

Mr. Addison . . . his Bees. " Alluding to a translation of the third book of the *Georgics,* exclusive of the story of Aristæus . . . by the famous Addison, then of Queen's College, Oxford " (Scott). Scott writes " third " by a slip of the pen. It is the fourth *Georgic* which deals with the management of bees.

the only one of them. Sir Richard Blackmore, court physician, and a voluminous writer in prose and verse. He was one of Dryden's old enemies. See further, pp. 289-291.

ON TRANSLATING THE POETS

P. 272. *a certain nobleman.* The Duke of Buckingham, "the tardy progress of whose great buildings at Cleveden was often the subject of satire" (Scott).

P. 273. *Godfrey of Bulloign.* Tasso's *Gerusalemme Liberata.*

P. 275. *a religious lawyer.* Jeremy Collier in his *Short View of the Immorality and Profaneness of the English Stage.* See p. 290, and compare Introduction, p. viii.

P. 277. *Homer . . . in the Second Book . . . hastens from the ships.* The dream of Agamemnon comes before, not after, the catalogue of the ships in the second *Iliad.*

P. 278. *Troilus and Cressida . . . Lombard author.* See note to p. 126.

P. 279. *Bartholomew Fair.* By Ben Jonson.

P. 280. *one of our late great poets.* Cowley.

If we may believe Catullus. This should be Martial (iii. 44).

P. 281. *he who published the last edition of him.* Thomas Speght, whose *Chaucer* appeared in 1597 and 1602. It is now of course well known that Speght's judgment was absolutely correct, and that Dryden in contradicting it was guilty of making hasty assertions about a subject with which he was very slightly acquainted.

P. 282. *the tale of Piers Plowman.* Dryden means *The Plowman's Tale,* a production belonging to the Chaucerian apocrypha.

the learned and ingenious Dr. Drake. In his reply to Collier's *Short View.*

P. 289. *Chaucer is now become an original.* Dryden evidently did not know that the groundwork of *Palamon and Arcite* was furnished by Boccaccio's *Teseide.*

M—. Luke Milbourne, one of Dryden's assailants.

B—. Blackmore.

P. 290. *his Arthurs.* Blackmore wrote two epics—*Prince Arthur* and *King Arthur.*

the whirl-bats of Eryx. *Æneid,* v. 400.

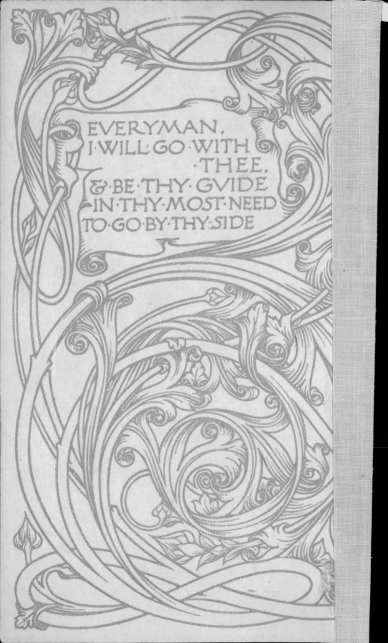

EVERYMAN,
I·WILL·GO·WITH
·THEE,
&·BE·THY·GVIDE
IN·THY·MOST·NEED
TO·GO·BY·THY·SIDE